# Innovations in Allied Health Fieldwork Education

# PRACTICE, EDUCATION WORK AND SOCIETY
Volume 4

**Other books in this Series:**
1. Higgs, J., Horsfall, D., & Grace, S. (2009). *Writing qualitative research on practice*. Rotterdam, The Netherlands: Sense Publishers.

2. Higgs, J., Cherry, N., Macklin, R., & Ajjawi, R. (2010). *Researching practice: A discourse on qualitative methodologies*. Rotterdam, The Netherlands: Sense Publishers.

3. Higgs, J., Fish, D., Goulter, I., Loftus, S., Reid, J., & Trede, F. (2010). *Education for future practice*, Rotterdam, The Netherlands: Sense Publishers.

# Innovations in Allied Health Fieldwork Education

*A Critical Appraisal*

**Edited by**

Lindy McAllister
*The University of Queensland, Australia*

Margo Paterson
*Queen's University, Canada*

Joy Higgs
*Charles Sturt University, Australia*

Christine Bithell
*St George's University of London and Kingston University, UK*

SENSE PUBLISHERS
ROTTERDAM/BOSTON/TAIPEI

A C.I.P. record for this book is available from the Library of Congress.

ISBN: 978-94-6091-321-1 (paperback)
ISBN: 978-94-6091-322-8 (hardback)
ISBN: 978-94-6091-323-5 (e-book)

Published by: Sense Publishers,
P.O. Box 21858,
3001 AW Rotterdam,
The Netherlands
http://www.sensepublishers.com

*Printed on acid-free paper*

# TABLE OF CONTENTS

JOY HIGGS

# SERIES INTRODUCTION

*Practice, Education, Work and Society*

This series examines research, theory and practice in the context of university education, professional practice, work and society. Rather than focussing on a single topic the series examines areas where two or more of these arenas come together. Themes that will be explored in the series include: university education of professions, society expectations of professional practice, professional practice workplaces and strategies for investigating each of these areas. There are many challenges facing researchers, educators, practitioners and students in today's practice worlds. The authors in this series bring a wealth of practice wisdom and experience to examine these issues, share their practice knowledge, report research into strategies that address these challenges, share approaches to working and learning and raise yet more questions.

The conversations conducted in the series will contribute to expanding the discourse around the way people encounter and experience practice, education, work and society.

*Joy Higgs, Charles Sturt University, Australia*

# FOREWORD

Fieldwork education is critically important to the education of professionals and their preparation for the workplace. Fieldwork education challenges students to transform their propositional (book or theoretical) knowledge into professional craft knowledge (the knowledge of how professionals get things done in practice) (Titchen & Ersser, 2001). Fieldwork education is primarily where professional identity is shaped and personal identity is challenged and extended. It is in fieldwork education settings that the many generic attributes required for successful professional practice develop more fully: capabilities such as teamwork, time management, prioritisation, conflict management and high-level communication skills.

Fieldwork education involves many stakeholders; not only students and their fieldwork educators, but also academic staff who help prepare students for entering practice settings, fieldwork education program managers at universities and in work-places, other professionals who deliver client care in the work settings in which students are placed or who manage such settings, and, most importantly, the clients themselves and their family and carer networks. The rewards for individual staff and agencies engaged in fieldwork education are many, as are the issues and challenges they must face.

## THE PURPOSE AND SCOPE OF THIS BOOK

Learning in the workplace, in professional practice or "in the field" has long been part of the education of health professionals. Today such learning is both highly valued and highly problematic, for many reasons including high workloads, the high cost of healthcare with limited time for "distractions" such as teaching students, and issues of accountability, litigation and quality assurance. In this context educators and practitioners, alongside researchers and managers, are asking the question: How can fieldwork education for health professionals move into the next era of innovative, sustainable as well as pedagogically sound educational programs and practices?

In several key articles (McAllister 2005a, 2005b), issues and challenges impacting on fieldwork education have been examined. These include changes to workplaces, changes in professional-entry education, the standards required by organisations accrediting university programs and registering or licensing graduates for practice, use of outdated approaches to fieldwork education, lack of preparation and support for fieldwork educators, systemic issues creating a shortage of fieldwork places, lack of funding for fieldwork, unrealistic expectations for new graduates, differences in philosophies and principles of fieldwork education, the need to focus on quality as well as quantity in fieldwork placements, and a need to view fieldwork education as a continuum from preparatory work in the classroom to actual practice in the field. From this work three key observations were made. First, there were few mechanisms for the sharing of innovations in fieldwork education. Second, the discourse around issues in fieldwork education was largely around quantity (getting more placements) rather than quality in those placements. Third, published research or evaluation of fieldwork education was scant, especially in comparison to research in the clinical aspects of the allied health professions. Based on these observations Lindy McAllister invited her colleagues Margo Paterson, Joy Higgs and Chris Bithell to produce a book that examined both the issues and the solutions or innovations that have emerged to address them.

This book presents innovations in fieldwork education that have been critically appraised or evaluated, and that could be used to create standards for fieldwork education and deliver high-quality learning experiences for students and staff engaged in fieldwork education. Because of the similarities in values, approaches and issues in fieldwork education shared by the allied health professions of occupational therapy, physiotherapy and speech language pathology, it made sense to have a book that shared innovations in these disciplines, so that fieldwork educators or managers in any one discipline could learn from developments in other disciplines.

The book presents international perspectives on fieldwork education, partly because preparing graduates for international mobility is increasingly important and partly because the ways in which programs around the world have addressed local concerns and needs point to new possibilities for programs in other countries grappling with similar issues. The four editors of this book are all leaders in fieldwork education in their disciplines in their own countries and internationally, and have been able to identify contributors and exemplars of innovation and best practice around the world, from English-speaking and non-English-speaking countries. In presenting innovations that have been critically evaluated, this book, with its international, interdisciplinary flavour, makes a unique contribution to the fieldwork education literature.

## TERMINOLOGY

We acknowledge that two of the three professions which are the focus of this book have different names in different countries. Australia uses speech pathologist where the U.S. uses speech language pathologist and the U.K. uses speech and language therapist. Physiotherapists in Australia and the U.K. are physical therapists in North America. For consistency, we have chosen to use the terms occupational therapist (which seems to be a worldwide term for that profession), speech language pathologist and physiotherapist.

As noted earlier, we use the term fieldwork education rather than clinical education, as it more appropriately describes the continuum of settings in which students obtain professional experience outside medical (clinical) settings. This term has been used in occupational therapy for some time, but may be new to some speech language pathologists and physiotherapists whose professions use the term clinical education.

The terms used to describe bodies which "approve" university education programs and the processes used to approve such programs, and then approve their graduates vary considerably within and between countries. The terms licensure, credentialing and registration are used in different chapters, depending on the country of origin of authors or literature sources used.

## STRUCTURE OF THIS BOOK

This book addresses major areas of innovation in fieldwork education in 9 sections. Section 1, **Fieldwork education: Students, settings and populations**, explores changing student populations, expectations of new graduates, workforce needs and strategies for enhancing the student experience, fieldwork education in non-traditional settings or with emerging client groups and community settings, and the provision of international fieldwork experiences in which students travel to placements outside their home country.

Section 2 is concerned with **Design and management of fieldwork education**. In this section we highlight issues in fieldwork education management, and the special skills needed to manage fieldwork education programs, alongside the frequent lack of knowledge, preparation and standards for effective fieldwork education management. We examine how business, governance, educational and service models can help assure quality standards in the delivery of fieldwork.

In Section 3, **Models of fieldwork education and supervision**, we consider the influences and contextual factors that can shape fieldwork education experiences, and the different types of fieldwork education programs that involve collaborative partnerships between universities and community agencies to provide new opportunities for student learning and service delivery. The importance of reflection and peer learning are highlighted in this section.

Section 4, **Using information and communication technology in fieldwork education**, presents a series of case studies to illustrate the opportunities that video-conferencing and new Web 2 technologies can offer to extend and support student learning, and to take fieldwork education into new settings.

Section 5, **Alternatives to practice in the field**, considers the continuum of fieldwork education from classroom and distance learning to real-world settings, using service learning, case-based teaching in the classroom and standardised patients as exemplars.

In Section 6, **Interprofessional fieldwork education**, we distil lessons learned from several programs that have undertaken extensive development and research in interprofessional learning. Issues of managing and sustaining such programs and ensuring that discipline-specific and student-specific learning outcomes are achieved, as well as interprofessional learning outcomes, are addressed.

In Section 7 we consider **Student assessment in fieldwork education** and discuss the challenges of assessing student performance in fieldwork settings, including achieving validity, reliability and authenticity, making quality judgements, providing formative and summative feedback, and using reflective self-assessment and peer feedback as well formal assessment by fieldwork educators.

Section 8, **Preparation and support of fieldwork educators and managers**, highlights the longstanding problem of lack of attention to these two important stakeholder groups. This section describes two approaches, both of which target fieldwork educators as well as managers (an often under-prepared stakeholder group in fieldwork education). One approach uses a formal program delivered in group mode, the other a workplace-based approach using mentoring and peer support.

In Section 9, **Preparation and support of students for fieldwork education**, we focus on strategies to prepare students for the increasingly common usage in fieldwork settings of peer learning, effective orientation of students to fieldwork settings, and the range of support provided to students from non-academic units of universities, which enable students and their fieldwork educators to undertake effective education programs.

In the chapters that follow, we present many examples, critiques, reflections and evaluations of fieldwork innovation. We hope the book will engage readers and stimulate further inquiry, research and innovation in fieldwork education.

## REFERENCES

McAllister, L. (2005a). Issues and innovations in clinical education. *Advances in Speech-Language Pathology*, 7(3), 138–148.

McAllister, L. (2005b). Issues, innovations and calls to action in clinical education: A response to Kathard, Lincoln and McCabe, Rose, Cruice, Pickering, van Dort, and Stansfield. *Advances in Speech-Language Pathology*, 7(3), 177–180.

Titchen, A., & Ersser, S. J. (2001). The nature of professional craft knowledge. In J. Higgs & A. Titchen (Eds.), *Practice knowledge and expertise in the health professions* (pp. 35–41). Oxford: Butterworth-Heinemann.

LINDY MCALLISTER, CHRISTINE BITHELL AND JOY HIGGS

# 1. INNOVATIONS IN FIELDWORK EDUCATION

*Current Trends and Future Directions*

Fieldwork education is a core learning endeavour within health professional education and it demands high quality strategies and innovative solutions to the many challenges it presents. This book, with its case studies and evaluation reports of cutting edge innovations in fieldwork education, provides a panorama of the diversity and vitality in this field of education and curriculum development. Since case studies are inherently highly situated, we present them as exemplary practice of the innovation in question and as a stimulus for further exploration and evaluation in other contexts. In this chapter we aim to draw together a synopsis of trends, challenges and lessons learned in order to point towards future directions as we currently see them.

## CHALLENGES AND CONTEXTS IN FIELDWORK EDUCATION

In framing this book we remind readers that globally there is no uniformity in health professions education. Early chapters set the stage for the book by discussing the changing contexts of fieldwork education in terms of changing student demographics and changing trends in higher education which impact on fieldwork education. Four chapters (2, 11, 14 and 29) consider the implications for fieldwork education of changing student demographics and attributes. These chapters ask us to consider the adjustments required of fieldwork education programs and educators from Generation Y students, and from a student body which is more culturally diverse, perhaps older, maybe time-poor because of family commitments or part-time work, and possibly living at a distance from the university. The authors of Chapter 2 write of fluidity in terms of the levels and lengths of initial qualifying programs. Students on fieldwork education programs will be at very different ages and stages of personal and educational development. Student debt is a reality for many and it affects their priorities, adding to pressures while on placement. Boudreau's analysis of the current generation of students (Boudreau, 2008), presuming this to mean those of traditional college age, known as Generation Y, or the Net Generation (Oblinger & Oblinger, 2005), described them as confident multitaskers and users of ICT, highly interactive and enjoying experiential and participatory learning but easily distracted and wanting immediate feedback. As one of the authors of Chapter 2 states, such student characteristics will determine the types of learning experience that are

*L. McAllister et al., (eds.), Innovations in Allied Health Fieldwork*
*Education: A Critical Appraisal, 1–13.*
© *2010 Sense Publishers. All rights reserved.*

appropriate and moreover the impact of professional socialisation processes upon them, a factor as yet unknown.

Challenges for fieldwork educators and their employing agencies may not be well understood by students and the universities from which they come. These challenges include:

- balancing the dual demands of student education with those of providing high quality client care
- ensuring that productivity targets in departments are not compromised by time directed to student teaching
- ensuring that income to agencies through health insurer reimbursements is not compromised by student delivery of services
- providing good learning experiences for students when models of client care are rapidly changing and may not meet the criteria for the types of placement requested by universities
- identifying adequate numbers of placements for an ever-growing number of students while not allowing fieldwork managers and educators to become burnt out
- dealing with the consequences of rapid turnover of staff, as well as providing space and other resources for students on site.

These challenges and other issues are addressed in Chapter 6.

The responses of workplaces to these growing pressures may be to withdraw from the provision of fieldwork placements or to reduce the number of placements offered. However, such reactions run the great risk of removing the long-established benefits of fieldwork education. Through fieldwork, students develop professional identities and competencies, particularly the ability to problem-solve and make professional decisions in unpredictable and complex human situations. Indeed, many agencies recognise the multiple benefits and rewards for staff and employers which students afford. These include contributions to the continued learning of staff through having to explain their practice or through professional development offered by universities for fieldwork educators (Ballinger & Diesen, 1994), improved staff morale, improved client throughput in well-designed fieldwork education programs (Ladyshewsky, Barrie, & Drake, 1998), and improved recruitment of new graduates. This last is particularly important in areas that suffer a chronic staff shortage, such as rural and remote areas and disability services (Iacono, Johnson, Humphreys, & McAllister, 2007).

With the need to produce the highest quality graduates possible to work in complex and rapidly changing workplaces, and the need to respond to issues and challenges in fieldwork education described above, university programs must be innovative in how they design, deliver and evaluate fieldwork education. The numerous drivers of innovation in fieldwork education include reduced funding, shrinking numbers of traditional fieldwork education placements, increasing student numbers, workplace demands, as well as client needs. Another driver is the desire of universities to market unique aspects of their programs in order to attract students in a competitive market. These and other drivers of innovation in fieldwork education are explored in more detail in Chapters 6 and 16.

## CURRENT TRENDS IN FIELDWORK EDUCATION

### Changes in Higher Education

Chapter 3 refers to the nexus between the university and the workplace as a key locus where current and future developments cluster. Partnership in the provision of fieldwork placements has always been essential, but the strengthening of this collaboration is driven by the requirements of a developing pedagogy of fieldwork education, and by profound and as yet not fully realised changes in the workplace. The authors identify four changes in higher education which influence fieldwork education. These are:

- changing approaches to teaching and learning
- expectations for new graduates in terms of evidence-based practice, high levels of competence, interprofessional and team practice, international mobility and meeting workforce needs
- requirements in terms of student numbers, funding, and policy compliance
- ways of enhancing students' experiences.

Strategies for enhancing the learning experience for students on fieldwork placements are also provided in Chapter 29. Over the last two decades international placements have become increasingly common in allied health professions. One driver for this is the pragmatic need to find additional placements, but more pedagogically sound drivers are the need to develop intercultural competence and preparation for international mobility amongst graduates. Intercultural skills developed in international placements are transferable back to the increasingly diverse domestic settings in which students and graduates in the Western world will work. The challenges and rewards of international placements are specifically addressed in Chapter 5.

### New Conceptions of Fieldwork Pedagogy

There is a developing pedagogy of fieldwork education, with newer theoretical constructs no longer dependent on understandings developed in the classroom. It is now well accepted that knowledge for clinical practice requires an integration between the propositional knowledge and research-based evidence learned in the classroom and professional craft knowledge derived from practice. The value of experiential learning that leads to ways of knowing and learning in practice is now well supported by research and theory, and embedded into practice by a number of different means. Examples in this book include Chapter 12, which explores the increasing adoption of learning portfolios as a means of promoting reflection on practice to promote transformative learning, although the authors comment on the detrimental effects of assessment as a function of the portfolio unless handled carefully. The use of different methods of peer learning to foster learning with and from others and to facilitate experiential learning through the use of open questions and a non-judgmental style is explained in Chapter 13.

### Changes in the Workplace

Health services demand not only that newly qualified graduates are safe and effective practitioners, able to manage their own caseloads, but also that they are better prepared to cope with the complex realities of becoming members of the workforce, equipped with a broader set of generic skills. New understandings of the role of fieldwork educators as managers of student learning experiences as a whole include designing placements, in collaboration with academic placement coordinators. The goal of these collaborations is to ensure that students develop the capabilities needed for employment, including independence and autonomy, teamwork, caseload management and communication skills, in addition to the clinical skills specific to their profession. In some places a specialist educator role has developed in response to these challenges, and everywhere the quality of the collaboration between academic placement coordinators and fieldwork educators is recognised as vital to the success of placements.

Schön (1987) catalysed intense interest in developing reflective practitioners, and the health professions quickly embraced reflection as both a learning strategy and outcome. Reflection was not always thoughtfully promoted or facilitated in students, and this book aims to provide not only innovations in the use of reflection in fieldwork education (Chapters 12, 17, 23 and 26), but also theoretical foundations for reflection and approaches to enabling students to reflect meaningfully and critically (Chapter 12). Chapter 26 discusses the use of reflection in the professional development of fieldwork educators.

Health systems in all developed countries have come under increased pressure as aging populations, expensive new technologies, increasing patient expectations and affluence change the profile of health and disease and generally increase the demand on the scarce resources – resources that are set to decrease further as a result of recent challenges to world economies. Disadvantaged or remote populations fare less well than urban or affluent populations under such circumstances. The scope of fieldwork placements is diversifying into non-traditional locations, often as a means of "re-engineering" healthcare provision, or encouraging graduates to take up their first posts in under-subscribed localities and services. Chapter 10 describes a fieldwork experience for speech language pathology students in schools in rural areas where no services currently exist, as a means of modelling the direction of change needed and encouraging students to show initiative and creativity, as well as challenging their strong sense of legitimate, medically oriented practice. In Chapter 4, three non-traditional placements are described that enable students to work with groups not normally encountered and to realise that they could devise appropriate services and derive personal satisfaction from working in new ways in relatively unstructured environments. The success of such placements depends upon careful planning and support for students, particularly those for whom lack of structure is a greater challenge.

*Diversification of Placement Models*

Many chapters consider well-established as well as new models and approaches to fieldwork education, particularly Chapter 9 which, in addition to reviewing curriculum-based, developmental and collaborative models of fieldwork education, also examines factors influencing the design of fieldwork placements. Consideration of such factors is illustrated in the design of a new fieldwork placement included as a case study. The move from apprenticeship models of fieldwork education to experiential but facilitated and supported learning is discussed in Chapters 3, 4, 5, 11 and 16. In Chapter 11, immersion in the field from day one is contrasted with the gradual introduction to fieldwork education outlined in many other chapters. The view that the unquestioned "gold standard" for professional education is actual placement in real-world field settings is shifting, and this changing perspective opens up the use of many different approaches to teaching and learning along the continuum from the classroom to the field (Chapter 15). Approaches considered include problem-based learning (Chapter 3), case-based teaching in the classroom (Chapter 16), project placements (Chapter 3), simulations and standardised patients (Chapters 3 and 17), service learning and volunteer placements (domestic or inter-national) (Chapters 16 and 5), whole-of-course internships and situated learning (Chapter 11).

Models of placement supervision have become increasingly heterogeneous for a number of reasons, but chiefly due to shortage of placements and the resulting diversification of placement supply. We suggest that previously the model of super-vision was a taken for granted concept and given no serious consideration. However, attempts to increase the number of placements led to testing of collaborative models of 2:1 and 3:1 student:supervisor ratios compared with the 1:1 ratio that many then considered ideal. In one study (Moore, Morris, Crouch, & Martin, 2003) 2:1 was considered the best compromise, giving sufficient individual supervision to each student as well as time to learn together. Time for 1:1 supervision and careful planning and preparation for the placement were found to be essential for a successful outcome. However, the most important finding from this and other studies was the benefit of peer learning for collaborative placements.

In the past, resistance to placement of more than one student with a fieldwork educator was considerable in some disciplines and in some countries where the old apprenticeship model of fieldwork education dominated, with one (apprentice/novice) student learning from one master, expert clinician. Economic as well as pedagogical drivers have seen increasing adoption of peer learning as an effective teaching and learning strategy in fieldwork education. When economic considerations are the major drivers for creating more placements this has sometimes led to ill-considered adoption of peer learning approaches. The benefits, risks and management issues in peer learning in fieldwork are considered in many chapters, notably Chapters 3, 9, 10, 13, 23, 26 and 27. Chapter 13 presents two perspectives on the usefulness of peer learning: as an activity-based approach where peers do things together and this creates learning opportunities; and as a dialogic tool where through discussion students can support and extend each other's learning. In combination, careful planning of peer learning activities and education of students in how to dialogically explore their learning can powerfully enhance peer learning in fieldwork education.

Pairing students of different levels and types can create problems if not well managed, as discussed in Chapters 21, 23, and 26. Data reported in Chapter 23 from senior students paired with more junior students showed that the senior students were not as satisfied with the experience as were the junior students. The need to prepare students to make the most of peer learning opportunities is addressed in Chapter 27.

The need to diversify placement provision has stimulated other innovations such as university-based clinics, presented in Chapter 8, where the pitfalls of attempting to provide a health service in a non-healthcare environment and guidelines for success are explained. Placements in non-traditional locations where services do not exist may require new models of intermittent supervision or reliance on communication technology. Students might not be managing a traditional caseload but instead might be engaged in a project which will benefit the placement host in some defined way. Such placements are likely to succeed when there is potential for reciprocal benefit for both the placement site and the student, which has been discussed and agreed before the placement begins; where written affiliation agreements are in place; and where students' learning goals and reflective assignments are designed to guide and enhance their placement experience.

International placements, or study abroad programs, have increased in quantity and diversity, and work best when they fulfil the aims of both home and overseas institutions. Development of intercultural understandings is of value in increasingly multicultural societies in home countries, and graduates increasingly need to be able to demonstrate international credibility. Chapter 5 describes the use of an international placement as a means of developing interprofessional teamwork. Finally, simulations, including standardised patients, both in the classroom and virtually by means of distance technologies, have been used as adjuncts and alternatives to fieldwork education. Such experiences can strengthen experiential learning in the curriculum while compensating for shortages of placements, or extending students' experience into areas they otherwise could not access, such as rural and remote areas or small specialist units offering few placements. A strong case can be made for using simulations or real patients as a means of controlled exposure to build students' confidence and reasoning skills, either individually or as a means of collaborative peer learning as they carry out group interviews.

*Interprofessional Fieldwork Education*

The requirement of health professionals to engage in interprofessional practice has driven (and in turn been shaped by) interprofessional education (IPE) of students. Section 6 of the book is devoted to interprofessional fieldwork education. IPE has many benefits for students, disciplines, workplaces and ultimately clients. But the development, implementation, and sustainability of sound IPE programs is fraught with barriers and often logistically difficult and costly in terms of time, staffing and resourcing. It can also be a challenge to obtain support for such programs from students and staff when they are seen as an "add-on" to existing fieldwork education programs, especially if not formally assessed. Chapters 18 and 20 describe successful IPE programs sustained over considerable periods of time. Chapter 19, on the other hand, describes the challenges to sustainability of an IPE program which ultimately led to its discontinuation, but with embedding of the IPE learning objectives and activities it had generated (such as shadowing a health professional from another discipline) into more routine fieldwork education within disciplines. Chapters 18 and 20 provide examples of rigorous evaluation of learning outcomes and program delivery and management, drawing upon several years of research and evaluation.

Collaborative practice is the essence of interprofessional teamwork, a concept extended to intraprofessional working with support personnel of the same profession in Chapter 21. Lessons learned include the value of key personnel such as an on-site coordinator; the need for additional resources to compensate for the time, space and management support that is required; and the importance of a pragmatic approach to overcome logistical difficulties. Many of the projects need to begin with good interprofessional work both among the educators and practitioners involved, as well as in the service units that will be the site for the placement. This entails staff development activities, that can include distance technologies, to reach the necessary understanding and commitment to foster a supportive interprofessional culture among those who must model an interprofessional team. Student learning is best served by explicit learning outcomes that are congruent with authentic active learning and assessment activities. Although examples of projects are numerous, sustainability has become a concern as projects come to an end and resources are withdrawn. Where there has been transformation of attitudes, beliefs and behaviours through change processes within the faculty and the clinical site, and continuing support from management at all levels, the chances of sustainability are higher.

With the development of IPE, partnership and service learning approaches to fieldwork education, a concomitant development is the education and supervision of students by professionals from disciplines other than those to which students on placements belong. For many decades there was resistance to cross-disciplinary or interdisciplinary supervision, with some disciplines, professions (and sometimes students) arguing that students could learn only from experts in their own fields. The shift in focus from illness to wellness models of care, the gradual move of health service delivery from medical settings to community and domiciliary settings, as well as interprofessional practice in those settings, together with the use of role-emerging placements in settings where disciplines are not currently present (such as those described in Chapters 4, 5, 9 and 16), further necessitate cross-disciplinary supervision on-site, sometimes supplemented with university-based educator support (as described in Chapter 9). Although there may be initial anxiety about supervision from someone outside a student's discipline, Chapters 5 and 10 suggest that students come to appreciate the unique learning this can offer.

*Work Readiness*

High expectations for graduates and the growing demand for graduates to be "work ready" are driving many innovations in fieldwork education that immerse students in the workplace from early in their programs of study (Chapter 11), or that utilise learning and teaching approaches which exemplify features of contemporary work-places. Approaches that construct learning as a social and collaborative activity, emphasise experiential learning, require students to own their learning and truly participate in work tasks, are described in Chapters 10, 11, 12. A theme in Section 3 is the need to provide structure, facilitation and support for students learning in more experiential and non-traditional models. Chapters 10 and 20 note the opportunities that innovation in fieldwork education offers in terms of shaping the future directions of classroom education as well as practice.

*Student Assessment*

No book on fieldwork education would be complete without discussion of assessment of student learning and performance. Assessment provides important feedback to students about their performance, learning needs and achievements, and to universities about the impact of their curricula and fieldwork programs. Moreover, assessment identifies those students ready to graduate and able to practise safely. The gatekeeper role which fieldwork educators undertake on behalf of the professions and society in assessing students' readiness for independent practice is a major source of anxiety for these educators. They need well-designed, valid, reliable, easy to use and efficient assessment tools in order to make sound judgments of student performance.

The challenges of assessing students' competence to practice with authenticity and in ways that do not impact negatively on learning are tackled in Chapters 22, 23 and 24. The authors rightly reject reductionism as a means to greater objectivity and determine that judgment either of observed performance, or of an oral discussion, is a valid discriminator and aligns well with real-life contexts and authentic assessment methods. Competency-based approaches to performance assessment must, authors argue, include assessment of a range of skills, but most importantly must encompass the processes required to practise in complex workplace environments, including generic skills such as reasoning and communication. Chapter 24 considers oral assessment as a complement to performance assessment, and discusses the benefits of oral assessment which specifically targets thinking processes based on a discussion of students' current caseloads, so possessing a high degree of authenticity in relation to real patients, but also perceived by students to be closely aligned with the professional communication skills required in practice. The authors emphasise the importance of gaining student perspectives on assessment design. Fairness and transparency are paramount, but not at the expense of assessing authentic processes of practice, a condition which the students in these studies appear to understand and accept.

The principles of good assessment of fieldwork performance are discussed in Chapter 22. This chapter presents COMPASS®, a tool for assessment of clinical competence in speech language pathology students (McAllister, Lincoln, Ferguson, & McAllister, 2006) as an example of a user-friendly, highly valid and reliable assessment tool, which can be used to provide formative as well as summative assessment feedback. This tool addresses concerns for authenticity in assessment, also raised in Chapter 24. The next stage in the research program using this tool is benchmarking programs and models of fieldwork education to begin to answer recurrent questions of quantity versus quality in fieldwork education, and timing and impact of different fieldwork education experiences across the continuum of student preparation.

To be able to engage in lifelong learning graduates need to have developed the capacity to self-assess and to provide feedback to peers to assist in their lifelong learning. Chapter 23 discusses approaches to fostering self- and peer assessment using reflective strategies, and considers the alignment between self, peer and supervisor assessment, which is important for realistically judging performance and subsequent learning needs.

*Partnerships and Collaborations*

The increasing use of partnerships and collaborations to meet both community needs, including the needs of unserved or under-serviced populations, and the need to generate more student placements is considered in Chapters 4, 5, 8, 9, and 10. The authors of Chapter 10 use the term "community responsive engaged learning" to define their dual approach to fieldwork education of students and service to clients (defined in the broadest terms), and describe how they educate students and serve the community using a non-impairment-focused approach to practice, notions that accord with discussions in Chapter 2 of a social ecological model for framing fieldwork and practice.

*The Impact of Information and Communication Technology*

Existing and emerging models and strategies in fieldwork education will be rapidly shaped by the increasing uptake of information and communication technologies (ICT). The capacity of ICT to allow real-time interaction of students and fieldwork educators who are remote from each other will open up new locations for fieldwork education and new approaches to teaching and learning. Chapter 29 shows how ICT can be used to enhance and support students whose fieldwork placements are remote from their campuses. Chapters 14 and 15 consider some of the opportunities currently available and the barriers and issues inherent in using ICT in fieldwork education. Many of these are the same as those that need to be attended to in the delivery of telehealth services (Dunkley, Pattie, Wilson, & McAllister, in press). These systemic and technical barriers, attitudinal issues, cultural concerns and the need to protect student/client privacy and confidentiality need to be addressed before ICT has significant uptake in fieldwork education.

*Management of Fieldwork Placement Systems*

The focus of this book has largely been on students and fieldwork educators. Although we have discussed challenges for fieldwork education managers we have not directed a great deal of attention to models of fieldwork management. One powerful but under-utilised model for assisting educators to think about and manage fieldwork experiences is the teacher-as-manager model (Romanini & Higgs, 1991).

Chapter 28 reports use of this model as the basis for preparing students for fieldwork, an application worthy of further exploration.

## Preparation for Fieldwork Educators and Students

Preparation of staff and students for fieldwork education is a key topic in this book. The use of different approaches to efficiently and effectively prepare students before they commence fieldwork is discussed in a range of Chapters, with in-depth discussion of preparing students for peer learning occurring in Chapter 27 and orientation to fieldwork placements considered in Chapter 28. Much of the guidance on preparation of students for peer learning placements in Chapter 27 may be usefully generalised to all placements, as many students are in groups on placement, either of their own profession or increasingly of other professions at the site at the same time. Learning the skills of peer learning not only enriches their placement learning but will build the social skills for collegiate relationships and teamwork as qualified professionals.

The lack of preparation of clinicians to be fieldwork educators has long been noted (Higgs & McAllister, 2007) and consequently we have included several chapters to address this topic (Chapters 25, 26, 28, and 29). Chapters 25 and 26 present advanced professional development programs for fieldwork educators. Chapter 25 describes a formal program running for more than a decade that is grounded in principles of evidence-based education and adult learning, using an interprofessional approach which models good teaching and learning practices as it educates participants about these approaches. Chapter 26 describes a less formal workplace-based approach, also grounded in educational theory. This chapter describes peer mentoring and support strategies used to prepare new fieldwork educators who are in the process of developing clinical expertise.

Preparation of those staff, typically based in universities, who manage fieldwork education programs is also lacking. Chapter 7 considers the special organisational, problem-solving, negotiation and conflict resolution skills required to undertake this management role. For most fieldwork education managers, learning the role and developing the skills needed happens "on the job". Some preparation programs do exist, and Chapters 25 and 26 provide examples of formal and informal preparation programs for fieldwork education managers. Chapter 25 presents an interprofessional program for fieldwork managers designed around the five themes of exploring expertise in professional practice as well as educational practice, creating learning relationships, managing learning programs and resources, and finally focusing on the role of personal knowledge in the fieldwork management role.

Face-to-face programs for fieldwork educators must demonstrate the learning approaches required in fieldwork education, such as role-modelling, the importance of relationships in person-centred approaches, and the application of the theories of adult learning. Programs need to teach the methods of learning from experience and the skills of reflection, as well as of learning from research, for those whose education may have pre-dated widespread adoption of these now core outcomes. Although on-line fieldwork educator programs can be added for those in rural and remote settings or otherwise unable to access face-to-face programs, learners often express a preference for a moderator to give feedback, demonstrating the value of human interaction when addressing such a person-centred topic.

## FUTURE DIRECTIONS IN FIELDWORK EDUCATION

To adapt the words of Thorne (2006) writing about key issues for 21st century nurse education, the core business for allied health professional educators is the preparation of the next generation of graduates to take their places in a world order that we can only begin to comprehend while ensuring that our core values are retained. Our values include a strong belief that fieldwork education must be based on sound educational principles, an evidence base derived from experiential learning, and attention to the scope and diversity of current and future practice. Fieldwork education is already adopting a wide range of non-traditional placement models that are pushing at the boundaries of what have previously been regarded as appropriate placements. Diversity will continue to increase as health services reach out to new client groups and hard-to-reach populations. Public health agendas to improve the health and wellbeing of populations will add an extra dimension to the provision of services for many professions and bring further diversity to placement provision. Rural and remote communities will benefit from advances in telemedicine, and students on placements where videoconferencing and Web-based technologies become the norm for receiving learning support will have valuable experience of their use.

Placement shortages are likely to continue as health services personnel come under more pressure to increase productivity. With further testing and evaluation it seems likely that simulations and technologically-based solutions will become increasingly trusted to increase exposure to experiential learning without direct patient contact, although work-based learning will remain crucial for the development of authentic practice-based skills and the opportunities for professional socialisation into a distinctive professional culture. Expanding placement capacity would be assisted by further research into the service contribution made by students on placement as well as the less tangible benefits to staff development and service quality.

Paradoxically, the value of work-based placements in health and other higher education programs has recently attracted government attention in a number of countries. Universities must see that graduates are more effectively prepared to enter the workforce able to deal with the complex realities of working environments. In Australia the state of Victoria is proposing an overall workforce strategy that will engage with placement arrangements for the first time, including providing funding, as well as planning for increased placement capacity and quality. The impact of such centralising changes has yet to be felt but it seems likely that other national bodies may follow suit. If placement provision becomes more centrally planned and administered, it will be important to retain the creativity and flexibility that can optimise learning outcomes currently possible in a locally managed placement system.

Student characteristics as members of Generation Y predispose to the enthusiastic acceptance of distance technologies and the possibilities of Web 2.0 tools that will open the way for interactive learning in flexible and geographically diverse locations. Provided that current barriers such as institutional firewalls and limited access to computers and the Internet can be overcome, the dream of true integration between the student experience at university, with its access to knowledge and evidence, and placement experience where real-world access to patients occurs, can become a reality. Curricula at entry level and continuing professional development for qualified staff will need to develop the skills required to engage with technology at all levels.

Preparation of fieldwork educators needs to expand and accelerate. Setting of standards and accreditation of educators are occurring in some places but change is slow. Pressures on staff time are such that programs of educator preparation must compete with other seemingly more urgent staff development needs. Newer initiatives may be difficult to roll out where staff are not prepared. Increasing uptake of programs of educator preparation that are delivered by electronic means would assist those who are time-poor or located in remote areas.

There are still numerous under-researched topics in the evidence base where further work is needed. Moreover, word limits have prevented coverage of many important topics in this book. We note a few topics here to stimulate future research and innovative practices:

- early identification and effective support for students who experience difficulty in fieldwork settings
- the perspectives of clients as major stakeholders in fieldwork education and the impact of students on them
- the changing demographics and work patterns of allied health professionals, and recruitment problems, increasing specialisation and mobility of the allied health workforce
- the types of placements that can maximise student learning outcomes at different points in their programs and the efficacy of different models of fieldwork education and supervision, in the face of expanding student numbers
- understanding if and how supervision actually makes a difference to student learning. This book suggests that peer learning and remote and cross-disciplinary supervision can facilitate effective student learning without direct supervision, so what then is the need, role and timing for effective supervision?

CONCLUSION

In 1997, Hagler, McFarlane, and McAllister identified six priority areas for research in fieldwork education: educator-student relationships, curriculum design, efficacy of models of fieldwork education, predictors of success, the economics of fieldwork education and assessment tools. These have been addressed in this book but continuing research in allied health fieldwork education remains a high priority.

## REFERENCES

Ballinger, P., & Diesen, M. (1994). The cost-effectiveness of clinical education. *Radiologic Technology, 66*(1), 41–45.

Boudreau, M.L. (2009). Is there a generation gap in occupational therapy? *Occupational Therapy Now, 11*(2), 16–18.

Dunkley, C., Pattie, L., Wilson, L., & McAllister, L. (in press). A comparison of rural speech-language pathologists' and residents' access to and attitudes towards the use of technology for speech-language pathology service delivery. *International Journal of Speech-Language Pathology*.

Hagler, P., McFarlane, L., & McAllister, L. (1997). Directions in clinical education research. In L. McAllister, M. Lincoln, S. McLeod, & D. Maloney (Eds.), *Facilitating learning in clinical settings* (pp. 214–251). London: Stanley Thornes.

Higgs, J., & McAllister, L. (2007). Educating clinical educators: Using a model of the experience of being a clinical educator. *Medical Teacher, 29*(2), e51-e57.

Iacono, T., Johnson, H., Humphreys, J., & McAllister, L. (2007). Recruitment of speech pathologists into Victorian positions including those considered less preferred. *Advances in Speech-Language Pathology, 9*(3), 204–212.

Ladyshewsky, R.K., Barrie, S.C., & Drake, V.M. (1998). A comparison of productivity and learning outcomes in individual and cooperative physical therapy clinical education models. *Physical Therapy, 78*(12), 1288–1298.

McAllister, S., Lincoln, M., Ferguson, A., & McAllister, L. (2006). *COMPASS®: Competency assessment in speech pathology*. Melbourne: Speech Pathology Association of Australia Ltd.

Moore, A., Morris, J., Crouch, V., & Martin, M. (2003). Evaluation of physiotherapy clinical education models: Comparing 1:1, 2:1 and 3:1 placements. *Physiotherapy, 89*(8), 489–501.

Oblinger, D.G., & Oblinger, J. (2005). Is it age or IT: First steps toward understanding the net generation. In D.G. Oblinger & J.L. Oblinger (Eds.), *Educating the net generation* (pp. 2.1–2.20). Available: http://www.educause.edu/ir/library/pdf/pub7101.pdf, accessed 30 October 2009.

Romanini, J., & Higgs, J. (1991). The teacher as manager in continuing and professional education. *Studies in Continuing Education, 13*, 41–52.

Schön, D.A. (1987). *Educating the reflective practitioner: Towards a new design for teaching and learning in professions*. San Francisco: Jossey-Bass.

Thorne, S.E. (2006). Nursing education: Key issues for the 21st century. *Nurse Education Today, 26*, 614–621.

*Lindy McAllister PhD*
*School of Medicine*
*The University of Queensland, Australia*

*Christine Bithell MA(Educ)*
*Faculty of Health and Social Care Sciences*
*St George's, University of London and Kingston University, UK*

*Joy Higgs AM PhD*
*The Education for Practice Institute*
*Charles Sturt University, Australia*

# SECTION I: FIELDWORK EDUCATION: STUDENTS, SETTINGS AND POPULATIONS

SUSAN RYAN AND MARGO PATERSON

# 2. TRENDS IN HEALTH PROFESSIONAL EDUCATION

*Changing Student Populations*

This chapter focuses on current trends impacting on professional education and provides a critical, interprofessional appraisal of these trends. Of necessity, the word "trend" denotes general tendencies, often in an upward direction, rather than hard facts. In fact the whole scene in both professional education and in descriptors of student populations is in a ferment of perpetual change, more so now than ever before. As you read this chapter and this book you must be a reader who is comfortable with the impermanence of knowledge and facts, realising that they are temporary, dynamic, constantly changing and therefore, of necessity, problematic and interesting enough to debate and to study (Fish & Twinn, 1995).

In this chapter we address some of the factors in these trends that we consider significant. First, we want to authenticate our credentials for writing an account about international trends. Second, we want to shine a different beam of light on the criticality that we believe needs to be applied to the literature and research about professional practice education and, indeed, on being *"a professional"* in these ever-changing times. By illustrating these complexities in a conceptual model (Figure 2.1) we want to give you a tool against which you can analyse and interpret your own professional educational scene, as well as compare your own experience with that of others from different parts of the world. Then, we examine the impact that credentialing could have on the professional orientation, level of reasoning and behaviours of students emerging from very different educational experiences. Finally, we consider the effects of all these external influences on the current "Generation Y" student population in two countries, Australia and Ireland, as their attitudes and behaviours also impact on professionalism.

## The Authors' Backgrounds

One of the requisites in any subjective account is the credibility of the authors and the perceived social relationship they have with each other, as well as with the conditional relationship they are attempting to develop with you, the reader! Bearing these factors in mind we want to tell you a little about our professional and international backgrounds and how they have come to merge together and influence writing this account. Both authors have been educators for many years and both are lifelong learners who studied for their successive higher degrees as mature students. The following two vignettes introduce you to our international and professional experiences.

*L. McAllister et al., (eds.), Innovations in Allied Health Fieldwork*
*Education: A Critical Appraisal, 17–28.*
© *2010 Sense Publishers. All rights reserved.*

## VIGNETTE 1: SUSAN'S STORY

Susan entered the profession of occupational therapy as a mature-aged student. She had lived in England, Ireland, India and Malaysia before she started studying occupational therapy at the University of Sydney, Australia. Her previous work background included teaching her own children in India and children with intellectual disabilities in Malaysia. Susan worked as an unqualified occupational therapy assistant in a large teaching hospital in Sydney before her course. She was married and had raised four children, one of whom was an adopted Tibetan daughter from another culture and religion. Despite this rich background of diverse international experiences being incorporated into her university learning, these different knowledges were not acknowledged by the university. University education in the late 1970s remained in the positivist, scientific era of thought and qualitative, interpretive work was not part of that scene. After qualification, Susan's professional life continued to be varied and colourful. Returning to India she and an Indian counterpart designed an integrated school for children with polio and for children from very poor socioeconomic backgrounds. A 50:50 mix of children with significant disabilities and those without gave the school a unique social edge in times when the medical background for occupational therapy was very strong. After 6 years a kaleidoscope of opportunities arose. These included working in England in a day-care centre, studying for a Masters degree in the U.S. at Columbia University, and designing and leading different Masters degrees at the University of East London, U.K., where she completed her PhD. Susan ran workshops in Finland, Sweden and Belgium. Then, as Professor she designed a suite of undergraduate and postgraduate programs at University College Cork, Ireland. Susan has returned to Australia and is working at the University of Newcastle researching "Generation Y" students' learning needs, that are different from other generations' needs and study habits. Throughout her career Susan has been interested in researching and listening to unheard student "voices".

## VIGNETTE 2: MARGO'S STORY

Margo took a more traditional path. She started in the occupational therapy profession with a diploma and then a Bachelor degree in occupational therapy (BScOT). She thought that she was "set for life" with the necessary credentials to carry out her career. Initially she worked for 2 years in Canada as a therapist in a rehabilitation setting. Then she travelled overland through Europe and Asia, working in a variety of jobs, and ended up working clinically as an occupational therapist in Australia in vocational rehabilitation and acute care settings. Eventually she returned to Canada to work in the community with home care clients. At this time she did not envision herself as an academic, although she supervised occupational therapy students as a preceptor in all these clinical settings. After 10 years of community practice and a period of leave to look after two young daughters, she was asked to take on the role of coordinating the fieldwork education program at Queen's University. As this new position required academic upgrading she completed a part-time masters degree in epidemiology, while working full time at the university. Margo was responsible for fieldwork education for 10 years until she became chair of the occupational therapy program and realised that she would need additional credentials at the doctoral level. She looked at many PhD programs around the world and noticed that there was a burgeoning interest in qualitative research and in professional reasoning. Therefore she commuted from Canada to Australia to complete her doctoral degree with Professor Joy Higgs at the University of Sydney a month before her 50th birthday, giving her the unique perspective of being a mature student while affiliated with the Canadian university in an administrative role. Following this she has embraced several wonderful opportunities to work as an educational consultant in a number of countries including Hong Kong, Sri Lanka and Russia.

These two vignettes illustrate the considerable international experience we both have experienced but they also illustrate that both of us were aware of international trends, both transferred our professional knowledge between countries and both took advantage of opportunities when they presented. Having introduced ourselves, we put forward our thoughts about the changing professional trends and student populations in the following sections.

## Becoming Even More Critical but in a Different Way

We are sure that anyone reading this chapter will be searching for new knowledge, ideas and innovations to apply to their practice or their research. Seeing things in a different light is a prerequisite for advancing professional knowledge bases. Most educational establishments, particularly those awarding higher degrees, insist that students can undertake comprehensive international database searches. This task is now so easy to accomplish if computerised data-bases are accessible, but that is not always the case in some countries. Criticality of research and its evidence for practice has long been an exhorted trend (Higgs & Titchen, 2007). However, this criticality is usually directed at the quality and integrity of the research methodologies, the researchers' credentials and their findings. We feel strongly that there has been too little emphasis on being critical about the transferability of these research findings into different international contexts. Not enough thought has gone into considering the multiple factors that need to be identified, debated and researched. This is the thrust of this chapter. So, while we give an overview of the current trends in health professional education and the patchy trends in the changing student populations, we also want you to become critical consumers of international papers in a different way. The trend towards globalisation needs to be counteracted by an intellectually challenging rigour of scholarship.

Hegemonic assumptions are made too easily. In our experience, what works in one culture or in one profession will not necessarily work in another. Or some aspects will work and other parts will not be appropriate. This critical, analytical perspective becomes a necessity for advancing health professions' many knowledges (Boud & Edwards, 1999), and these extra layers take our collective knowledge to a deeper level. You need to become a critical consumer of information so that you can manoeuvre your knowledge, adapt it and make it accessible and appropriate in your work context. This is indeed higher level thinking and doing, and should manifest in an altered research focus.

Different trends are evident in collaborative international research. We are starting to see international comparison studies being developed in the health professions (Paterson & Adamson, 2001; Paterson, 2003). These studies often illustrate differences but do not address the outcomes of any transferability. Now, with the advent of Web 2 research, the interconnectedness between teams of researchers brings possibilities of immediate research thoughts being brought together. The advent of telemedicine and teleconferencing brings critical discussions to other levels. All these possibilities are seemingly successful in the scientific realm of knowledge, but it is human, cultural and educational factors that appear to cause transferability or generalisability problems.

19

*The Social Ecological Model*

To illustrate the complexity of the factors we put forward in Figure 2.1 a social ecological model to conceptualise some of the main elements that need to be taken into consideration. This model recognises local and global trends and then identifies major forces that dictate change. The framework is intersectoral and multi-level. It is drawn as a fluid structure to denote changing circumstances at all levels of the physical and social environments (Higgs, Neubauer, & Higgs, 1999).

Each separate portion of the model illustrates a profound body of constructed knowledge. For example, the idea of the interactive practitioner at the centre, a concept first proposed by Higgs and Hunt in 1999, has been developed to encompass constructs from the previous two decades in a newly graduated professional of the 21st century. These include reflection, clinical reasoning development, reflexivity, person-centred care, other interpretations of science, the legitimising of qualitative research methodologies, and the notion of practice artistry rather than technical specialism. All these areas have discrete bodies of knowledge and at this point in the new millennium, an amalgam and integration needs to occur.

---

### SCHOLARLY QUESTIONING

* Taking the concept of an *interactional professional*, ask various colleagues from different professions and from different countries how they interpret this phrase.
* Working from an accepted/agreed interpretation from the original authors, study the other layers in the social ecological model to see how each part is affected by the other and to understand how intermingled each stratum is. Do this with colleagues from other countries.

---

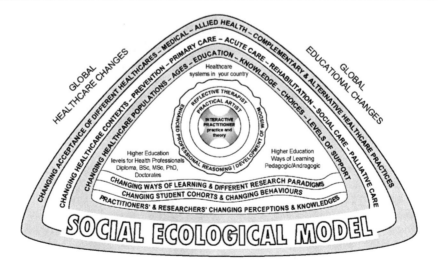

*Figure 2.1. Social ecological model.*

This complex social ecological model can be used as a basis for many different aspects of interpreting practice knowledge and practice behaviours. It can be used as a foundation for international research. Indeed, this scene is so complex that, to make sense of this information in a worldwide sense, rationalisations and professional connections have to be made. International organisations such as the World Federation of Occupational Therapists (WFOT) need to construct guidelines that seek to unify members while still incorporating local contexts (Hocking & Ness, 2005). In the next section we examine a few significant trends and change factors shown in the model that we believe you should consider in your debates.

*So what are the Facts About these Changes?*

We start with trying to identify the current professional entry level for the health disciplines represented in this book. We feel that it could be helpful to provide a sample of the different entry level programs (Bachelors, Masters, doctoral levels) and length of program for four disciplines: audiology (audio), occupational therapy (OT), physiotherapy (PT) and speech language pathology (SLP). In Australia, there are a number of options available for entry level programs with 3- or 4-year (embedded or add-on honours) Bachelors degrees as well as 1–2 year Masters programs in OT, PT, SLP and audio. In Canada all four disciplines' entry level programs are 2-year Masters degrees. In Europe there are parallel tracks in both college and university programs with quite a bit of variation. In South Africa the entry level credential is a 4-year Bachelors degree and in some cases such as SLP the student must do an extra year of community service in underserviced areas. In South America the educational programs are 5-years Bachelor level. In the U.S. the trend is to move toward a professional entry level doctoral degree by 2012 for audio and 2013 for PT. SLP will remain as Masters' entry and OT is deliberating multiple levels of entry including both Masters and doctoral level. It is possible to infer an average age of students in these programs where undergraduates are approximately 18 years of age on entry to a 3- or 4-year program and thus graduate at 21 years. In contrast, Masters level students could be 22 years or older coming into a profession-specific 2-year program and graduating at 24 years or older. It is difficult to obtain accurate statistics about gender; the majority of students in the health professions are female, although this statistic is gradually changing in English-speaking countries, whereas in many Asian countries there is definitely a higher proportion of men.

Commenting on the socioeconomic status of students is also problematic, as student funding requirements and support are variable across countries. But it is safe to say that many students graduate with significant debt loads that need to be repaid once they enter practice. Conversely, many students choose to work long hours during the course of a full-time program. This has consequences in their level of knowledge, the amount of effort put into learning, or in their health status and their work/life balance. Either way, from the student perspective, can be very difficult. For instance, a Canadian OT, PT or SLT student will pay $38,000 for 6 years at university in tuition fees alone. Most students incur other expenses with social expenditure, housing, food and travel. Moreover, going to fieldwork education sites that are often a long way from campus can entail duplicate expenditure for housing to participate in this valuable and often compulsory learning experience. All these factors affect the depth of knowledge gained and alter students' behaviours and priorities.

*How has Credentialing Affected the Student Population in the Professions?*

Depending on your location, you may or may not be aware of a profound shift in the academic level of "entry level" education in professional programs. Upwardly moving degree enhancement or academic drift started in the mid-1990s in the U.S. and has had a cascading effect on many other areas of the world. It began with the PT profession trying to keep up with the chiropractic profession which had doctoral level degrees in the U.S. The first step was to require Masters level as the basic level of education. At the time of writing this chapter, this status had been achieved and now there is a movement to upgrade again to the doctoral level as the minimum criterion by 2013. Canadian PTs followed suit with a decision that Masters level education would be the minimum entry level for PTs effective from 2009. So there has been an international domino effect, with pressure for higher and higher degree qualifications in the PT profession.

In the U.S. other professions such as audio and OT are following suit. The 1997 Commission on Education (Coppard et al., 2009) articulated eight reasons for moving to postbaccalaureate education in OT. As a result, Masters level preparation was expected as the standard entry to practice. These reasons are as follows:

1. OTs and new graduates must demonstrate an unprecedented need for advanced clinical reasoning.
2. New graduates must define and demonstrate the uniqueness of OT.
3. New graduates must view themselves and function as autonomous practitioners.
4. The environment showed readiness to move to postbaccalaureate education.
5. Postbaccalaureate education will better prepare therapists to conduct outcomes research and serve on interdisciplinary teams.
6. Many graduates of baccalaureate programs have received a Bachelor's degree that was equivalent to a Masters degree level education.
7. Postbaccalaureate education would assist in clarifying the role between "professional and technical education".
8. Postbaccalaureate education is in keeping with related fields. (p. 11)

The Canadian Association of OT provided a strong incentive for similar change in minimum standards with a decision that Bachelor level academic programs would not be accredited after 2010. This decision was controversial at the time, with some educators not agreeing that Masters level was necessary for educating competent therapists. This debate is continuing. In the U.K. and Ireland, as well as in Australia, there is a mix being offered at either Bachelor degree with honours or Masters level, and currently, there is no professional preference.

These changes in credentialing have been applauded in many corners but there are those, particularly government officials, who view these processes as simply "creeping credentialing", and have blocked or slowed the process of conversion of degree requirements. Many of these decisions have financial implications for studying and, later, for employing therapists. In some countries the desire to upgrade minimum entry level standards has been denied because their universities do not provide programs for applied professions. This raises important questions concerning the implications for each profession at the international level, for students who wish to make exchanges and therapists who wish to work in different countries after graduation. Although many of these credentialing changes are very recent it is expected that all educational programs will be reviewed by some accreditation process to evaluate the outcomes.

### What Educational Approaches are most Effective with Diverse Student Populations?

An exciting aspect of these trends is much greater diversity in the student population, leading to other changes. We established at the beginning of this chapter that knowledge is so impermanent that other ways of learning which embrace uncertainty would seem to be preferred. There is thus a trend towards using different educational approaches such as inquiry-based learning (IBL) or problem-based learning (PBL) (ENOTHE, 2004) rather than the more traditional approaches which fix a more permanent knowledge marker. ENOTHE argues that student-centred, self-directed teaching and learning are prerequisites for developing lifelong learners. Also, the inductive IBL/PBL methods should create independent creative thinkers who have the capability of moving their professions forward. Higher level awards are thus creating practitioners who are wider in their interpretations and who are also more critical and research minded, and who will incorporate research and evidence into their ongoing practice (Strzelecki, 2009).

Students are older and, we expect, more mature if they have four years of generic education, and many have additional years of life experience before they begin their professional program, as Susan had when she entered the university. There are other advantages to widening access to education programming, as some students are not firm in their career choices until they have completed their undergraduate degree or, as in many cases, have worked in related fields and come into the health disciplines as mature students. Shanahan (2000), interviewing mature students in the U.K., indicated that the "experience of life and the world of work is stated as one of the great advantages of being a mature student, and one that adds to their level of confidence as they prepare to qualify and enter the workforce" (p. 153). However, raising the age bar may exclude other groups of potential students, such as those who could not afford or would be frightened at the thought of 6 years of tertiary study unless specific arrangements are made such as bridging or access courses. There are a great many other arguments in favour of widening access for these seemingly disadvantaged groups, as they bring with them cultural and ethnic richness (Boylan, 2001) as well as possibly being more representative of the potential recipients of therapy.

Educationally, we know that there have been various approaches to the issue of raising minimum entry level standards. These range from educational programs that combine Bachelor and Masters degrees, resulting in a total of 5 years of education, to professional Masters programs generally of 2 years' duration that follow on from an undergraduate degree. There are many other combinations of degrees, including online education at the Masters and doctoral level to allow access to education from remote locations. Hollis and Madill (2006) provided a thoughtful review of the many approaches to online learning in conjunction with campus-based delivery of curricula. They concluded that "evidence suggests that blending combinations of technologies with computer mediated learning enhances interaction and could address higher order learning needs in professional programs" (p. 61). You have seen from this section that professional education is currently in a state of fluidity and varies considerably around the world. Many countries still have diploma entry level programs; others, like New Zealand and Japan, have their programs in both technical colleges and in universities, and yet others are providing doctoral programs.

*What about the Behavioural Changes?*

Although there are significant differences in healthcare trends and in the student populations and levels at which they study, there has been little research so far into the observed changing expectations and behaviours of some of the healthcare student populations in different countries (Fisher & Crabtree, 2009). However, these changing student learning behaviours must be taken into account as they are forcing great debate and educational changes in curricula and educational practices in higher education.

Table 2.1 (adapted from Boudreau, 2009) illustrates the different characteristics of the generations as seen from a Western perspective. Social commentators such as Twenge (2006) from the U.S. have stated that "today's young Americans are more confident, assertive, entitled – and more miserable than ever before". Boudreau's analysis highlights generational differences strongly. Most academics in healthcare and most experienced practising therapists belong to one of the previous generations. Their thinking has been defined as being more logical/linear and traditional, whereas the "net generation" or "millenials" or "Generation Ys" are used to multi-tasking, reading and moving several windows on the computer monitor almost simultaneously. These differences have implications for ways of learning and for developing thinking and reasoning strategies.

In their preliminary research in Australia on "Generation Y" undergraduate students, Ryan and Hills (2010) found that these students are easily distracted and, indeed, bored with knowledge, particularly theoretical knowledge, and wish to be active and "doing" practice. This behaviour trend in learning is only just surfacing and the outcomes for professional integrity cannot yet be determined. For readers of this chapter this is an emerging area that needs to be noted and incorporated into future research about professions. There are evidently significant differences between professional students in different countries, as the vignette below indicates.

*Table 2.1. Generational differences that affect education and ways of learning and working (adapted from Boudreau, 2009)*

|  | *Baby Boomers* | *Generation X* | *Generation Y or Millenials* |
|---|---|---|---|
| They grew up in: | Born 1946–1960 | Born 1961–1978 | Born after 1978 |
| Technology: | Information age just beginning Introduction of calculators, automation and computers | Born in computer age, used them from infancy and comfortable with them | Gaming generation; technology is both a tool for work and a source of entertainment |
| Typical characteristics: | The "Me" generation – because of their numbers attention focused on them | Assertive, self-directed, clever, resourceful Sceptical, put more faith in themselves and less in institutions that have failed them | "Just do it" Practical, techno-savvy Realistic about challenges of modern life, aware of threats of violence, illegal drugs Grew up with the internet, expect many choices |
| Learning styles: | Prefer interactive learning sessions more than lectures, providing a variety of means of learning (books, videos, someone to answer questions) | True multi-taskers Like to learn with CD-ROM, interactive video, internet resources Role play is seen as an opportunity to practise skills and get feedback and coaching on the spot Can learn from experience of others and appreciate shared stories of own shortcomings and learning experiences | Grew up in computer and gaming age – don't want to be shown how to do things, just jump in and try it Used to dealing with simulated situations and environments Contradiction of spending a lot of time working alone on computers but structured into group work in schools |
| Views of work: | Select profession based on intent to make the world a better place Inherited the model of working vertically – enter at ground level and work way up | Want to make money but want job that can balance job satisfaction and quality of life Expect to change jobs and move laterally – no commitment "Build a portable career" – career stability rather than job stability | Saw young entrepreneurs become millionaires at early age Build parallel careers – have multi-tasked and expect to be able to do more than one job at a time |

**VIGNETTE THREE: SUSAN'S PRELIMINARY OBSERVATIONS**

**Ireland and Australia** *Please consult Table 2.1 when reading this comparison*

Susan's experiences of working with undergraduates in two regional universities in Ireland (2001–2006) and Australia (2007 to date) were the start of her fascination with looking at this current generation of students. In Ireland, students had to receive very high points in their Higher School Leaving Certificate to gain entry into the occupational therapy program. There was a great demand for places at the regional university, and only 30 students were accepted from a pool of approximately 500 applicants. Competition encouraged students to familiarise themselves with occupational therapy websites and make visits to practice sites to have a better chance of entry. In Australia, students had also to gain high entry level points, but there was a greater choice of courses within and beyond the regional university. There was also a larger cohort of 100 first year students, and as there was a higher number of places nationally due to the greater choice of universities and programs, many students who entered knew little about the profession they found themselves studying. Many had not gained the points to enter other programs and this profession was not their first choice. Studying Table 2.1 you can see that these two groups had different starting points.

You can see that the motivation and attitudes for studying a particular profession in these two groups would be dissimilar. Furthermore, the social backgrounds of the two groups were different. Ireland, an "old" country, entered into relative prosperity in the 1990s whereas Australia, a "new" country, has had relative prosperity for several decades. The influences of family, parental support and religion were widely different as well. Irish children still came from or were surrounded by larger families. Many helped to look after younger children or had exposure to them. Although losing its domination, the Catholic Church still influenced students through school if not through the church. Australian children in "Generation Y" or otherwise known as "The Millenials" had been brought up in smaller families that involved positive psychology, semi-independence, and computerised environments of quite a sophisticated nature. Most were from two-parent working families.

Students in Ireland had to pay registration fees but no additional fees. Many did not work at all during the semester, and those who did worked to fund their social lives. In contrast, Australian students had to pay full higher education fees amounting to nearly A$10,000 per year in addition to their living, subsistence and social needs. Most students worked during the delivery of their courses. Thus they had to be strategic when deciding into what learning they put their energies. The studying behaviours of the undergraduate students of the same age in the two universities were also widely different. In Ireland, students followed a task-based learning (TBL) curriculum. Tasks were interwoven throughout the courses and were often situated in the community, but always in "real life" contexts that mirrored transferable practice attributes. Readings were done more or less regularly and there was a great involvement of the students in the program as they were so keen to study this profession. By the third year most students were reflective; they questioned established practices and were innovative in their ideas for future practice. In contrast, in Australia, students would not do any tasks unless they were directly linked to an assignment. Readings were strategically followed only if they were being tested. Teaching methods were altered to "fit in" with the students' study and work behaviours. A great deal of time and effort was put in to make these educational accommodations. It is too early to see whether these changes still result in really "interactive therapists".

It could be argued that *"the professional as the outcome"* is the criterion that matters. Comprehensive, multi-faceted research is now delving into these questions. Longitudinal research will also show whether the graduated therapist at the end is deemed comparable and accountable (Cappetta & Haskins, 2009). As we argued at the beginning of this chapter, it is only international, comparative research that will paint in the gaps in this picture.

## What about the Future?

Thorne (2006) has written a thoughtful reflection on key issues for the 21$^{st}$ century in nursing education which has many parallels with other health professions. She stated that our "core business is the preparation of the next generation of nurses [health professionals] so that they can take their rightful place in a world order that we can only begin to comprehend. We craft knowledge frameworks, conceptualizations, and theoretical structures so that an infinite set of new ideas will arise out of the mist and take shape ... key issues for all of us to grapple with in our quest for ensuring the core values" (p. 615). This chapter has highlighted the extreme fluidity of the different trends in professional education that could have real international repercussions. It has also highlighted areas in which future scholarly debate needs to take place. We hope it has aroused your research interest in these practice and educational areas.

## ACKNOWLEDGMENTS

The authors wish to acknowledge the contribution of Paola Durando, librarian at Queen's University Health Sciences, who assisted with a literature search. In addition, Mary Lou Boudreau of the occupational therapy program at Queen's University prepared the original Table 2.1.

## REFERENCES

Boud, D., & Edwards, H. (1999). Learning for practice: Promoting learning in clinical and community settings. In J. Higgs & H. Edwards (Eds.), *Educating beginning practitioners: Challenges for health professional education* (pp. 173–179). Oxford: Butterworth-Heinemann.

Boudreau, M.L. (2009). Is there a generation gap in Occupational Therapy? *Occupational Therapy Now*, *11*(2), 16–18.

Boylan, H. (2001). Broadening access through higher education research in the United States of America: A legacy of the 1960s. Oral presentation at *Researching widening access: International perspectives* symposium, Glasgow Caledonian University, July.

Cappetta, M., & Haskins, A. (2009). Perspectives on accountability: Considerations for occupational therapy faculty and students. *OT Practice*, *14*(3), 11–14.

Coppard, B., Berthelette, M., Gaffney, D., Muir, S., Reitz, S.M., & Slater, D.Y. (2009). Why continue 2 points of entry education for occupational therapists? *OT Practice*, *14*, March 9, 10–14.

ENOTHE. (2004). *PBL stories and signposts: Towards a problem based learning oriented curriculum.* Amsterdam: ENOTHE, P/A Hogeschool van Amsterdam.

Fish, D., & Twinn, S. (1995). *Quality clinical supervision in the health care professions: Principled approaches to practice.* Oxford: Butterworth-Heinemann.

Fisher, T.F. & Crabtree, J.L. (2009). Generational cohort theory: Have we overlooked an important aspect of the entry-level occupational therapy doctorate debate? *American Journal of Occupational Therapy*, *63*(5), 656–660.

Higgs, C., Neubauer, D., & Higgs, J. (1999). The changing health care context: Globalization and social ecology. In J. Higgs & H. Edwards (Eds.), *Educating beginning practitioners: Challenges for health professional education* (pp. 30–37). Oxford: Butterworth-Heinemann.

Higgs, J., & Hunt, A. (1999). Rethinking the beginning practitioner: The interactional professional. In J. Higgs & H. Edwards (Eds.), *Educating beginning practitioners: Challenges for health professional education* (pp. 10–18). Oxford: Butterworth-Heinemann.

Higgs, J., & Titchen, A. (2007). Becoming critical and creative in qualitative research. In J. Higgs, A. Titchen, D. Horsfall & H. Armstrong (Eds.), *Being critical and creative in qualitative research* (pp. 1–10). Sydney: Hampden Press.

Hocking, C., & Ness, E. (2005). Professional education in context. In G. Whiteford & V. Wright-St Clair (Eds.), *Occupation and practice in context* (51–86). Sydney: Elsevier, Churchill Livingstone.

Hollis, V., & Madill, H. (2006). Online learning: The potential for occupational therapy education. *Occupational Therapy International, 13*(2), 61–78.

Paterson, M. (2003). *Understanding "professional practice judgement artistry" in occupational therapy practice*. Unpublished PhD Thesis, The University of Sydney, Australia.

Paterson, M., & Adamson, L. (2001). An international study of educational approaches to clinical reasoning. *British Journal of Occupational Therapy, 64*(8), 403–405.

Ryan, S., & Hills, C. (2010). Generation Y students studying occupational therapy at the University of Newcastle. Unpublished work in progress.

Shanahan, M. (2000). Being a bit older: Mature students' experience of university and healthcare education. *Occupational Therapy International, 7*(3), 153–162.

Strzelecki, M.V. (2009). Doctoral degrees, moving forward going further. *OT Practice, 14*(3), pp. 9–10.

Thorne, S.E. (2006). Nursing education: Key issues for the 21st century. *Nurse Education Today, 26*, 614–621.

Twenge, J. (2006). *Generation me*. New York: Free Press.

*Susan Ryan PhD*
*School of Health Sciences*
*University of Newcastle, Australia*

*Margo Paterson PhD*
*School of Rehabilitation Therapy*
*Queen's University, Canada*

MEGAN SMITH AND JOY HIGGS

# 3. TRENDS IN FIELDWORK EDUCATION

## INTRODUCTION

Fieldwork education has a long-established tradition in health professional education. The sustained and widespread inclusion of fieldwork education in health professional curricula indicates recognition that optimal preparation of health professionals requires students to actively engage with clients in realistic workplace settings. A number of trends are evident in the conduct of fieldwork education. These trends relate to learning and teaching in fieldwork education settings, expectations of graduate capabilities, workplace changes, and enhancing the student experience. In this chapter we explore these emerging trends and the factors that we consider instrumental in driving them. One of the key driving factors is the nexus between workplace and education trends which influence practices of fieldwork education. We complete the chapter by exploring new models of fieldwork education and pose questions about future directions in fieldwork education. This review is developed from a review of contemporary fieldwork education literature and our collective experience in the practice and management of fieldwork. There is a focus on the Australian examples, reflecting the context of our practice; however, many of the examples should have international salience.

## LEARNING AND TEACHING IN CLINICAL SETTINGS

Higgs (2009) described the progressive evolution of health professional education from apprenticeship-style training, with a predominantly experiential model of education, to a contemporary view of education where there is a broader under-standing of the nature of knowledge required for clinical practice and how this knowledge is acquired. Knowledge for clinical practice requires propositional (i.e. research or theoretical) knowledge that is integrated with practice-based know-ledge developed through experience (Higgs, 2009). It is our observation that this evolution in health professional education is reflected in fieldwork education trends. Traditional models of fieldwork education, which replicated the apprenticeship model where students were taught by a more experienced practitioner, are being challenged by a developing pedagogy of fieldwork education, as reflected in subsequent chapters in this book. Importantly, experiential learning is a part of the emerging pedagogy, supported by research and theory, and valuing such learning as a critical way of knowing and learning in the complex, human world of professional practice.

*L. McAllister et al., (eds.), Innovations in Allied Health Fieldwork*
*Education: A Critical Appraisal, 29–38.*
*© 2010 Sense Publishers. All rights reserved.*

Increasingly within the literature is a trend towards applying theoretical perspectives of learning in workplaces to the practice of fieldwork. Where there may have been a tendency to apply concepts relevant to the classroom to the practice of fieldwork education, there now appears to be a developing understanding of learning and practice as it occurs in workplaces and the meaning this has for fieldwork education. Kilminster (2009) argued for the application of theory to the understanding, research and application of fieldwork education in ways that have not been widely done to date. Examples of theories being applied to fieldwork education include those with a focus on the sociocultural and contextual nature of learning (see Eraut, 1994; Billett, 2009).

Another trend in the area of teaching and learning is the promotion of structured learning activities and supported facilitation of student learning in workplace (fieldwork education) *placements*. Whereas in the past it was considered that students learned by immersion as novice practitioners in the clinical context, it is now recognised that optimal student learning requires specific learning activities. Examples include teaching and supporting students to incorporate critical reflective processes (Delaney & Molloy, 2009) and using a problem-based learning approach to facilitate the transfer of learning skills from the university to the workplace (Rose, 2005). Research is emerging (Dornan, Boshuizen, King, & Scherpbier, 2007; Patton, Higgs, & Smith, 2009) that explores how workplace factors (e.g. resources, workplace climate) influence student learning in fieldwork education settings, with potential implications for how learning opportunities are structured by educators. Dornan et al. noted, however, that fieldwork education is a relatively under-researched area of student education in comparison to learning in academic settings.

Although there is expanding discussion in the literature regarding these educational trends and their relevance to fieldwork education we do not know the rate and extent to which actual fieldwork education practices are being substantially changed. It is our observation that many such practices continue to have their basis in traditional models of apprenticeship, where the emphasis is on students observing or participating in guided practice to gain experience. A number of key factors contribute to this situation. Some factors relate to fieldwork educators, such as the reliance in many cases on practitioners to take on students as well as their practice load, the rapid turnover of this "volunteer" pool of fieldwork educators and the consequent difficulty in preparing them for their educator role. Curriculum factors include the relative place of fieldwork education in curricula compared to the dominance of the "academic" curriculum components in terms of prestige and available pedagogy. The academic component of courses is owned by the academic community including senior academics, while fieldwork education is often managed by a few more junior academics and administrative staff whose role is seen more as management or administration than academic. Consequently they have more limited career advancement opportunities. Moreover, when fieldwork education occurs largely off campus, it often fails to take best advantage of both student preparation prior to placements and reflection and consolidation of learning after placements. Not only does this failure limit the success and effectiveness of learning on placements, it also fails to value and incorporate the rich learning from the workplace back into academic learning.

The preparedness of fieldwork educators for their teaching role is emerging as a significant issue. Whereas practitioners had previously been expected to supervise students' practice, there is emerging recognition and expectation that practitioners will also take on a teaching and assessment role. They need to develop teaching skills and strategies, such as structuring learning opportunities, providing feedback on performance to enhance learning, and assessing student performance. Practitioners need and are asking for university support to prepare them for a role for which many have not received formal or even informal training. McAllister (2005) noted that a number of courses exist within the Australian context to prepare fieldwork educators, but the proportion of practitioners accessing these courses remains low.

## EXPECTATIONS OF GRADUATE CAPABILITIES

Trends in the challenges faced by fieldwork education also stem from changing expectations of (and by) graduates on entry to the workforce. Four key trends in this area are the growing interest in the high degree of entry-level competence expected of graduates, the demand for graduates to be able to justify their practice in a evidence-based practice environment, the focus on interprofessional practice and teamwork as a norm (occurring in the face of high levels of workplace competition for employment), and the expectation that graduates have the status and competence to be internationally mobile. Fieldwork education addresses these challenges through such strategies as setting high performance expectations for placements, focusing on assessment strategies and supervisor training, identifying fieldwork education standards, emphasising interprofessional education, and expanding student mobility through international placement opportunities.

Many health professions have identified and developed standards and expectations of competency for new graduates (e.g. Australian Physiotherapy Standards (Australian Physiotherapy Council, 2006) and Australian Competency Standards for entry-level occupational therapists (OT Australia, 1994). Documented standards for practice result in expectations that providers of health professional education will demonstrate how students have achieved the relevant standards and competency. In this way these competencies shape fieldwork education practices by determining the nature of the experiences expected for students during their education and the behaviours they are expected to demonstrate upon completion of their degrees. For example, in some professions students are expected to have worked with specific client groups and in particular settings to ensure they have demonstrated the competencies identified in the professional standards (McAllister, 2005). Further there is greater focus on the assessment of students' performance, with fieldwork educators playing a critical role in the determination of students' readiness for practice (Courtney & Wilcock, 2005). Within Australia a number of health professions have engaged in the development of national forms for the assessment of competency. Examples of such assessment programs are the Australian Competency Assessment in Speech Pathology tool (Speech Pathology Australia, 2009) and the Student Practice

Evaluation Form used in occupational therapy (Allison & Turpin, 2004). As mentioned above, fieldwork educators are required to develop skills in the assessment of competence in practice settings. Although fieldwork educators have often engaged in assessment, the nature and quality of their assessment practices are emerging as critical focal points for both research and professional development.

Many allied health professional graduates are now expected, upon entry to practice, to display a high level of work readiness and to have the capacity to engage in independent practice. Whereas traditionally there was an emphasis on the post-graduate education opportunities for an expanded scope of practice learning and skills development, workforce pressures (e.g. higher workloads and decreased staff numbers) are shifting these expectations to entry-level education. Consequently, workplace placements are critical in preparing work-ready graduates, and the types of experiences students are exposed to in senior years are expected to approximate the first year of professional practice (Hummell & Williamson, 1999; Hummell, 2007). There is also a growing need to facilitate the transition from student to graduate during professional entry programs rather than after graduation.

A further trend that has emerged related to expectation of graduates' capabilities has been the increasing expectation of graduate readiness for interprofessional practice. Interprofessional practice has been supported as an optimal approach for client care (Zwarenstein, Goldman, & Reeves, 2009). Consequently there have been strong calls for students to engage in interprofessional educational opportunities, particularly interprofessional placements (World Health Organization Technical Series Report, 1988). A number of challenges exist to developing interprofessional educational placement opportunities. These include issues of the structure and logistics of coordinating students from different disciplines to complete placements at the same time, and the absence of examples of good interprofessional practice occurring systematically within the workplace that provide student experience opportunities (Davidson, Smith, & Stone, 2009).

Expectations that graduates will be effective global citizens and will positively contribute to increased workforce mobility have spurred interest in providing students with international experiences. This trend is reflected in opportunities for placements in international settings. Students find these placements attractive (Kinsella, Bossers, & Ferreira, 2008). Initiatives such as the "Go Global" program offered for health students through Curtin University in Western Australia (http://ot.curtin.edu.au/go_global/) provide opportunities for students to complete international and inter-professional fieldwork education placements.

## WORKFORCE NEEDS

Many of the trends in fieldwork education are occurring in response to the nexus between the workplace as a provider of placements and educators requiring place-ments to ensure that students can complete their education. In many countries the situation relating to the demand and supply of placements for health professionals has been described as critical (McAllister, 2005; Rose, 2005; Thomas et al., 2007; National Health Workforce Taskforce, 2008). Rose (2005) described a cycle of crisis in which critical health workforce shortages have resulted in a dramatic growth in the number of health professional students being educated. In Australia this was reflected in a 46% increase in the number of students requiring placements in the period 2006 to 2010. However, increased student numbers correspondingly increased the pressure for clinical placements on health care systems that are ill-equipped to manage the number and types of placements required, given the very workforce shortages that the expanding student numbers are intended to address. Rose noted that a critical factor contributing to this problem has been a failure by governments, employers and universities to recognise and respond to the costs of providing fieldwork education, with a consequent lack of sufficient and dedicated funding for fieldwork education. Employers often respond by declining to accept students, citing their over-stretched staff and resources, yet expect well educated, work-ready graduates. Universities often respond by looking for alternatives to real-world fieldwork education practice, which can result in positive and effective learning opportunities to supplement fieldwork but can also result in decreasing real-world learning experiences, thus losing these powerful and essential learning opportunities for students.

The demand for placements has seen a shift from a taken-for-granted expectation that students will be provided with placement opportunities to a situation where a clinical placement is seen as a commodity that is viewed as costly as well as valuable. This has given rise to expectations that funding should flow from educational institutions to providers of placements. In some circumstances this has resulted in placement providers being in a position to offer placements to the highest (university) bidder. This situation is less than desirable, and the issue of payment for placements is controversial. There is evidence that the contribution of students to service provision negates any costs associated with student education (Jones & Akehurst, 1999; McAllister, 2005). However, this argument does not refute that there are costs associated with providing fieldwork placements. Argument over who should pay and how funds should be transferred from universities to workplaces overshadows the reality that there are insufficient funds in the system to conduct fieldwork education. The problems associated with the demand for enhanced capacity and ensuring quality placements can be meaningfully addressed by the injection of funding to universities that recognises the costs of health professional education.

In Australia these issues are gaining attention. The Council of Australian Governments has recognised the issues of placements and the relationship to the health workforce and has implemented a strategy via the Health Workforce Agency directed toward clinical training (fieldwork education) reform. The scope of the agency's activities encompasses data, organisation and capacity; funding arrange-ments and responsibilities; new models and innovation; governance and organisation; and quality, efficiency and effectiveness (National Health Workforce Taskforce, 2008). Critical elements of this strategy are accurately quantifying the demand for placements and the capacity of the healthcare system to supply these placements, dedicated funding to support placements, and governance approaches that have a national agenda. A similar shortage of placements has been described in other countries and therefore this remains an important issue shaping future fieldwork education practices (Baldry Currens and Bithell, 2003; Thomas et al., 2007; Blakely, Rigg, Joynson, & Oldfield, 2009).

Practitioners with a fieldwork educator role have been largely unrecognised members of the health workforce. Increasingly, the demands and importance of skilled educators are being recognised and explored (Irby, 1994; McAllister, Higgs, & Smith, 2008). The growing demand for fieldwork education placements is increasing the expectations that clinical staff will be involved in an educational role as a core component of their practice. It is likely and desirable that we will continue to see the emergence of defined and specialist educator roles across the health professions. To enhance fieldwork education practices this role expansion will ideally be linked with appropriate career structures, support and remuneration.

A final example where the workplace–education nexus is shaping fieldwork education practices is the growing demand for students to meet compulsory legal expectations and policy directives set by workplaces (e.g. health service systems) prior to commencing placements. These directives relate to activities such as students' mandatory completion of police checks and immunisation requirements. These mandatory requirements, together with expanded reporting requirements of health agencies and difficulties in locating placements, have seen a trend towards high workloads for staff involved in the management and administration of fieldwork placements. Orrell, Cooper, and Jones (1999) reported on these issues and high-lighted the complex nature of fieldwork education management. Technological solutions are being investigated to assist in the data management and process elements of managing placements.

## ENHANCING THE STUDENT EXPERIENCE

The final trend we have observed in fieldwork education has been in recognising and managing the student experience. Understanding and enhancing students' experiences is a particularly popular goal in higher education today (Richardson, 2005). Fieldwork education placements are challenging for students in many ways, ranging from learning demands and pressure to perform in their future practice arena to coping with the logistics of engaging in placements. Coping with placement logistics can place a considerable burden on students, particularly if the placement requires relocation to a place away from their home. Murdoch (2003) identified factors outside the placement, such as accommodation, transport and associated costs, that impacted upon student learning during the placement. These concerns are being recognised, and in our local experience scholarships are being introduced to support students undertaking fieldwork education placements. Likewise improved methods are being developed for maintaining contact between university educators and students and providing access to learning resources for students on placement, to support their learning. Such resources include technologies such as mobile phones and distance access to library resources (Callaghan, Newcombe, Abey, Gore, & Lea, 2007–08; Callaghan, Doherty, Lea, & Webster, 2008).

## NEW MODELS OF FIELDWORK EDUCATION PLACEMENTS

We have observed that the above trends are manifest in innovations and emerging models of fieldwork that commonly fit into two categories. In the first category, models demonstrate the emergent adoption of placements with educator:student ratios of 1:2, 1:3 and 1:4, based on recognition of the value of peer learning (Ladyshewsky, Barrie, & Drake, 1998) (see Chapter 13). Although placements with these ratios have existed for some time there is now greater preference for them than for 1:1 placements. A second trend has been the emergence of non-traditional placement models, for instance where students complete placements with intermittent rather than continuous support from a qualified health professional (McAllister, 2005), or where the focus is on students completing projects for health care services (see Chapter 16). Fieldwork education placements are being recognised as having the potential to provide reciprocal benefits to sites and students; students have a learning opportunity and the site receives input to its service provision.

Although the value of a real-world placement where students can experience client care in all its reality continues to be valued, there has been the emergence of alternatives and complements to placements, with increasing interest in the use of simulated learning environments (SLEs) (Issenberg, McGaghie, Petrusa, Gordon, & Scalese, 2005). In SLEs students apply their skills using simulations designed to replicate the workplace setting, such as high-fidelity devices and models, trained actors and virtual reality programs (e.g. Broom, Lynch, & Preece, 2009; Warburton, 2009) (see also Chapter 17). The emergence of these tools reflects an interest in providing learning environments for students that allow them to practise skills in safe and controlled environments. High-tech SLEs have only recently been mad possible by developments in technology and as such are in early stages of develop-ment and application. These developments are receiving increased attention due to the current limitations in supply of traditional placements, and SLEs are being considered as potential substitutes for or supplements to workplace placements; this decreases the number and types of placements for universities to locate in a highly competitive environment. The growth in the use of these technologies (Warburton, for example, reported that 75% of UK universities were using or developing "Second Life" initiatives), would suggest that these initiatives will be a sustained trend, leading to the need to explore their integration with traditional fieldwork education practices.

Although new models of fieldwork education are emerging, the current challenges affecting the demand and supply of placements are driving further calls for new models of clinical education to address the problems being faced. With expanding research and interest in fieldwork education it is possible that new models may emerge and existing models may be enhanced. However, we suggest that it is unlikely for new models to completely resolve the existing problems.

## CONCLUSION

There are a number of significant trends in fieldwork education. We foresee that in the future many of the current trends will continue. Critical factors driving fieldwork education will be the nexus between the workplace and education, and technological advances that provide new options. Some key questions we have identified are:

– Will the crisis in fieldwork education placement supply continue or will government, industry or university actions significantly increase the capacity to provide placements?

– Will the strategies employed to address the placement supply problem support the developing pedagogy for best practice in learning in fieldwork education?

– What future directions will research related to fieldwork education take, and how will research findings influence practice? As it is recognised that research is often poorly incorporated into practice, will this be an issue for fieldwork education and how might it be addressed?

– Which innovations and new models of practice will gain traction and how will existing models be modified? Will a robust model of supervisor-student relationship be sustained in the future?

– How will the role of fieldwork educator evolve? Will this position continue to emerge as a significant and important role in health professional practice?

– How will the student voice impact on fieldwork education practices?

– How will continued developments in technology shape fieldwork education?

## REFERENCES

Allison, H., & Turpin, M. (2004). Development of the student placement evaluation form: A tool for assessing student fieldwork performance. *Australian Occupational Therapy Journal, 51*(3), 125–132.

Australian Physiotherapy Council. (2006). *Australian Standards for Physiotherapy.* Available: http://www.physiocouncil.com.au/file_folder/AustralianStandardsforPhysiotherapySummary, accessed 27 January 2009.

Baldry Currens, J.A., & Bithell, C.P. (2003). The 2:1 clinical placement model: Perceptions of clinical educators and students. *Physiotherapy, 89*(4), 204–218.

Billett, S. (2009). Conceptualizing learning experiences: Contributions and mediations of the social, personal, and brute. *Mind, Culture, and Activity, 16*(1), 32–47.

Blakely, C., Rigg, J., Joynson, K., & Oldfield, S. (2009). Supervision models in a 2:1 acute care placement. *British Journal of Occupational Therapy, 72*(11), 515–517.

Broom, M., Lynch, M., & Preece, W. (2009). Using online simulation in child health nurse education. *Paediatric Nursing 21*(8), 32–36.

Callaghan, L., Doherty, A., Lea, S.J., & Webster, D. (2008). Understanding the information and resource needs of UK health and social care placement students. *Health Information and Libraries Journal, 25*, 253–260.

Callaghan, L., Newcombe, M., Abey, S., Gore, O., & Lea, S. J. (2007-08). Trials and tribulations: Three key elements in running a successful mobile learning trial in a health care setting. *Learning and Teaching in Higher Education, 2*, 71–73.

Courtney, M., & Wilcock, A. (2005). The Deakin experience: Using national competency standards to drive undergraduate education. *Australian Occupational Therapy Journal, 52*(4), 360–362.

Davidson, M., Smith, R., & Stone, N. (2009). Interprofessional education: Sharing the wealth. In C. Delaney & E. Molloy (Eds.), *Clinical education in the health professions* (pp. 70–91). Chatswood, NSW: Elsevier.

Delaney, C., & Molloy, E. (2009). Critical reflection in clinical education: Beyond the "swampy lowlands". In C. Delaney & E. Molloy (Eds.), *Clinical education in the health professions* (pp. 3–24). Chatswood, NSW: Elsevier.

Dornan, T., Boshuizen, H., King, N., & Scherpbier, A. (2007). Experience-based learning: A model linking the process and outcomes of medical students' workplace learning. *Medical Education, 41*, 84–91.

Eraut, M. (1994). *Developing professional knowledge and competence.* London: Falmer Press.

Higgs, J. (2009). Ways of knowing for clinical practice. In C. Delaney & E. Molloy (Eds.), *Clinical education in the health professions* (pp. 25–37). Chatswood, NSW: Elsevier Churchill Livingstone.

Hummell, J. (2007). *Allied health graduates' first year of employment.* Unpublished PhD thesis, The University of Sydney, Australia.

Hummell, J., & Williamson, P. (1999). Fieldwork in occupational therapy: Close to the edge. *Focus on Health Professional Education: A Multi-disciplinary Journal, 1*(2), 33–49.

Irby, D.M. (1994). What clinical teachers in medicine need to know. *Academic Medicine, 69*(5), 333–342.

Issenberg, S.B., McGaghie, W.C., Petrusa, E.R., Gordon, D.L., & Scalese, R.J. (2005). Features and uses of high-fidelity medical simulations that lead to effective learning: A BEME systematic review. *Medical Teacher, 27*(1), 10–28.

Jones, M.L., & Akehurst, R. (1999). The cost and value of pre-registration clinical placements for Project 2000 students. *Journal of Advanced Nursing, 30*(1), 169-178.

Kilminster, S. (2009). Recognising and bridging gaps: Theory, research and practice in clinical education. In C. Delaney & E. Molloy (Eds.), *Clinical education in the health professions* (pp. 38–49). Chatswood, NSW: Elsevier.

Kinsella, E.A., Bossers, A., & Ferreira, D. (2008). Enablers and challenges to international practice education: A case study. *Learning in Health and Social Care, 7*(2), 79–92.

Ladyshewsky, R.K., Barrie, S., & Drake, V.M. (1998). A comparison of productivity and learning outcomes in individual and cooperative physical therapy clinical education models. *Physical Therapy, 78*(12), 1288–1298.

McAllister, L. (2005). Issues and innovations in clinical education. *International Journal of Speech-Language Pathology, 7*(3), 138–148.

McAllister, L., Higgs, J., & Smith, D. (2008). Facing and managing dilemmas as a clinical educator. *Higher Education Research and Development, 27*(1), 1–13.

Murdoch, J. (2003). *Lifestyle change and financial demands as contributing factors to stress for rural allied health students during clinical placement.* Dissertation completed as a requirement of Bachelor of Physiotherapy (Honours), Charles Sturt University.

National Health Workforce Taskforce. (2008). *Data, capacity and clinical placements across Australia: a discussion paper.* Available: http://www.nhwt.gov.au, accessed 19 April 2010.

Orrell, J., Cooper, L., & Jones, R. (1999). Making the practicum visible. Paper presented at the HERDSA Annual International Conference, Melbourne, July.

OT Australia. (1994). *The Australian Competency Standards for Entry-Level Occupational Therapists.* Available: http://www.ausot.com.au/inner.asp?relid=11&pageid=22, accessed 27 January 2009.

Patton, N., Higgs, J., & Smith, M. (2009, June). Work integrated learning: Physiotherapy clinical education experience. Paper presented at the 16th World Conference on Co-operative Education and Work Integrated Learning, Vancouver.

Richardson, J.T.E. (2005). Instruments for obtaining student feedback: A review of the literature. *Assessment & Evaluation in Higher Education, 30*(4), 387–415.

Rose, M.L. (2005). The cycle of crisis in clinical education: Why national-level strategies must be prioritized. *International Journal of Speech-Language Pathology, 7*(3), 158–161.

Speech Pathology Australia. (2009). *COMPASS®: Competency Assessment in Speech Pathology.* Available: http://www.speechpathologyaustralia.org.au/resources/compassr, accessed 18 January 2010.

Thomas, Y., Dickson, D., Broadbridge, J., Hopper, L., Hawkins, R., Edwards, A., et al. (2007). Benefits and challenges of supervising occupational therapy fieldwork students: Supervisors' perspectives. *Australian Occupational Therapy Journal, 54*, S2-S12.

Warburton, S. (2009). Second life in higher education: Assessing the potential for and the barriers to deploying virtual worlds in learning and teaching. *British Journal of Educational Technology, 40*(3), 414–426.

World Health Organization Technical Series Report. (1988). *Learning together to work together for health. Report of a WHO Study Group on Multiprofessional Education of Health Personnel: The Team Approach.* Geneva: World Health Organization.

Zwarenstein, M., Goldman, J., & Reeves, S. (2009). Interprofessional collaboration: Effects of practice-based interventions on professional practice and healthcare outcomes. *Cochrane Database of Systematic Reviews, 3* (Art. No. CD000072).

*Megan Smith PhD*
*School of Community Health*
*Charles Sturt University, Australia*

*Joy Higgs AM PhD*
*The Education for Practice Institute*
*Charles Sturt University, Australia*

LINDY MCALLISTER, CLAIRE PENN, YDA SMITH,
SANDRA VAN DORT AND LINDA WILSON

# 4. FIELDWORK EDUCATION IN NON-TRADITIONAL SETTINGS OR WITH NON-TRADITIONAL CASELOADS

Many factors motivate the development of fieldwork education placements in non-traditional settings or with non-traditional caseloads. Changing population demographics have been recognised in both developed and developing countries (see e.g. Pickering et al., 1998). Such demographic factors include migration, increasing disability rates, aging populations, and rural-urban as well as urban-rural population drifts. Social changes, including widening gaps between the wealthy and the impoverished, people with low socio-economic status and recent migrant arrivals living in outer urban areas which may have poor public transport and hence poorer access to services, and homelessness, have led some groups to become disenfranchised from traditional services. Changes in information technology which support tele-health create the potential for both increased access to healthcare for some groups in society, and further disenfranchisement for other groups who do not have such IT access (Baur, 2008). The shift of healthcare from hospital to community settings, driven partly by political and financial considerations and partly by philosophical changes that see a move from a medical model to a social model of health care, require practitioners to involve clients and their families in healthcare decisions and planning, and direct intervention beyond impairment towards participation in society.

This chapter presents three case studies which describe the need for and rationales of innovative fieldwork placements with non-traditional client groups or with clients in non-traditional settings. Van Dort and colleagues outline work done in Malaysia to provide speech language pathology for low income families and their children with disabilities who attend an early intervention program, a context in which services are not well developed and in which speech language pathology is not typically provided. In Malaysia, as in other developing countries, a growing middle-class and their desire for rehabilitation services for their family members with disabilities is driving expansion of services, necessitating educational preparation of professionals who will provide such services in the future. Smith, in contrast writes from the U.S., a country with highly developed healthcare and social services, and describes innovative occupational therapy fieldwork in a community-based service for resettled refugees. In the third case study, Penn writes from a whole-of-curriculum perspective about preparing speech language pathology students for work in South Africa, a country with a mix of highly developed and developing healthcare services. South Africa has had world-leading healthcare for its white citizens for many decades. A compulsory community service (CS) year for doctors was first introduced there

L. McAllister et al., (eds.), Innovations in Allied Health Fieldwork
Education: A Critical Appraisal, 39–47.

in 1998, expanding to other health professions, including speech language pathology in 2003. The goal of CS was to "distribute health personnel throughout the country in an equitable manner" (Department of Health, 1997) and "to ensure improved service provision to all the citizens of our country". The aim was also "to provide our young professionals with an opportunity to develop skills, acquire knowledge, behaviour patterns and critical thinking that will help them in professional development". A further implicit aim for CS was in counteracting (or at least delaying) emigration trends of health professionals (Reid, 2000).

## CASE STUDY 1: SANDRA VAN DORT, LINDY MCALLISTER AND LINDA WILSON

### Introduction and Context for the Case Study

Speech language pathology services in Malaysia are typically available only in traditional medical model settings such as hospitals, and university and private clinics (Van Dort, 2005). Due to the limited number of speech language pathologists in the country and the critical need for equitable and accessible services for communication disability, alternative service delivery models need to be explored. The placement described in this case study was part of a capacity building action research project which aimed at pioneering a student speech language pathology placement in an urban community-based rehabilitation (CBR) setting. The CBR setting was chosen for its emphasis on increasing the equitability and accessibility of services for persons with disability. The intention of this innovation was to educate students for working in such settings and thus to prepare them to advocate for speech language pathology services in this and other disability settings.

The CBR centre where this placement occurred had an enrolment of 27 children with a range of developmental disabilities and was staffed by five CBR grassroots workers, three of whom were parents of a child with disability. The CBR team conducted mainly centre-based activities with occasional home visits. The centre was situated on the ground floor of a low-cost apartment block and activities ran five mornings a week. All the activities proceeded in the one moderately-sized rehabilitation room, in extremely noisy conditions and with a limited set of appropriate resources.

### Planning the Placement

Before the student placement began, the centre stakeholder committee for this project discussed and agreed on some key issues, namely that the students would be at the centre three mornings a week over a 10-week block; the majority of the sessions would take place in a quieter room near the rehabilitation room; and there would be a focus on transferring appropriate skills and knowledge to the CBR workers and parents.

### The Students

Two final year students, Meela and Maggie (their chosen pseudonyms), opted for this placement. Consistent with other student clinics run by our university department, the supervisor (author Van Dort) accompanied the students into their placement. The students agreed to write a short journal entry each week about their learning experience. At the end of the placement they were involved in a focus group discussion (FGD) with another staff member in our department about the placement. The following description of learning experiences and outcomes is based on student data.

*Learning Experiences*

Both students described a range of learning experiences which were based on their initial observations, individual and group therapy sessions, planning and review sessions with the CBR workers, home and community visits, CBR worker/parent workshops, and informal interactions.

*Learning Outcomes*

Both students perceived a mutual learning/teaching relationship between themselves and the CBR workers in their collaborations. For instance, Meela learned from the CBR workers, wealth of experience and knowledge of the children but felt she could contribute by helping the workers put communication goals into the activities they conducted.

Maggie noted that her initial fear that the CBR workers would not trust students disappeared over time as she got to know the workers better:

Initially I felt that it would be a bit difficult to transfer the skills because the CBR workers were older than us and we were student clinicians but as time went on we built up rapport. Then they began to trust us and they often asked questions about how to carry out certain things; for example how to do prompting.

Further, both students noted that they could understand their clients and families more comprehensively in the community setting. For instance, Maggie commented how home visits were a real "eye-opener" for her. This was different from her previous placements, where she had just been "sitting in the therapy room". These visits had allowed her to "imagine and empathise" with the real-world difficulties her clients and their families faced.

*Challenges Faced*

While the benefits were obvious, there were challenges. The most significant challenge faced was in terms of the lack of structure in the environment. Meela found the context overwhelming at times, "nothing had been set up!" and no structure established, and recorded this in her journal. Another challenge that both Maggie and Meela faced was in terms of defining their roles. Maggie perceived that the informal atmosphere of the CBR meant that she had to "work much harder" at convincing parents and CBR workers to adopt certain measures, as compared to hospital settings where the speech language pathologist's role is clearer. Meela worked with two mothers who were often absent from therapy sessions. Factors such as the families' low income status and personal struggles explained this, but it had the effect of dampening Meela's confidence and limiting the carryover of goals. It was hard to immediately change the culture of the centre in this respect.

*Supervisor Reflections*

Speech language pathology service delivery should be adapted to the context and needs of each country, and the above example demonstrates that it is possible for students to work successfully in non-traditional contexts. It must be noted that initially a weaker student is likely to need more structured support (e.g., a more careful selection of clients and increased supervisor-student contact). A notable characteristic of this community setting was that it allowed the students to gain a deeper understanding of their clients and their families, which informed their practice. "Walking out of the therapy room" of a traditional medical model setting and into the CBR had indeed helped them grow as clinicians.

## CASE STUDY 2: YDA SMITH

*Introduction and Context for the Case Study*

Since the fall of 2004, University of Utah occupational therapy students have been participating in fieldwork experiences at University Neighbourhood Partners – Hartland Partnership (UNP-Hartland), a university-community partnership that brings together students and faculty, community organisations, and residents in a traditionally low-income, culturally diverse section of the city. Many of the residents at the centre are from villages in Somalia or Myanmar where they had no access to electricity or indoor plumbing. When they arrive in the U.S. most do not speak English and have no familiarity with technology such as the use of computers. Many are illiterate in their own language. After fleeing their homelands and surviving in refugee camps for as long as 20 years they may struggle with mental health issues; some arrive with physical disabilities as well. It is not uncommon for women to become isolated in their new homes, as they lack the skills to access community resources and are often caring for small children. Many of these residents are at risk for the development of depression due to the occupational deprivation they are experiencing. Life skills training, aimed at increasing participation in meaningful occupations, is provided one-on-one, in groups in the centre, in the home with families and, in the case of gardening and weaving, with specific communities.

*The Students and their Supervision*

Fieldwork settings such as this one can provide students with the educational back-ground they need to respond to the contemporary demands of an ever-changing society. To date over 40 occupational therapy students have completed fieldwork experiences in this setting, working with students from social work, linguistics, and nursing. OT students are supervised using a collaborative learning model (Cohn, Dooley & Simmons, 2001) designed to provide students with opportunities to learn from each other with a moderate amount of on-site supervision. They have to organise their own schedules, set priorities and collaborate with staff and students from other disciplines. Often an interpreter is not available and students must be creative and use gestures and modelling to explain a new skill.

## The Learning Experience and Learning Outcomes

Each new group of refugees accessing services at the centre brings with them needs that are different from those of the residents before them. As a result, there are no fixed programs with established curriculum content. Students are placed in a position where they must listen for current interests and concerns and then develop programming to fit. By working in the community with an underprivileged population, they come to realise that healthcare is part of a broad complex of inter-woven issues which include access to education, employment, and differences in cultural values and beliefs. Examples of student comments include, "The benefit of doing this kind of fieldwork is learning how to help clients from diverse backgrounds with respect and understanding." Another student stated, "I learned that I can be pushed out of my comfort zone and still be OK… It also helped sensitize me to the fact that my values are not universal and not the only ones that count."

This setting provides students with experiences that are in perfect alignment with the underlying constructs of occupational therapy. Students do not provide services "to", but work "with" residents to help them achieve their goals. Occupational therapy students provide life skills training which includes education on use of public transportation, home safety and cleaning, rules of the road for driving, access to healthcare and other community resources, pre-employment skills, computer literacy, and money management. Moreover, students have helped to develop gardening programs and functional English classes, and have been involved in restoring weaving as an occupation for Karen women from Myanmar. The very nature of the setting highlights the value and significance of participation in meaningful occupations, and students have ample opportunity to develop their observation skills, practise grading of activities and therapeutic use of self. One student commented, "It is a chance for us to truly try our skill at remaining occupation-based in any setting". Another student said, "I am learning how to identify needs and provide assistance so refugees learn how to help themselves now that they live in America. Teaching independence is what OT is all about".

Students provide program evaluation data through reflection papers, fieldwork evaluation forms and individual interviews with their supervisor. They consistently express that they are challenged in multiple ways and are transformed by the experience while gaining critical skills that will generalise to any treatment setting.

## CASE STUDY 3: CLAIRE PENN

### Introduction and Context for the Case Study

South Africa is a country characterised by great linguistic and cultural diversity. Limited professional resources exist for the population and there are barriers to care imposed by issues such as poverty, illiteracy, the legacy of apartheid and the specific illness profile of the population. A large proportion of the country's population resides in rural areas and continues to have limited access to rehabilitation. Newly qualified speech language pathology and audiology graduates working in such under-serviced areas have described the experience as "culture shock", moving from the initial stage of feeling "Overwhelmed" through phases of "Fascination, Irritation, Depression, and then Adjustment" (Penn & Stein, in press).

This case study describes the factors that have influenced the curriculum of the Department of Speech Pathology and Audiology at the University of the Witwatersrand, that aims to equip graduates with the knowledge, confidence, resilience and values needed to deliver effective services under these conditions. Much of our experience is based on the training of community-based rehabilitation workers and our two-year diploma course for speech and hearing therapy community workers which ran until 1994 (Bortz, Schoub, & McKenzie, 1992). A further major influence on our curriculum as well as on the development of the profession has been the introduction in 2003 of Community Service (CS). Published accounts suggest that CS has generally been successful in achieving its goals (Bateman, 2004). For the past 7 years, in order to gain insight into concerns in practice, and to evaluate and engage in ongoing refinement of our curriculum in preparing graduates for CS, our Department has hosted a feedback session for our new graduates in the middle of their CS year. Details of this process have been described by Penn and Stein (in press) and our findings in summary relate to the challenges and demands around professional and technical issues, systemic and managerial issues, interpersonal issues and ethical issues. The curriculum implications of these findings are considered below.

*Curriculum Implications*

1. *Philosophy.* An underlying principle of the curriculum is to embed culture into every aspect of teaching and to develop a critical attitude which integrates theory and application. This may be described as a framework of cultural (as opposed to cross-cultural) speech language pathology and audiology and aligns to the need to recognise that the clinician working in this complex world should remain reflective and in a permanent state of feeling "culturally incompetent" (Swartz, 2007). The cultural diversity of our staff and student body as well as the clients whom they serve is an excellent springboard for self-awareness and clinical training. Creation of a culturally aware graduate incorporates exposure to a range of traditional customs and beliefs regarding illness, different client- and family-centred approaches, and an understanding of how public health issues and sociopolitical context influence service delivery. Each unit of the undergraduate syllabus is coordinated with clinical work, most of which takes place off-campus at one of the 41 community-based sites (these include hospitals, schools, centres for the aged, orphanages, non-government organisations, and stroke groups).

As a second main governing principle of the curriculum, we continue to prepare graduates for dual registration as both speech language pathologists and audiologists. This has been controversial, but our commitment has been strengthened by graduates' recent feedback that there remain limited opportunities in the public sector to employ singly qualified audiologists. The majority of our graduates indicate a preference for a dual qualification and with it a level of preparedness for the types of problems they encounter.

2. *Language issues.* The long-standing inclusion in the curriculum of a course in an indigenous language has had mixed results and has been controversial, as the language of the workplace often did not match the language studied, there being 11 official languages in South Africa. Sign language is also seen as a useful option for language study. There is greater emphasis in the curriculum on addressing language diversity and working with mid-level workers and interpreters (Penn, 2000). Particular attention has been paid in lectures and practicals to asserting the role of our profession in advocating language services at clinical sites and promoting the critical potential role of the third party as cultural broker as well as interpreter.

3. *Ethics training.* Many of our graduates have reported a high level of ethical distress linking to service delivery in a context of poverty, vulnerability and unique disease burden, particularly for HIV/AIDS patients. Ethics has always been an essential part of the training in our course, and over recent years the course has been modified to include a component and an assignment on ethical problem-solving based on real incidents encountered in the clinical setting of our final year students. Students are urged to describe and analyse the ethical dimensions of a case, and to use problem-solving strategies including a cost-benefit analysis in the context of scarce resources. The consequences of political unrest, xenophobia, a high number of orphans in caseloads, lack of equipment and suitable assessment measures are all reflected in these cases.

4. *Community work input.* Lectures on counselling and community work are an integral part of our training and these are reinforced by a service learning opportunity in a third year course which involves the development of a workshop within a community of students' choice (see Mophosho & Stein, 2008, for details of this component). Students are exposed to the practice of community work, principles of community development and local social and health policy issues, and they are assessed by a group project involving engagement in a situation, needs analysis, development of a community profile, and demonstration of an ability to encourage community representation and participation.

5. *Curriculum content.* Other recent curriculum developments arising from new-graduate feedback include expansion in areas such as multiple and severe handicap, dysphagia, early intervention, multilingualism, augmentative and alternative communication, and HIV/AIDS. Perceived areas for additional input include budget writing and grant management, meeting protocol, home visits, developing home programs, ENT procedures including cerumen removal and syringing, assertiveness skills, and a better understanding of legal issues around abuse.

Feedback on aspects of our curriculum has been particularly positive regarding clinical placements in hospitals, field trips and exposure to culturally diverse case-loads. Graduates have also commented on the value of the resource portfolios, which they prepared throughout their program, and practical assignments (e.g. on the development of culturally relevant materials for language and aphasia assessment).

6. *Research.*   Pleasingly, the benefit of our community experiences has also been an increase in the number of research projects at an undergraduate and postgraduate level which have been motivated by such placements and experiences. Such research has required the application of novel research methodologies, including those drawn from sociology and anthropology. Topics include the perception of caregivers in rural areas regarding disability, the development of communication skills in other medical professionals, exploring traditional models of causation of various genetic illnesses, and surveys concerning barriers to care. Such research evidence should clearly continue to inform our future educational practice.

*Outcomes*

The context of service has profoundly influenced the content, methods, sequence and evaluation frameworks of our program and the expected roles that our graduates will play. Assessment and treatment of communication disorders is as much influenced by history, geography, language, gender, age and culture as by the factors contained in our traditional curriculum. It is our firm belief that training clinicians for managing cultural diversity enriches and enhances skills and attitudes in practitioners for every context, regardless of whether it is with non-traditional client groups and whether it is in a developed or a developing country.

CONCLUSION

The case studies in this chapter highlight a number of factors for educators to consider when establishing non-traditional or role-emerging placements. As Smith and Van Dort and colleagues note, different models of supervision are required that can assist students to work with often reduced levels of supervision but which still provide support for weaker students and help students manage often unstructured environments for service delivery and increased demands for organisation. Students in such role-emerging placements (Bossers, Cook, Polatajko, & Laine, 1997) need to learn to educate others in the placement setting about their roles as health professionals, and to sell the value of their role.

Students in the placements described in this chapter had unique opportunities to develop truly client-focused care, meeting the needs of their clients as their awareness grew of what could be offered. Students were also able to develop wide-ranging generic professional skills, including high levels of self-awareness provoked by the cultural diversity with which they worked. This cultural diversity also provides experience in working with interpreters. Students became aware of issues of access and equity and, as Penn highlights, ethics in everyday practice, all important attributes for future practice. If the factors summarised here are carefully planned for and managed, non-traditional placements have the capacity to be personally and professionally transforming for the students, surely a desired goal of effective professional education.

## REFERENCES

Bateman, C. (2004). Community service six years on. *South African Medical Journal, 94*, 408–409.

Baur, C. (2008). An analysis of factors underlying e-health disparities. *Cambridge Quarterly of Healthcare Ethics, 17*, 417–428.

Bortz, M., Schoub, B., & McKenzie, J. (1992). Community work project in Gazankulu: A community-based training experience. *South African Journal of Communication Disorders, 39*, 62–68.

Bossers, A., Cook, J., Polatajko, H., & Laine, C. (1997). Understanding the role-emerging fieldwork placement. *Canadian Journal of Occupational Therapy, 64*(2), 70–81.

Cohn, E.S., Dooley, N.R., & Simmons, L.A. (2001). Collaborative learning applied to fieldwork education. In P. Crist & M. Scaffa (Eds.), *Education for occupational therapy in health care: Strategies for the new millennium* (pp. 69–83). New York: Haworth.

Department of Health. (1997). *White paper for the transformation of the health system in South Africa.* Pretoria: Government Press.

Mophosho, M., & Stein, J. (2008). Learning about life: Academic service learning in the Department of Speech Pathology and Audiology, University of the Witwatersrand, South Africa. In M. Moore & P. Lan Lin (Eds.), *Service-learning in higher education: Paradigms and challenges.* (pp. 209–220). Indianapolis: University of Indianapolis Press.

Penn, C. (2000) Cultural narratives: Bridging the gap. *South African Journal of Communication Disorders* (Special edition on communication disorders in multilingual populations) *47*, 71–78.

Penn, C., & Stein, J. (in press). From pillars to posts: Some reflections on community service six years on. *South African Journal of Communication Disorders.*

Pickering, M., McAllister, L., Hagler, P., Whitehill, T.L., Penn, C., Robertson, S.J., & McCready, V. (1998.) External factors influencing the profession in six societies. *American Journal of Speech Language Pathology, 7*, 5–11.

Reid, S. (2000). An overview of the first two years of community service. *Health Systems Trust Update, 57.* Available: http://www.hst.org.za/uploads/files/upd57.pdf, accessed 13 March 2007.

Swartz, L. (2007). The virtues of feeling culturally incompetent. *Monash Bioethics Review, 26*(4) 36–46.

Van Dort, S. (2005). Issues and innovations in clinical education: A perspective from Malaysia. *Advances in Speech-Language Pathology, 7*(3), 170–172.

*Lindy McAllister PhD*
*School of Medicine*
*The University of Queensland, Australia*

*Claire Penn PhD*
*Department of Speech Pathology and Audiology*
*University of Witwatersrand, South Africa*

*Yda Smith MOT*
*Division of Occupational Therapy*
*University of Utah, USA*

*Sandra Van Dort MA (SLP)*
*Department of Audiology and Speech Sciences*
*University Kebangsan, Malaysia*

*Linda Wilson PhD*
*School of Community Health*
*Charles Sturt University, Australia*

LINDY MCALLISTER, MICHAEL CURTIN, BRIDGET
O'CONNOR AND KERRYELLEN VROMAN

# 5. INTERNATIONAL FIELDWORK
# EDUCATION PLACEMENTS

Study abroad programs for students in the last few decades have increased in quantity
and diversity in terms of student types, destinations, duration and type of program
(Godkin & Savageau, 2001). Allied health students are increasingly involved in
international fieldwork placements which have the potential to address goals of both
home institutions (where students come from) and host institutions (where students
go to) (Pechak & Thompson, 2009). Home institutions see international placements
as opportunities for students to develop intercultural skills for transfer back to
domestic healthcare settings; setting which provide services to the home countries'
increasingly multicultural populations. Some, as in both case studies presented in
this chapter, see the international placement as a unique context for the development
of interprofessional skills. For some home institutions the international setting may
offer students experience with caseload types not readily secured in the home
location, as seen in Case Study 1 where students worked with children with complex
disabilities. Host institutions in developing countries may see international students
and their fieldwork educators as an opportunity to provide services for huge unserved caseloads in their country. Further, host institutions may wish to build partnerships which facilitate knowledge and skills transfer, staff professional development
or research opportunities.

The goals of both institutions need to be understood by each other from the outset
and continuously renegotiated, so that unrealistic expectations, power imbalances,
and the risks of cultural tourism or postcolonial practice by students and staff from
the home institution are managed. Threats to sustainability can also be addressed from
the outset in such dialogues. The two case studies in this chapter illustrate many
of the aspects of best practice in international fieldwork education placements. In
addition to well considered and structured programs of preparation, in-country support
and debriefing, both the programs have built evaluation into their cycle of activity.

## CASE STUDY 1: TRUNG THI NGHÈ: AN INTERNATIONAL
## INTERPROFESSIONAL FIELDWORK PLACEMENT

Since 2001, the School of Community Health, Charles Sturt University (CSU),
has taken 12 final year occupational therapy, physiotherapy and speech language
pathology students to work for 6 weeks at Thi Nghè Orphanage in Ho Chi Minh City,

L. McAllister et al., (eds.), Innovations in Allied Health Fieldwork
Education: A Critical Appraisal, 49–58.

Vietnam. Ideally, four students are selected from each discipline, so as to achieve the desired balance for interprofessional teamwork during the placement. Experience has shown that more than 12 students, or a large imbalance in discipline numbers, is detrimental to the interprofessional and student experience.

Thi Nghè Orphanage provides care for up to 400 children with physical and cognitive impairments, most of whom have cerebral palsy, though a number of children also have autism spectrum disorders and other associated impairments. Children spend much of their day in their assigned living area, referred to as their "room", where they eat, sleep, and play unless they are mobile enough to go to school. Children remain at the orphanage until the age of 18 years when they are moved to other institutions which cater for adults.

Around 60 people are employed at Thi Nghè Orphanage. The majority are carers who look after the children in their room. There are approximately 10 teachers for children who are able to go to school, 15 Vietnamese trained physiotherapists, one paediatrician, a number of nurses, a pharmacist and a dentist, and several administrative and maintenance staff. In addition, many Vietnamese and expatriate volunteers regularly assist with the daily care of the children, either on a short- or long-term basis.

CSU actively supports placements which provide culturally diverse experiences. The university is based in several regional locations with comparatively small immigrant populations and the small scale of service providers in the region can limit opportunities for interdisciplinary practice in the field of disability. To address these contextual limitations, an interprofessional, intercultural placement was developed in 2001 in response to a request for assistance by the management of Thi Nghè Orphanage while CSU staff were on a field visit to Vietnam.

*Aims and Goals of the Program*

The aims of the program are twofold:

1. To build the capacity of Vietnamese carers, via education and training, to improve the opportunities for the children through optimising feeding, communication, play, mobility, and other activities of daily living.
2. To develop students' basic competence in:
   - working with children with physical and cognitive impairments
   - assessing needs and building the capacity of staff and volunteers
   - working in an interprofessional way
   - working in resource-poor environments
   - intercultural competence and communication including working with interpreters.

Generic and discipline-specific learning goals are developed with students for the duration of their placement. Table 5.1 outlines the preparation process for students going to Vietnam. The timelines and content for preparation, in-country support and debriefing on return home have been refined over the years based on evaluation of the placement outcomes and management issues. Selection and preparation of students starts several months before departure.

*Table 5.1. Application process and preparation for placement*

| | |
|---|---|
| 1. Information session for all students interested in a placement at Thi Nghè Orphanage | Session includes:<br>– a presentation on the nature and objectives of the placement<br>– costs<br>– safety<br>– a video of previous students working at the orphanage<br>– the personal experiences of students who had recently completed working at the orphanage. |
| 2. Written application from interested students | Application states:<br>– reasons for wanting to do this placement<br>– capacity to meet the learning goals of the program<br>– capacity to self-fund. |
| 3. Heads of programs select students | Selection based on written application and on the student's previous academic and practice performance. |
| 4. Pre-departure briefings at university to prepare for placement at Thi Nghè Orphanage | Students attend three to four 1-hour briefing sessions. Topics covered include:<br>– what to expect<br>– working in an interdisciplinary team<br>– working with children with complex impairments<br>– the experience and work of previous programs run at the orphanage<br>– working with interpreters<br>– intercultural competence<br>– intercultural "safe" communication<br>– culture shock and personal management.<br>In addition, travel arrangements are checked and confirmed. Students are expected to make their own travel and accommodation arrangements, with copies of their itinerary and insurance details forwarded to the university. |
| 5. Pre-departure briefing | 2-day practical briefing run by therapy and education staff from a disability service, to provide students with practical experience and focused theory on working with children. Students learn:<br>– the range of impairments that children at the orphanage may have<br>– practical positioning and handling techniques and assistance at meal times<br>– planning and running play groups<br>– play techniques and evaluating equipment options. |

## Structure of the Program

Prior to departure, students conduct a number of fund-raising activities to enable equipment and local resources to be purchased for projects in the orphanage, and to assist with covering the costs of interpreters and language classes. During the first week at the orphanage the students settle in and become familiar with the institution's structures and routines, and begin to work with the carers and interpreters. Students also attend two 2-hour Vietnamese language classes to equip them with some understanding of the language. They are encouraged to spend time with the children and to assist the carers with mealtimes as much as possible. Students then choose which rooms they will work in and separate into working groups of three or four, with each group having at least one student from each discipline.

To assist students to develop working relationships with the staff and children, each group is assigned one interpreter who works for approximately 4 hours per day. Professional interpreters are not used due to the cost. Instead, we employ Vietnamese university students who are studying English and enjoy the paid opportunity to practise their English language skills.

By the end of the first week students should have drafted timetables, goals and plans for each room, and suggestions for a project that could be completed either for their assigned room or for the orphanage overall. This is a working document which is refined as students become more familiar with the children and staff. In the past, students have completed a range of projects such as building a sensory room, installing a sensory frame on the wall of a room, making cushions to support children in chairs, and creating volunteer resources to inform volunteers about what they can do to assist the children. All goals, plans and project suggestions are negotiated with the room staff. Over the course of the following 5 weeks, students implement a variety of activities for children, staff and volunteers.

Students are supported for the first 2 weeks by the University coordinator, whose role is to facilitate the students' settling in. Since 2009, the coordinator's work is then dovetailed with that of three practitioners (an occupational therapist, a physiotherapist and a speech language pathologist) from Yooralla, a Melbourne based multi-faceted community-based disability service provider, operating professional disability services in communities across Victoria, Australia. Each of these practitioners spends 2 weeks at the orphanage, overlapping for 1 week with the next arrival, with the aim of having two therapists available for student supervision and to demonstrate interdisciplinary practice.

*Project Evaluation*

Evaluation of the Vietnam placement is done from the perspectives of students, university staff and orphanage staff and management, with the aim of improving preparation and learning experiences and to capture impacts on students, staff and supervisors. This has taken the form of group debriefings, student and staff interviews and written student reflections. Changes in care staff practice, interactions and activities with the children have been informally observed since the students began work at the orphanage in 2001. Some of the outcomes of the project have been published by McAllister, Whiteford, Hill, and Thomas (2006) Whiteford and McAllister (2006) and McAllister and Whiteford (2008).

The outcome of the Vietnam placement for the students is overwhelmingly positive. The in-country and return-to-Australia interviews with students, along with students' written reflections and presentations to their peers, show that their learning goals of developing generic and discipline-specific skills are achieved. Many students have reflected on their Vietnam experience as a life-changing event. This is reflected in the comments of students who returned from the 2009 trip to Vietnam (pseudonyms used):

During my Vietnam placement I learnt a lot about my own practice as [a therapist]. I learnt how to work as a team member in an interdisciplinary setting ... It also assisted with my reasoning and problem solving skills ... I believe I also improved in being able to adapt my listening skills and communication style ... to talk to my peers in a professional manner and respect their point of view even when they differed from my own. (Kim)

[Thi Nghè] was an incredibly challenging placement. I was at times very far removed from my comfort zone and needed to think outside of the square ... not only will I be a better therapist for [this experience], I am a better person because of it. This experience challenged and changed my views of humanity. (Phoebe)

The impact on employment prospects of doing a placement in Vietnam can be demonstrated by the outcomes experienced by Sarah. When she graduated Sarah was fortunate to be offered a prestigious new-graduate position at a major Australian children's hospital. Her employer said:

With so many undergraduates vying for the one position each year, the culling process is always difficult. Therefore, indicating on your resume that you've done a placement in an orphanage in Vietnam was certainly going to get noticed. Sarah didn't disappoint. I do believe that her overseas experience added to her confidence and ability to negotiate successfully, to her creativity in therapy and made her more sensitive and appropriate in her dealings with people of other cultural and linguistic backgrounds; all hugely important skills for working in a team in a large metropolitan paediatric hospital.

Some things that have contributed to the success and sustainability of this program include:
- Returning every year to enable relationships and trust to be established between CSU staff and the orphanage staff;
- Ensuring that students do large negotiated room-based projects as a way of establishing mutual respect and rapport between carer staff and students and to provide the orphanage with concrete visible changes lasting beyond the time the students are there;
- Taking time for students to learn from and understand the orphanage staff – and not to go in with an attitude of "we know best";
- Spending time preparing students thoroughly prior to travel, which is essential to enable them to settle in and quickly commence work towards their objectives;
- Ensuring philosophical, financial and staff support from the university, especially as the placements involve some costs; and
- Supporting the interprofessional nature of this placement by ensuring that students learn from and observe practitioners from different disciplines.

## CASE STUDY 2: INTERDISCIPLINARY FIELDWORK
## IN BELIZE, CENTRAL AMERICA

This case study describes an interdisciplinary fieldwork experience for pairs of nursing and occupational therapy students from the USA who were placed throughout Belize with District Nurses who provide primary healthcare services, especially maternal and child health. Students participate in natural settings rather than function as "foreign" observers. Belize is a lesser developed nation with a population of approximately 311,500 who live predominantly in small towns or rural communities. The country has a rich ethnically diverse culture and population consisting of people who are Mestizo, Creole, Ketchi, Mayan, Garifuna, and immigrants from neighbouring Central American countries as well as countries further afield. The official language of Belize is English and the adult literacy rate is estimated at 70% but Spanish is spoken extensively and increasingly is the first language of many Belizeans (Belize Development Trust, 2000).

### Background, Objectives, Practicalities and Structure of the Program

The fieldwork experience was a collaborative project between nursing and occupational therapy fieldwork educators, who through their volunteer work in Belize had established a network of colleagues in non-governmental organisations, education, human services, and healthcare, subsequently enabling the development of fieldwork placements with local healthcare providers. Official permission from the appropriate governmental agencies such as Nursing and the Department of Human Services was important prior to establishing the fieldwork programme. The fieldwork placement was conducted in the 2-week spring break including weekends for travelling. The overarching objectives for the placements were for students to observe and participate in the healthcare system of a lesser developed nation and achieve a mutually beneficial exchange of information with their Belizean mentors and hosts. Attention to planning, preparation, and educational and emotional support provided to students, and inclusion of debriefing sessions as well as collaboration with personnel in Belize ensured that student learning was meaningful, culturally respectful, and that their experience was safe.

The costs of the travel and expenses incurred in this fieldwork were met by the students and fieldwork educators, although some students sought and received some university travel grants. Students had either no or limited travel experience outside of the USA. Therefore, preparation in the culture, language and knowledge of the host country were crucial. These topics were addressed during a pre- and post-fieldwork three credit course with a predominant public health focus, which also included the issues and practice of healthcare in developing nations, team building, and interdisciplinary awareness. The practicalities of travel in a developing nation, such as organising vaccinations, travel documentation, awareness of how to practise universal precautions in a variety of settings with limited resources, and managing minor health conditions associated with travel, were also covered in the pre-course work. Table 5.2 shows the structure and timeline of the fieldwork placement and includes excerpts from student journals used in evaluation of the fieldwork placement.

*Table 5.2. Structure of the fieldwork programme*

| | Pre-fieldwork course - 6 weeks – 3 hours per week |
|---|---|
| Days 1–3 Travel to Belize and orientation | Transition time – activities with fieldwork educators in Belize City 1-day workshop hosted by the Belize School of Nursing - introductions, lectures. <br> – Member of the Ministry presented a public health perspective which offered a broad sociopolitical and economic framework for the delivery and challenges of public health services in Belize <br> – Nursing faculty member presented overview of healthcare in Belize <br> – District Nurse described her work as a primary healthcare provider |
| Days 3–4 Travel to San Ignacio | Visits to the Hospital and Residential Home for the Elderly and also to cultural and significant Mayan historical sites. Rehab equipment which had been previously identified as needed was provided through OT Student Association fund raising (e.g. stainless bathroom rails, shower chairs). These first few days were used to orient and adjust to Belize, its culture, climate, and familiarise students with travelling on public transportation and problem-solving before the students independently travelled to their fieldwork sites. This independence contributed to personal growth gained by students from a successful international experience. A typically positive student experience is reflected in this excerpt from a student diary: <br> *We gave everyone a quick hug good bye and then we were swiftly on the bus. That is the moment it hit me, we are on our own in BELIZE! This is the moment that stood out for me today. All the security that I had been feeling with the* [fieldwork educators] *who were savvy to the ways of Belizean travel* [was gone]. *We were traveling to a foreign place in a foreign country with foreign people. A woman pushed her three children over and offered me a seat, the bus was very crowded...* |
| Days 5–10 (approx.) Fieldwork Education | Students travelled to their District Nurse mentors in fieldwork sites throughout Belize. Fieldwork experiences included giving vaccinations and performing infant checks in community child and maternal clinics in small communities. An excerpt from a student's journal describes her day in such a clinic: <br> *Another task of the clinic was the developmental scale of the babies, which I did. The developmental scale that Belize uses is extremely basic compared to ours. With the amount of children that they have to see it is necessary to have a short and basic developmental description. I was surprised that two babies were developmentally delayed according to their developmental scale and were very delayed according to... I provided the mother with some suggestions* [from the play] *manual* [we developed]. <br> Other fieldwork experiences included working in community programs for elders at residential homes, time with community psychiatric nurses, and participating in programs for children with disabilities. OT students became involved in activity programming. They modified assistive devices to improve safety at the homes for elders and performed home visits to improve independence and quality of life for adults who had disabilities. Fieldwork educators travelled to all locations to visit students to offer input and support. Contact was maintained by email and phone. Students were encouraged to plan weekend activities to explore their placement communities. |
| Final weekend: Debriefing | Relaxing before returning to the USA and structured debriefing sessions immediately following the fieldwork were facilitated by fieldwork educators to process experiences. Cultural adjustment can occur in both directions – going to a developing nation and new culture, and returning to one's own affluent culture. Transitions occurred more easily with debriefing when all experiences could be discussed in a supportive context. Fieldwork educators used this time to assist students to place their experiences in the context of a broader sociocultural and political-economic climate and relate their experiences to their future practice as illustrated in this student journal excerpt: <br> *The large group then broke into nursing and OT. This part of the night was very interesting to me to hear how different everyone's experience was and the impact on them personally and professionally that the experience had on them as individuals.* |

*Table 5.2. (Continued)*

| |
|---|
| Post-fieldwork course (3 wks) |
| Relating fieldwork to theory and course content, completion of assignments and discussions on issues of public health, healthcare and therapy in Belize. |

Typically the accommodation arrangements for international fieldwork are that students stay as a group, often with fieldwork educators who provide oversight and input and provide a perception of increased personal safety. The disadvantages of this type of accommodation are that students socialise predominantly with their peers and the group experience can shape the learning and the interpretation of the experience. In this fieldwork programme, students stayed with local families as much as possible or in locally owned hotels. Staying with families increased students' cultural experience through inclusion in family and local activities.

*Project Evaluation*

The main evaluation methods for this fieldwork and course were class presentations, peer interviews pre- and post-fieldwork experience, and a final paper. All students also prepared resources or public information materials related to their placements and worked on personal diaries in which they included responses to specific questions such as reflecting on an experience for the day that was distinctive or challenging.

The peer pre- and post-fieldwork interviews explored expectations and attitudes. In writing up the interviews students linked the data with concepts such as cultural sensitivity, prejudice and personal biases that could influence healthcare delivery in their future work as healthcare practitioners. The assignment that required students to develop materials for client education was assessed on criteria such as how well it integrated principles of health information literacy and relevance to the target population. The final paper required students to select a learning issue they identified during fieldwork. They researched the issue and examined it in relation to public health, healthcare priorities, or delivery in a developing nation. The course grade also considered professional behaviours and collaborative teamwork during the academic and fieldwork components of the course.

*Outcomes of the Placements*

My [KV] experience of fieldwork in developing nations is that the student outcomes have outweighed the challenges. In addition to achieving course objectives, it is the attitudinal and cognitive shifts that are most noteworthy. Many students who return from fieldwork placements like these recognise the needs of individuals within their own country, and take action through volunteerism. For example:

> I hope I will be able to carry over what I learned from the experiences that I have had with the people because a lot of people in the US are very under-privileged too and don't have all the necessities that you might want.

There is a strong sense of professional identity that emerges when students observe what their profession can offer outside the infrastructure of modern healthcare, and they gain respect for each other's professions through the relationships forged, as is evident in this extract from a student journal:

> As S and I reflected on the bus for our 5-hour bus trip we talked about the amount of fun that we had this week and how the week went by so fast. It seemed as if it wasn't enough time. But what I learned was such an experience. I learned a lot about what a nurse's role is in both the US and in a 3rd world country. I also learned a lot about Belize's healthcare system and areas of improvements. I also thought about how therapy can be implemented into this area and the benefits that [...] would have with the use of therapy.

Lastly, the insights and attitudinal changes realised by the students cannot be orchestrated, even using the best pedagogical strategies. International fieldwork which takes students away from their familiar environment and out of their comfort zone is rich with such learning. A final example captures the unquantifiable but valuable dimension of fieldwork in developing nations. At a debriefing session, a student reflected on her time spent in rural villages and in a moment of unguarded honesty she remarked "I didn't know you could be poor and happy".

## CONCLUSION

The two case studies in this chapter reveal a deep consideration by staff involved of the milieu in which the fieldwork activities are located, and awareness of the power dynamics and misunderstandings that can arise in intercultural interactions between people from resource-poor and resource-rich settings. This attention, coupled with evaluation of perceptions and outcomes, with subsequent refinements of the programs' structures, has allowed sustainability of the placement programs over considerable spans of time. Both programs exemplify factors which have been described as contributing to effective international fieldwork placements (Balandin, Lincoln, Sen, Wilkins, & Trembath, 2007). They have established partnerships with local service providers; they maintain clear and ongoing communication between institutions prior to, during and after placements; students attend regular, planned orientation in the period leading up to departure for the host country; there is clarity about the roles of students on placement; students have clear goals and projects for the placements; students keep reflective journals to maximise personal and professional learning; there is regular briefing and debriefing throughout the placement; and a cycle of debrief, evaluate, review, rebuild/refine is evident. These case studies demonstrate the personal and professional growth that can be achieved through well planned, carefully implemented and thoroughly evaluated international, intercultural fieldwork education placements.

## REFERENCES

Balandin, S., Lincoln, M., Sen, R., Wilkins, D., & Trembath, D. (2007). Twelve tips for effective international clinical placements. *Medical Teacher, 29*(9), 872–877.
Belize Development Trust. (2000). REPORT #209: *Literacy of a nation and comprehension.* Available: http://www.belize1.com/BzLibrary/trust209.html.

Godkin, M., & Savageau, J. (2001). The effect of a global multiculturalism track on cultural competence of preclinical medical students. *Family Medicine, 33*, 178–186.

McAllister, L., & Whiteford, G. (2008). Facilitating clinical decision making in students in intercultural fieldwork placements. In J. Higgs, M. Jones, S. Loftus & N. Christensen (Eds.), *Clinical reasoning in the health professions* (3rd ed., pp. 357–365). Edinburgh: Elsevier.

McAllister, L., Whiteford, G., Hill, R., & Thomas, N. (2006). Learning and reflection in professional inter-cultural experience: A qualitative study. *Journal of Reflective Practice, 7*(3), 367–381.

Pechak, C.M., & Thompson, M. (2009). A conceptual model of optimal international service-learning and its application to global health initiatives in rehabilitation. *Physical Therapy, 89*(11), 1192–1204.

Whiteford, G., & McAllister, L. (2006). Politics and complexity in intercultural fieldwork: The Vietnam experience. *Australian Occupational Therapy Journal, 54*(1), S74–83.

*Lindy McAllister PhD*
*School of Medicine*
*The University of Queensland, Australia*

*Michael Curtin PhD*
*School of Community Health*
*Charles Sturt University, Australia*

*Bridget O'Connor BPT*
*School of Community Health*
*Charles Sturt University, Australia*

*Kerryellen Vroman PhD*
*College of Health and Human Services*
*University of New Hampshire, USA*

# SECTION II: DESIGN AND MANAGEMENT OF FIELDWORK EDUCATION

CHRISTINE BITHELL, WENDY BOWLES
AND NICOLE CHRISTENSEN

# 6. ISSUES IN DESIGN AND MANAGEMENT OF FIELDWORK EDUCATION

Fieldwork education forms an essential component of all health and social care professional programs, yet universities must rely upon employers and healthcare providers for an appropriate, sufficient and sustainable source of placements, over which they have little direct control. This chapter explores the challenges faced when designing and managing fieldwork education programs within the context of the health systems and policies in Australia, the U.K. and the U.S. We all have experience from a university perspective of managing fieldwork placement provision for one or more of the health and social care professions, and our different voices identify the issues which seem to each of us the most important within our own contexts.

## CHALLENGES IN DESIGN AND MANAGEMENT OF FIELDWORK EDUCATION PROGRAMS IN AUSTRALIA

The population of Australia is mostly highly urbanised (70%) and clustered around the eastern seaboard. Australian's overall level of health is good and continues to improve in relation to comparable countries. Yet people living in rural and remote areas die younger and experience higher levels of illness and disease risk factors than their counterparts in cities (Australian Institute of Health and Welfare, 2008).

The Australian health system operates as a complex mosaic of public and privately funded services, under a variety of regulatory and funding mechanisms. Although almost 70% of total health expenditure is funded by government, Australians also have a wide range of private health insurance options. Negotiating the complexity of this "mixed economy" healthcare system is a major challenge for universities designing and managing fieldwork education programs. Challenges also come from national policy sources and international pressures. A brief discussion of some of the factors impinging on the design and management of Australian fieldwork education programs illustrates the scope of these challenges.

### De-Professionalisation

Many authors have discussed how forces in postmodern society, which becomes ever more globalised, highly regulated, risk-averse and dependent on expensive technology, push healthcare disciplines towards de-professionalisation. Writers such as Bauman (2000) in Europe, Banks (2004) in the U.K., Bisman (2004) in the U.S.,

*L. McAllister et al., (eds.), Innovations in Allied Health Fieldwork Education: A Critical Appraisal, 61–73.*

and Hugman (2005) and Bowles, Collingridge, Curry, and Valentine (2006) in Australia have argued that the increasing pressures to be accountable and to conform to detailed checklists and risk management procedures within highly specialised health and welfare bureaucracies reduce professional discretion and push practitioners from all disciplines into defensive, technical types of practice. Such practice bears little resemblance to the traditional view of autonomous professionals making considered judgements in the best interests of their client/patient.

These pressures widen the gap between university and the clinical worlds, encouraging students to experience a dichotomy between the "ivory tower" vision of professionalism espoused by academics and the "real world" experience of work inside healthcare facilities. The challenge for allied health academics designing fieldwork education programs is to find ways to bridge this gap and to offer practice approaches that will enhance professionalism and resist the pressure toward practitioners becoming mere technicians.

In this highly specialised multidisciplinary clinical environment, designers of fieldwork education programs need to become increasingly innovative. The recent move to focus more strongly on learning and teaching ethics within fieldwork education curricula (Banks, 2004; Hugman, 2005; Bowles et al., 2006) is one strategy to raise student and practitioner awareness of their potential power as autonomous professionals. However, potential ethical conflicts between the interests in fieldwork education, such as the duty to disclose and duty of care versus the duty to protect student privacy, remain serious issues (Hicks & Swain, 2007).

*Enthusiasm for Fieldwork Education*

More and more, professional educators in Australia are recognising the value of fieldwork education, or workplace learning as it is sometimes termed. The national voice for the higher education sector, Universities Australia, recently released a position paper arguing for the federal government to adopt a national internship scheme (Universities Australia, 2008), and a range of ministers from the Rudd federal Labor government have promoted partnerships between educational providers and industry to encourage a range of fieldwork education initiatives.

With so many disciplines within universities initiating fieldwork education programs as part of their course structures, there is increasing pressure on a limited pool of qualified practitioners to supervise student placements as part of their professional role, at a time when funding pressures are demanding more from a reduced workforce. Designers of fieldwork education programs need to incorporate a "win-win" approach, with tangible benefits for the industry partner as well as for the student and university.

Australian research into the costs and benefits of fieldwork education for the industry partner is beginning to explore these issues. In one small study, social work student supervisors concluded that in most instances the benefits of fieldwork placements outweighed the costs for the industry partner, with the major benefits including improvements in service delivery, completion of projects that other staff lacked the time to undertake, and professional development opportunities for the supervisors themselves, including increased access to professional literature and debates and critical reflection on their own practice (Darton, Bell, & Bowles, 2005).

## National Standards in Fieldwork Education

Partly in response to the increasing pressure on the limited pool of fieldwork educators across the diverse range of fieldwork settings in health, several allied health disciplines in Australia are moving towards adopting national standards for fieldwork education, developed by national accreditation bodies. In some disciplines, universities are cooperating with the accreditation bodies to develop shared assessment tools as well. This means that fieldwork educators in a given profession use the same assessment tool and educational approach regardless of the university in which students are enrolled, leading to more efficient use of educator time and energy.

For example, a single assessment tool for physiotherapy courses, developed in a project funded by the Australian Learning and Teaching Council, will replace over 25 distinct assessment practices used by different Australian and New Zealand universities (Australian Learning and Teaching Council, 2009a). With most physiotherapy courses agreeing to adopt it over the next 2 years, the *Assessment of Physiotherapy Practice* was developed in field trials involving nine universities and over 1000 clinical educators. It provides a valid, reliable and standardised approach to fieldwork assessment practices and procedures, according to the chief investigator, Megan Dalton (Australian Learning and Teaching Council, 2009a).

Similarly, a collaborative national project also funded by the Australian Learning and Teaching Council involving several universities and the peak professional body, Speech Pathology Australia, has developed a valid and reliable tool, COMPASS®: Competency assessment in speech language pathology (McAllister, Lincoln, Ferguson, & McAllister, 2006), to assess speech language pathology students' performance in workplace settings (see also Chapter 22). All universities offering speech language pathology courses in Australia and New Zealand have adopted this competency-based tool, which also leads to a shared fieldwork education curriculum in speech language pathology (Australian Learning and Teaching Council, 2009a).

Approaching the issue from a different angle, a project involving 24 of the 26 university social work programs, two industry partners and the professional body, the Australian Association of Social Work, is developing an online program to prepare practitioners to become fieldwork educators of social work students. It is hoped that two of the outcomes of this project will be more accessible resources for rural and remote social work fieldwork educators and national standards for student supervision (Australian Learning and Teaching Council, 2009c).

## Fieldwork Education in Rural and Remote Areas

Issues of recruitment and retention of healthcare professionals, and the lack of a critical mass of health care professionals in rural and remote areas of Australia to support activities such as fieldwork programs, have plagued Australian rural and remote health care for years (Lonne & Cheers, 2004). The online student supervision project mentioned earlier is a strategy that attempts to ameliorate the situation by providing access to professional development to promote practitioner confidence to accept fieldwork education placements. Online technology such as videoconferencing is also being used to overcome the shortage of suitably qualified and experienced student supervisors in rural areas (McLeod & Barbara, 2005).

Several Australian universities require fieldwork education students to undertake at least one fieldwork placement in a rural area, in the hope that this will inspire new graduates to apply for jobs in regional and rural areas. The evidence, however, is that decreasing support for professionals, combined with longer working hours than city counterparts and fewer colleagues available for support, leads to burnout, loss of professionals in rural areas, and difficulty in recruitment. Clearly, finding ways to populate rural and remote health care settings with properly supported professionals is a priority if rural communities are to be sustainable. Offering innovative fieldwork education programs is one way to encourage this. Innovative employment structures to support senior health staff to mentor student placements and supervise practitioners, with joint appointments between health departments and universities in rural areas, is another strategy that has been explored in rural Australia to address this issue (Bowles & Duncombe, 2005).

*Interprofessional Approaches to Fieldwork Education*

Another trend developing in fieldwork education in Australia and internationally, in response to the contextual issues discussed in this chapter, is to seek opportunities for interprofessional practice, and to recognise the benefits of working collaboratively to achieve the best outcomes for clients/patients. A related strategy to address interprofessional issues is interdisciplinary cooperation in the design of fieldwork education programs and management systems within the university community. At Charles Sturt University, for example, the Field Education Network is an inter-disciplinary, cross-faculty network of academics and administrative staff who share resources and strategies to improve fieldwork education and to raise its profile within the university. This network is hosted and resourced by the university's Education For Practice Institute (EFPI) and offers online resources, debates, email distribution lists, workshops and teaching fellowships to develop high-quality field-work education programs in the university (EFPI, 2009). EFPI also participates in APROPOS, an international network for practice-based and interprofessional education.

## CHALLENGES IN DESIGN AND MANAGEMENT OF FIELDWORK EDUCATION PROGRAMS IN THE UNITED KINGDOM

The majority of allied health professionals (AHPs) in the U.K. are employed by the National Health Service (NHS), the state healthcare system that is funded from general taxation. The NHS also directly funds AHP education in England and

Wales by contracting with universities for an agreed number of places, thus exerting a degree of control over the number of healthcare workers entering the workforce. In addition to the NHS workforce, social care agencies, independent hospitals and private practices provide further opportunities for the employment of AHPs, but the NHS provides almost all fieldwork placements for the majority of AHP students.

Proposed changes in health policy (Department of Health, 2008) are intended to make profound changes to the way healthcare is delivered, in order to improve the quality of services within existing budgets. The impact upon AHP services and fieldwork placements is beginning to be felt, although, due to the devolved nature of decision making in the NHS, specific local changes and the pace of implementation differ widely across the U.K. Placement coordinators in universities must work closely with NHS managers to keep abreast of changes in the way NHS staff are deployed and to ensure that students' placements continue to prepare them appropriately for practice in a new NHS that is as yet not fully realised. The major challenge faced by educators in all the AHPs is to provide sufficient fieldwork placements to enable all students to complete mandatory program requirements while meeting the high standards set by professional and regulatory bodies, and the universities themselves, for placement quality.

All AHP programs leading to national registration must provide at least the required minimum hours of supervised and assessed fieldwork practice. However universities do not have control of the supply of placements. Although this section now focuses mainly on physiotherapy as an example of AHP placement management in the U.K. and examines some of the specific initiatives to address placement shortages, the same issues and challenges exist for educators in other AHP professions (Craik & Turner, 2005; Rodger et al., 2008).

*Fieldwork Placements in Physiotherapy*

To be eligible for registration in the U.K., students must successfully complete a minimum of 1000 hours of fieldwork practice-based learning. The distribution and length of placements within the program design are decided by program planners who aim for a balance of experiences for each student in both acute and primary care, reflecting the increasingly diverse settings in which physiotherapy services are delivered. Placement scarcity renders it impossible to provide each student with a program of placements in specialist units, although many students continue to believe that specialist units provide superior learning experiences. The management of student expectations of placement learning and practice can pose difficult questions about equity of access to learning experiences, and also about what is an appropriate fieldwork learning experience in a context of uncertainty about future service delivery. Fieldwork designers increasingly adopt the view that transferable skills can be learned by treating patients in a wide range of hospital and community settings, and it seems that this will be the way that physiotherapists will increasingly work. For example, many patients with acute exacerbations of chronic respiratory conditions are now managed at home, whereas less than a decade ago they would have been admitted to acute respiratory units.

*Responsibility for Placement Provision*

As universities do not have responsibility for the healthcare facilities providing placements, efforts have been made through the NHS commissioning process to ensure that NHS Trusts, which are responsible for all NHS hospitals, primary care and community services, cooperate in providing sufficient fieldwork placements and sign a Placement Agreement that sets out the basis for cooperation. Due to the complexity and volume of placement providers there have been difficulties in ensuring that all Placement Agreements are in place. For example, in London a typical physiotherapy program with an intake of 70 students uses around 50 different NHS Trusts each year. The extent to which Placement Agreements have been fully implemented in all of the 10 Strategic Health Authorities in England and for all professions is unknown. The provision of placements has historically been dependent upon the goodwill and enthusiasm of AHP services managers and individuals willing to become clinical educators and supervise students, and so it continues to be.

Placements attract no additional funding and clinical educators are unpaid for their roles. Where AHP managers actively promote the benefits of student placements and ensure the quality of the placement learning environment with appropriate support for staff with student supervision roles, students frequently evaluate their placements highly, and many seek first posts in Trusts where they have had a positive placement experience (CSP, 2003). However findings from a study by Baldry Currens and Bithell (2000) suggested that for some managers placement education was not a priority, with the result that clinical educators in the study felt unsupported in their role. Both the number and the quality of fieldwork placements are dependent upon the support and enthusiasm of service managers.

*Increasing Placement Capacity*

Two major factors have endangered the supply of sufficient placements in the past decade. Physiotherapy student numbers increased by over 50% as a result of a government commitment in *The NHS Plan: a plan for investment, a plan for reform* (DOH, 2000), and there were similar increases in other health professions between 2002 and 2006, with commensurate increased demand for placements. Although student entry numbers are now returning to pre-2002 levels, the developments that increased placement capacity have endured. The second factor, the intense pressures experienced by NHS staff as a result of financial stringencies in recent years, tends to have had a damaging effect on placement capacity. Lack of formal arrangements between Trust and university can lead to a lower priority given to placements when unanticipated events occur, such as pressures to meet targets with reduced resources or staff shortages. Late cancellations of placements occur quite frequently, and because placements are scarce there may be difficulty in finding suitable alternatives at short notice. In the absence of additional funding to ensure the supply of placements, two approaches have been taken: (a) improving the management and sharing of placements as a scarce resource, and (b) increasing the number of placements through different models of supervision.

Collaborations between universities to share placements are now common, making greater use of placements that would previously have been unused for long periods during the year. One such collaboration, started in 1995 by three universities in the North Thames area, has now developed to include 10 universities and all placement providers across the South East of England and East Anglia. Jointly funded administrators maintain a database, the Physiotherapy Placement Information Management System (PPIMS), that facilitates the co-ordination of placement offers and uptake, including taking measures to identify placements for students affected by cancellations, and provides management information that enables the placement system to be monitored and evaluated. Collaboration between the academic clinical co-ordinators of the 10 universities has led to the development of common student assessment, placement evaluation and audit tools that ensure that placement educators need to be familiar with only one set of documentation, although taking students from several universities at different times in the year. There is work ongoing in London to establish a similar database for occupational therapy programs.

A second approach set out to increase the number of placements through new models of supervision. A preference had developed in the U.K. for a 1:1 ratio of student to supervisor, despite lack of evidence to support its continuation. Recent studies examined collaborative or multiple placement models, with the aim of expanding placement capacity (Baldry Currens & Bithell, 2003; Moore, Morris, Crouch, & Martin, 2003), investigating models where two or more students were placed with one clinical educator. Team models of supervision, where a team of clinicians of different levels of experience was jointly responsible for the clinical education of a number of students, have also been evaluated (Bennett, 2003). Both models increased the number of placements, and findings based on the perceptions of students and supervisors indicated that students' learning also benefited from peer support (Baldry Currens & Bithell, 2000).

*Future Challenges for Fieldwork Placements in the U.K.*

Current health policy in England is based upon the strategic directions set by the NHS Next Stage Review (DOH, 2008). Scotland, Wales and Northern Ireland have similar strategic visions. The most important changes for the organisation of fieldwork placements include the delivery of the majority of services in or closer to patients' homes in community and primary care settings; changing patterns of staffing with fewer senior staff to supervise placements; new and emerging roles for AHPs and nurses; and NHS services sub-contracted to independent provider agencies who may not include provision of student placements in their business plans.

Fieldwork placements for physiotherapy students in community settings are already well established, although individuals may have only one such experience during their program. When the majority of placement hours are spent in such settings, matters such as how closely a student should be supervised, whether a multiprofessional team could take responsibility for students, and whether other professions could contribute to student assessment must be resolved. Ways of providing students with experience of new or emerging roles will challenge current placement models further, although occupational therapists are adopting role-emerging placement models successfully in a variety of settings where services do not currently exist, such as primary schools and prisons, with "long arm" supervision arrangements (e.g. Thew, Hargreaves, & Cronin-Davis, 2008).

## CHALLENGES IN DESIGN AND MANAGEMENT OF FIELDWORK EDUCATION PROGRAMS IN THE UNITED STATES OF AMERICA

Fieldwork placements for students in professional-entry allied health education programs in the U.S.A., including various rehabilitation professions such as physiotherapy, occupational therapy, and speech language pathology, are organised within the context of a mixed health care system, where publicly and privately funded insurance systems co-exist. The influence of the context of the larger health care system and both its publicly and privately funded payer components can be seen in fieldwork experiences of allied health rehabilitation students in the U.S.A. Students involved in clinical education at the professional entry level are fulfilling requirements for their professional training and therefore are not yet graduated or licensed ("qualified"). These students are placed in various clinical settings, spanning the typical spectrum of acute inpatient settings, sub-acute transitional care and rehabilitation inpatient settings, outpatient ambulatory care settings, both within and outside of hospitals, home care settings, and school settings.

### Clinical Education in Physiotherapy Programs

In physiotherapy education programs, the fieldwork placements are administered by an Academic Coordinator of Clinical Education (ACCE) within each academic program, but the individual clinical educators most often are not part of the academic program faculty. Most clinical educators work primarily as clinicians, and volunteer to supervise students from one or more academic programs.

Assessment of clinical competence is performed by these volunteer clinical educators. A standardised assessment tool was developed and adopted by most physiotherapy academic programs (APTA, 2006), but because curricular sequencing and specific content varies between academic programs students from different programs present to their volunteer clinical educators with varying levels of exposure, and also with approaches to different knowledge and skill content areas according to the particular academic program they attend, even when at the same chronological stage in their education.

Neither the clinical educators nor the clinical facility within which they are employed are reimbursed by the academic program for their clinical education services to students. As is common in all clinical education programs, the level of direct supervision provided to students is expected to be high early in students' progression, diminishing over time as students gain in knowledge and skill. To fulfil the requirements of their entry-level professional education programs (e.g. APTA, 2006), students are required to demonstrate independence in clinical practice by the end of their training.

*Effects of Public Payment System Regulations on Clinical Education*

The most significant issue for clinical education arising from within the health care system over the past decade has been the regulatory restrictions enacted on reimbursement of services provided by students to patients covered under the publicly funded Medicare health insurance program. Although it is the subject of current national political debate and legislative activity, the U.S.A. does not now provide universal medical care coverage for its citizens. However, since 1965 the Medicare system has provided publicly funded health care insurance for all over the age of 65, and for those with permanent disabilities (Sandstrom, Lohman, & Bramble, 2009). Given the large percentage that older adults represent within the population in need of rehabilitation services, restricting reimbursement of services provided to this population by students is indeed a significant challenge to clinical education.

As the largest payer of healthcare services in the USA, the publicly funded Medicare system has significant influence within the healthcare economy, and its reimbursement policies and procedures not only affect individuals covered by Medicare (and their healthcare providers), but also influence many of the private insurance systems' policies and procedures. These regulatory policies restricting reimbursement for services provided by rehabilitation professionals are developed and implemented by the Centers for Medicare and Medicaid Services (CMS), part of the federal government's Department of Health and Human Services (Sandstrom et al., 2009). It is worth noting that recent changes in federal health care legislation under the Obama administration are expected to further regulate reimbursement of healthcare in the near future.

For the past decade, only services provided by physicians and practitioners authorised by statute (i.e., post-entry level, licensed practitioners) can be billed and reimbursed by Medicare when conducted in outpatient and skilled nursing facility settings (CMS, 2001, 2008). When services occur in acute-care hospital settings, reimbursement is possible if delivered by students within the line of sight of their clinical instructor. Given that clinical education is voluntarily provided by practitioners in various settings, the effect of eliminating reimbursement for student-delivered services for patients in these settings is clearly prohibitive to providing students with experiences where they are the primary caregivers for older adults or for permanently disabled individuals insured through Medicare (Gwyer, Odom, & Gandy, 2003) As noted by the American Physical Therapy Association (APTA), along with the associations of other allied health professions (American Speech-Language-Hearing Association, American Occupational Therapy Association), this policy has had significantly detrimental effects on the clinical education of students who are not yet graduated or licensed, and therefore whose services cannot be billed for or reimbursed by Medicare (APTA, 2005, 2009a, b).

A well-accepted mandate in current professional education systems in the U.S.A. is that for students to gain both the technical and the clinical reasoning skills necessary to work safely and competently with older adults or severely disabled individuals upon entry into the profession, they must be provided opportunities, under the guidance of a clinical educator, to experience and successfully manage working with these very people. Indeed, recent research exploring the development of clinical reasoning capability in student physical therapists in the U.S.A. found that a key factor identified by students in developing experiential knowledge and confidence in their practice abilities was the opportunity for facilitated experiential learning under the guidance of a skilled clinical educator (Christensen, Jones, Edwards, & Higgs, 2008; Christensen, 2009).

As was anticipated, these regulations have now been more widely adopted by other private health care insurers, as many tend to be guided by and choose to adopt Medicare regulations, especially if perceived that they might be financially beneficial for the private insurers. Therefore the Medicare regulations limiting reimbursement for student-delivered services now have an even more significant negative impact on the potential for students to gain experience working with patient populations in a wider range of settings (Gwyer et al., 2003).

Additionally, some health care systems/institutions themselves have chosen to limit students' experiences with all older adults, even for individuals with other primary or supplemental insurance coverage for whom reimbursement for student-delivered services would currently not be restricted. The rationale for these decisions at the local health care facility level is that they do not wish to appear to be violating any ethical boundaries by treating individuals "differently" due to their different health care insurance coverage. This is a result of the perception by some individuals that receiving care provided by a student is receiving a standard of care inferior to that from a qualified, licensed practitioner.

The inherent challenges are clear when ACCEs face the task of obtaining suitable fieldwork placements for students in the face of these restrictions on delivery of services to clients with publicly funded Medicare and other similarly regulated private health care insurances, and individual facilities choosing to apply these regulations uniformly, whether required or not, to all their older adult clients. However, this challenge arising from the publicly funded insurance component of the system is not the only challenge faced when finding volunteer clinicians to serve as clinical instructors for students.

*Effects of Private Insurance Systems and Self-Pay Situations on Clinical Education*

There are also inherent issues that arise when placing students in clinical settings where the dominant form of insurance reimbursement comes from private insurance companies, or where clients pay for a percentage or for their entire services themselves. In many outpatient private practice health care settings, practitioners work to build their reputation and practice by providing those individuals paying privately for their care (partially or completely) with a higher level of customer service and clinical expertise, when compared to the care they could receive at many competing typical larger hospital-based outpatient settings. Because many of their clients are "paying for" their expertise, these private practitioners perceive an ethical dilemma inherent in having a student provide non-expert, potentially inefficient or ineffective care. Private practitioners are therefore commonly resistant to taking on students due to the concern that they would be risking their reputation and consequently also potentially losing business if allowing a student to work with their clients.

## Effects of Concerns for Productivity on Clinical Education

Another concern arising in multiple-practice settings is related to the perception that volunteering to provide clinical placements for students could result in a decrease in productivity and/or generation of revenue. This concern arises across the spectrum of practice settings, including managed care practice settings and settings relying on income from billing in a fee-for-service system. The perception is that taking a student requires extra time from clinical educators, thereby reducing their overall productivity. Especially during times such as these, when the economy is unstable or down, the prospect of losing potential income and/or sacrificing time that could be used to see more clients is not appealing to many potential volunteer clinical educators and their clinical practice administrators. This is not a new concern, and is one that has persisted despite published research demonstrating financial and quality of care benefits contributed by the presence of students in clinical education placements (e.g. Paterson, 1997; Ladyshewsky, Barrie, & Drake, 1998). However, with rising productivity expectations and in the context of the current unstable economy, this concern has recently become strengthened again, resulting in further challenges for ACCEs attempting to secure placements for students' fieldwork experiences.

## REFLECTIONS

We have stated the major challenges that need to be overcome in order to provide students with learning experiences essential to their development as independent practitioners, so that they are appropriately prepared to take their place in our health systems. Although the systems are funded in different ways, many of the same issues arise in our three countries, but for different reasons. In the U.S.A. public and private insurance systems seek to limit professional choices, whereas risk aversion in publicly funded systems has similar effects. Scarcity of placements occurs for different reasons, but in each case the issue is met with a pragmatic, problem-solving approach to the development of more placements and the preparation of more supervisors. The issue of the cost-benefits of student placements arises in all three countries. Fieldwork placement systems seldom attract funding for allied health professions, and the costs to the placement provider are perceived differently, whether in terms of productivity, time lost from other opportunities, or alleged lower standards of client care. Although there is some evidence to counter these beliefs and to suggest that students contribute to improved quality of services, further studies, grounded in the context of each national health system, are needed.

## REFERENCES

American Physical Therapy Association. (2005). *Physical therapy clinical instructor educator credentialing manual.* Alexandria, VA: APTA.

American Physical Therapy Association. (2006). *Physical therapist clinical performance instrument for students.* Alexandria, VA: APTA.

American Physical Therapy Association. (2009a). *Clarification of provision of therapy services by students under Medicare Part B.* Available: http://www.apta.org/AM/Template.cfm?Section=Home& TEMPLATE=/CM/ContentDisplay.cfm&CONTENTID=31946, accessed 21 September 2009.

American Physical Therapy Association. (2009b). APTA letter to MedPAC on student services under Part B Medicare. Available: http://www.apta.org/AM/Template.cfm? Section=Home& TEMPLATE =/ CM/ContentDisplay.cfm&CONTENTID=18236, accessed 21 September 2009.

Australian Institute of Health and Welfare. (2008). *Australia's Health 2008.* Cat no AUS 99. Canberra: AIHW. Available: http://www.aihw.gov.au, accessed 15 December 2009.

Australian Learning and Teaching Council. (2009a). *Benchmarking clinical learning in speech pathology to support assessment, discipline standards, teaching innovation and student learning.* Media release. Available: http://www.altc.edu.au/project-benchmarking-clinical-learning-speech-pathology-sydney-2006, accessed 23 December 2009.

Australian Learning and Teaching Council. (2009b). *Development of AAP.* Available: http://www.altc.edu. au/july2009-Development-of-the-APP, accessed 23 December 2009.

Australian Learning and Teaching Council. (2009c). Online student supervision training – accessible and cooperative learning in social work. Media Release, available: http://www.altc.edu.au/project-online-student-supervision-training-csu-2007, accessed 23 December 2009.

Baldry Currens, J.A., & Bithell, C.P. (2000). Clinical education: Listening to different perspectives. *Physiotherapy, 86*(12), 645-653.

Baldry Currens, J.A., & Bithell, C.P. (2003). The 2:1 clinical placement model: Perceptions of clinical educators and students. *Physiotherapy, 89*(4), 204-218.

Banks, S. (2004). *Ethics, accountability and the social professions.* New York: Palgrave Macmillan.

Barton, H., Bell, K., & Bowles, W. (2005). Help or hindrance? Outcomes of social work student placements. *Australian Social Work, 58*(3), 301–312.

Bauman, Z. (2000). *A meeting with Zygmunt Bauman.* Video. Norway: Oslo University College.

Bennett, R. (2003). Perceived abilities / qualities of clinical educators and team supervision of students. *Physiotherapy, 89*(7), 432–42.

Bisman, C. (2004). Social work values: The moral core of the profession. *British Journal of Social Work, 34*(1), 109–23.

Bowles, W., & Duncombe, R. (2005). A satellite model for rural and remote education. *Rural Society, 15*(3), 284–295.

Bowles, W., Collingridge, M., Curry, S., & Valentine B. (2006). *Ethical practice in social work: An applied approach.* Sydney: Allen and Unwin.

Centers for Medicare & Medicaid Services (CMS), Department of Health & Human Services, USA. (2001). *Program Memorandum Intermediaries/Carriers (Transmittal AB-01-56).* Health Care Financing Administration (HCFA) Pub. 60 AB. Available: http://www.cms.hhs.gov/Transmittals/ downloads/AB0156.pdf, accessed 22 September 2009.

Centers for Medicare & Medicaid Services (CMS), Department of Health & Human Services, USA. (2008). *Guidelines for teaching physicians, interns, and residents.* Available: http://www.cms.hhs. gov/MLNProducts/downloads/gdelinesteachgresfctsht.pdf, accessed 19 September 2009.

Chartered Society of Physiotherapy. (2003). *Clinical Education Placement Guidelines.* London: CSP.

Christensen, N. 2009. *Development of clinical reasoning capability in student physical therapists.* Unpublished PhD thesis. University of South Australia. Available: http://arrow.unisa.edu.au/vital/ access/manager/Repository/unisa:40761?exact=title%3A%22Development+of+clinical+reasoning+c apability+in+student+physical+therapists%22, accessed 22 November 2009.

Christensen, N., Jones, M., Edwards, I., & Higgs, J. (2008). Helping physiotherapy students develop clinical reasoning capability. In: J. Higgs, M. Jones, S. Loftus, & N. Christensen (Eds.), *Clinical reasoning in the health professions* (3rd ed., pp. 389–396). Amsterdam: Elsevier.

Craik, C., & Turner, A. (2005). A chronic shortage of practice placements: Whose responsibility? (Editorial). *British Journal of Occupational Therapy, 68*(5), 195.

Department of Health. (2000). *The NHS Plan: A plan for investment, a plan for reform.* London: DOH.

Department of Health. (2008). *High quality care for all: The NHS Next Stage Review Final Report.* London: DOH.

Education for Practice Institute. (2009). Available on Charles Sturt University website: http://www.csu. edu.au/division/landt/efp/index.html, accessed 10 December 2009.

Gwyer, J., Odom, C., & Gandy, J. (2003). History of clinical education in physical therapy in the United States. *Journal of Physical Therapy Education, 17*(3), 34–43.

Hicks, H., & Swain, P. (2007). Direct, facilitate, enable—the juxtaposition of the duty of care and the duty of disclosure in social work field education. *Social Work Education, 26*(1), 69–85.

Hugman, R. (2005). *New approaches in ethics in the caring professions.* Houndmills: Palgrave Macmillan.

Ladyshewsky, R.K., Barrie, S.C., & Drake, V.M. (1998). A comparison of productivity and learning outcome in individual and cooperative physical therapy clinical education models. *Physical Therapy, 78*(12), 1288–1298.

Lonne, B., & Cheers, B. (2004). Retaining rural social workers: An Australian study. *Rural Society, 14*(2), 163–177.

McAllister, S., Lincoln, M., Ferguson, A., & McAllister, L. (2006). *COMPASS®: Competency assessment in speech pathology.* Melbourne: Speech Pathology Association of Australia Ltd.

McLeod, S., & Barbara, A. (2005). Online technology in rural health: Supporting students to overcome the tyranny of distance. *Australian Journal of Rural Health, 13*(5), 276–281.

Moore, A., Morris, J., Crouch, V., & Martin, M. (2003). Evaluation of physiotherapy clinical education models: Comparing 1:1, 2:1 and 3:1 placements. *Physiotherapy, 89*(8), 489–501.

Paterson, M. (1997). Clinician productivity with and without students. *Occupational Therapy Journal of Research, 17*(1), 48–54.

Rodger, S., Webb, G., Devitt, L., Gilbert, J., Wrightson, P., & McMeeken, J. (2008). Clinical education and practice placements in the allied health professions: An international perspective. *Journal of Allied Health, 37*(1), 53–62.

Sandstrom, R.W., Lohman, H., & Bramble, J.D. (2009). *Health services: Policy and systems for therapists* (2nd ed., pp. 133–137). Upper Saddle River, NJ: Pearson.

Thew, M., Hargreaves, A., & Cronin-Davis, J. (2008). An evaluation of a role-emerging practice placement model for a full cohort of occupational therapy students. *British Journal of Occupational Therapy, 71*(8), 348–53.

Universities Australia. (2008). *Universities Australia Position Paper No3/08 – A national internship scheme: Enhancing the skills and work readiness of Australian university graduates.* Available: http://www.universitiesaustralia.edu.au/documents/publications/discussion/National-Internship-scheme-May08.pdf, accessed 22 December 2009.

*Christine Bithell MA(Educ)*
*Faculty of Health and Social Care Sciences*
*St George's, University of London and Kingston University, UK*

*Wendy Bowles PhD*
*School of Humanities and Social Sciences*
*Charles Sturt University, Australia*

*Nicole Christensen PhD*
*Department of Physical Therapy*
*Samuel Merritt University, USA*

# 7. MANAGING REAL WORLD PLACEMENTS

*Examples of Good Practice*

Managing fieldwork education placements is integral to ensuring that fieldwork learning objectives are achieved. Fieldwork programs that achieve student learning involve tripartite organisation between students, fieldwork educators and academic coordinators, embedded within the context of education and healthcare organisations. The relationship between each of these partners has been found to be critical to the success of the placement (Waryszak, 1999).

Effective fieldwork management is required to establish, implement and operate placements and to ensure the sustainability of a fieldwork education program. Orell, Cooper, and Jones (1999, p. 7) referred to the management of placement as an "intensive and complex interpersonal and organisational activity". Fieldwork management requires a diverse and sophisticated level of capabilities from those involved. These skills can include organisational capabilities, problem-solving skills, conflict-resolution and negotiation skills, the capacity to develop partnerships and manage and sustain relationships, understanding and application of policy, adherence to legal and ethical issues, the capacity to provide professional development and support for students with fieldwork performance difficulty, and change-management skills to respond to and lead new developments.

Despite the importance of good management of fieldwork placements, this essential dimension of fieldwork is largely unrecognised and unexplored for examples of best practice. Orell et al. (1999) noted that this aspect of placements is largely invisible within university processes. It is not unusual for individuals involved in fieldwork management to develop their skills "on the job" and in the absence of coordinated induction and professional support activities. We interpret the notion of *real world* to refer to the activities that impact on the day to day functioning of those engaged in placements. In this chapter we present three facets of real-world practices in effective fieldwork placement management. We explore the activities of university fieldwork coordinators and site-based fieldwork educators, and we consider organisation-wide approaches to management.

## UNIVERSITY FIELDWORK COORDINATORS
### BRIDGING THE UNIVERSITY–PRACTICE DIVIDE

The focus of a successful fieldwork placement program should be on student learning. The connection of academic theory with practice in the workplace is of

*L. McAllister et al., (eds.), Innovations in Allied Health Fieldwork*
*Education: A Critical Appraisal, 75–83.*

central importance to the development of the associated profession and the emerging professional (Mau, 1997; Cates & Jones, 1999). The academic coordinator selects and arranges the content of the fieldwork experience to align with and support the mission and goals of the program and to maximise students' learning (Cates & Jones, 1999). Students need to be provided with a range of fieldwork experiences that help them to develop a greater understanding of themselves and their practice (Bates, Bates, & Bates, 2004).

Our collective experience as university fieldwork coordinators and fieldwork educators has led to a conviction that effective management of fieldwork placements can be facilitated by having a university fieldwork coordinator with a strong professional background. These fieldwork coordinator are likely to have networks already established with professional partners, many of which can be subsequently maintained when they join a university faculty. Such previously established networks can provide substantial support and resilience for an ongoing university fieldwork program. To be effective in this role, university fieldwork coordinators of health profession programs draw upon their discipline-specific knowledge of practice and their knowledge of academia. Optimally they will have at least:

– Knowledge of the conditions that promote optimal learning from fieldwork experiences
– Knowledge of their discipline and the real world of the relevant work practices
– Knowledge of teaching and assessment practices and strategies to support students' learning in the fieldwork setting.

The combination of the personal and professional credibility of a university fieldwork coordinator in association with a fieldwork program that also demonstrates educational quality can encourage recurring professional partnerships. The coordinator can also build authentic relationships with professional partners, which can develop into collaborative research and potentially make substantial contributions for both the partner and the university.

Established professional partnerships can also be very useful when challenges arise during a student's fieldwork placement; for example, if a student is underperforming. The university fieldwork coordinator has to consider and integrate workplace interests as well as the student's learning. Addressing problems that may arise is facilitated because of the professional relationships that have been previously developed and when good knowledge of the practice environment exists. A strong professional background can also provide university fieldwork coordinators with a range of skills (e.g. specific professional knowledge and skills, interpersonal skills, personnel management, administrative skills, clear understanding of the integration of practice and academic theory) that promote the depth and strength of the fieldwork programs and partner relationships. The university fieldwork coordinator involved in fieldwork programs has the responsibility to develop and maintain contact with the "real" world, forge and sustain collaborative research with the relevant profession, spend time researching work-oriented projects, and focus on the relevance and design of the program's content ensuring that it meets the needs of both student and employer (Weisz & Chapman, 2005).

A fieldwork placement is a complex, intense and often relatively brief learning experience. There can be considerable risk involved, therefore, if the student "doesn't get it right" the first time. Problems that arise need to be handled promptly and flexibly, according to their nature. If the fieldwork experience is handled poorly, risk is involved for the student as a learner and a person, for the workplace as the provider of goods and services, and for the university, both legally and ethically. There is also considerable onus upon university fieldwork coordinators to minimise any potential damage to the relationship that might occur from negative experiences in the placement context. These coordinators need to function within an environment where clear policies exist to guide the conduct of fieldwork. The effectiveness of these policies should be monitored throughout the fieldwork placements (Bates, Bates, & Bates, 2004).

## EFFECTIVE PLACEMENT MANAGEMENT BY FIELDWORK EDUCATORS

Fieldwork educators located at fieldwork sites frequently assume the role of managers of fieldwork education programs (Brown & Kennedy-Jones, 2005). Core components of this management role are organising and structuring placements in collaboration with key stakeholders, providing a supportive learning environment for students, ensuring that adequate physical and educational resources are available for students, understanding the university's requirements for placements including the learning goals and assessment processes, using appropriate supervision and teaching/learning strategies to facilitate student learning, and completing placement evaluations (McLeod, Romanini, Cohn, & Higgs, 1997; Brown & Kennedy-Jones, 2005).

Researchers including Roe-Shaw (2004) and Brumfitt, Enderby, and Hoben (2005) have found that to optimise student learning outcomes, fieldwork placements need to be structured to provide (a) increasing levels of student learning opportunities and skill development and (b) decreasing levels of direct supervision, within and across placements throughout professional entry programs. Final year fieldwork placements need to approximate the early months of graduates' first year of employment, including the levels of responsibility and autonomy, the style and content of supervision, the working relationships and workload. Assessment conditions need to be created to determine the extent to which students have achieved the expected level of performance (Hummell, 2007). Research findings with new graduates (Adamson, Harris, Heard, & Hunt, 1996; Adamson, Cant, & Hummell, 2001) suggest that final year students' workloads need to include non-direct client tasks and a focus on teamwork skills, prioritising tasks, time management skills and managing workplace stressors.

A core aspect of the fieldwork educator manager role is effectively developing, implementing and evaluating fieldwork placements that incorporate research findings. Hummell and Williamson (1999) and Clouder and Dalley (2002) have provided examples of innovative final year fieldwork placements, which underline the importance of the fieldwork educator's management role to positive outcomes. These authors evaluated placements which had been specifically structured, based on research findings of the workforce experiences of newly qualified allied health graduates, with the intent of enhancing the preparation of final year students for the realities of their initial employment.

Hummell and Williamson (1999) reported on a study that evaluated a range of innovative final year fieldwork placements for occupational therapy (OT) students that reflected developing areas of practice. The placements were established by fieldwork academics with the intent of promoting the development of students' skills in self-directed learning, peer learning, clinical reasoning, reflection, problem solving, teamwork, and evaluation. Small groups of two to six students were allocated to each fieldwork site, with supervision provided by one fieldwork academic/ educator, using a collaborative consultative framework. In accordance with the writing of Higgs (1992), the students were encouraged to be co-managers of their learning program.

The fieldwork sites did not employ an occupational therapist for the services provided by the students. Each placement was established following a series of meetings and negotiations between OT fieldwork academics and relevant people in interested organisations. These discussions determined the specific aims of the placement from each organisation's perspective as well as the anticipated outcomes for the students, clients and university. The fieldwork academics also aimed to ensure that an appropriate learning environment for the students was available at the fieldwork site. This included respect for students, provision of adequate space, a minimum of one on-site contact person, and an ability to meet the identified learning objectives for the placement as documented by the university. Such pre-placement planning was perceived by all concerned as crucial to the success of the placements.

The fieldwork academic who negotiated the specific placement subsequently became the placement fieldwork educator. Each student group received an orientation to the placement that incorporated information about expectations and responsibilities of the fieldwork site, the students and the fieldwork educator, the style and frequency of support/supervision and the requirement for the students to engage in self-directed learning. The fieldwork educator provided each student with support/ supervision for approximately 3 hours per week. The level of support/supervision and its content was negotiated between the fieldwork educator and students on an ongoing basis and varied throughout the placement. Support/supervision included regular workplace visits by the designated academic fieldwork educator and tele-phone contact as required. During the regular visits, the fieldwork educator and students met individually and as a group for discussion, the fieldwork educator observed students engaged in direct client service provision, assessed student performance and reviewed their documents, and met with staff employed by the organisation.

The placements were evaluated using focus group methodology. Findings indicated that students perceived their autonomy to be high during these place-ments and identified a range of skills that had increased during the placement: most notable were their teamwork skills (multidisciplinary, with peers and with their fieldwork educator, communication and time management skills) and skills in evaluating practice and managing conflict. The students indicated that although the style of supervision had initially created anxiety it had marked overall benefits for their development as emerging occupational therapists. They believed it gave them independence, compelled them to take responsibility for their decisions, created a sense of competence through working autonomously and contributed to the development of their communication and teamwork skills. They gained an appreciation of their own skills and the skills of other team members.

Clouder and Dalley (2002) reported on a study that evaluated a 4-week caseload management module that was collaboratively developed by physiotherapy academics and fieldwork educators and implemented at the end of physiotherapy students' final fieldwork placement. The module's aim was to equip students for their work roles as beginning physiotherapists by facilitating the generic transferable skills required to manage a client caseload, including prioritisation of clients and work tasks. The students provided therapy to a familiar client caseload to allow for an increase in the "complexity and pace of work" (p. 197) and in the level of responsibility and autonomy. They developed learning objectives "appropriate to their perceived needs as newly appointed junior therapists" (p. 193) and were required to communicate with other team members. Assessment was ongoing, with performance criteria relevant to "practical skills, professional behaviour, self-management/caseload management and meeting personal objectives" (p. 193), and student learning was facilitated through formal and informal systems of support and supervision, with fieldwork educators implementing a style of supervision that encouraged student initiative, problem solving and self-direction. By retaining overall responsibility for client care the fieldwork educator provided a "safety net" for the students.

The placement caseload management module was evaluated by obtaining student feedback at its conclusion, using the standard placement evaluation form and a small group discussion, and questionnaire-based feedback from graduates 6 months after course completion. Feedback from both groups was positive. Student feedback indicated that they had functioned at an increased level of independence and accountability, taken increased responsibility for the organisation of their client caseload, and developed collegial relationships with team members. Feedback from the new graduates indicated that the module had assisted their transition from student to employee by developing their skills to manage workplace realities, developed their self-management abilities through the acquisition of transferable skills across client caseloads in time management, prioritisation, goal planning, accountability and working autonomously, and promoted social inclusion through the provision of opportunities to communicate with team members in a collegial manner. Both groups indicated that the style of supervision was an important component in the achievement of these outcomes, and in the development of their professional identity.

In both studies, the fieldwork educators' management role was complex and an important contributor to the positive placement outcomes. The fieldwork educators collaborated with key stakeholders, assisted in the creation of a supportive learning environment for the students, utilised a collaborative supervisory style and teaching/ learning strategies that addressed the goals of the placement.

The findings of Hummell and Williamson (1999) and Clouder and Dalley (2002) provide evidence of positive student learning experiences and outcomes when fieldwork educators are effective placement managers. Current research findings relevant to the fieldwork educators' manager role continue to support the approaches taken by these authors in final fieldwork education placements, and underline the importance of collaboration across all fieldwork education stakeholders (Kirke, Layton, & Sim, 2007), grading learning experiences (Fish & Coles, 2005), using sound educational principles including facilitating clinical reasoning, reflection and self direction (Donaghy & Morss, 2007; Ryan & Higgs, 2008), and the workplace experiences of allied health graduates in their initial employment (Roe-Shaw, 2004; Hummell, 2007).

## BUILDING A CULTURE OF EDUCATION IN FIELDWORK PLACEMENT SETTINGS

Organisations are seldom considered in the day-to-day management of fieldwork. However, when an organisational culture supports fieldwork many management challenges can be addressed systematically and greater degrees of change achieved. As an example of good organisational practice we offer the activities being led through the State Government Department of Health (DoH), Victoria, Australia and exemplified in allied health departments within Victoria. We acknowledge that the activities of the Victorian DoH have been undertaken with an awareness of a National Council of Australian Governments (COAG) agenda to address fieldwork placement issues as a component of an overall health workforce strategy. This will see the establishment of Health Workforce Australia in 2010.

Within the state of Victoria, the DoH is responsible for, among other things, the provision of health services for the people of the state. Whereas the health care sector has traditionally emphasised its responsibility for patient/client health care, the initiative we describe is intended to reflect the recognised role of healthcare facilities in educating the future healthcare workforce. Through recognition and systematic addressing of issues of management and coordination at an organisational level, coordinated resources are being made available to many staff involved in fieldwork placements across the health sector. We have become aware of this example through our partnerships with Victorian DoH healthcare facilities, communication by the Victorian DoH with education facilities, and by reviewing the DoH web site established to support the Department's activities (http://www.health.vic.gov.au/workforce/placements).

The key aspects of the statewide approach are to address objectives and act in five broad areas: governance and coordination, funding, innovation, data and planning, and enhanced capacity and quality. Of these, governance and coordination and data and planning are two key aspects that should directly impact on the resources required to manage placements. A DoH note states:

> The Victorian DoH is committed to promoting efficient and effective approaches to the management and delivery of clinical placements. This includes implementing systems and supports that streamline processes for the organisation,

allocation, delivery and reporting of clinical placements. It also involves developing tools and resources that can be used by health services and other stakeholders to achieve consistency, where desirable, and to minimise administrative burden. These measures aim to build broader system capacity and improve linkages across organisations and sectors. (State Government of Victoria, DoH, 2009)

There are advantages and disadvantages associated with adopting an organisational and centralised approach to fieldwork management. The potential advantages are readily apparent, including:
- the capacity to address systemic issues centrally rather than relying on local initiatives that would be limited in scope of impact
- absence of duplication of management activities
- improved coordination of placements, enhanced capacity to identify placements
- an enhanced profile of fieldwork education and management issues within organisations
- the establishment of communication and information sharing pathways that provide a framework for sharing and disseminating good practice
- organisational support which encourages local organisations to actively engage in fieldwork education and potentially establish more effective learning partnerships with education providers
- provision of funding to support local facilities to enhance their capacity.

There are also potential disadvantages or less comprehensive advantages. For example, establishing sector-wide approaches does not remove the need for local management. When local agencies rely on large-scale data collection and allocation systems there can be a detrimental effect on establishing and maintaining local partnerships. A centralised view may also erode local differences and scope for individuality according to local needs, when those involved do not recognise the value of their own contextual needs. A centralised focus on efficiency in locating placements and allocating students to them can undermine the pedagogic motivations for placements and the focus on ensuring student learning, when a placement begins to be represented as a commodity. The DoH has included a focus on ensuring the quality of placements, and it will be important to see how partnerships between health organisations and universities define the nature of quality. Although these systems have been put in place it is yet to be established how these initiatives are impacting on the experiences of those with responsibility for managing placements. It will be important to monitor these outcomes to ensure that such system wide approaches are effective.

## CONCLUSION

In this chapter we have reviewed the tripartite dimensions of fieldwork management, with academic staff, fieldwork educators and students having key roles within their organisational contexts of health care and education. To bridge the nexus between universities and the workplace, good management practice requires an understanding of the diverse and complex nature of fieldwork management and a capacity to draw upon knowledge of professional practice, the workplace and students' learning needs. Research and scholarship exploring best practice in this area have been limited, and there is great scope to explore the relationship between management and optimal learning outcomes in fieldwork settings.

## REFERENCES

Adamson, B., Harris, L., Heard, R., & Hunt, A. (1996). *University education and workplace requirements: evaluating the skills and attributes of health science graduates.* Sydney: The University of Sydney.

Adamson, B.J., Cant, R.V., & Hummell, J. (2001). What managerial skills do newly graduated occupational therapists need? A view from their managers. *British Journal of Occupational Therapy, 64*(4), 184–192.

Bates, A., Bates, M., & Bates, L. (2004). Weaving the threads of knowledge: A focus on students. In C. Eames (Ed.), *Proceedings of the 5th Asia Pacific Cooperative Education Conference*, Hamilton: New Zealand Association for Cooperative Education. Available: http://eprints.qut.edu.au /11668/1/11668.pdf, accessed 19 March 2010.

Brown, L., & Kennedy-Jones, M. (2005). Exploring the roles of the clinical educator: The manager role. In M. Rose & D. Best (Eds.), *Transforming practice through clinical education, professional supervision and mentoring* (pp. 49–58). Sydney: Elsevier.

Brumfitt, S.M., Enderby, P.M., & Hoben, K. (2005). The transition to work of newly qualified speech and language therapists: Implications for the curriculum. *Learning in Health and Social Care, 4*(3), 142–155.

Cates, C., & Jones, P. (1999). *Learning outcomes and the educational value of cooperative education.* Paper presented at the 1999 WACE/CEA International Conference on Cooperative Education, World Association for Cooperative Education, Boston.

Clouder, L., & Dalley, J. (2002). Providing a 'safety net': Fine-tuning preparation of undergraduate physiotherapists for contemporary professional practice. *Learning in Health and Social Care, 1*(4), 191–201.

Donaghy, M., & Morss, K. (2007). An evaluation of a framework for facilitating and assessing physiotherapy students' reflection on practice. *Physiotherapy Theory & Practice, 23*(2), 83–94.

Fish, D., & Coles, C. (2005). *Medical education: Developing a curriculum for practice.* Berkshire: Open University Press.

Higgs, J. (1992). Managing clinical education: The educator-manager and the self-directed learner. *Physiotherapy, 78*, 822–828.

Hummell, J. (2007). *Allied health graduates' first year of employment.* Unpublished PhD thesis, The University of Sydney, Australia.

Hummell, J., & Williamson, P. (1999). Fieldwork in occupational therapy: Close to the edge. *Focus on Health Professional Education: A Multi-disciplinary Journal, 1*(2), 33–49.

Kirke, P., Layton, N., & Sim, J. (2007). Informing fieldwork design: Key elements to quality in fieldwork education for undergraduate occupational therapy students. *Australian Occupational Therapy Journal, 54*, S13–S22.

Mau, R.Y. (1997). Concerns of student teachers: Implications for improving the practicum. *Asia-Pacific Journal of Teacher Education, 25*(1), 53–64.

McLeod, S., Romanini, J., Cohn, E., & Higgs, J. (1997). Models and roles in clinical education. In L. McAllister, M. Lincoln, S. McLeod & D. Maloney (Eds.), *Facilitating learning in clinical settings* (pp. 27–64). Sydney: Nelson Thornes.

Orell, J., Cooper, L., & Jones, R. (1999). Making the practicum visible. Paper presented at the HERDSA Annual International Conference, Melbourne, July.

Roe-Shaw, M.M. (2004). *Workplace realities and professional socialization of recently graduated physiotherapists in New Zealand.* Unpublished PhD thesis, University of Otago, Dunedin.

Ryan, S., & Higgs, J. (2008). Teaching and learning clinical reasoning. In J. Higgs, M. Jones, S. Loftus & N. Christensen (Eds.), *Clinical reasoning in the health professions* (3rd ed., pp. 379–387). Sydney: Elsevier.

State Government of Victoria, DOH. (2009). *Clinical placements in Victoria*. Available: http://health.vic. gov.au/workforce/placements, accessed 28 October 2009.

Waryszak, R. (1999). Assessing students' perceptions of their cooperative education placements in the tourism industry: International perspective. Paper presented at the WACE/CEA International Conference on Cooperative Education, World Association for Cooperative Education, Boston.

Weisz, M., & Chapman, R. (2005). Benefits of cooperative education for educational institutions. In R. Coll & C. Eames (Eds.), *International handbook for cooperative education* (pp. 247–258). Boston: World Association for Cooperative Education.

*Megan Smith PhD*
*School of Community Health*
*Charles Sturt University, Australia*

*Carol Burgess MEd*
*School of Teacher Education*
*Charles Sturt University, Australia*

*Jill Hummell PhD*
*Community Integration Program*
*Westmead Brain Injury Rehabilitation Service, Australia*

JOY HIGGS, RODNEY POPE, JENNY KENT,
PETER O'MEARA AND JULAINE ALLAN

# 8. UNIVERSITY CLINICS

## Practice and Education Dimensions

At a time when fieldwork education placements in the real world of health care are becoming more, scarce universities are looking for other means of providing student placements. University clinics address this need and also provide benefits such as offering community services, developing partnerships with local industry, allowing students to work in professional practice settings with their academic role models and providing a means for academic faculty members to engage in professional practice and professional development.

In this chapter we use the term university clinics to refer to university-operated health science clinical practice units that both provide health services to the public and provide student placements in actual health care venues. In such units, set up by universities, students and educators are likely to play a more prominent role than in a typical health industry setting, although the service provision offered by the clinic is an authentic part of the operation of the clinic. In both settings there is a balance to be found between the education and the health care practices and priorities. This is discussed further below.

### A STUDY OF UNIVERSITY CLINICS

We report in this chapter on a research study we conducted to investigate the practices of university clinics in Australia and New Zealand across the health and veterinary sciences and to develop guidelines for our university for the establishment and operation of clinics. This chapter focuses on the health sciences aspects of the study. Charles Sturt University (CSU) in Australia provides education across many professions including nursing and allied health. CSU is a regional university, located across multiple campuses in rural and regional areas of Australia, mainly in the state of New South Wales (NSW) (see Figure 8.1). The challenges faced by CSU fieldwork education staff in organising fieldwork placements are exacerbated by vast distances, sparse populations and limited numbers of health professionals working in rural and regional areas, in rural cities (with populations often below 50,000), small towns and "outback" areas. Most of Australia's population is concentrated in largely urban populations in two widely separated coastal regions, the largest being in the south-east and east. Population density ranges from around 8000 people per km$^2$ in

*L. McAllister et al., (eds.), Innovations in Allied Health Fieldwork
Education: A Critical Appraisal, 85–93.*

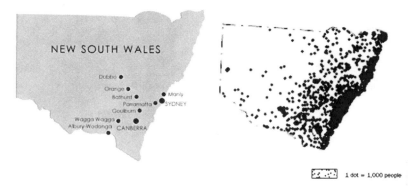

1 dot = 1,000 people

*Figure 8.1. CSU Campuses.*          *Figure 8.2. NSW Population Density 2006.*
*http://www.csu.edu.au/about/maps/*          *http://www.abs.gov.au/ausstats*

some capital city areas to around 0.2 in remote areas, with the national average being around three people per km[21] (see Figure 8.2 for NSW population density 2006). NSW covers a large area, 800,628 km². Placements occur in NSW, interstate and overseas, hundreds (sometimes thousands) of kilometres away from the campus locations where students are enrolled (e.g. Albury-Wodonga).

Rural health science education programs are acknowledged as an effective way of increasing the numbers of health professionals in rural communities (Dunbabin & Levitt, 2003; Western Research Institute, 2006). However, a scarcity of regional and rural clinical placements limits the ability of regional universities to obtain sufficient workplace locations to place students for clinical education. University clinics can help overcome this shortfall in clinical placements and at the same time deliver quality health services to under-serviced communities.

## THE PROJECT

This research was conducted as a consultative inquiry that examined the goals, possibilities and challenges of university clinics by reviewing and critically appraising:

a) documents and literature relating to clinical education models and clinics
b) 20 existing clinics, across a range of health and veterinary disciplines, associated with Australian and New Zealand universities and private sector health service providers that offered places for students undertaking clinical education.

An advisory group was established to provide discipline-related advice to the project team and to review the draft report and recommendations from the study.

## CONSIDERATIONS IN ESTABLISHING UNIVERSITY CLINICS

The operation of a university clinic involves a number of dimensions: education, service delivery, business and finance, and governance (Pope, Allan, Kent, Higgs, & O'Meara, 2008) (see discussion below). In this chapter the primary focus is on the education and service delivery dimensions. Our study of health and veterinary clinics identified a number of factors that can influence the clinic model adopted by universities. Practice and service-related factors include the history and culture of the clinic, including the associated professional practice and community expectations, and population demographics; the services otherwise missing or less available in the clinic region; the availability of clients[2]; the location of clients relative to the clinic. Infrastructure factors include available infrastructure and funding; clinic space; and the capacity of the venue for flexible usage. Educational factors include the education needs of students; the type of student placement; the availability of mentors, specialists and teachers.

The clinical model, aims, location and procedures in turn influence the client population attracted to the clinic and the learning opportunities available to students (including such variables as number of clients, range of conditions represented by client group, mode of supervision, background of clinical educator).

From an education perspective, university clinics present a number of challenges. These include achieving appropriate student preparation for placements; maximising the benefits from learning in a clinical environment; facilitating learning to gain understanding of workplace and community responsibilities, rules and cultures; dealing with changing client populations and client availability and coping with different student needs. Of particular concern is the need to convince patients that they are receiving quality care from students as opposed to graduate practitioners. This matter requires sensitive marketing, good supervision by competent practitioners, and positive patient experiences and outcomes. Students need appropriate time and space in clinics to work at their required pace and supervision level. Our project identified a number of key issues to be considered within the service delivery dimension of university clinic models:

—  *The community contexts, needs and markets within which university clinics operate.* Included in these considerations are the availability of providers, population density, the types of service that are demanded by policy or lobby groups and not yet supplied, and the extent of socioeconomic disadvantage in the community (impacting on the affordability of services).

—  *The available health care workforce.* The disciplinary focus and potential client group of each university clinic model determines the likely mix of clinical providers attached to the clinic and the frameworks under which they operate. For instance, it is unlikely that health professionals from local private practices would participate in a clinic that was in direct competition with their own clinic. They might, however, be willing and able to support a clinic that provided services to under-serviced populations. This would achieve dual aims of improving health outcomes for the disadvantaged and educating future professionals in their discipline.

—  *Available resources and facilities within each location.* Resources and facilities available in particular locations can be a problem in providing services and meeting demand. The problem most frequently noted in our study was that clinic premises were not designed for the dual roles of service provision and education. This limited either the services provided or the number of students that could be supervised or work at any one time. Often clinic facilities were teaching rooms turned into clinics and there were problems with layout and room design. Access for clients was also noted as a problem, with stairs, signage, parking and location identified as barriers to clients locating the clinic or even knowing that it existed. Some clinics also experienced problems maintaining resources and clinic facilities.

- *The scope/attractiveness of clinics and access to particular services.* Many clinics had problems recruiting enough clients for student needs. This can be a consequence of inaccessible and poorly identified locations within university campuses, sporadic and ineffective marketing, competition from other providers, or lack of a range of client types or problem types in the nearby area. The study also revealed considerable difficulty in matching curriculum requirements with client needs.

In dealing with the dual roles of education and health services provision in university health services clinics, there are many matters for clinic managers, health service practitioners, clinical educators and students to deal with in terms of managing the multiple responsibilities of clinics towards students, the university, clients and the community. Managers and educators need to balance their duty of care to patients/clients and students and to help students balance their learning and service provision responsibilities.

## CHALLENGES FOR UNIVERSITIES IN PROVIDING QUALITY CLINICAL SERVICES

Underpinning university clinic models is an understanding that benefits will accrue to the university, students and clients through the provision of services that also provide clinical education to students. At a societal level, clinics provide value through the provision of clinical care and opportunities for health-care-related research that contribute to improving health care quality, availability and access.

In choosing to operate health clinics, universities are addressing their commitment to serve the community, thereby accepting that the quality of services must be a high priority. The dual obligation of enhancing students' clinical education and providing clinical services to clients confronts universities with the challenge of ensuring that their staff and students provide care to clients that meets contemporary quality standards across a range of clinical disciplines. In Australia, for example, The Australian National Health Performance Framework (National Health Performance Committee, 2001) divides quality into the four dimensions of safety, responsiveness, capability and continuity.

*safety:* the avoidance, or reduction to acceptable levels, of actual or potential harm from health care services or environments, and the prevention or mini-misation of adverse events associated with health care delivery

*responsiveness:* the provision of services that are client orientated and respectful of clients' dignity, autonomy, confidentiality, amenity, choices, and social and cultural needs *capability:* the capacity of an organisation, program or individual to provide health care services based on appropriate skills and knowledge

*continuity:* the provision of uninterrupted, timely, coordinated health care, interventions and actions across programs, practitioners and organisations (Australian Government Productivity Commission, 2009, Health Preface, p. E.26).

In the establishment of university clinics it is important to consider the sustainability of the clinic, to avoid encouraging expectations that cannot be realised in the longer term through a lack of capacity to provide the necessary infrastructure, to be innovative or to respond to emerging health care needs. Clinics also have an obligation to ensure that quality standards are established and maintained, through attention to the service delivery dimensions that underpin the viability and sustainability of university clinics.

Table 8.1 demonstrates in a generic fashion how university clinics might consider each of the service delivery dimensions in relation to satisfying this obligation to provide high quality clinical service to clients on the same basis as any other health service provider.

Although there is no absolute best model for university clinics there is a common requirement to provide quality clinical services and to control the risks to clients, staff and students. Health care providers increasingly emphasise and address clinical and professional governance issues, to deal with concerns across the health sector and in the community about quality of care, and university clinics need to perform at the same standard in their role as providers of clinical care.

*Table 8.1. Quality standards and service delivery dimensions*
*(adapted from O'Meara & Strasser, 2002 and Humphreys et al., 2008)*

| Service delivery dimensions | DIMENSIONS OF QUALITY | | | |
| --- | --- | --- | --- | --- |
| | *Safety* | *Responsiveness* | *Capability* | *Continuity* |
| **Location and infrastructure** | Safe working environment for staff, students and clients<br>Co-location may be an option | Clinics located to maximise access and equity<br>Public transport availability<br>Disabled access | Contemporary standards for facilities, equipment and information systems. Some technological requirements may be beyond capacity | Locations of clinics limited to where students are located<br>Provision to offer outreach services |
| **Processes of service delivery** | Clinical practice standards<br>Risk management policies and processes | Clinics are often walk-in clinics<br>Operate as interdisciplinary workplaces when possible | With regular clientele, booking systems may be required | Referral system for clients to other providers |

*Table 8.1. (Continued)*

| Workforce | Students practise under supervision of experienced and skilled professionals | Sufficient staffing (and students) to provide timely services | Academics, clinical staff and students provide services | Succession-planning strategies in place |
|---|---|---|---|---|
| **Times of operation** | Security of staff, students and clients considered | Consider client needs, expectations and ethical issues Manage within business constraints | Hire staff to operate clinic over student vacation periods? | Clinical services limited due to student and staff availability |
| **Funding** | Adequate funding to ensure safe working environment | Adequate budget to allow management flexibility | Recurrent budgets to cover salaries and infrastructure | Funding and performance agreements Funded from a variety of sources |
| **Governance** | Clinic accreditation and clinical governance system | Professional and community involvement | Appropriate management structures and processes | Clearly defined governance structures and processes |
| **Integration and co-ordination** | Clinical and management information systems | Agreed clinical referral pathways | Management and information systems | Key stakeholders identified and roles defined |

## MANAGING RISKS

The primary objectives of university clinics include quality clinical education, service provision and clinical research. Additionally, objectives of such university enterprises include business sustainability, reputation management and regulatory compliance. A *risk* can be defined (Standards Australia/ Standards New Zealand, 2004a) as "the chance of something happening that will have an impact on objectives" and that "impact" can be either positive or negative.

Risk management (Standards Australia/ Standards New Zealand 2004a, b) for university clinics is complex. In addition to the business risks that must be managed by any organisation, risks associated with clinical practice, patient care and professional competence demand special care (Irvine 2004; Braithwaite & Travaglia, 2008). Risks associated with the delivery of services by students under supervision and with student education and supervision further complicate the situation. Critical incidents arising from these risks have the potential to significantly compromise and damage a university clinic and those it serves. Effective management of these risks requires robust and comprehensive governance arrangements and information systems, which encompass clinical, academic, professional and business governance domains.

A DECISION-MAKING FRAMEWORK FOR ESTABLISHING
AND OPERATING UNIVERSITY CLINICS

The flowchart in Figure 8.3 provides a decision making framework developed from
our study of university clinics in Australia and internationally, which can be employed
when establishing or reviewing university clinics. The framework considers the

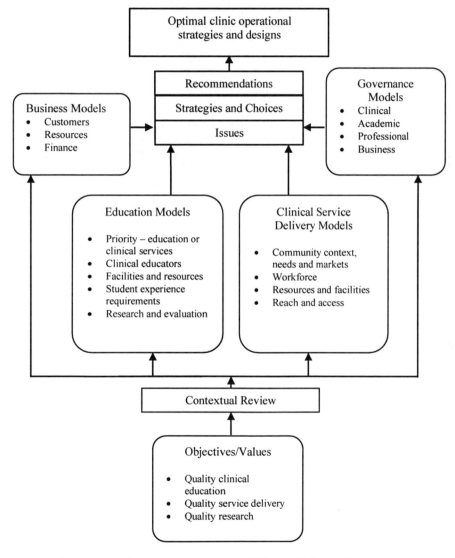

*Figure 8.3. A decision-making framework for establishing and operating
university clinics. (Pope et al., 2008).*

underpinning values and key objectives we consider are necessary for university clinics, and the contexts in which the clinics are to operate. On this basis, decisions can then be made regarding preferred models for *clinical education, clinical service delivery, business and financial management,* and *governance and risk management.* The 'issues' element in the decision-making framework is the point in the decision-making process at which conflicts between alternate models are identified and resolved. This is likely to require modification of at least some of the initially preferred models. The weightings given to specific concerns in this phase of the decision-making process should reflect the underpinning clinic objectives, values and contextual sensitivities.

## CONCLUSION

University clinics provide an alternative and supplement to industry workplaces as a means of clinical education alongside health care services delivery. In the study we have reported, issues related to decision making about optimal practice models for the given university/community/health care industry setting were examined. We have provided findings from our study that emphasise the need for this decision making to be informed by considerations of various interests and imperatives: clinical education, service delivery, business and financial management, and governance and risk management.

## NOTES

[1] Australian Bureau of Statistics http://www.abs.gov.au/ausstats
[2] In this chapter the terms *clinical* and *patient* are used to fit with the setting of health sciences clinics.

## REFERENCES

Australian Government Productivity Commission. (2009). *Report on Government Services 2009.* Chapter 1, p. 1.20. Australian Government. Available: http://www.pc.gov.au/gsp/reports/rogs/2009, accessed 15 March 2010.

Braithwaite, J., & Travaglia, J.F. (2008). An overview of clinical governance policies, practices and initiatives. *Australian Health Review, 32*(1), 10–22.

Dunbabin, J., & Levitt, L. (2003). Rural origin and rural medical exposure: Their impact on the rural and remote medical workforce in Australia. *Rural and Remote Health, 3,* Art. 212 (online). Available: http://www.rrh.org.au/articles/defaultnew.asp?IssueNo=3x, accessed 15 March 2010.

Humphreys, J., Wakerman, J., Wells, R., Kuipers, P., Jones, J., & Entwistle, P. (2008). "Beyond workforce": A systematic solution for health service provision in small rural and remote communities. *Medical Journal of Australia, 188*(8), S77–S80.

Irvine, D. (2004). Time for hard decisions on patient-centred professionalism. *Medical Journal of Australia, 181*(5), 271–274.

National Health Performance Committee. (2001). *National Health Performance Framework Report: A report to the Australian Health Ministers' Conference.* Canberra: Australian Government.

O'Meara, P., & Strasser, R. (2002). More after hours medical service: "Pillars" of success. *Australian Health Review, 25*(2), 104–114.

Pope, R., Allan, J., Kent, J., Higgs, J., & O'Meara, P. (2008). *Optimising university clinics for clinical education and community care in inland NSW.* Wagga Wagga, NSW: Charles Sturt University.

Standards Australia/ Standards New Zealand. (2004a). *AS/NZS 4360:2004 Risk Management*. Sydney: Standards Australia International.

Standards Australia/ Standards New Zealand. (2004b). *HB 436 Risk Management Guidelines - Companion to AS/NZS 4360:2004*. Sydney: Standards Australia International.

Western Research Institute. (2006). *The destination of on-campus graduates of Charles Sturt University: 2006 update*. Bathurst, NSW: Charles Sturt University.

*Joy Higgs AM PhD*
*The Education for Practice Institute*
*Charles Sturt University, Australia*

*Rodney Pope PhD*
*Centre for Inland Health*
*Charles Sturt University, Australia*

*Jenny Kent PhD*
*Institute for Land Water and Society*
*Charles Sturt University, Australia*

*Peter O'Meara PhD*
*Centre for Inland Health*
*Charles Sturt University, Australia*

*Julaine Allan PhD*
*Centre for Inland Health*
*Charles Sturt University, Australia*

# SECTION III: MODELS OF FIELDWORK EDUCATION AND SUPERVISION

JILL HUMMELL, JOY HIGGS AND SUSAN MULHOLLAND

# 9. MODELS OF FIELDWORK EDUCATION

*Influences and Approaches*

Fieldwork education plays a vital and highly influential role in the education and professional socialisation of health science students. The complex and diverse nature of fieldwork education placements and their impact on students and graduates cannot be underestimated. Due consideration must therefore be given to the nature of the fieldwork education experience and opportunities available to students and to the model of fieldwork education that optimises learning and socialisation experiences and outcomes for the given course, setting, student population and system (e.g., country, healthcare model, industry partners, society, population/s). Informed decision making aims to optimise outcomes for all involved, most notably clients, students, fieldwork educators and workplaces. In making these statements we are clearly saying that best practice in determining (choosing, planning, creating) a model for fieldwork education is a situational rather than universal matter.

In this chapter we reflect on the goals of fieldwork education as the framework for shaping fieldwork education models; we review different fieldwork education models and research reviewing them, context parameters and the decision-making concerns that influence fieldwork education approaches. The model of fieldwork education in operation at any venue is influenced by many factors, including tradition, the influence of individuals conducting the program (e.g., their values, preferences, experiences), trends in higher education, evolutions in health sciences education, and local contextual factors including policies, economics and the availability of fieldwork education sites.

GOALS AND MODELS OF FIELDWORK EDUCATION

On completion of their professional entry courses allied health graduates are expected by the workplace to be work-ready to engage in their work roles competently and autonomously with limited supervision and to engage in ongoing professional development (Higgs & Edwards, 2002). They are expected to be technically competent and able to communicate effectively with all relevant personnel, to work effectively within multidisciplinary teams, evaluate existing practices, and engage in management tasks at an entry level. Graduates are also expected to demonstrate a range of generic attributes such as problem-solving, analytical and lifelong learning skills (Adamson, Harris, Heard, & Hunt, 1996). Fieldwork placement experiences during

*L. McAllister et al., (eds.), Innovations in Allied Health Fieldwork*
*Education: A Critical Appraisal, 97–110.*

entry-level allied health courses have a crucial role in preparing students for the reality and responsibilities of work roles post-graduation (Roe-Shaw, 2004; Hummell, 2007).

Fieldwork education does not occur in isolation; it is part of a curriculum. Before we consider models of fieldwork education, then, we need to reflect upon the broader picture of curriculum models. The health sciences are a diverse group of professions with equally diverse curriculum frameworks linked to such factors as the nature of the profession's role (ranging from very technical, as in radiography, to highly interpersonal as in occupational therapy (OT)), the place the profession occupies in healthcare (e.g., enmeshed in people's lives, such as social work), and educational trends (e.g., graduate entry compared to undergraduate). Despite these differences there are some broad similarities that reflect the evolution of healthcare from practical caring occupations to the emergence of the health professions, the rise of higher education, the knowledge explosion of the twentieth century, and today's emphasis on the competing demands for evidence-based and patient-centred healthcare. Matching these evolutions, health sciences education, as described by Higgs and Hunt (1999), has followed some key transitions:

- Traditionally, education of healthcare workers followed the apprenticeship model, where apprentices studied practical knowledge, craft and art of the practice role with a master practitioner in the workplace setting, progressing from high levels of supervision to increasing independence. The success or failure of this system rested largely on the masters' technical and educational abilities and willingness to share their learning.
- The rise and proliferation of the health professions called for a greater degree of shared knowledge and skill as well as a collective responsibility for the quality of practice and education. Educating the health professional became the focus of curricula, with a shift from practical knowledge and pursuit of mastery to clinical–technical competence supported by a scientific knowledge base and the pursuit of professionalism (i.e., a responsibility for knowledge generation and quality regulation).
- A key response to the knowledge and technology explosions was an increased emphasis on the skills of problem solving, with a diminishing emphasis on knowledge acquisition (Norman, 1990). Problem-based education became a key trend in health sciences education.
- With the emergence of professionalism across the allied health professions came a focus on identifying and teaching professional competencies. A down-side of competency-based education curricula often tended to be a lack of attention to caring for the whole person in the midst of attending to atomised competencies.
- During the second half of the twentieth century, attention to shifted to the need for reflective practice to face the challenge of professional practice with its uncertainties, ill-defined problems, complex goals and outcomes that are difficult to predict (Schön, 1983).
- In the latter twentieth century the scientific basis for healthcare was clearly established as the grounds for credibility of health services (Michels, 1982).

Health professional educators were called to engage in research and pursue the scientific foundations for what they were teaching the next generation. The model of the scientist-practitioner reflected the commitment of professional groups to scientific rigour (James, 1994).

– Current expectations of health sciences curricula face two seemingly opposing challenges: to meet the rigours of evidence-based practice of the professional, scientific and managerial communities, and to fulfil society's calls for client-centred care and client engagement in healthcare decision-making.

Fieldwork education has evolved alongside these curriculum trends. Models of fieldwork education can be described and classified in many ways. Some models focus on the *curriculum*; for instance, integration of the desired knowledge, skills and attitudes across all dimensions of the curriculum including classroom and fieldwork education. Other models emphasise the *development* of students throughout the curriculum and the styles of supervision most relevant to these developmental stages. Anderson (1988), for example, proposed a continuum of supervision approach which aimed to develop independent clinicians capable of self-supervision. That continuum of supervision involves three developmental stages: evaluation–feedback, transition, and self-supervision. This model reflects concepts inherent in the apprenticeship and the reflective practitioner education frameworks. A further group of models highlights interaction between fieldwork educators and students (and sometimes clients). Goldhammer (1969) proposed five stages in the sequence of clinical supervision within a cycle of supervision: pre-observation conference, observation, analysis and strategy, supervision conference, post-conference analysis.

A set of *collaborative* models was also identified, including Dowling's (1979) Teaching Clinic model involving a six-phase group supervisory approach: review of previous clinic, planning, observation, critique preparation, critique and strategy development, and clinic review. The fieldwork educator's role is emphasised in Romanini and Higgs' (1991) teacher-manager model, which recognises the educator's role in overall management of the fieldwork education program as well as management of multiple dimensions of the program, including the learning environment, student participation in the learning task, group process and individual student development. Throughout this section of the book recent models are presented to complement this brief overview.

Fieldwork education models can also be classified by the fieldwork educator:student ratio. In the allied health literature, these models include one student to one fieldwork educator (1:1), two students to one fieldwork educator (2:1), three students to one fieldwork educator (3:1), small groups of students to one fieldwork educator, and one student to two or more fieldwork educators who share the responsibility for facilitating student learning (1:2 or shared responsibility).

Internationally, over the past two decades, there has been a growth in 2:1, small group, shared responsibility and inter-professional fieldwork education models in allied health professions (see Moore, Morris, Crouch, & Martin, 2003) although the 1:1 model continues to be the most common approach used in Western countries (Lekkas et al., 2007). A recent paper by Roberts et al. (2009) reported a tendency for models to incorporate varying levels of student self-directed and peer-assisted learning in conjunction with student learning facilitated by the fieldwork educator.

An overview of research findings on fieldwork education models follows, with a focus on collaborative models. The 2:1, 3:1 and other small groups of student to one fieldwork educator are commonly referred to as collaborative models. Role-emerging placements, that invariably involve a small group of students supervised by a fieldwork educator in newly developing practice settings, and inter-professional placements, which tend to occur in small groups, are also included in the overview of research findings on collaborative models. Research on the 1:1 model is very limited. Examples of placements that have utilised a particular model of fieldwork education are included in other chapters in this book.

In reports of research on collaborative learning models, both fieldwork educators and students have identified that the key advantages of these models for students are enhanced student learning through the provision of peer support, peer learning and self-directed learning opportunities (Ladyshewsky, Barrie, & Drake, 1998; McAllister & Lincoln, 2004). Increased student independence and enhanced teamwork skills have also been identified as outcomes of collaborative learning models (Hummell & Williamson, 1999; Baldry Currens, 2003). It is important to note, however, that in these studies the fieldwork educators had commonly received education on managing collaborative placements prior to the placement. In role-emerging placements, students were also provided with an orientation to the placement, which included information on the collaborative supervisory style to be implemented (Hummell & Williamson, 1999).

Key components for the success of collaborative models are well planned placements, adequate education of fieldwork educators on the use of collaborative teaching/learning strategies, their skill in implementing such strategies, adequate time for fieldwork educators to regularly meet students individually throughout the placement, primarily through delegating their client caseload to students, and adequate client numbers to enable each student to develop skills to the required competency level (Moore et al., 2003; Bartholomai & Fitzgerald, 2007). Further essential components for the success of collaborative placements are adequate physical space and resources – even desks – for the number of students.

Students and fieldwork educators report more advantages and fewer disadvantages with the 2:1 model than the 1:1 and 3:1 models (Moore et al., 2003). The key disadvantage of the 1:1 model is the lack of peer support, and the key disadvantage of the 3:1 model is the limited individual time spent between educator and student, which tends to compromise the adequacy of their relationship and the effective monitoring of student progress. The anticipated disadvantages identified by fieldwork educators prior to using the 2:1 model, including increased stress and student competitiveness, have not been supported in research (Baldry Currens, 2003). A minority of students, however, identified negative competitiveness as a disadvantage of 2:1 and 3:1 fieldwork placements (Moore et al., 2003). Fieldwork educators identified the key disadvantages of small group placements compared with 1:1 placements as the increased paperwork and organisation required (Moore et al., 2003).

In summary, current research findings indicate that there is inadequate evidence to favour one fieldwork education model over another. Each provides valuable and different learning opportunities and has advantages and disadvantages. Stakeholder perspectives require consideration when determining the optimal model for individual fieldwork sites. Key consistent findings, however, are that students value the peer support and peer learning, in combination with group and individual supervision from the fieldwork educator, in the collaborative models (Moore et al., 2003), that fieldwork educators benefit from education on effective teaching/learning strategies for small group placements (Baldry Currens, 2003; Moore et al., 2003) and that effective placement planning contributes strongly to successful outcomes (Hummell & Williamson, 1999; Moore et al., 2003). When 1:1, 2:1 and 3:1 fieldwork placement models are compared, the 2:1 model is viewed as optimal by both educators and students as long as the key components identified previously are included (see Moore et al., 2003). The comment by Aiken, Menaker, and Barsky (2001) that there is no perfect fieldwork placement model and that the allied health professions need to strive for flexible and varied student fieldwork experiences is most astute. Further research is required into current and potential fieldwork education models, including outcomes for clients, students, and fieldwork educators, cost–benefit analyses and productivity levels of students and fieldwork educators, to further guide decision-making. Adequate education of fieldwork educators is essential for their success (McAllister, 2005).

Perhaps the most significant or prevalent trends shaping these models in recent and coming years are (a) a move towards new areas of practice, (b) an increasing shift towards interprofessional initiatives, and (c) advances in communication technologies. As disciplines move into new areas of practice their fieldwork education placements also need to reflect these changes by both following and leading these trends. Many students are now given opportunities to participate in placements beyond the more traditional clinical practice realm, such as those focused on administration and professional issues, including within professional organisations, regulatory bodies, or with industrial businesses. The need for students to graduate with interprofessional competencies or team skills has been gaining attention at local, national and international levels. A number of fieldwork education placement models are now being used to provide students with interprofessional experiences. Traditionally, individual students have been integrated into well-functioning teams with the focus on team interaction versus student-to-student interaction (Hilton & Morris, 2001). Newer models strive to have two or more students from different professions on placement at the same time and integrated into an effective multidisciplinary team, with the aim for them to work together as a "student team" with particular clients and/or projects (Stew, 2005; Nisbet, Hendry, Rolls, & Field, 2008). The efficacy of these models continues to be studied to determine the value of these placements and models in facilitating the development of these competencies.

Advances in communication and Web-based technologies will perhaps provide the greatest opportunities for change within practice education models. Over the years new technologies have been integrated into supervision models with varying degrees of success. Tele- and video-conferencing, WebChat and support sites, as well as cell phones and texting, can be used to support students and site supervisors (see Chapter 14 for more examples). It will be interesting to track the future benefits of such technologies, including the impact on the availability of placements and the quality of the learning experience.

## CONTEXT PARAMETERS SHAPING OPTIMAL FIELDWORK EDUCATION MODELS AND APPROACHES

Many context parameters, including the adequacy of the entry-level curriculum in preparing graduates for their initial workforce experiences, professional socialisation during fieldwork placements and the influence of workplaces on students' fieldwork placement experiences, influence the models and approaches used in fieldwork education settings. Earlier chapters have explored the impact on fieldwork placements of health professionals' contexts of practice, health/social care, and education, as well as their sociocultural, political and economic contexts.

### The Adequacy of Entry Curricula in Preparing Graduates for Workforce Roles

Qualified allied health professionals are expected to function as independent professionals from their first day of employment, commonly with limited or no professional supervision or mentoring from senior staff members (Steenbergen & Mackenzie, 2004; McAllister, 2005). Research findings on the workplace experiences of newly qualified allied health graduates has an essential role in informing fieldwork placement models and approaches. Research with allied health graduates in Australia has identified that managers and graduates perceived that professional entry programs prepared newly qualified allied health graduates adequately for some aspects of their workplace role but inadequately for others (Adamson et al., 1996; Brumfitt, Enderby, & Hoben, 2005). These studies indicated that newly qualified graduates were adequately prepared for specific workplace tasks, including carrying out their clinical duties with confidence, engaging in ethical practice, evaluating professional literature, documenting reports and seeking help from peers. In another Australian study, therapy graduates were also perceived as being adequately equipped with generic skills and attributes including problem-solving, communication and lifelong learning skills; new graduates were client- and family-centred, flexible, adaptable and action-oriented (Hummell, 2007). However, these new graduates were inadequately prepared for the complex lived realities of their work roles and the work stressors they experienced (Hummell, 2007; see also Tryssenaar & Perkins, 2001). Several studies have identified key workplace tasks for which newly qualified graduates were not adequately prepared: these included time management and prioritisation skills; managing challenging clients, interpersonal conflict and workplace stress; and applying academic knowledge to practice (Ferguson, 2000; Roe-Shaw, 2004).

Fieldwork placements can facilitate or impair students' preparation for the realities of their initial work roles after graduation. Allied health graduates have consistently identified student fieldwork placements as important sources of the knowledge and skills required for their successful integration into the workplace and workforce

(Brumfitt et al., 2005; Hodgetts et al., 2007). Fieldwork placements are often perceived as both the most difficult and the most rewarding components of entry-level courses (Axford, 2005), providing opportunities to gain practical skills with clients as well as skills in critical thinking, analysis and synthesis. They are also viewed as contributing to confidence in work roles and in understanding workplace systems, with final year placements considered to be the most important in this preparation for the workforce (Hummell, 2007).

The rather idealistic portrayals of work roles and workplaces in entry-level courses, including during fieldwork placements, and the subsequent lack of congruence between graduates' expectations and actual experiences of initial employment, may be a key contributor to the shock experienced by allied health graduates in their initial employment (Tryssenaar & Perkins, 2001; Roe-Shaw, 2004). Research findings about the workplace experiences of newly qualified allied health professionals clearly indicate that university curricula, including fieldwork curricula, require revisions to provide students with more realistic expectations of their initial employment. To address this issue we recommend implementation of fieldwork education models that promote student reflection, collaboration and self-directed learning, and the use of styles of supervision that aim to increase independence throughout courses.

*Fieldwork Placements Influence Students' Professional Socialisation*

Cant and Higgs (1999) described professional socialisation as the process of induction into a distinctive professional culture. This includes learning the accepted values, attitudes, codes of practice/behaviour, language, knowledge, skills and roles of a profession. It is perceived as a process which starts during the professional entry course and continues throughout a professional's career. Professional socialisation encompasses the notion of professions as communities of practice (Richardson, 2001) which individuals adapt to and learn from over time (Davis, 2006). Davis found that a cohesive community of practice enhanced the development of a professional identity in final year OT students whereas an individualistic community impeded this development. Positive role models and mentors are important during the professional socialisation process (Kasar & Muscari, 2000). Collaborative fieldwork education models have the potential to facilitate positive socialisation experiences in entry-level professional education.

Fieldwork placements contribute to the professional socialisation and professional identity development of students. They provide opportunities to induct students into the workplace realities of their profession in a graded manner across a variety of workplace settings and areas of practice (Bartlett, Lucy, Bisbee, & Conti-Becker, 2009; Higgs, Hummell, & Roe-Shaw, 2009). During fieldwork placements, students engage in a range of professional tasks and learn that their interventions make a difference (Crowe & Mackenzie, 2002). A study by Roe-Shaw (2004) indicated that experiences in physiotherapists' university courses affected their professional socialisation. Positive fieldwork experiences enhanced professional socialisation, but negative fieldwork experiences, including a lack of positive physiotherapy role models and a lack of enthusiastic and skilled physiotherapists, undermined novices' sense of professional identity and commitment to their profession.

Fieldwork placements can also have a long-term effect on professional socialisation. Research over two decades with occupational therapists (Crowe & Mackenzie, 2002) has indicated that fieldwork placement experiences affect graduates' employment choices for a significant length of time. Graduates chose to work in workplaces and areas of professional practice in which they had had positive field-work experiences and avoided those in which their placement experiences had been negative. The quality of student–supervisor relationships was a key component in this decision-making. Academics are encouraged to educate fieldwork educators and managers about the benefits of collaborative fieldwork education models and models which focus on the style and cycle of supervision. These models aim to enhance the quality of the student–supervisor relationship as an important contributor to positive learning experiences during placements.

*The Influence of Workplace Environments on Fieldwork Placement Experiences*

Fieldwork placements occur in "real world" workplaces. Research across a range of professions has consistently indicated that such placements are crucial in developing the "authentic" practice-based skills required by students prior to graduation: such placements enable students to learn that professional practice varies across settings, practitioners and client groups (Fish & Coles, 2005).

The quality of fieldwork education placements is enhanced when workplaces have a supportive management approach, welcome students, promote student learning and provide skilled fieldwork supervision (Mulholland, Derdall, & Roy, 2006). Work-place managers in collaboration with fieldwork educators also have an important role in determining the fieldwork education model/s appropriate to the individual workplace setting, including the number of students per placement and the practice areas in which students complete placements.

Expertise of fieldwork educators is highly valued by students and is perceived by them as essential for successful learning; unfortunately, however, this expertise tends not to be highly valued by workplace managers (Baldry Currens & Bithell, 2000). Students have described effective fieldwork supervisors as essentially skilled and enthusiastic therapists and educators who behave in a professional manner and function as role models. Effective fieldwork educators also have high level inter-personal, organisational and communication skills, provide constructive feedback, use effective teaching/learning strategies to promote student learning, provide graded and challenging learning experiences which promote increasing student knowledge, skills, independence and responsibility during their placements, and engage in student supervision in a supportive manner (Hummell, 1997; Mulholland et al., 2006).

### DESIGNING A FIELDWORK EDUCATION MODEL FOR PLACEMENTS: THE FIELDWORK EDUCATOR'S PERSPECTIVE

Designing a fieldwork education model for a particular program is often a complex decision-making process. Who will supervise students and how they will be supervised are key questions that need to be answered to ensure the availability of a placement and to make that placement a quality learning and teaching experience for all involved. But who makes these decisions and how are they made, specifically regarding the best model to use for clinical placements? The decision-making process regarding the best model of supervision is a complex process with multiple stakeholders and related considerations. Figure 9.1 provides a visual representation of the decision-making process.

Although many people are typically involved in this decision-making process, the two primary players could best be identified as the fieldwork education co-ordinator (university staff member) and the fieldwork educator (a practitioner from industry). Often the fieldwork education coordinator initiates the clinical education planning process and takes the lead on collaborating and negotiating. The decision-making process is typically pragmatic and often reliant on the generosity and professional commitment of the clinicians. The coordinator and educator are situated within the context of the educational institution (e.g., university or college) and the healthcare site (e.g., hospital, community centre), respectively. Although student learning is the primary focus of a fieldwork education placement, students ultimately may have limited input into the decision-making process. However, individual students need to be considered within the context of their class cohort. Similarly, the institutional, cultural, physical and social parameters of all key stakeholders need to be considered (Townsend & Polatajko, 2007). The stakeholders collaborate and negotiate in a process to come to a conclusion regarding the most appropriate model of supervision to be used. Clients may be involved in this decision-making process where feasible.

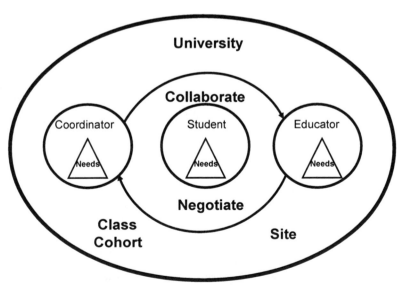

*Figure 9.1. Context and considerations when selecting a fieldwork education model.*

The coordinator and educator each have specific needs that must be met in order for a placement to be feasible and for a model of supervision to be decided upon. The coordinator must take into account many factors, including the quality of the potential learning/teaching experience, pedagogy, timing within the curriculum and level of placement, type of clinical experience, geographical location, site culture, potential models of supervision, legal and liability issues, and being evidence-based in the decision making. The educator may have a similar list of considerations, as well as staffing logistics and available peer support, caseload availability, personal interest in offering a placement or explicit job expectations to offer a placement, previous supervision experience and abilities, and the professional commitment and culture of the work site. Student considerations may also include financial concerns if relocation is necessary, personal interest in particular areas of practice, and strategies to ensure post-graduation employment. More and more there is a shift in health and education towards being evidence-based in practice. Decision making regarding supervision models for fieldwork education placements is no different. There is growing literature evidence regarding different supervision models, but often these are based on a "case study" approach and are therefore situationally relevant rather than generalisable.

*Need Drives Innovation: An Example of Designing Fieldwork Education*

Although decisions regarding the most appropriate model of supervision often follow the tradition of a profession or institution, fieldwork education is sensitive to external factors outside the control of stakeholders. These factors include logistics such as staffing and holidays, caseload availability, and changes in healthcare budgets and restructuring. The following example from OT at the University of Alberta in Edmonton, Canada (Mulholland & Derdall, 2005), illustrates two points: first, how need and demand often drive change and innovation, and second how the model of decision making was applied.

Internationally in OT, one of the more innovative supervision strategies used over the years has involved students participating in fieldwork education placements at sites where there is no occupational therapist and no well-defined OT role. Fieldwork has sometimes been divided into two broad types of placement that are often referred to as traditional (or role-established) and non-traditional (role-emerging or alternative) (Bossers, Cook, Polatajko, & Lane, 1997). At the University of Alberta the latter are called independent community placements (ICPs). These placements have occurred in a wide variety of community and non-profit settings including inner-city community drop-in centres and homeless shelters (Heubner & Tryssenaar, 1996; Totten & Pratt, 2001) and schools (Hubbard, 2000).

In traditional placements, students are typically supervised directly by an occupational therapist and perform tasks within a well-established role. In non-traditional placements students typically explore the potential role of OT within a new setting. Because there are no OT services on site, various supervisory models have been used to provide students with an appropriate level and quality of supervision and to ensure that they are able to focus on and learn OT skills.

In typical non-traditional placements or ICPs, in the absence of an occupational therapist, another professional (e.g., a social worker, psychologist, nurse) at the site is identified as the primary supervisor and provides day-to-day direction, guidance and feedback to the student. The university ensures that the student has off-site or indirect OT supervision by using one of two strategies. Most commonly, a university faculty member with academic commitments acts as a resource on a limited basis and provides feedback and guidance specific to OT skills and issues (Hubbard, 2000; Totten & Pratt, 2001). Another model recommends identifying an OT working in a similar area of practice or setting who is willing and interested to mentor a student off-site (Bossers et al., 1997; Friedland, Polatajko, & Gage, 2001).

In 2003 the University of Alberta OT program underwent a significant increase in demand for student fieldwork education placements due to increased admission numbers and curriculum changes that resulted in two overlapping graduating classes. Over a 2-year span the number of required placements jumped from 290 to 550, with a significantly increased demand for community settings and mental health populations. Although the university had a long history of developing and using ICPs, excessive teaching commitments of faculty in a new curriculum and the higher than usual number of students participating in the ICPs forced OT academics to seek a new strategy of supervision for this particular time period.

In response to these challenges, the fieldwork education coordinator was proactive and initiated a solution. As the research literature yielded no appropriate alternative model of supervision, brainstorming resulted in the development of a staffing position called the Fieldwork Educator for Independent Community Placements (FEICP). This individual was responsible for overseeing ICPs and providing OT-specific guidance and feedback to the students. A proposal was developed to pilot this model as a new temporary faculty position entirely dedicated to providing appropriate supervision for students in ICPs. In this scenario the model of decision making had an added layer of complexity in that both the FEICP and site primary supervisor (e.g., social worker) were identified as fieldwork educators. Through pragmatic decision making, planning, collaboration and negotiation with stakeholders including university administration and both fieldwork educators, the new supervision model was implemented. Although student input was not directly sought, student safety and learning experience quality were foremost. From the university's perspective, sustainability of this model of supervision at these placements sites was critical.

To ensure evidence-based practice, a written survey was developed to collect feedback in order to determine the impact of the FEICP position on the fieldwork experience for both sites and students. This feedback would play an important part in determining the value of continuing this position. In summary, the feedback from both sites and students strongly supported continuation of the FEICP position. The roles of the FEICP that the sites and student class cohort identified as most important included providing support, providing information, acting as liaison, and helping to identify the OT perspective and role. The feedback collected provided substantial evidence that the position was of value to all stakeholders and hence the position has continued. This model of fieldwork education placement supervision is now used for all ICPs at the University of Alberta.

## CONCLUSIONS

The quality of health professional education is influenced by the quality of fieldwork education within curricula. Thus the development, implementation and evaluation of fieldwork education models which incorporate sound educational principles and reflect the scope and diversity of current and anticipated future practice for allied health professions are essential in striving to achieve the goals of entry-level health professional education.

Models of fieldwork education are being adapted, developed and invented every day. This book, with its various case studies and research reports, provides cutting edge evidence in support of innovative models for exploration and further testing in other contexts. Research in education is a challenge and an important goal for the health professions.

## REFERENCES

Adamson, B., Harris, L., Heard, R., & Hunt, A. (1996). *University education and workplace requirements: evaluating the skills and attributes of health science graduates.* Sydney: The University of Sydney.

Aiken, F., Menaker, L., & Barsky, L. (2001). Fieldwork education: The future of occupational therapy depends on it. *Occupational Therapy International, 8,* 86-95.

Anderson, J.L. (1988). *The supervisory process in speech-language pathology and audiology.* Boston, MA: College Hill.

Axford, B. (2005). Entering professional practice in the new work order: A study of undergraduate students and their induction into professional work. *The Australian Educational Researcher, 32*(2), 87–104.

Baldry Currens, J.A. (2003a). The 2:1 clinical placement model: Review. *Physiotherapy, 89*(9), 540–554.

Baldry Currens, J.A., & Bithell, C.P. (2000). Clinical education: Listening to different perspectives. *Physiotherapy, 86*(12), 645–653.

Bartholomai, S., & Fitzgerald, C. (2007). The collaborative model of fieldwork education: Implementation of the model in a regional hospital rehabilitation setting. *Australian Occupational Therapy Journal, 54,* S23–S30.

Bartlett, D.J., Lucy, S.D., Bisbee, L., & Conti-Becker, A. (2009). Understanding the professional socialization of Canadian physical therapy students: A qualitative investigation. *Physiotherapy Canada, 61,* 15–25.

Bossers, A., Cook, J., Polatajko, H., & Laine, C. (1997). Understanding the role-emerging fieldwork placement. *Canadian Journal of Occupational Therapy, 64(2),* 70–81.

Brumfitt, S.M., Enderby, P.M., & Hoben, K. (2005). The transition to work of newly qualified speech and language therapists: Implications for the curriculum. *Learning in Health and Social Care, 4*(3), 142–155.

Cant, R., & Higgs, J. (1999). Professional socialization. In J. Higgs & H. Edwards (Eds.), *Educating beginning practitioners: Challenges for health professional education* (pp. 46–51). Oxford: Butterworth-Heinemann.

Crowe, M.J., & Mackenzie, L. (2002). The influence of fieldwork on the preferred future practice areas of final year occupational therapy students. *Australian Occupational Therapy Journal, 49,* 25–36.

Davis, J. (2006). The importance of the community of practice in identity development. *The Internet Journal of Allied Health Sciences and Practice, 4*(3), 1–8. Available: http://ijahsp.nova.edu, accessed 5 August 2006.

Dowling, S. (1979). The teaching clinic: A supervisory alternative. *Asha, 21,* 646–649.

Ferguson, A. (2000). Feedback from Newcastle graduates. *Australian Communication Quarterly, 2*(1), 11–12.

Fish, D., & Coles, C. (2005). *Medical education: Developing a curriculum for practice*. Berkshire: Open University Press.

Friedland, J., Polatajko, H., & Gage, M. (2001). Expanding the boundaries of occupational therapy practice through student fieldwork experiences: Description of a provincially-funded community development project. *Canadian Journal of Occupational Therapy, 68*(5), 301–309.

Goldhammer, R. (1969). *Clinical supervision: Special methods for the supervision of teachers*. New York: Holt, Rinehart and Winston.

Heubner, J., & Tryssenaar, J. (1996). Development of an occupational therapy practice perspective in a homeless shelter: A fieldwork experience. *Canadian Journal of Occupational Therapy, 63*, 24–32.

Higgs, J., & Edwards, H. (2002). Challenges facing health professional education in the changing context of university education. *British Journal of Occupational Therapy, 65*(7), 315–320.

Higgs, J., & Hunt, A. (1999). Redefining the beginning practitioner. *Focus on Health Professional Education: A Multi-Disciplinary Journal, 1*(1), 34–48.

Higgs, J., Hummell, J., & Roe-Shaw, M. (2009). Becoming a member of a health profession: A journey of socialisation. In J. Higgs, M. Smith, G. Webb, M. Skinner & A. Croker (Eds.), *Contexts of physiotherapy practice* (pp. 58–71). Melbourne: Elsevier Australia.

Hilton, R., & Morris, J. (2001). Student placements: Is there evidence supporting team skill development in clinical practice settings? *Journal of Interprofessional Care, 15*, 171–183.

Hodgetts, S., Hollis, V., Triska, O., Dennis, S., Madill, H., & Taylor, E. (2007). Occupational therapy students' and graduates' satisfaction with professional education and preparedness for practice. *Canadian Journal of Occupational Therapy, 74*(3), 148–160.

Hubbard, S. (2000). A case example of remote supervision. *OT Practice, 5*(24), 16–18.

Hummell, J. (1997). Effective fieldwork supervision: Occupational therapy student perspectives. *Australian Occupational Therapy Journal, 44*, 147–157.

Hummell, J. (2007). *Allied health graduates' first year of employment*. Unpublished PhD thesis, The University of Sydney, Australia.

Hummell, J., & Williamson, P. (1999). Fieldwork in occupational therapy: Close to the edge. *Focus on Health Professional Education: A Multi-disciplinary Journal, 1*(2), 33–49.

James, J.E. (1994). Health care, psychology, and the scientist-practitioner model. *Australian Psychologist 29*(1), 5–11.

Kasar, J., & Muscari, M.E. (2000). A conceptual model for the development of professional behaviours in occupational therapists. *Canadian Journal of Occupational Therapy, 67*(1), 42–50.

Ladyshewsky, R.K., Barrie, S., & Drake, V.M. (1998). A comparison of productivity and learning outcomes in individual and cooperative physical therapy clinical education models. *Physical Therapy, 78*(12), 1288–1298.

Lekkas, P., Larsen, T., Kumar, S., Grimmer, K., Nyland, L., Chipchase, L. et al. (2007). No model of clinical education for physiotherapy students is superior to another: A systematic review. *Australian Journal of Physiotherapy, 53*, 19–28.

McAllister, L. (2005). Issues and innovations in clinical education. *Advances in Speech-Language Pathology, 7*(3), 138–148.

McAllister, L., & Lincoln, M. (2004). *Clinical education in speech-language pathology*. London: Whurr.

Michels, E. (1982). Evaluation and research in physical therapy. *Physical Therapy, 62*(6), 828–834.

Moore, A., Morris, J., Crouch, V., & Martin, M. (2003). Evaluation of physiotherapy clinical education models: Comparing 1:1, 2:1 and 3:1 placements. *Physiotherapy, 89*(8), 489–501.

Mulholland, S., & Derdall, M. (2005). A strategy for supervising occupational therapy students at community sites. *Occupational Therapy International, 2*, 28–43.

Mulholland, S., Derdall, M., & Roy, B. (2006). The student's perspective on what makes an exceptional practice placement educator. *British Journal of Occupational Therapy, 69*(12), 567–571.

Nisbet, G., Hendry, G.D., Rolls, G., & Field, M.J. (2008). Interprofessional learning for pre-qualification health care students: An outcomes-based evaluation. *Journal of Interprofessional Care, 22*(1), 57–68.

Norman, G.R. (1990). Editorial: Problem-solving skills and problem-based learning. *Physiotherapy Theory and Practice, 6*, 53–54.

Richardson, B. (2001). Professionalisation and professional craft knowledge. In J. Higgs & A. Titchen (Eds.), *Practice knowledge and expertise in the health professions* (pp. 42–47). Sydney: Butterworth-Heinemann.

Roberts, N., Brockington, S., Doyle, E., Pearce, L., Bowie, A., Simmance, N. et al. (2009). Pilot study of an innovative model for clinical education in dietetics. *Journal of Nutrition and Dietetics, 66*, 39–46.

Roe-Shaw, M.M. (2004). *Workplace realities and professional socialization of recently graduated physiotherapists in New Zealand.* Unpublished PhD thesis, University of Otago, Dunedin.

Romanini, J., & Higgs, J. (1991). The teacher as manager in continuing and professional education. *Studies in Continuing Education, 13*, 41–52.

Schön, D.A. (1983). *The reflective practitioner: How professionals think in action.* London: Temple Smith.

Steenbergen, K., & Mackenzie, L. (2004). Professional support in rural New South Wales: Perceptions of new graduate occupational therapists. *Australian Journal of Rural Health, 12*(4), 160–165.

Stew, G. (2005). Learning together in practice: A survey of interprofessional education in clinical settings in South-East England. *Journal of Interprofessional Care, 19*, 223–235.

Totten, C., & Pratt, J. (2001). Innovation in fieldwork education: Working with members of the homeless population in Glasgow. *British Journal of Occupational Therapy, 64*, 559–563.

Townsend, A., & Polatajko, H. (2007). *Enabling occupation II: Advancing an occupational therapy vision for health, well-being and justice through occupation.* Ottawa: CAOT Publications.

Tryssenaar, J., & Perkins, J. (2001). From student to graduate: Exploring the first year of practice. *American Journal of Occupational Therapy, 55*(1):19–27

*Jill Hummell PhD*
*Community Integration Program*
*Westmead Brain Injury Rehabilitation Service, Australia*

*Joy Higgs AM PhD*
*The Education for Practice Institute*
*Charles Sturt University, Australia*

*Susan Mulholland MScRehab*
*Department of Occupational Therapy*
*University of Alberta, Canada*

RUTH BEECHAM AND MARIJKE DENTON

# 10. COLLABORATIVE ENGAGEMENT IN FIELDWORK EDUCATION

## The Schools Project

### EXPLORING ALTERNATIVE CONCEPTIONS OF FIELDWORK

In this chapter we describe a three-way fieldwork education partnership between nearly 30 public schools, a local public community health service, and the speech language pathology program of a university. All three partners service regional and rural communities in inland Australia, communities historically underserved by health, health education, welfare and disability agencies. A key management strategy of organisations responsible for ensuring public health and education is to encourage collaboration between agencies in order to maximise the use of scant resources and to solve complex social problems by forming networks at local levels. This and the general assumption that there will never be enough health professionals to serve rural and regional (let alone remote) Australia, means that Australian universities need to prepare students very differently from historical educational models (Beecham et al., 2006).

A crucial component of allied health education is the practical experiential learning that has historically helped frame what, where and how therapists define their professional role in society. As part of accepting that our educational models need to change we must find fieldwork experiences that model the direction of the change needed. Given this, the Schools Project (hereafter referred to as the Project) represents an attempt to explore alternative conceptions of fieldwork education for speech therapy practice, conceptions that are influenced by the elements of a resource-poor context, organisational approval to collaborate, and the values of the speech language pathology educational program.

### THE PROJECT: DESCRIPTION

Up to 13% of New South Wales school-age children have some kind of communication impairment that interferes with their ability to learn (McLeod & McKinnon, 2007), yet there is no state wide school-based speech language pathology service. Instead, teachers refer children they believe require communication services to external agencies such as community health centres. A frequent result is long delays and/or significant reduction in the scope of communication services offered to this population; another is that many children showing more subtle signs

L. McAllister et al., (eds.), Innovations in Allied Health Fieldwork
Education: A Critical Appraisal, 111–119.

of communication problem may escape referral altogether or may be deemed ineligible for services even after assessment. Resource shortages in rural areas may exacerbate these problems.

This issue was identified in 2004 by two 4th (final) year students as part of a program of renewal in speech language pathology fieldwork education at Charles Sturt University (CSU) (Millar & Reid, 2006). It led to the establishment of a partnership between local representatives from the Department of Education (DET), CSU, and a Community Health Speech Pathology Department (CHSP). A practising speech language pathologist, an academic clinician, and a learning support teacher became the partnership steering committee who, in addition to supporting the educational philosophy of the CSU program, adopted the Health Promotion with Schools Policy (NSW Health Department, 2000) as the theoretical framework informing the direction of the Project. Importantly, this policy describes a three-way interface between the curriculum, the physical and social environment of the school, and the school-home-community. This interface lies at the heart of all Project activities.

Each semester, teams of speech language pathology students (three to five 2nd year students mentored by one 4th year student) work with teachers in five schools around the region to develop school-specific projects. As well as supporting achievement of the NSW schools K-6 English Syllabus outcomes (Board of Studies New South Wales, 1998), these projects must also address the schools' individual needs while embedding the relationship between language and learning in the school ethos. In collaboration with school staff, the speech language pathology student teams plan, implement and finally evaluate projects aimed at developing the communication skills of school-age children. Importantly, no child is identified or assessed for specific problems of speech, language or communication. Over the life of the Project, 27 of 29 schools in the region have been serviced, and 15 have hosted the Project more than once.

Each year, in two 8-week cycles, placements are created for the entire 2nd year cohort of speech language pathology students (up to 50), as well as 10 4th year students. Supervision of students is supplied by the CHSP, while the DET offers access to schools in the local area, as well as administrative and schools-based support. Supervision is thus collaborative and cross-disciplinary, a factor discussed later in this chapter.

## EVALUATION DATA

The Project has been evaluated annually since its inception. However, each year the emphasis of evaluation has shifted. Originally, the evaluations were designed primarily to guide planning for the following year, and secondly to provide justification to the organisational partners that the Project was of educational value (Beecham et al., 2006; Baily & Hampton, 2007). As the years have progressed, however, we have been focusing evaluation on gaining understanding of what lies below the surface of what students report as learning. Specifically, we have attempted to understand the relevance of these reports to changing speech language pathology practice.

Data sources and informants over the past 5 years include written and verbal reports and interviews from teachers, teacher-managers, learning assistance personnel, speech language pathology students and new graduates, and various managers of the organisations involved in the Project.

As an introduction to the main themes distilled from this data, what follows is a vignette created from the speech language pathology supervisor's reflections regarding the Project. It highlights the complex contexts, the types of teaching and learning that occur, and the multiple layers of collaborative opportunity offered by the Project.

### Vignette of Teaching and Learning in the Schools Project

*I remember one [student speech language pathologist] team telling me about the positive post-test results on the class of students they'd been working with. The numbers had no statistical validity, but I was stunned by one of the [school] children's comments. A boy in grade five said, as a result of the project encouraging "reading with expression", he finally understood what he was reading.*

*This child had missed out on 5 years of reading for meaning and therefore a good portion of his learning. It was devastating to realise that this boy, never recognised as struggling with learning, was one of many children in Australia who have access to schools but potentially poor educational outcomes as a result of poor communication skills. I think it's these poor outcomes that justifies projects like making a baby record album promoting early childhood communication to its small rural community and a project enhancing social communication, such as conflict resolution, in a large urban primary school that had recently attracted notoriety as a result of weapons being found there.*

*While the schools are usually delighted with the project outcomes, the speech language pathology student team can really struggle with the process. As a supervisor it can be difficult to deal with the 2nd years' distrust of the Project being a valid clinical learning experience. They say things like, "You're [supervisor] not demonstrating the skills I need. You're supposed to show me [how to administer a test and do therapy]", and "This [project] is a waste of time ...[it] is not what I'm going to do when I'm qualified!" It's also common for the 2nd years to be critical of their peers' abilities. I can recall numerous comments between students like, "You've got to learn how to speak to the kids. You sounded like a robot!" or "Even though I've got so much to do, I don't trust anyone else to do it!"*

*A critical element of the Project is a philosophy of guiding and supporting rather than dictating to students. This philosophy also permeates how they engage with the schools. As a result, the relationship formed between the team and the school is a very important motivator. Despite the students' struggle with the process, I'm pleasantly surprised that by the end of the projects, students not only rate highly the professional skills they have acquired but also demonstrate significant pride in what they have contributed to the school.*

*At the completion ceremony of the Reading with Meaning project I mentioned at the beginning, that same Grade Five boy read a few words: "On behalf of all the children, parents and teachers…" He gathered confidence as he read and finished strongly with, "It's been great having you guys come. Your games were really fun. It didn't seem like work at all! We're going to miss you. Good luck!" Everyone applauded as we all felt we shared in the success, that he had read it well, and more, that he had read it with meaning.*

Several of the prominent themes from this vignette are discussed below, and are linked to our ongoing discussion of the theoretical understandings around speech language pathology practice.

## LEGITIMACY OF NON-IMPAIRMENT-FOCUSED PRACTICE

The speech language pathology profession has a tradition of approaching difficulties of human communication in a sequence of problem identification, assessment, diagnosis and treatment. The majority of these problems fall within one or more classifications of communication impairment, such as stuttering or language delay. The implication of this tradition is that getting to the root of the problem means getting to the core of the impairment. In the traditional model of speech language pathology practice, therefore, the impairment becomes the object of treatment.

Even though there is growing literature suggesting this may not be the optimal, and certainly not the only way of conceiving our practice (Kathard, 2005), our experience in the Project suggests that speech language pathology students develop an early and strong sense of *legitimate* practice being at an impairment level, in one-to-one contexts (or with small groups of children/adults with the same/similar impairment), and most often in a separate room, away from the distractions of peers and/or family. They also generally believe that the focus of their future work lies at the level of cure or rehabilitation into the community, rather than health promotion.

The Project challenges this construction of legitimate practice, and therefore initially appears almost universally confronting to 2nd year students. Yet, by the end of the Project, negative comments like *"I still don't know how you administer a language test [assessment]. I mean, that's what we're supposed to do"*, are paired with positive evaluations such as, *"We really made a difference"* and *"It was incredibly hard work, but the kids really liked us coming and so did the teachers."*

By 4th year, when students are asked to express preferences for their final year placements, there is a regular over-subscription to become a mentor for the Project. When asked to justify their preference, students express sentiments such as *"I can see why it's so important now. The projects are really making a difference and it's fun"* and *"I know I can get a job working with schools [interstate] because of this."*

Comments from graduates now working with school-age children include: *"It sort of freed me up. Most of the time I have to do it [practice] the 1:1 way because that's the way the job's set up, but I feel okay about having bigger ideas and talking to teachers [about them]"*. When asked whether she felt disadvantaged with regard to more traditional skills of assessment with the paediatric population, another graduate responded, *"No! You've got years of doing the [name of test]. That's what the manuals are for!"*

## COMMUNITY-RESPONSIVE ENGAGED LEARNING

There is clear evidence of the educational effectiveness of students learning in an engaged manner (Zhao & Kuh, 2004), that is, using activities that that are out-of-class and involve real world problems. It is believed that the life skills gained from such learning increase students' employability and help them understand their role as knowledgeable and active citizens of their region (Australian Universities Community Engagement Alliance, 2006). The primary motivator for directing students towards real life, community-responsive and engaged learning contexts has been to maximise the opportunity to broaden their professional identities, in an effort to develop skills more appropriate to rural contexts, where there is a high demand for service commitment despite resource limitations.

In an attempt to counter the influence of the apprentice/expert model of clinical education, the Project admits other professionals into the supervisory process. Thus by changing the "rules" of professional participation in student learning, and by legitimising teachers, who are also the clients, we aim to demonstrate to students that practice occurs in a social community. In this community, collaborative solutions need to be made in response to complex, community-based problems, where democratic values such as seeking the common good displace profession-specific interests. Second year students generally seem to progress from resentment of teachers supervising their activities to an acceptance that the project can become more useful if teachers are actively involved. Only in 4th year do students begin to acknowledge an actual benefit from other perspectives, for example, *"If she [teacher] hadn't put us right, it [the project] would have been just a waste of time."*

After two years of graduate professional practice, the perspective seems to change once more. For example, *"You know, I always wanted to rush in and fix things, but then I remember [doing the project], feeling so completely stupid not knowing what to do, and then this [teacher's] aide came over and said, 'Don't you worry, we'll all help. We're just glad you're here.' And that was the best thing. Now I just try to settle down and think, 'Don't you worry, everyone'll help. There's just one of me but loads of everyone else'"*.

## COMPLEX, CONTEXT-SPECIFIC LEARNING

In our vignette we referred to the variety of schools that have participated in the Project. They range from a flexible single-class rural school to a 20-class school faced with problems of antisocial behaviour. Schools also vary socio-economically, some receiving funding to support disadvantaged students, and some with a computer for every student. These various contexts mean that varied solutions need to be found for sometimes similar problems. For example, teachers often express a need for improvement of children's classroom listening skills, yet the unique influence of each school context means that the resulting team project must be individually tailored to the school's culture. Because of this, students learn that practice solutions are shaped by the distinctive features of the context. They also learn, usually quite uncomfortably, that time is needed to fully engage with the nuances of this context: *"I'm worried. It's week three and we still don't know what our project is"* (comment from a 2nd year student's journal).

The challenge for the supervisory team is to balance the benefits of the authentic working environment with the high levels of anxiety that arise. Piaget (1971) was the first to emphasise that the cognitive conflict arising from multiple perspectives is important for developing the ability to critically reflect and be objective about experiences. However, our experience in the Project suggests that unless a number of support mechanisms are put in place, students will be overwhelmed by conflict and unable to learn. Although these support mechanisms differ for the different year levels, there is a single guiding principle, that of providing support for student learning rather than simplifying or decontextualising the task itself. The reason is to encourage students to view the challenges of the Project as rich sources of learning.

The 2nd year students are more intensely supported by the project team. Strategies include encouraging the practice of self-reflection and professional development through weekly reflective journals, individual goal setting, tutorials and small supervised debriefing groups. Most of these strategies offer the Project team almost immediate feedback about the levels of anxiety in the group, and allow swift intervention. The success of this can be judged from this 2nd year's reflective journal entry: *"I attended the debrief and put forward how I was feeling about the lack of achievement with the schools project so far. Everyone was very assuring and [supervisor] made some great suggestions about how I could tackle the problem. Having this support helped me to think about the situation more open-mindedly and to look at the entire picture."*

With 4th year students we have found that the most important foci of internal conflict and anxiety are not the level of their clinical skills or their ability to lead and project manage, but the need to be recognised as having their own burgeoning professional identity and to be considered capable of authentic practice in authentic contexts, by their professional supervisors. For example, *"I'm nervous about your feedback because you're a real clinician not just one of the lecturers. I won't be able to fake it with you!"* Support strategies used by the project team include weekly 1:1 mentoring and coaching appointments, most commonly giving feedback with the aim of motivating, reassuring and developing self-reliance. This intensely social set of support strategies relies heavily on the success of the final aspect of student learning to be discussed here: peer learning.

## LEARNING IS INHERENTLY SOCIAL AND COOPERATIVE

We have already suggested that a "traditional model of practice might not best serve the complex contexts of rural public health practice. One key aspect of this context is the need to learn from others and to apply one's skills in a flexible and extended scope of practice. The key driver of this cooperative learning is peer coaching. Although we encourage students to consider peer coaching and peer learning as occurring with people who are not necessarily members of a speech language pathology team, including parents, teachers, school students, and all other personnel supporting the school experience, students themselves identify their student team as the locus of the peer learning experience. The development of collegial relationships and individual growth that occurs from peer learning has been noticeable in the way students manage conflict and internal team discord. Entries from reflective journals frequently track a journey from team conflict to conflict avoidance; one frequently marked linguistically with a move from the pronoun "I" to "we". Examples of early 2nd year reflections include *"I was a bit ashamed of myself for shouting at her [peer group member]"*, and *"I walked outside so as to stop myself saying anything"*, to later entries such as *"We talked about it and I think it's sorted"*, and *"We just need to get the work done, so we all do what we can. We're pretty sure we can manage it."*

The peer group allows the revelation of how the students view themselves in relation to personal power and responsibility in the educational process. Our goal has always been to facilitate the movement of students from the unequal relationship between teacher/supervisor and student to the more reciprocal relationships between equals and professional colleagues, but we have noted that this process is neither smooth nor guaranteed. There are graduates of several years' standing who, when asked about their Project experience as a 2nd year, respond with comments such as: *"I wanted to work fast, and to know what I was doing. I like to work alone. I want to do the best I can. And I'll tell you: I was in pain with the Project. I never knew what I was doing. The kids were sweet, but I never saw myself working with kids. I just hated the messiness of it."*

Peer learning, group problem-solving, collaboration and negotiation are transparently messy. Yet they are all essential components of speech language pathology practice in rural contexts, where roles blur, resources need to be shared, and communication needs to be both effective and trusted across both vastly different and geographically vast contexts.

## REFLECTIONS

The strength as well as the sustainability of the Project lies in it being a locally developed response to a locally developed philosophy of the values speech language pathology practice should encompass. The most difficult issue in assessing the value of the Project is precisely its local nature.

The partnership emerged from an intersection of three organisational needs: the schools' need for support in gaining better learning outcomes, the need for the health service to promote better communication outcomes within school-age children, and the need for CSU students to gain alternative clinical practice placements. The very strong benefits accruing to all parties promote an atmosphere of goodwill among the project team that survives changes of personnel, lack of dedicated funding, and the influences of our respective organisations.

The Project can claim several benefits regarding teaching and learning. For example, this comment comes from a recent job-seeking graduate, *"I must tell you, the Project really impressed [the interviewers]. They said it was really different and like the real world. They've asked if they can use some of the Project in their school"*. Equally, the schools hosting the Project have provided positive feedback, stating that they *"will continue to use the resources"* as they are *"of high quality," "meet a need"* and have been communicated in *"teacher friendly formats like posters and lesson plans, identifying relevant learning outcomes"* (post-project principal surveys 2006–2008).

That schools evaluate the Project positively translates to an annual over-subscription of schools to host the speech language pathology teams. More importantly, the experience of learning how each profession contributes to the enrichment of outcomes for school students has forged relationships between teaching and speech language pathology which flow much deeper than a mutual transfer of knowledge between professionals. For example, a teacher interviewed in 2007 commented, *"It's like we're the client, and the [speech language pathology] teams go all out to give us what we say we want. And then we find out that what we wanted, was really what we needed, but never knew it before. So it's like they teach us, but they do it without teaching."*

This articulation of the value of negotiating and collaborating to advance mutually beneficial relationships leads to our final point. Our large organisations are responsive to policies and directives that accommodate changes to public health and education. The changes are expressed publicly as vision and value statements containing phrases like "equitable access" and "shared responsibility." But in a climate of over-stretched resources there is little time to properly examine these terms and their implications with our managers. Without this opportunity, we have been unable to share how our experiences of the Project have come to shape our interpretations of these very concepts or to influence the learning of our respective organisations. The result is that we believe that the Project, for all its internal sustainability, is externally fragile, subject to changes in not only its vision but also in its variable interpretation by management, policy-makers and other pragmatic decision-makers.

We experience a sense of frustration with the limited opportunities to share our insight that cost-effective solutions can be found to improve health and education outcomes in rural areas. Our experience tells us that answers will be rooted in the goodwill created from addressing mutual needs; from collaborating, negotiating and engaging co-operatively. Along the way, we also have no doubt that an immensely rich and complex range of educational experiences is created for everyone involved.

## REFERENCES

Australian Universities Community Engagement Alliance. (2006). *Universities and community engagement* [Position paper].Unpublished manuscript.

Baily, S., & Hampton I. (2007). *Sustainable speech therapy in schools.* Paper presented at the 2007 Successful Learning Conference, Sydney, 25 June.

Beecham, R., Clark, L., Denton, M., McAllister, L., Shanahan, L., Wilson, L., & Winkworth, A. (2006). Speech pathology clinical education at CSU: Using a partnership model to expand service opportunities in rural areas. Paper presented at the 2006 Sarrah Conference, Albury, 26 September.

Board of Studies New South Wales. (1998). *English K-6 syllabus.* Sydney: Board of Studies NSW.

Kathard, H. (2005). Clinical education in transition: Creating viable futures. *International Journal of Speech-Language Pathology, 7*(3), 149–152.

McLeod, S., & McKinnon, D.H. (2007). The prevalence of communication disorders compared with other learning needs in 14,500 primary and secondary school students. *International Journal of Language and Communication Disorders, 42*(S1), 37–59.

Millar, C., & Reid, K. (2006). A clinical education alternative: Creating a link between students, schools and community health. Paper presented at the 2006 Speech Pathology Australia National Conference, Fremantle, 21–25 May.

NSW Health Department. (2000). *Health promotion with schools: A policy for the health system.* Sydney: NSW Health Department.

Piaget, J. (1971). *Biology and knowledge.* Chicago, IL: University of Chicago Press.

Zhao, C.M., & Kuh, G.D. (2004). Adding value: Learning communities and student engagement. *Research in Higher Education, 45*(2), 115–138.

*Ruth Beecham D.Ed*
*Consultant, Yackandandah, Australia*

*Marijke Denton CPSP*
*Albury Community Health Centre*
*Greater Southern Area Health Service, Australia*

# 11. SITUATED LEARNING IN PRACTICE

Situated learning theory identifies learning as a function of the activity, context and culture in which it takes place. A learner is seen less as one who will acquire a set of abstract knowledge and apply it to later contexts, and more as one who will acquire skills and knowledge through participation and engagement in an authentic process. The situated character of learning emphasises interaction, collaboration and participation in a community of practice (Lave & Wenger, 1991). In this chapter we describe a model of physiotherapy education that embraces situated learning theory. Acknowledging that fieldwork facilitates the experience of situatedness, we extend this further. We describe a situated learning physiotherapy degree program, where the majority of learning is situated in fieldwork experience and supported by university-based study. This is contrasted with traditional full-time or part-time models of physiotherapy program delivery, where the student experience is university-based, supported by periodic fieldwork experience.

Situated learning theory proposes "legitimate peripheral participation" (Lave & Wenger, 1991, p. 29) as a dynamic concept of engagement and the means by which participation in a community is achieved. This involves working alongside experts and participating in their practice to a limited degree and with limited responsibility. Their theory originated from ethnographic research among communities of Liberian tailors, recovering alcoholics and midwives (Lave & Wenger, 1991). Although expert and apprentice relationships are traditionally hierarchical, such interactions are not the preferred pedagogy in situated learning. Instead, improvised practice and learning with peers is favoured in preference to instruction-oriented and directive teaching. In our view, the concepts of evolving participation, progressive engagement and peer learning offered by situated learning resonate strongly with the ethos of professional healthcare education and offer a theoretical basis worthy of exploration.

Within Great Britain at least, the situated learning program (SLP) for undergraduate physiotherapists at the University of East London appears unique. Drawing on our experience of partnership with six physiotherapy service providers, we explore issues arising in program design and delivery. We refer to SLP students as interns. We define interns as full-time undergraduate students enrolled in the SLP. They are employed and paid a salary by a physiotherapy service provider for the three year duration of the degree program. Interns are engaged in structured learning for 33 hours per week. They learn in the university two days per week and through fieldwork for the other three. We later identify the key differences between the SLP and traditional physiotherapy programs.

*L. McAllister et al., (eds.), Innovations in Allied Health Fieldwork*
*Education: A Critical Appraisal, 121–130.*
© *2010 Sense Publishers. All rights reserved.*

DEVELOPMENT

In an increasingly competitive environment we identified SLP as offering a unique departure from existing undergraduate and Masters entry level physiotherapy programs in the London area. Extensive consultation was undertaken with clinicians, managers, students, recent graduates, academic staff, commissioners of physiotherapy education and the UK's professional body, The Chartered Society of Physiotherapy. Although the need for more efficient utilisation of scarce fieldwork placements was a significant driver, all partners envisaged additional potential benefits for the new program in providing:
– Closer relationships between local physiotherapy services and university
– Enhanced local employment opportunities for our physiotherapy graduates
– Opportunity for students to "earn while they learn".
Our attempts to realise these benefits are considered below.

*Closer Relationships with Local Physiotherapy Service Providers*

Delivery of the SLP requires a sustained relationship and regular communication between academics and clinicians. The latter engage with discussion of curriculum, and develop "ownership" of the interns as members of their workforce, rather than regarding them as visiting students and therefore the responsibility of the university. The increased frequency of meetings and of opportunities for mutual collaboration on projects facilitates clearer understanding and appreciation of organisational perspectives.

*Enhanced Local Employment Opportunities for Our Physiotherapy Graduates*

As with most major world cities, London experiences the phenomenon of attracting students, relatively few of whom seek local employment while most move away upon graduation. Increasing pressure to recruit a workforce that more closely reflects the ethnicity and changing cultural patterns of inner city migration confirmed a need for service providers to recruit locally.

*Opportunities for Students to "Earn while they Learn"*

The potential for interns to earn from work that contributes to their degree is appealing. Interns are often mature students with family commitments in the local area and may have substantial work experience but are seeking a career change. Acquiring significant debts from full-time study is unappealing, and an intern's salary obviates the need to combine full-time study with part-time work.

A guiding principle of the consultation process was the desire to situate learners in the clinical setting. The enculturation of interns resulting from weekly immersion in an authentic practice setting reflects the realities of working life in the healthcare environment. As employees and team members, interns participate in the range of normal day-to-day workplace activities, including staff meetings and staff-room exchanges. Interns' situated experiences provide opportunities for learning that is embedded in fieldwork. Rather than attempting to learn abstract facts out of context with delayed clinical application, interns are stimulated to enquire and explore formal and informal theory in order to make sense of their experiences. Through observation and discussion, interns are encouraged to identify relevant workplace skills and to develop them through supervised clinical application.

## KEY FEATURES OF SLP

Before we identify some of the significant differences between the SLP and traditional physiotherapy programs it may be helpful to define *traditional*. Although variations exist, a traditional model for physiotherapy qualifying programs in the UK typically involves a BSc (Hons) degree program, taken in a full-time or part-time mode. Protection of title requires all programs to be approved by statutory regulatory and professional bodies. Programs are usually modular and semestered. Periods of university-based teaching introduce propositional knowledge and basic clinical skills. Fieldwork placement blocks (each usually 5–6 weeks long) are interspersed throughout the program. Students' professional performance on placement is assessed by fieldwork educators, using standardised assessment criteria provided by the host university. Clinical performance marks contribute to student attainment and final degree classifications.

From the outset, SLP delivery was intended to run alongside a pre-existing traditional physiotherapy program. A common modular structure, semestered delivery and program outcomes were adopted for both programs. Accommodating different attendance patterns for SLP and traditional students was complex, yet essential to ensuring coherent learning opportunities, integrated delivery and efficient use of finite resources. Although integration is desirable for the reasons stated, there are many significant differences from traditional programs:

- SLP interns are full-time students who commence learning in a fieldwork setting from the first week of the SLP.
- They are appointed on a three-year salaried contract with a physiotherapy service provider. They are situated with this same provider for the duration of the program. Interns are not employed as physiotherapy assistants but have their own job description, reflecting their evolving role and responsibilities.
- Each provider employs two interns per year who learn and work as peers.
- Physiotherapy skills are taught by fieldwork educators and learned by interns in practice, rather than the classroom.
- Fieldwork learning is carefully planned to support the achievement of learning outcomes of concurrent university-based modules.
- A weekly attendance pattern of three consecutive days in practice and two in the university occurs in each semester and continues throughout the program.
- Lectures and seminars shared with traditional peers occur on days when the interns attend university, providing teaching of theory.

- Achievement of module learning outcomes is assessed in the university, at the same time points and using the same assessment methods, for both SLP and the traditional program.
- Interns have prolonged exposure to learning and working in the practice environment. Fieldwork experience exceeds 1500 practice hours and is far in excess of the notional 1000 hours required by UK professional and statutory bodies.

*The Role of the Fieldwork Educator in SLP*

As facilitators of learning, fieldwork educators are crucial to the success of interns and the SLP program. Educators must be confident with the nature of their role in relation to the program. They teach skills and deliver some curriculum content in the fieldwork setting and must be familiar with the program structure, module learning outcomes and available resources. An appreciation of experiential and adult learning is required, since educators do not merely supervise professional performance. In SLP, theory is not "front loaded" but is encountered in parallel with fieldwork. Educators must be comfortable with the concept of facilitating engagement with the subject matter through direct experience. For example, in a module that introduces interns to neurology, they may learn about stroke in the university while fieldwork provides synchronous opportunities to experience relevant assessment and treatment skills, which are not taught in the university. Alternatively, interns may encounter stroke prior to engaging with theory and will need guidance from the educator to develop appropriate scope and depth of theoretical knowledge to support their practice at that time.

*Situated Learning Coordinators*

Coordinators support interns and fieldwork educators in each service. They provide a permanent presence for SLP in the organisation and have in-depth knowledge of program requirements and interns' progress. They act as conduits, offering an invaluable link between university and clinical teams. Partly funded by the university, they are responsible for planning interns' fieldwork education to dovetail with the modular program and learning outcomes. Coordinators meet regularly both as a group, to share ideas and problem solve, and with university staff, contributing to program monitoring and enhancement.

*Program Leader*

This role is central to all aspects of program management and especially in facilitating inter-organisational communication, creating a mutually supportive relationship with all stakeholders and ensuring the quality of the student experience.

*University Tutors*

Tutors familiar with the SLP visit interns and their educators on a regular basis, throughout their first year. Visits provide valuable support to new interns as they become accustomed to both clinical and university environments.

*Recruitment*

The SLP recruitment process requires applicants to meet prescribed academic entry criteria. Short-listed applicants are then interviewed by a panel consisting of representatives from practice and education. This process is essential, since interns are employees. It offers an invaluable opportunity to explore an intern's insight into and preparedness for the demands of learning in the workplace environment. Interviews also provide an opportunity to explore any experience of teamwork and expectations of delivering safe and effective physiotherapy in a diverse city environment.

*Accessible Learning Resources*

These are essential for interns and their educators. The resources include module workbooks and access to the university's virtual learning environment which provides teaching and learning material for the entire program.

*Intern Relationships*

The social and contextual nature of situated learning emphasises the importance of relationships of various types to the learning process (Lave & Wenger, 1991). Interns are placed in learning pairs in their clinical service and meet together at the university on a weekly basis. Action learning sets, student-led discussions and structured activities enhance their community, identity and learning. The SLP cohort bond closely, which may be seen as exclusive when within the university environment. Tutors may need to manage group work to ensure group diversity including both traditional and SLP students.

Interns are placed with the same peer within the workplace for the duration of the program. Although they work with many clinicians and with other visiting students, the prime learning relationship is with one another. As an intensive and long-term relationship, it is inevitable that peers experience "ups and downs", though relationships are most effective when based on mutual trust, respect, a shared commitment to the learning experience and to supporting one another's development. Educators and coordinators who plan the student experience must be aware of the dynamics of these peer relationships and be sensitive to their different learning needs and interactions. Difficulties arise if confidentiality is not strictly observed regarding an intern's performance, since the interns will remain in the organisation for the full three years "for better or worse".

## CONSIDERATION OF EMERGING ISSUES

Relationships between participating organisations have been strengthened by the SLP delivery, an original objective for program development. We now explore emergent issues which influence the delivery of SLP, and considerations for its future development.

*Interns' Learning Experiences*

The quality of the interns' experience is our main concern in program design and delivery. In order to manage working and learning in the fieldwork setting a supportive, understanding approach towards interns is essential. They must learn to interpret the formal curriculum as their framework for learning and to recognise, with their educators, the relationship between experiences and program learning outcomes. Initially, it is helpful to make explicit links between structured field-work experiences and identified skills and knowledge. Intern and educator refer to module study guides as a framework from which to structure manageable learning activities, map fieldwork to learning outcomes and engage in critical reflection. This helps interns to avoid feeling overwhelmed, identify learning opportunities of appropriate breadth and depth, and achieve recognised milestones. Although the formulation of manageable learning experiences may be reductionist, this pragmatic approach to experiential learning is crucial and provides structure within a challenging practice environment.

Interns and clinicians need help in recognising the many types of learning that are available within the broad curriculum of professional knowledge. An area that may be overlooked, yet is vital for interns' success, is the extent of their engagement with informal and hidden curricula (Mann, 2002). Interns need to achieve credibility as contributing team members and engaged learners. This links closely to their developing "craft knowledge" (Titchen & Higgs, 1999) and includes informal learning and appreciation of "the way we do things here". Although such learning is important to interns' performance in the workplace and to their acceptance as members of the team, they may perceive it as peripheral compared to the formal espoused knowledge delivered in the university. Consequently they may need support to ensure that it is not given lower priority.

From the outset interns are confronted by, and must become comfortable with, variations in practice. In comparison with traditional students, interns need to apply classroom taught skills into the practice setting less frequently. A common challenge, however, is to reconcile practice learned in the field and espoused theory. They must also become cognisant of the value afforded to criticality and research evidence, a core value of university degrees. Although interns need to be supported as they navigate these challenges, early exposure to the theory–practice dichotomy is distinctive of the SLP and contributes to the development of mature professional practice.

*Assessment*

Since learning outcomes are shared across the SLP and traditional programs, a pragmatic decision was taken at the outset to retain a common set of assessment methods. Broadly, professional performance is assessed by fieldwork educators in the practice setting. All other module learning outcomes are assessed in the university. This allows comparative assessment across both programs. To enhance university and practice links, fieldwork educators are encouraged into the university to participate in assessment. A natural progression will be to assess a greater proportion of practice skills in the fieldwork setting. Situated learning deserves situated assessment.

## EVALUATION OF OUTCOMES

Evaluation of the SLP has been ongoing since program commencement. Interns provide feedback on their fieldwork experiences each semester. An evaluation of all stakeholders' perspectives, including those of intern representatives and fieldwork educators, was conducted after the first cohort had graduated in 2007 (Baldry Currens, King, & Potter, 2007). It evidenced wide support, and found that the SLP provides confident and competent interns who appreciate the realities of clinical practice.

Interns' perspectives of peer learning have also been explored, using Q-methodology with 25 interns (Baldry Currens, 2007) and a case study of 12 Level one interns as part of a wider study (Baldry Currens, 2008). The performance of the SLP is encouraging, showing a progressive improvement of interns' performance. Across the first four cohorts graduating since 2006, 86% have achieved First and Upper Second Class Honours degree classifications. The SLP has low attrition, with 10% of students leaving or transferring into the traditional program. Reasons for leaving include early acknowledgement that physiotherapy is no longer a preferred career; academic failure; a preference for the traditional pattern of program delivery in which placements are separate from periods of university-based study. Interns' academic performance and low attrition compares favourably with our traditional program and the national average.

With increasing experience, interns are able to offer greater levels of professional skill to their employing service and become valued members of the team. After graduation, exit data relating to first destination within six months of graduation is sought. At least 75% of students graduating since 2006 have achieved work within physiotherapy. Against a difficult national picture with high levels of unemployment amongst new healthcare graduates, these figures are extremely positive. In the main, prolonged exposure of interns to learning in the workplace appears to develop their confidence and prepares them to step into practice as qualified clinicians:

*I feel confident that I can hit the ground running as soon as I graduate. Working as an intern means you've had three years experience of how it all works.* (Intern, 3rd year)

## REVISITING SITUATED LEARNING PROGRAM PROPOSITIONS

We now return to our motivations for establishing SLP, which have been realised to a large extent, in both program development and delivery.

Firstly, we desired closer relationships with local physiotherapy services. The creation of the new role of SLP coordinator has proved effective in linking university and clinical practice and in providing a sustained presence for SLP in the workplace. It also offers development for clinicians who are interested in professional education, in a role that differs from that of fieldwork educator. Clinicians were part of the original program design team, continue their involvement through teaching and assessment, and are essential to ongoing quality review and enhancement. Just as the clinical service feels greater ownership of interns who are their employees, the university enjoys closer links with its practice partners. A deeper, mutual understanding and acceptance of organisational perspectives has evolved over the duration of the program.

*The relationship's much closer now, we've far more contact with the [university] staff and more say in the course.* (Physiotherapy manager)

Secondly, we wished to enhance local employment opportunities for physiotherapy graduates. Although the SLP recruits nationally, it continues to have particular appeal to local applicants. The ethnicity and cultural backgrounds of the diverse local population are reflected in our interns. Interns are employed on a fixed-term contract that does not extend beyond the duration of the degree. Graduates, therefore, are required to apply for any available vacancies using normal recruitment procedures in accordance with equal opportunities legislation. We have been greatly encouraged by their success in obtaining employment within six months of graduation. The majority of interns have been recruited within the same group of physiotherapy services that participate in the SLP, though not necessarily the one in which they were originally placed as an intern. This suggests both familiarity with the program on the part of employers and confidence on the part of its graduates.

Thirdly, we sought to create opportunities for students to "earn while you learn". The capacity to earn a wage while being a full-time student is certainly an initial attraction to SLP applicants. In our opinion the value of this incentive should not be overstated. On its own, financial remuneration provides inadequate motivation for entry into SLP. It has the capacity to attract applicants with either the wrong motivation or insufficient insight into the demands of working and learning simultaneously. However, it also creates genuine opportunity for those who would not otherwise be in a position to undertake full-time study.

Further, we sought to create an innovative program design. Because learning opportunities are situated within the workplace, interns can develop their practice and use their skills immediately. This synchronous development of learning with evolving practice is valued by interns and their clinical team. The SLP recruits from a broad range of applicants and has consistently appealed to those who already work as physiotherapy assistants and wish to undertake a different experience. Those who have made the transition from assistant to intern recognise that their experience offers a helpful basis, though reporting significant differences in their new role:

*When I was an assistant they used to tell me what to do and when, now they explain why.* (Intern, Level one)

Not all interns have previous clinical experience from which to draw. We recognise that placing new interns in the practice setting from the first week of the program requires considerable investment in their support and development. The continuous weekly immersion in practice enables interns to assimilate working knowledge rapidly; fieldwork educators have not found this unmanageable. As interns' knowledge and skills progress, their independence grows and they begin to contribute more fully to service delivery and to some extent repay the initial investment.

We were also keen to acculturate interns within an authentic practice setting. Interns engage in a variety of work that reflects the full range of professional practice, including administration, teaching, assistant duties and clinical work. While we recognise that this embeds and consolidates an understanding of the realities of practice, this depth of understanding may be achieved at the expense of breadth. Interns are limited to experiencing a scope of practice within the opportunities available in their employing service. Moreover, consistent exposure to the practices of one particular service might limit an appreciation of possible variations. To counteract this, interns are encouraged to participate in an elective placement at the end of their second year. This placement may be in any setting within the UK or internationally. Some interns use this to experience clinical provision which is not available within their employing service, such as in a special care baby unit or in community based mental health, whereas others explore an alternative provision of particular interest, such as a leprosy clinic in India or a professional sports team.

SLP aims to enhance theory–practice links, which we acknowledge to be complex and interdependent. We sought closer integration of university-based study with fieldwork. To achieve this, a predisposition towards "learning through doing" and workplace learning is essential for interns. Support is vital as they learn how to learn in the practice setting. This includes being able to maintain focus, develop structure, and extract meaningful and relevant learning from the plethora of possible experiences. A continuing challenge for future SLP development is to further embed assessment in the reality of practice.

We have set out to explain the motivations for developing this unique physiotherapy program. We have attempted to clarify some differences between this and traditional program design and explored emergent issues from the seven years in which SLP has run. We acknowledge the real challenges in delivering any new program, particularly one which spans organisational boundaries and utilises a previously untested design in physiotherapy education. For all stakeholders the benefits are tangible, outweighing the challenges of program delivery. Situated learning as a model of fieldwork education is attractive, successful and worthy of consideration for wider adoption within professional healthcare education.

## REFERENCES

Baldry Currens, J.A. (2007). Student perceptions of peer learning in the practice setting: A Q-methodological study. Paper presented at 15th World Confederation for Physical Therapy Conference, Vancouver, June.

Baldry Currens, J.A. (2008). Peer assisted learning: Embracing learner choice in the practice setting. Paper presented at International Society for the Scholarship of Teaching and Learning Conference, Edmonton.

Baldry Currens, J.A., King, R., & Potter, J. (2007). Situated learning - creating an innovative model for physiotherapy education: Enhancing university and hospital partnerships. Paper presented at 15th World Confederation for Physical Therapy Conference, Vancouver, June.

Lave, J., & Wenger, E. (1991). *Situated learning: Legitimate peripheral participation.* Cambridge: Cambridge University Press.

Mann, K. (2002). Thinking about learning: Implications for principle-based professional education. *The Journal of Continuing Education in The Health Professions, 22,* 69–76.

Titchen, A., & Higgs, J. (1999). Facilitating the development of knowledge. In J. Higgs & H. Edwards (Eds.), *Educating beginning practitioners* (pp. 180–188). Oxford: Butterworth-Heinemann.

Wenger, E. (1998). *Communities of practice: Learning, meaning, and identity.* Cambridge: Cambridge University Press.

*Julie Baldry Currens PhD*
*Learning, Teaching and Assessment*
*University of East London, UK*

*Julian Hargreaves MSc*
*School of Health and Bioscience*
*University of East London, UK*

LESTER E. JONES, JOHN A. HAMMOND
AND JEAN-PASCAL BEAUDOIN

# 12. CLINICALLY-BASED LEARNING PORTFOLIOS

*Guiding Reflection and Professional Development*

Fieldwork learning experiences require careful management if they are to facilitate reflection for professional development. In particular, frequent opportunities for feedback and self-review should be provided throughout the curriculum. This enables learners to refine their understanding of personal strengths and areas for improvement, and to formulate a plan of action to optimise personal and professional development. A learning portfolio, either paper-based or electronic, can provide an appropriate framework to support self-review, including reflection and analysis, and in a collaborative learning environment will also be valuable in the feedback process. This chapter explores how these processes can be promoted in fieldwork experiences, using two case studies that describe the implementation of learning portfolios in health professional education.

*Theoretical Perspectives on Reflective Learning for Professional Development*

Reflective learning in allied health professions has been influenced by three major theoretical perspectives as we see it. As decisions in skilled everyday work are made in contexts characterised by uncertainty, the first perspective advocates that professional practice is not just about technical expertise (Schön, 1983). It follows that process knowledge – or a professional's "know-how" – is of similar importance to propositional knowledge – or "knowing what" (Eraut, 1994; and for further reading Higgs, 2009). Becoming aware of this know-how is a desirable outcome of reflection on one's thoughts and behaviour. The second perspective supports the use of models of experiential learning as a framework for organising reflective thinking. Many tools designed to facilitate reflection in the health professions are based on Kolb's reflective learning cycle (Kolb, Rubin, & Osland, 1994; see Burns & Bulman, 2000, and Jafari & Kaufman, 2006 for examples). The third perspective recognises that professionals' feelings and beliefs may influence their practice and need to be taken into account in order to achieve a more holistic approach to reflective learning. The merging of these perspectives leads to "critical reflection", allowing an understanding of multiple perspectives and the opportunity to gain greater insight into relationships with others; it can also reveal contradictions in the context of practice (White, Fook, & Gardiner, 2006).

*L. McAllister et al., (eds.), Innovations in Allied Health Fieldwork*
*Education: A Critical Appraisal, 131–140.*
© *2010 Sense Publishers. All rights reserved.*

*Reflective Learning for Professional Development*

It is proposed that a reflective practitioner demonstrates qualities that enhance professional practice (Delany & Molloy, 2009). These qualities may be difficult to observe, but can be shared through discourse and writing, forming the basis for both continuing professional development and portfolio keeping. A guide for learners and a hierarchical framework that ranges from superficial descriptive writing to deeper critical reflection has been proposed (Hatton & Smith, 1995). Some examples are provided in Table 12.1.

*Table 12.1. Levels of reflection in writing*

| | | |
|---|---|---|
| **Superficial →** | Descriptive writing | Provides description of situation or experience and does not demonstrate any discussion beyond this. *"Saw Patient X with TB who appeared anxious. I made sure I communicated clearly so he had confidence in me."* |
| | Descriptive reflection | Provides description of situation or experience and presents some alternative perspectives uncritically. *"Saw Patient X with TB who appeared anxious. I remember also feeling anxious and I think this influenced how I asked my questions, for example...."* |
| | Dialogic reflection | Shows ability to step back from the situation to explore different perspectives, judgements or explanations in a discourse with self. Considers how different actions might lead to different possibilities. *"Saw Patient X with TB who appeared anxious. I wonder why? Was it just that he was concerned about the diagnosis? Was it that he was unfamiliar with the environment? I remember also feeling anxious and maybe this was because he was too. Perhaps I could ask about the patient's concerns in situations like this in the future."* |
| **← Deeper** | Critical reflection | Shows awareness that multiple perspectives (historical, social or political) that may be hidden, can influence the situation or experience. *"Saw Patient X with TB who appeared anxious. I wonder why? Was it just that he was concerned about the diagnosis? I remember also feeling anxious and maybe he could sense this. Was I feeling anxious because I was pre-judging him? Based on the prevalence of TB, was I assuming that he might be homeless or an IV drug user? My reactions may also be biased because of my comfortable upbringing. I have never known anyone who has been in this situation. How might I deal with these perceptions in the future to ensure I am treating all patients equally?"* |

*The Challenges of Engaging Students with Reflective Tasks*

Clinical educators are often faced with students keen to build up their "patient mileage" in preference to fostering reflective practice. Reflective writing activities may be encouraged and a reflective learning portfolio compiled. However, unless the reflective purpose is clear, the compilation of a portfolio risks becoming a repository of achievements and may not be representative of how professionals develop (Edwards & Nicoll, 2006). Notably, deeper reflection may be inhibited if the reflective writing is to be viewed by others and, more critically, if it is to be assessed (Moon, 2004). Educational professionals therefore need to consider strategies that could facilitate the development of safe, collaborative relationships between reflector and assessor. The following cases provide examples.

*Case Study 1: Experience of using a paper-based portfolio to support learning in a physiotherapy education programme, St. George's University of London, UK.*
During a period of curriculum review, questions arose amongst staff about the sustainability of existing assessment processes used for fieldwork learning experiences. Developing a portfolio of reflective tasks was seen as a promising way of sampling student performance. Also, it would enable students to express some of the thinking behind their decisions and actions (e.g., "what shapes and has shaped their perspective? what do they do with what they have found?") (Delany & Molloy, 2009, p. 9). Staff were also interested in providing a structure for students' personal development, to promote lifelong learning. As well, the United Kingdom Health Professionals Council (HPC) was developing a mandatory process for re-registration, and this involved the keeping of a professional development portfolio (HPC, 2002). Staff developed the student portfolio tasks based on these requirements for re-registration. This gave students a head start in their professional responsibilities, and also provided strong leverage for student and staff engagement (Jones, Hammond, & Horgan, 2007).

As a form of introduction to reflective practice, Year 2 students were asked to create, collect and complete specific evidence of their clinically-based learning. The required content included analyses of strengths, weaknesses, opportunities, threats (SWOT), "significant incident forms", a weekly reflective journal, annotated references of research relevant to their practice, and clinical reasoning proformas (see Appendix). A number of these were derived from professional sources, including the Chartered Society of Physiotherapy (UK) (2008). It was hoped at the end of Year 2 that students would have a clear idea of types of evidence, and that they would also be valuing the reflective activities as a way of advancing their development.

To promote the completion of portfolio tasks as a reflective and development activity there were two phases of assessment. In the first phase, students submitted their entire portfolio – minus a private section that they were encouraged to keep – after the second of three fieldwork education placements. Students' university-based personal tutors provided formative feedback on the depth of reflection, the selection of "significant incidents", the quality of the annotated references and the logic and comprehensiveness of the clinical reasoning. The students then had the opportunity to use the feedback to develop their portfolio during their third placement. From this final Year 2 placement, personal tutors then completed the summative assessment of the portfolio. In the review of students' attempts at the required tasks several commonalities were identified. In keeping a journal some students demonstrated deeper levels of reflection whereas others did little more than keep a diary, describing – but not analysing – the activities from week to week. Some students were able to explore learning experiences that were "significant", appropriately owning their responsibility in the situation reported, as well as their role in improving performance. Other students were less keen to own the experience, especially when it could reflect negatively on them, and either wrote "we" (that is, sharing the blame for a negative situation) or even blamed others. The differences noted here may be indicative of varying levels of so-called "emotional intelligence", or simply a matter of some students trusting the process more than others. The students' responses might also be explained by "positioning theory", which allows analysis of people's actions and language in relation to the position they hold in a social or a professional interaction (Webb, Fawns, & Harré, 2009). Therefore the responses described might be reflective of the students' perception of their rights and duties in the significant learning incident. A common problem with students completing annotated references was that they gave no indication of how the research had influenced their thinking or their actions in the clinical context. Completion of the clinical reasoning form often highlighted where students were not linking subjective interviews to physical examination or treatment planning, and when they were not using an evidence-based approach.

Although not a requirement, students were encouraged to share aspects of their portfolio with their fieldwork educator to demonstrate their development. Initially it was thought that both students and fieldwork educators might be reluctant to do this. However, feedback from the clinic-based staff was overwhelmingly positive (Jones, unpublished data). Initiation of this sharing, and the decision as to what degree, were left entirely to the student. Anecdotal evidence suggested that discussions about student reflections were time efficient and allowed the fieldwork educators to emphasise their role as facilitators of student learning rather than as assessors. As the benefits became apparent, university-based staff began to encourage students not performing well to use some of the required-content tasks as tools for working with their fieldwork educator to improve performance (notably the "significant incident forms" and the clinical reasoning forms).

An unexpected outcome was the improved interaction between students and their university-based personal tutors. Prior to the implementation of the portfolio activity, most personal tutor–student interactions were based on problems related to poor performance. However, the portfolio facilitated constructive communication that related to learning, achievement and professional development. Having interacted with students in this way, tutors commented that it was easier to construct employment references for them, and that they were better placed for giving advice about curriculum vitae construction and interview preparation.

In the final year of the course (Year 3), guidance for the portfolio was less instructive in terms of required content. Students were asked to create a "profile" of their portfolio to demonstrate how they had satisfied the learning outcomes of the clinical component of the course. Students could draw on their preferred evidence for support, allowing them to be more creative and resulting in greater ownership of their portfolio. A requirement of the final year portfolio was the identification by students of their learning needs. The aim of this strategy was to contextualise for students the level of practice they had reached, and also to set the scene for an iterative process of self-reflection, self-assessment and action planning for ongoing development. During Year 3 it was evident that some students began to use their portfolio more effectively, intuitively and with broader purpose. For some it became routine to complete a "significant incident form" or clinical reasoning form, as a process of communication between themselves and the fieldwork educator. As well, students were increasingly aware of the value of having an up-to-date organised portfolio as part of the job-seeking process. An important purpose of the fieldwork-based learning portfolio was to facilitate the integration of the university-based curriculum with the rationale and delivery of clinical practice. Through ongoing review this integration has become increasingly formalised. Curriculum revision has seen the portfolio and associated tasks embedded in the university-based subjects. This has put an even greater emphasis on the role of the portfolio as a tool for the integration of theoretical perspectives and fieldwork experiences.

Overall, the clinically-based learning portfolio has provided an opportunity for students to engage in reflective activities that promote transformative learning experiences. Additional benefits have included more profitable interactions with clinical educators and university educators. However, this requires students to share their reflections, which may compromise the honesty and genuineness of the content they create. The portfolio may also facilitate an evidence-based approach, including the integration of theory into practice. Increasing numbers of students found the activity of keeping a portfolio relevant (Jones et al., 2007) and this may have a lot to do with the similarities with the professional re-registration process.

*Case Study 2: Developing and implementing an electronic student professional portfolio (e-SPP) in an occupational therapy program, University of Ottawa.*
This project emerged from discussions on how to facilitate student reflective learning and also meet the professional regulatory body competency development requirements (College of Occupational Therapists of Ontario, 2005). It started with implementation of a paper-based portfolio, similar to that in Case Study 1. Selected occupational therapy students were given initial guidance as to the purpose and use of a portfolio. A mentor supported students to complete the portfolio documents and inspected the portfolio at regular intervals throughout the academic year.

At the end of the first year, survey and focus group interview data was collected from students to evaluate the e-SPP as a learning tool. Analysis identified several emerging themes. The students valued the opportunity to (1) archive pertinent documentation, (2) reflect and grow, and (3) have a means of communication with university-based staff. As well, they felt that the portfolio would be more valued if it was integrated into the curriculum and not perceived as an add-on. They reported that the inspection process was stressful and not conducive to learning. They strongly advocated the move to an electronic portfolio to reduce the paper trail and the need to carry a large binder (Hébert, Beaudoin, Thibeault, & Pitre, 2007).

The project team, including an information technology professional (ITP), selected a web-based portfolio platform that would best suit the set criteria (e.g., user friendliness, types of functions, adaptability, price, transferability). The ITP met with the platform developers to set the menu functions and to insert the portfolio's base structure (see Table 12.2). Students were provided with an initial training session and technical support throughout the piloting phase.

Analysis of survey data at the end of the second year identified a new set of themes. The students felt that the electronic portfolio was helpful in (1) organising and archiving meaningful material using multimedia, (2) structuring thoughts and learning, and (3) sharing information with classmates, university-based staff, field-work educators and potential employers. The students recommended improvements for the e-SPP. These included (1) increasing the number of reflective activities to improve linking theory with practice and to further develop clinical reasoning and critical thinking, (2) simplifying the e-SPP's navigating process (e.g., fewer steps, no need to scan documents, fewer glitches) and allowing more personalisation of the menu, structure and functions of the portfolio, (3) increasing data transferability from the university's web platform to a personal computer or to the professional regulatory body portfolio, and (4) phasing out the "professional inspection" process by having university-based staff review selected assignments within specific courses (Hébert et al., in press).

During the last phase of the project, the program went through a transition from Bachelor to Masters level. The e-SPP was given a central role, and course designers integrated portfolio requirements with most components of the new curriculum. The focus changed from policing by staff to student self-directed learning. From this point on, students were given the responsibility to include required assignments in their e-SPP. Also at this time, the web-based platform was discontinued and each student was provided with a memory stick (USB key) with the e-SPP base software structure installed for personal use (see Table 12.2 for content). The memory stick had most of the advantages of the internet platform but addressed earlier student concerns. Over the last 3 years, use of the e-SPP has been incorporated within the annual curriculum evaluation process. Students have agreed that the e-SPP allows them to reflect and learn, to be aware of the regulatory responsibilities and accountabilities and to document professional competency from an early stage in their professional development. Senior students found that the e-SPP promoted a more active approach to learning and helped them to link theory to practice. Students realised that what they were learning was connected to the complexity of "real life" practice. Also, metacognitive learning activities such as journalling, where students reflected on their learning processes, increased their engagement in the learning.

As predicted, students suggested that the e-SPP fostered discussions with peers and academic staff mostly through the integrative activities included at key points of the curriculum. For example, seminars held at the end of the program allowed students to share and reflect on their overall learning experience, through case studies, discussions, and going back to previous assignments and reflection pieces. Overall, the use of an electronic portfolio has had an impact on professional preparedness and supports progress toward achieving entry level competency (Hébert et al., in press).

*Table 12.2. Sample content of the University of Ottawa OT electronic
student professional portfolio (e-SPP)*

| |
|---|
| *1. Introduction to Portfolio:* |
|    – Welcome letter from Programme Chair<br>   – Portfolio definition<br>   – User guide<br>   – Programme's teaching philosophy<br>   – Students' code of conduct |
| *2. Personal and Professional Background:* |
|    – Student's biography (including values, culture, etc.)<br>   – Curriculum vitae (resume)<br>   – Recommendation letters<br>   – Diplomas, certificates, awards |
| *3. Education Plan:* |
|    – Informative documentation:<br>    (e.g., course syllabus, curriculum mapping, professional guidelines, web links,<br>    fieldwork guides) |
| *4. Reflective Journal:* |
|    – Journal entries from each course<br>   – Journal entries from fieldwork experiences<br>   – Personal initiative journal entries |
| *5. Monitoring of Competency Development:* |
|    – Specific assignments from each course<br>   – Feedback from academic staff and clinical educators<br>   – Continuing education plan |
| *6. Personal Section:* |
|    – Meaningful documentation from courses or fieldwork that will help students<br>    with the transition from student to practitioner.<br>   – Daily practice tools of importance to student. |

## CONCLUSION

The literature on reflective practice has been particularly significant in shaping professional accountability in health professions. This chapter has provided an overview of some of these influences, using two cases to illustrate how portfolios may be used to guide reflection and professional development.

Drawing from the two case studies, we highlight the following points:
- Learning portfolios can be a private record of sensitive and significant experiences that can shape and drive personal and professional development.
- In safe and collaborative learning environments, a learning portfolio can be a means for promoting student and staff relationships.
- The reflection that is facilitated by the compilation of a portfolio can assist students to become reflective practitioners.

137

Finally, recommendations to improve the chances of success when developing and implementing a portfolio include:
– Address potential pitfalls while developing the critical path for the implementation phase.
– Gain support from academic and administrative staff to deal with workload and resources issues.
– Link the portfolio to the program's curriculum (classroom and fieldwork) and to the regulatory body's requirements.
– Avoid complexity of format and content.
– Involve students within the development team to identify learner needs.

Student preparedness for clinical practice, including meeting the requirements of professional bodies, can be enhanced by using learning portfolios and promoting a process of continuing professional development. The case studies have provided evidence of students self-managing their learning. It could be argued that, by adopting a reflective approach by using learning portfolios, students attained many of the desirable attributes of reflective practitioners and lifelong learners.

## ADDITIONAL RESOURCES

*Australian ePortfolio project.* Available: http://www.eportfoliopractice.qut.edu.au/, accessed 6 December 2009.

*Chartered Society of Physiotherapy (UK) – portfolio resources.* Available: http://www.csp.org.uk/ uploads/ documents/csp_PD010_keepingAportfolio.pdf, accessed 6 December 2009.

*Making practice-based learning work.* Available: http://www.practicebasedlearning.org/resources/materials/ intro.htm, accessed 6 December 2009.

## APPENDIX – ST GEORGE'S UNIVERSITY OF LONDON, CLINICAL REASONING FORM

| | |
|---|---|
| **STUDENT NAME:** | **DATE:** |
| *CLINICAL REASONING FORM* | |
| *To be completed after initial assessment* | |
| **PATIENT ID:** | **DOB:** |
| (first name or initials or number or code) | |
| **Gender:** | **Occupation:** |
| **Lifestyle (active/sedentary):** | |
| **What is/are the main reason(s) for attendance/referral? (as stated by patient)** | |
| 1. | |
| 2. | |
| List the main **subjective** findings: | |
| 1. | |
| 2. | |
| 3. | |
| List the main **objective** findings for each of the aforementioned symptoms: | |
| 1. | |
| 2. | |
| 3. | |

Are there any **safety issues** (e.g., redflags / SIN / BP / O2 sats)? If so, briefly explain
.....................................................................................

*Are there **any other contributing factors** that will influence management (e.g., work or home situation, health beliefs or behaviours)? if so, briefly explain*
.....................................................................................

**Problems: List & describe**

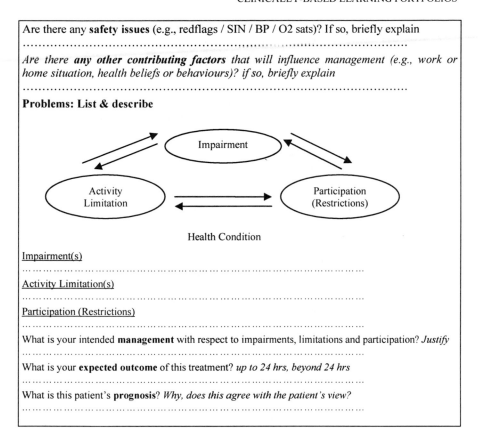

Health Condition

Impairment(s)
.....................................................................................

Activity Limitation(s)
.....................................................................................

Participation (Restrictions)
.....................................................................................

What is your intended **management** with respect to impairments, limitations and participation? *Justify*
.....................................................................................

What is your **expected outcome** of this treatment? *up to 24 hrs, beyond 24 hrs*
.....................................................................................

What is this patient's **prognosis**? *Why, does this agree with the patient's view?*
.....................................................................................

## REFERENCES

Burns, S., & Bulman, C. (2000). *Reflective practice in nursing.* Oxford: Blackwell Scientific.

Chartered Society of Physiotherapy. (2008). *Keeping a portfolio: Getting started.* Information paper: PD010 (formerly CPD6). Available: http://www.csp.org.uk/director/libraryandpublications/publicati ons.cfm?item_id=74C877D7C2F372207CD8793005F2691B, accessed 13 October 2008.

College of Occupational Therapists of Ontario. (2005). *Professional portfolio.* Available: http://www.coto. org/media/documents/PP-Interior.pdf, accessed 25 June 2009.

Delany, C., & Molloy, E. (2009). Critical reflection in clinical education: Beyond the "swampy lowlands". In C. Delany & E. Molloy (Eds.), *Clinical education in the health professions* (pp. 3–24). Chatswood, Australia: Elsevier Churchill Livingstone.

Edwards, R., & Nicoll, K. (2006). Expertise, competence and reflection in the rhetoric of professional development. *British Educational Research Journal, 32*(1), 115–131.

Eraut, M. (1994). *Developing professional knowledge and competence.* London: Falmer Press.

Hatton, N., & Smith, D. (1995). Reflection in teacher education: Towards definition and implementation. *Teaching and Teacher Education, 11*(1), 33–49.

Health Professions Council. (2002). *The future: A mini prospectus.* Available: http://www.hpc-uk.org/ assets/documents/100005DCHPC_Consultation2002_The_future_mini_prospectus.pdf, accessed 10 August 2009.

Hébert, M., Beaudoin, J.-P., Thibeault, R., & Pitre, R. (2007). Conception, implantation et utilisation d'un portfolio professionnel étudiant dans un programme de formation en ergothérapie. *Revue internationale de pédagogie de l'enseignement supérieur, 25*(1), 80–95.

Hébert, M., Thibeault, R., Beaudoin, J.P., Tremblay, M., Séguin, A., & Zamor, A. (in press). Format numérique? Un portfolio étudiant pour la formation en ergothérapie. *La Revue des sciences de l'éducation.*

Higgs, J. (2009). Ways of knowing for clinical practice. In C. Delany & E. Molloy (Eds.), *Clinical education in the health professions* (pp. 25–37). Chatswood, NSW: Elsevier Churchill Livingstone.

Jafari, A., & Kaufman, C. (2006). *Handbook of research on ePortfolios.* Hershey, PA: Idea Group Reference.

Jones, L.E., Hammond, J.A., & Horgan, T. (2007). The use of a clinically-based reflective practice portfolio: A survey of undergraduate students' opinion. WPCT World Congress platform presentation, Vancouver.

Kolb, D.A., Rubin, I.M., & Osland, J. (1994). Individual and organisational learning. In D.A. Kolb, J. Osland, & I.M. Rubin (Eds.), *Organisational behaviours: An experiential approach* (6th ed., pp. 41–70). Engelwood Cliffs, NJ: Prentice Hall.

Moon, J.A. (2004). *A handbook of reflective and experiential learning: Theory and practice.* London: Routledge Falmer.

Schön, D.A. (1983). *The reflective practitioner: How professionals think in action.* Aldershot, Hants: Arena Ashgate Publishing.

Webb, G., Fawns, R., & Harré, R. (2009). Professional identities and communities of practice. In C. Delany & E. Molloy (Eds.), *Clinical education in the health professions* (pp. 53-69). Chatswood, NSW: Elsevier Churchill Livingstone.

White, S., Fook, J., & Gardiner, F. (2006). *Critical reflection in health and social care.* Maidenhead: Open University Press.

*Lester E Jones MSc MEd(PM)*
*School of Physiotherapy*
*La Trobe University, Australia*

*John Hammond MSc*
*Faculty of Health and Social Care Sciences*
*St George's University of London and Kingston University, UK*

*Jean-Pascal Beaudoin M.A.P.*
*Formation clinique - ergothérapie*
*Université d'Ottawa, Canada*

JULIE BALDRY CURRENS AND RICHARD LADYSHEWSKY

# 13. LEARNING WITH AND FROM PEERS IN FIELDWORK EDUCATION SETTINGS

## INTRODUCTION

Learning with and from one another is fundamental to our practice as healthcare professionals. Through engagement with peers, we share ideas that help to enhance our practice and solve the clinical challenges we often encounter. High quality field-work education empowers learners to function as effective team players, and to become as comfortable with collaborative approaches as with independent, auto-nomous practice. Learning is evident in the development of knowledge, the transfer and consolidation of skills, and the acquisition of new attitudes to self, others and academic content. Rather than merely being an organised response to placement scarcity, peer learning models should be valued and recognised as a way of fostering high quality learning experiences.

In this chapter we identify theories underlying peer learning. We explore peer coaching and the more generic "2:1" model (two students placed with one fieldwork educator). We consider practical perspectives for application of peer learning and we acknowledge the challenges and the advantages of these models from the perspectives of students and their fieldwork educators.

## THEORIES SUPPORTING PEER LEARNING

We accept that learning is a socially constructed activity. Peer learning draws on constructivist theories of sociocognitive and sociocultural development. During peer discussion, learners question and challenge their own and one another's thinking, knowledge, and underlying assumptions. Students defend and consolidate their own understanding, assimilating new ideas and concepts as a result of structured disagree-ment. This is in keeping with Jean Piaget's (1926) theories of cognitive development and learning through sociocognitive conflict, in which learning occurs through a process of conflict and reconciliation between prior and new information. Similarly, Vygotsky (1978) argued that the skill development that is achieved with the help of another person exceeds that of an individual attempting to acquire a skill alone.

Within fieldwork settings, learners regularly support each other's attempts to master treatment techniques, construct and co-construct new knowledge and skills. In observing each other's practice and that of more experienced clinicians, peers learn to model and replicate successful and appropriate behaviours. This is in keeping with social learning theory (Bandura, 1971), in which modelling and

L. McAllister et al., (eds.), Innovations in Allied Health Fieldwork
Education: A Critical Appraisal, 141–149.
© 2010 Sense Publishers. All rights reserved.

reinforcement guide learning. Topping and Ehly (1998) have argued that peer modelling is highly influential, heightening metacognitive awareness, insight and self-regulation.

Language and dialogue also play a key role in sociocultural theories of learning (Bakhtin 1983; Wertsch, 1991) and peer learning (Renshaw, 2004). Conversations between learners incorporate simple question and answers as well as highly sophisticated dialogic patterns. They include speaking one's thoughts aloud, and helping to clarify a peer's understanding through prompts and open-ended questions. Cognitive elaboration theory is part of this dialogic learning process, since peers help each other to extend their thinking and co-construct deeper understanding of ideas and concepts (King, 1999).

## PEER LEARNING APPROACHES

Over 30 years ago, pioneering approaches known collectively as "cooperative learning" introduced small group learning to school children. This entailed working together in goal-directed team activities, with shared responsibility for learning. Achievement was measured by grade, with rewards for team or individual success (Johnson & Johnson, 1987; Sharan & Sharan, 1992; Slavin, 1995). Johnson and Johnson emphasised the place of learning social skills to support development of effective peer relationships and collaboration, and described five crucial elements of group processing: positive interdependence; face-to-face interaction; individual accountability for learning assigned material; appropriate interpersonal and small-group skills; and developing procedures to analyse group activity. Direct translation of these five crucial elements into fieldwork education settings is not straightforward, but it could be said to underpin successful peer learning strategies.

A plethora of predominantly British and American classroom applications of peer learning subsequently emerged, and the generic title "peer assisted learning" (PAL) now embraces many approaches using both pairs and small groups, and is known variously as peer tutoring, peer mentoring, peer collaboration, cooperative learning, small group teaching, group instruction, and reciprocal peer learning. Innovative teaching and learning practices have been created, with literally hundreds of attempts to evaluate their effectiveness. Although proponents cite credible research demonstrating the effectiveness of a favoured approach, little agreement exists in relation to the preferred method or conditions under which optimal peer learning might be achieved (Slavin, 1990).

In contemporary education, PAL has proliferated widely in further and higher education, such that Cohen and Sampson (2001, p. 35) observed that there were "as many ways of using peer learning in courses as there are courses". Peer tutoring, peer coaching and the 2:1 model have received particular attention, and are discussed below.

### Peer Tutoring

Although early approaches to peer tutoring involved a linear transmission of knowledge from a more able peer as surrogate teacher to less able or younger pupils, newer definitions include similar pairs and reciprocal peer tutoring in which teaching and learning roles are shared (Topping, 1996). Higher education models often incorporate peer monitoring and assessment, mentoring and counselling. Reviews have consistently identified significant advantages for both tutors and tutees across a range of ages and subjects. Greater cognitive benefits are often experienced by the tutor who, in the process of explaining material to the tutee, cognitively reorganises the material and gains a deeper understanding (Sharpley & Sharpley, 1981; Topping, 1996). Benefits reported among psychology and economics students in higher education include gains in academic achievement and student satisfaction, reduced stress, lower drop-out rates and improved transferable skills (Topping, 1996).

Health professional education has seen several novel initiatives using peer tutoring and assessment. In nursing, significantly higher performance in surgical dressing technique was achieved by students acting as both peer tutor and tutee, compared to those taught by a clinical teacher (Iwasiw & Goldenberg, 1993). In medicine, first year students performed similarly in clinical examinations, regardless of being taught by fourth year medical students or faculty teachers, with student teachers rated more highly (Nestel & Kidd, 2003). Tutorials in "difficult" topics devised and led by medical students were viewed positively, with significant improvement in post-tutorial scores (Hurley, McKay, Scott, & James, 2003). Dental students assessed medical students' mouth examinations, with scores close to those of medical faculty (Ogden, Green, & Kerr, 2000). As Rushton and Lindsay (2003) have explained, the potential for comparison of fieldwork research is limited by restricted descriptions of pedagogical processes, although findings present innovative approaches that are clearly of use to and valued by students.

*Peer Coaching*

Peer coaching (PC) is one of a suite of peer learning strategies that can be used to promote learning and professional development (Ladyshewsky, 2000). It was originally developed as a strategy to support the development of teachers, who often work in isolation in the classroom (Joyce & Showers 1982). As a strategy, it was highly effective for supporting teachers in adopting and implementing new models of curriculum. Since then, PC has been used in a wide range of settings, including the education of health professionals, with evidence to suggest that it has been used effectively in medicine (Sekerka & Chao, 2003), nursing (Waddell & Dunn, 2005), and physiotherapy education and practice (Ladyshewsky, 2002, 2004).

Much of the early health sciences literature on PC focused on the model and its associated benefits and challenges (Gandy & Jensen 1992; Lincoln & McAllister 1993; Ladyshewsky, 2004). For example, reductions in student stress and anxiety, increased confidence and opportunities for enhanced learning and practice were often cited. Other studies have focused on outcomes (DeClute & Ladyshewsky, 1993; Ladyshewsky, 2002), with findings suggesting that the model increased competence, attention to clinical reasoning, clinical performance and productivity.

Waddell and Dunn (2005) defined PC as a voluntary and non-evaluative relationship between two practitioners who share similar experience and training and wish to embed knowledge and skill into practice. It is a planned and systematic approach to building competence and professional practice in a fieldwork setting. Central to the success of PC is the aim of ensuring that evaluation does not become a focus of the relationship, otherwise a status difference emerges. Peer coaches must learn to ask open-ended questions about what they have observed and heard. This encourages reflection and revisitation of knowledge networks by the coachee, leading in turn to transformative changes in knowledge, skill and attitude. If peer coaches engage in evaluation or "confrontational coaching" (Veenman & Denessen, 2001) by telling coachees what they are doing wrong, the coaches begin to take the unintended and undesired role of evaluator. If peer coaches adopt this quasi-supervisory role relative status changes, and coachees are likely to disengage from the experience because the important tenets of equality and mutuality in the peer learning relationship (Damon & Phelps, 1989) have become violated. In these circumstances coachees begin to withhold information and opportunities for learning, to avoid being evaluated.

There are appropriate question formats for coaching that encourage self-disclosure (Zeus & Skiffington, 2002). These are part of the skill base learners must acquire for a PC relationship to be successful. As noted by Johnson and Johnson (1987), participants in peer learning relationships must have certain skills to make these learning arrangements successful. These questions are usually preceded by "who", "what", "where", and "how". When coaches ask open-ended questions with these prompts, employing active listening, and probing coachees about their actions, coachees are assisted in the self-assessment process. They can link their action to their knowledge and performance, and can formulate conclusions about how to restructure knowledge and enhance their professional practice. This is the experiential learning process (see Kolb, 1984) in action, which supports clinical reasoning through a PC methodology.

*The 2:1 Model*

Placing two students together in practice settings with a shared clinician in the role of fieldwork educator has become known as the "2:1" model. The 2:1 model offers considerable opportunity for shared learning activities. For example, shared learning activities may be planned and facilitated by the educator, or the students, through the use of structured learning objectives. Learning experiences may also be unscripted, informal and spontaneous. They may be opportunistic, since they occur through peers asking questions, sharing ideas, and preferring to practise techniques without the gaze (or judgment) of the fieldwork educator.

In keeping with many aspects of fieldwork education, much of the research relating to the 2:1 model has been pragmatic, driven by the need to address the problem of placement scarcity and improve organisation and service delivery (Baldry Currens, 2003a; Rushton & Lindsay, 2003), often to the detriment of students' learning experiences. Despite some methodological limitations, findings are relatively consistent across studies, and evidence supports valuing the presence of a peer. Mutual support, a less threatening atmosphere, and lower levels of anxiety that can occur with peer learning, are especially valued (Baldry Currens & Bithell, 2003)

Student peers offer each other *companionship* (Baldry Currens, 2003b) in which emotional support features highly. Fieldwork can be daunting, especially for less experienced students, and peers represent a "familiar face", "ally" or "buddy". Peers share common experiences and have similar worries and fears. Peers voice their concerns to each other, and in mutual recognition of similar circumstances they form allegiances and offer reassurance and support. They help each other adjust their emotional landscape to better participate in and benefit from their learning experiences (Baldry Currens, 2008).

Learning in 2:1 situations occurs through individual and shared activities. *Collaboration* is fundamental to peer learning (Baldry Currens, 2003b), and both planned and spontaneous learning activities fall broadly into *dialogic* or *activity-oriented* categories of collaborative activity, summarised in Table 13.1. These learning activities can occur separately, but more frequently in tandem. Peers who achieve greater levels of companionship achieve more collaboration, with richer learning dialogues and more effective practice.

*Table 13.1. Collaborative peer learning activities*

| Dialogic collaboration | Activity-oriented collaboration |
| --- | --- |
| Questioning: ranging from simple requests for information to more complex exchanges | Modelling: peers observe and emulate successful practice |
| Clarifying: expressing, consolidating or reframing information | Rehearsing: peers practise therapeutic techniques to achieve confidence and competence |
| Exchanging: sharing information and ideas | Reviewing: peers offer non-judgmental, supportive feedback |
| Rich dialogue: probing, challenging, elaborating ideas, constructing and co-constructing knowledge | Tutoring: peers teach one another techniques and strategies |

## Organisational Challenges

Although advantages of the PC and 2:1 models have been noted above, implementing these models poses some challenges. Perhaps the greatest obstacle to success is lack of preparation and confidence by fieldwork educators and students. In this respect, universities have a considerable role in facilitating a paradigm shift away from the traditional role of teacher as instructor and gatekeeper of knowledge. Constructivist approaches are more helpful, since they locate educators as facilitators of learning, and value enquiry-based, experiential and collaborative learning. Since the dominant model largely remains one of instruction (Watkins, Carnell, Lodge, Wagner, & Whalley, 2002) whether in schools or fieldwork contexts, there is much to be done. Attempts to challenge this dominance may be met with suspicion and cynicism, even when alternative proposed models offer demonstrable solutions to identified problems (Huddlestone, 1999). Acknowledged challenges, however, do exist. For instance, clinicians need to learn new strategies and adapt to role changes, especially when students have different learning styles and abilities (Baldry Currens, 2003a). Despite these reservations, many fieldwork educators report positive experiences once they attempt the 2:1 model. These positive experiences include greater time for fieldwork education, reduced stress associated with greater student independence, and more satisfying clinical teaching with fewer "superficial" questions (Baldry Currens, 2003a).

Students also need support to appreciate the many opportunities offered through peer learning. Many do not recognise their own learning style and activities. A paradigm shift is necessary here too. Some students may be challenged by the need to develop trusting, respectful and confidential relationships, since the typical paradigm in university settings emphasises competing against one another for grades. Although such relationships are essential for effective professional practice and teamwork, they can be hard to achieve in a learning context. Some individuals find it difficult to build supportive learning relationships given their underlying personality structure, the short length of placements, or their values in relation to learning, motivation and performance.

It is not necessary to try to match students in learning pairs according to ability or clinical performance. However, significant differences between peers may result in a less satisfying learning experience. Perceived difficulties include feeling burdened by an overly dependent peer, feeling constrained, and being reluctant to answer an educator's questions for fear of upsetting the peer or influencing the educator's opinion. Such experiences may reduce the desire to participate in peer learning. Nevertheless, students commonly acknowledge that different levels of ability need not be problematic (since the less able peer benefits from the teaching, skills and knowledge of the more able peer while the more able peer gains because explanation to a less able peer offers the opportunity to consolidate understanding), although many prefer to be placed with someone at a broadly similar level.

Comparison and competition are aspects of concern which frequently blight discussion of peer learning unnecessarily. Many students acknowledge that it is helpful to monitor and benchmark their own development by comparing it with that of a peer. This is natural, and even helpful, yet it can become problematic if overemphasised, or if an educator verbalises similar comparisons, leaving a student feeling judged, vulnerable and exposed. Some students acknowledge their own competitive tendencies, which provide a personal spur to encourage their performance. Nevertheless, individual competition to out-perform a peer is unhelpful in a 2:1 or coaching context. Instead, it is desirable to encourage and reward cooperation and collaboration; this can be achieved by including this aspect in evaluation of professional behaviour by the supervisor.

The short term nature of placements and the requirements of fieldwork education programs offer few opportunities for individuals to select their peer. Consequently, building trust and respect may be difficult, but not impossible. Facilitating attitudes include commitment to the confidential nature of the relationship; negotiated and shared learning experiences; mutual tolerance, respect and trust; sufficient self-knowledge and self-esteem to permit self-disclosure; and a willingness to support a peer's development alongside one's own. Peer relationships flourish quickly when built on these principles. Friendship is not a prerequisite, although a degree of interpersonal compatibility is helpful, and peers should take time to get to know each other, familiarise themselves with learning needs and make a commitment to the relationship and the learning that will follow.

## CONCLUSION

Learning with and from peers in the fieldwork setting offers both student and fieldwork educator unique benefits. Peer learning has a strong theoretical base and provides learners in the fieldwork setting with additional learning resources to support their development towards competency. For fieldwork educators, peer learning approaches extend their development as educators, yield positive outcomes for the healthcare facility (e.g. increasing service provision), and enrich the educators' professional practice development. Although 2:1 and PC models have been the main focus of this chapter, the use of peer tutoring can also be embedded into many models, extending the boundaries of fieldwork education. Peer tutoring also yields many benefits that are not available in independent learning models.

Since the early 1990s the use of peer learning models has increased in the health sciences sector. With this expansion has come a growing body of literature which supports the model as a means of enriching the learning environment. Research is also now revealing that peer learning can increase the depth of clinical reasoning in learners, enhancing the achievement of professional competency and performance.

With evidence-based practice increasingly driving clinical activity, it is important to acknowledge the evidence in support of peer learning and to extend this practice in both university and fieldwork education settings. When carried out effectively using the principles outlined in this chapter, peer learning can produce the positive outcomes which all health disciplines seek to achieve in their fieldwork education programs and curricula.

Peer learning requires that all involved students, fieldwork educators and academics understand how this approach works. Universities, therefore, must develop strategies and implement systems that promote collaborative practice in the classroom so that students are prepared with the requisite skills to execute this kind of learning in the fieldwork setting. Programs that support fieldwork educators also need to be developed to assist them in the transition towards more constructivist teaching practices.

# REFERENCES

Bakhtin, M. (1983). *The dialogic imagination: Four essays* (M. Holquist, Ed.; C. Emerson & M. Holquist, Trans.). Austin, TX: University of Texas Press.

Baldry Currens, J.A., & Bithell, C.P. (2003). The 2:1 clinical placement model: Perceptions of clinical educators and students. *Physiotherapy, 89*(4), 204–218.

Baldry Currens, J.A. (2003a). The 2:1 clinical placement model: Review. *Physiotherapy, 89*(9), 540–554.

Baldry Currens, J.A. (2003b). Physiotherapy student perceptions of peer assisted learning. Paper presented at 14th World Confederation for Physical Therapy Conference, Barcelona.

Baldry Currens, J.A. (2008). Peer assisted learning: Embracing learner choice in the practice setting. Paper presented at International Society for the Scholarship of Teaching and Learning Conference, Edmonton.

Bandura, A. (1971). *Social learning theory.* New York: General Learning Press.

Cohen, R., & Sampson, J. (2001). Strategies for peer learning: Some examples. In D. Boud, R. Cohen, & J. Sampson (Eds.), *Peer learning in higher education: Learning with and from each other* (pp. 35–49). London: Kogan Page.

Damon, W., & Phelps, E. (1989). Critical distinctions among three approaches to peer education. *International Journal of Educational Research, 13*, 9–19.

DeClute, J., & Ladyshewsky, R. (1993). Enhancing clinical competence using a collaborative clinical education model. *Physical Therapy, 73*(10), 683–689.

Gandy, J., & Jensen, G. (1992). Group work and reflective practicums in physical therapy education: Models for professional behavior development. *Journal of Physical Therapy Education, 6*(1), 6–10.

Huddlestone, R. (1999). Clinical placements for the professions allied to medicine, Part 2: Placement shortages? Two models that can solve the problem. *British Journal of Occupational Therapy, 62*(7) 295–298.

Hurley, K.F., McKay, D.W., Scott, T.M., & James, B.M. (2003). The Supplementary Instruction Project: Peer-devised and delivered tutorials, *Medical Teacher, 25*(4), 404–407.

Iwasiw, C., & Goldenberg, D. (1993). Peer teaching among nursing students in the clinical area: Effects on student learning. *Journal of Advanced Nursing, 18*, 659–68.

Johnson, D.W., & Johnson, R.T. (1987). *Learning together and alone: Cooperative, competitive and individualistic learning.* Englewood Cliffs, NJ: Prentice-Hall.

Joyce, B., & Showers, B. (1982). The coaching of teaching. *Educational Leadership, 40*(1), 4–8.

King, A. (1999). Discourse patterns for mediating peer learning. In A.M. O'Donnell & A. King (Eds.), *Cognitive perspectives on peer learning* (87–115). Mahwah, NJ: Lawrence Erlbaum.

Kolb, D.A. (1984). *Experiential learning: Experience as the source of learning and development.* Englewood Cliffs, NJ: Prentice-Hall.

Ladyshewsky, R. (2000). Peer assisted learning in clinical education: A review of terms and learning principles. *Journal of Physical Therapy Education, 14*(2), 15–22.

Ladyshewsky, R. (2002). A quasi-experimental study of the differences in performance and clinical reasoning using individual learning versus reciprocal peer coaching. *Physiotherapy Theory and Practice, 18*(1), 17–31.

Ladyshewsky, R. (2004). The impact of peer coaching on the clinical reasoning of the novice practitioner. *Physiotherapy Canada, 56*(1), 15–25.

Lincoln, M., & McAllister, L. (1993). Peer learning in clinical education. *Medical Teacher, 15*(1), 17–25.

Nestel, D., & Kidd, J. (2003). Peer tutoring in patient-centred interviewing skills: Experience of a project for first-year students. *Medical Teacher, 25*(4), 398–403.

Ogden, G.R., Green, M., & Kerr, J.S. (2000). The use of interprofessional peer examiners in an objective structured clinical examination: Can dental students act as examiners? *British Dental Journal, 12*(3), 160–164.

Piaget, J. (1926). *The language and thought of the child.* New York: Harcourt Brace.

Renshaw, P.D. (2004). Dialogic learning, teaching and instruction: Theoretical roots and analytical frameworks. In J. van der Linden & P. Renshaw (Eds.), *Dialogic learning: Shifting perspectives to learning, instruction and teaching.* Dordrecht: Kluwer Academic Publishers.

Rushton, A., & Lindsay, G. (2003). Clinical education: A critical analysis using soft systems methodology. *International Journal of Therapy and Rehabilitation, 10*(6), 271–279.

Sekerka, L., & Chao, J. (2003). Peer coaching as a technique to foster professional development in clinical ambulatory settings. *Journal of Continuing Education in the Health Professions, 23*, 30–37.

Sharan, Y., & Sharan, S. (1992). Expanding cooperative learning through group investigation. New York: Teachers' College Press.

Sharpley, A., & Sharpley, C. (1981). Peer tutoring: A review of the literature, *Collected Original Resources in Education, 5*(3), 1–63.

Slavin, R.E. (1990). Research on cooperative learning: Consensus and controversy. *Educational Leadership, 47*(4), 52–54.

Slavin, R.E. (1995). *Cooperative learning: Theory, research and practice.* Needham Heights, MA: Allyn and Bacon.

Topping, K., & Ehly, S. (Eds.) (1998). *Peer-assisted learning.* Mahwah, NJ: Lawrence Erlbaum.

Topping, K.J. (1996). The effectiveness of peer tutoring in further and higher education: A typology and review of the literature. *Higher Education, 32*, 321–345.

Veenman, S., & Denessen, E. (2001). The coaching of teachers: Results of five training studies. *Educational Research and Evaluation, 7*, 84–91.

Vygotsky, L.S. (1978). *Mind in society: The development of higher psychological processes.* Cambridge, MA: Harvard University Press.

Waddell, D., & Dunn, N. (2005). Peer coaching: The next step in staff development. *Journal of Continuing Education in Nursing, 36*(2), 84–91.

Watkins, C., Carnell, E., Lodge, C., Wagner, P., & Whalley, C. (2002). Effective learning. *National School Improvement Network Research Matters Bulletin, 17* (Summer).

Wertsch, J.W. (1991). *Voices of the mind: A sociocultural approach to mediated action.* Cambridge, MA: Harvard University Press.

Zeus, P., & Skiffington, S. (2002). *The Coaching at Work tool kit.* Roseville, NSW: McGraw Hill Australia.

*Julie Baldry Currens PhD*
*Learning, Teaching and Assessment*
*University of East London, UK*

*Richard Ladyshewsky PhD*
*Graduate School of Business*
*Curtin University of Technology, Australia*

# SECTION IV: USING INFORMATION AND COMMUNICATION TECHNOLOGY IN FIELDWORK EDUCATION

MERROLEE PENMAN, CATHERINE DONNELLY
AND DONNA DRYNAN

# 14. USING INFORMATION AND COMMUNICATION TECHNOLOGY IN FIELDWORK EDUCATION

*Issues and Possibilities*

In responding to the changing needs and expectations of the workplace, academic institutions and students, fieldwork staff increasingly need to find innovative solutions to complex issues. In general, these innovations have focused on developing different teaching models or alternative fieldwork opportunities. However, the use of information and communication technologies (ICT) to support students' learning as they engage in these innovative or alternative opportunities has received less attention. Although researchers have explored the use and value of ICT to support student learning on-campus, little attention has been given to how ICT may support fieldwork education. We aim to highlight how ICT is being or could be used to support the work of fieldwork staff. Where available, evidence from the research is used to support the claims made. We are aware, however, that with the speed at which ICT is changing, especially with the emergence of the interactive, social and media-intensive Web 2.0 technologies (Skiba, Connors, & Jeffries, 2008), research in this area often lags behind actual practice.

Before discussing how ICT can support the development of innovative solutions for the challenges faced in fieldwork, we begin by defining the terms ICT and Web 2.0, and providing a brief overview of how learning is viewed by the users of these technologies. We briefly look at why ICTs should be used to support fieldwork, before presenting case examples of the use of websites, blogs and wikis. We conclude with discussing barriers to the use of ICTs in fieldwork, and ways to overcome them.

## WHAT ARE ICT AND WEB 2.0?

Information and communication technology/ies (ICTs) is an all-encompassing term used to describe the "technologies that process information and aid communication" (Schaper & Pervan, 2007, p. S217) such as personal computers, online video games, interactive TV, cell phones, iPods, PDAs or the Internet (Young et al., 2010). Effective use of these networked and non-networked technologies to access, create and use information (Sandars & Haythornthwaite, 2007) can enhance the learning of students and fieldwork staff, as they facilitate the "rapid and efficient communication of information ... to support clinical and educational processes"

L. McAllister et al., (eds.), Innovations in Allied Health Fieldwork
Education: A Critical Appraisal, 153–165.

(Levett-Jones et al., 2009, p. 612), anytime and anywhere (Boulos, Maramba, & Wheeler, 2006).

In contrast, the term Web 2.0 (or the social networking tools) is used to encompass not only a number of technologies but also what the technologies can offer the user (Lupiáñez-Villanueva, Mayer, & Torrent, 2009). Web 2.0 tools are interactive, facilitating communications, connections and collaborative activity between people who may be geographically and chronologically dispersed (McGee & Begg, 2008). Users are active in the creating, sharing, remixing and repurposing of content (Boulos & Wheeler, 2007), thus developing the collective wisdom of the learning community (Skiba et al., 2008). For this reason Web 2.0 tools are ideal for fieldwork, as the literature has demonstrated that the socially interactive process of feedback and reflection promotes deeper learning during fieldwork (Best, 2005; Richard, 2008). In Web 1.0, information was disseminated through the use of static websites created by experts for others to access (Lemley & Burnham, 2009) in a one-to-many model (McGee & Begg, 2008). Typically, allied health professional associations' websites are examples of Web 1.0. In contrast, Web 2.0 supports inter-action across a range of media by many-to-many (McGee & Begg, 2008). Lemley and Burnham (2009) have suggested that these tools can "augment the educational method and increase its efficacy" (p. 50), and others (Boulos & Wheeler, 2007; Michael, 2009) have argued that networked collaboration creates new possibilities for learning in health and health care that cannot be underestimated.

## WHY USE ICT TO SUPPORT FIELDWORK PROCESSES?

Most fieldwork staff use telephone and email to support student learning. But although the potential of ICTs to support nursing students in distant placements was proposed as early as 1995 (see Ward & Moule, 2007), the uptake of ICTs by the health professions continues to be slow (Abbott & Coenen, 2008) and somewhat haphazard (Lemley & Burnham, 2009). With a seeming reluctance by many to engage the use of ICTs to support student learning, we have asked why health professionals should invest time and energy in exploring these ever-changing technologies. There are a number of reasons.

Clearly, students are changing, and although we would argue that generational divides have almost always existed, previous divides did not appear to significantly influence how students were taught and supervised (Boudreau, 2008). However, the current Net Generation members (Tapscott, 2009) or Digital Natives (Prensky, 2001) are different, being confident users of ICTs (Skiba et al., 2008; Tapscott, 2009), although this may be with the more youth-oriented, social networking sites (McGee & Begg, 2008) than in their professional learning. Given the Net Generation's experiences with the tools, Oblinger and Oblinger (2005) have argued that these students are experiential or participatory learners, preferring group to individual learning, interaction to solitary study, wanting immediate responses to what they are seeking, and preferably visual than just text-based. Thus, tools that have proven effective for supporting student learning may no longer meet the needs of our current students.

Educational pedagogy is also changing. One example is the "authentic learning movement" or learning by doing. This movement is described as "making use of a variety of emerging technologies to provide a highly interactive, collaborative and reflective learning environment" (Skiba et al., 2008, p. 226) that is "engaging and student-focused, self-generating and sustainable" (McGee & Begg, 2008, p. 169). Social constructivist theory is another pedagogy that informs the use of ICTs, with knowledge individually constructed. Learners take an active role in their learning, creating meaning from their experiences through discussion and interactions (Boulos & Wheeler, 2007), often in the context of a community of practice (Wenger, 1998). These face-to-face or online communities support student learning through the provision of a social context in which to understand knowledge. More than a social meeting place, online learning communities enable the exploration of ideas, allowing students to engage in collaborative learning and reflective practice (Palloff & Pratt, 2007) with the teacher guiding the learner.

Although it is possible to design learning environments that are constructivist in nature or to provide authentic learning without using any ICTs, these tools can enhance or support the learning experience. ICTs allow fieldwork staff to focus less on content and more on the learning process (Skiba et al., 2008), assisting graduating students to be "life-long participants in their continuing education" (McGee & Begg, 2008, p. 169). Furthermore, the use of ICTs facilitates the development of collaborative skills, something all health professionals are expected to possess (Lemley & Burnham, 2009). If all of this is true, then how might we use ICTs effectively?

## WAYS IN WHICH ICT CAN BE USED EFFECTIVELY

Before we talk about what is possible we need to remind ourselves of the reason for using ICTs. At some point, students and fieldwork staff need to address an identified knowledge or skill deficit. In identifying a need for more information, individuals need to know not only where the information may be, but how good it is and how they may ethically use that information. They also need to be able to reflect on the learning gained through processing the information and to be able to integrate this new learning with previous experiences, thus constructing new understandings (21st Century Information Fluency Project, 2009).

Some ICTs provide access, others provide opportunity for reflection and others construction of new understandings, although this is a somewhat artificial division, especially when one tool can provide all three processes depending on who uses it, how and for what purpose. Given the diversity of ICTs it is difficult in one chapter to present all the ways all tools could be used. Rather than present an exhaustive list of the tools of choice in 2010 (some of which may no longer be used in 2015), we have chosen instead to consider those processes of learning that remain constant, that is, accessing information, reflection and construction of knowledge, and to give examples of how ICTs are currently being used to support those learning processes.

*Accessing Information: Sharing Existing Knowledge*

Fieldwork academic coordinators have spent much time developing manuals to support the fieldwork learning experience and in delivering face-to-face workshops to prepare students and fieldwork educators for placements. In our experience, however, fieldwork educators' attendance is often influenced by barriers such as geographical location, financial issues including the provision of release time and cover for those attending, and/or time constraints. Students may also choose not to attend for a myriad of reasons. Thus both students and fieldwork educators may not have the information they need, when they most need it – during the fieldwork placement. Students and fieldwork educators can seek support or information from their peers or the fieldwork staff (Ward & Moule, 2007) but ICTs can provide a viable alternative. The following case example demonstrates how a Web 1.0 resource was developed to facilitate sharing of existing knowledge at the time that it is most needed.

*Case Example: Supporting Students and Fieldwork Educators through the Provision of a Web-Based Resource.*

To address the knowledge and skill gap and the challenges of attendance at face-to-face workshops, E-Tips (www.practiceeducation.ca) was developed by Kassam et al. (2008) as a viable and sustainable web-based fieldwork educator support program. Intended to provide an introductory and interactive web-based program, E-tips is aimed at increasing the knowledge, skills and thus confidence of practitioners offering student placements. Based on a needs assessment[1] of over 400 healthcare fieldwork educators and an extensive literature review, the modules were developed by a healthcare professional interdisciplinary team[2] to cover cross-disciplinary essential educational concepts. Free and accessible to anyone at any time, E-Tips consists of eight modules designed to be completed within 15 to 30 minutes. The modules are titled:

1. Setting the stage for clinical teaching
2. The role learning plays in the practice education experience
3. Enhancing your teaching skills
4. Fostering clinical reasoning
5. Giving feedback
6. The evaluation process in practice education
7. Supporting the struggling student
8. Strategies for resolving conflicts

Using the metaphor of film and acting as analogous to the various roles of fieldwork educators, each module follows a consistent framework, beginning with objectives and concluding with a "that's a wrap" screen. Key content is presented through a variety of teaching strategies including points to stimulate self-reflection, quizzes, self-assessments, quick tips, video clips and flash cards which illustrate points or provide information.

Pilot testing of the technical aspects of the online platform as well as the content was undertaken prior to the release of E-Tips (D. Drynan, personal communication, January 8, 2010). Fieldwork academic coordinators from professions such as occupational therapy, physiotherapy, nursing, social work, pharmacy, dietetics, speech language pathology, audiology and medicine sent email invitations to their clinical educators to pilot E-Tips. All 86 respondents were accepted. In this phase, respondents were asked to provide feedback on the applicability and usefulness of the modules, what they learned and how that learning could be applied in their clinical teaching, and the appropriateness of the size of the module.

Results from the pilot test revealed that 100% of the respondents found the modules extremely or very applicable, with the content presented in an engaging and manageable format. Ninety five percent of respondents stated that E-Tips increased their confidence for educating a student. Some comments included "As a [fieldwork educator] in the north, I value online education opportunities. Thank you" and "The modules were extremely user-friendly. They were thorough without being too much. The short funny videos illustrated the points well and made it interesting to continue. I found the visual diagrams to be very helpful".

Based on the formative feedback and ongoing summative evaluation, it appears that online fieldwork educator programs such as E-Tips are valued and useful. While some perceive the modules to augment to face-to-face sessions, the modules are also seen to provide information at the "just in time" moment when clinicians have a student in the fieldwork setting. As there are a number of online programs available ranging from open access to registered continuing education resources, diversity among online programs is appreciated in meeting users' varied needs.

E-Tips is an excellent example of what can be achieved with external funding and a team approach to developing an online resource relevant for a range of allied health professionals. However, websites such as E-Tips have their limitations. The website needs to be hosted somewhere and maintained. Although interactive, it does not allow for interactivity among all fieldwork staff and students. Real examples as they are experienced are not shared, and a community of learners is unlikely to be fostered around a site such as E-Tips. To create a community, interactive tools such as blogging would be more effective.

## Reflection: Making Sense of the Learning Experience

Although E-Tips is a valuable Web 1.0 resource for the transmission of information from one or few to many, social networking tools or Web 2.0 tools such as blogging can not only support reflection, but ultimately facilitate the coming together of a community of learners. The concept of reflective journaling in fieldwork is not new, being a process that assists students' learning as they strive to make sense of rich and varied albeit unfamiliar situations. Reflective journaling enables students to connect theory to practice, to generate new knowledge and to shift attitude (Kessler & Lund, 2004).

With postings in reverse chronological order, blogs are essentially an extension of the written fieldwork journal, but with the additional benefit of authentic feedback from both peers and an open audience via reader comment (Penman, 2008). The interaction that is possible between blog owner/poster and reader is the ultimate example of active learning and creation of meaning endorsed by social constructivists (Palloff & Pratt, 2007). The interactive nature of the blog allows students to reflect and revisit concepts, and the use of hyperlinks offers the opportunity for students to situate their learning in a broader context by connecting with others both within and across educational programmes and geographies. Three case examples are presented demonstrating different ways of using blogging to support student learning in fieldwork.

### Case Examples: Using Blogging to Facilitate Reflection.

This first case is an example of the use of a blog situated in an academic course, whose goal was to link disability theory to practice over the duration of a fieldwork placement (Villeneuve, Jamieson, Donnelly, White, & Lava, in press). Villeneuve et al. used blogs in a disability theory course for first year Master's students in occupational therapy. The course coupled face-to-face interaction with weekly blogs that extended over an 8-week fieldwork placement. This structure provided students with a blend designed to maximise opportunities for them to apply disability theory to their fieldwork experiences.

In answering set questions drawn from assigned disability-related readings chosen for their provocative nature, 64 students individually posted weekly reflections in their blogs for two guided questions. Three course instructors were each assigned a group of students, reviewing their blogs and providing early informal feedback followed by formal feedback at midterm and post-placement. Students were expected to build an understanding of disability concepts and consider the impact of different perspectives for people with disabilities. Students were also encouraged to consider the implications of these interpretations for their future practice. Evaluation of this blended learning is currently underway. Anecdotally this format offered students the opportunity to explicitly reflect on practice and theory and to reshape their understanding of this knowledge in light of their fieldwork contexts and personal experiences (C. Donnelly, personal communication, November 30, 2009).

The findings of Villeneuve et al. (2009) are similar to those of Ladyshewsky and Gardner (2008) which we discuss as our second case example. They examined the use of group-authored blogs designed to facilitate reflection by final year physiotherapy students in the latter part of their final fieldwork placements. Each group consisted of five students and an academic moderator. To evaluate the effectiveness of blogging compared with a written examination to assess clinically-based reflective practice, the authors used focus groups to gain insight into the students' perspectives of the value and challenges of blogging. Ladyshewsky and Gardner determined that blogging assisted students in their clinical reasoning and overall reflective practice. Students commented that the blogs provided a non-threatening medium through which to discuss clinical examples, and exposed them to a range of student learning experiences that enhanced their own learning. The authors suggested that blogging can "provide students with extended opportunities to build reflective practice networks" (Ladyshewsky & Gardner, 2008, p. 254).

The third case example demonstrates blogs created by students outside of any course requirement. Requiring a high level of commitment, the benefits can outweigh any drawbacks. Now a licensed occupational therapist, Karen Dobyns created her blog to chronicle her life as a student in the Master of Occupational Therapy programme, University of Tennessee Health Science Center (K. Dobyns, personal communication, October 26, 2009). Karen created entries on a range of topics from coursework through to her fieldwork experiences (http://otstudents. blogspot.com/). Active knowledge construction through fieldwork postings was evident as Karen continually linked new experiences to previous learning, integrating theory with authentic learning experiences that occurred through her placements. Karen effectively used narrative with continual interaction between herself and her audience to enhance knowledge construction. Karen responded to feedback and integrated comments to build expertise in topics of interest to her. For Karen, blogging perhaps provided a non-threatening medium in which to discuss clinical examples. The lack of academic facilitator creates genuineness in the blog entries, illustrating student-driven, active learning and avoiding the concerns that physio-therapy students in the study by Ladyshewsky and Gardner (2008) had in relation to the presence of academic facilitators in their blogs.

However, while there are many benefits for blogging, the challenge to move on from one writer sharing reflections with many readers is still present. Another ICT that allows a community to work and learn together is wikis, which can facilitate the third learning process mentioned earlier, construction of knowledge.

*Constructing Knowledge: Creating Learning Communities*

Initially one of the lesser known of the Web 2.0 tools, wikis are fast becoming the tool of choice for groups of people coming together in learning communities. Wikis enable the collective wisdom of many to be located in a web-based collaborative space (Erardi & Hartmann, 2008) allowing for easy adding, editing, critiquing and removal of content. Cadogan (2009) described wikis as "essentially a web-based word processor, which any one can edit" (p. 166), and they have the added value of "rollback functionality" allowing users to refer back to earlier versions of the document (Erardi & Hartmann, 2008). Wikis provide a place for discussion about the collaborative work undertaken and can be fully open or with restricted access. Thus they appear to be excellent tools for use by health professions, allowing ongoing construction of understandings, and in the process enabling a learning community to form and learn together.

While Wikipedia is perhaps one of the better known wikis and similar medical type wikis such as Ganfyd (www.ganfyd.org) have emerged, there are few public examples to illustrate the value of wikis as a collaborative tool to be used in field-work learning and thus little published research. No specific fieldwork-related case examples could be found in the literature, but the following case examples demonstrate the use of wikis in related areas.

*Case Examples: Using Wikis for Knowledge Construction.*

The first case example is use of the wiki in a qualitative research course offered as part of the post-professional Master of Occupational Therapy programme at Otago Polytechnic. The lecturer of this course was seeking ways of engaging registered health professionals in the experience of planning and undertaking a small, short research project within their 14 week distance based course. Her aim was to demystify research by encouraging different members of the class to undertake parts of the research project (L.H. Wilson, personal communication, November 1, 2009). Each student was responsible for interviewing a colleague about his or her perceptions of client-centred practice. Students also volunteered to complete other parts of the study, for example contributing to the literature review, reviewing the posted transcripts and collating themes or identifying points for the discussion. The work of the wiki was made public (http://occtherotagoqrip.Wiki spaces.com), and although only enrolled students were able to contribute to it, visitors were encouraged to send comments to the lecturer. Although not formally evaluated, this project appears to have been successful, with a compiled report made available for the postgraduate students and their participants. Students who completed the course evaluation reported that they had found the experience in the main positive. The project wiki supported the learning of the students, fostering collaboration amongst a group of 15 students living and working throughout New Zealand.

This project has many similarities to the projects in our second case example of the use of wikis by allied health professionals. Post-professional nursing students enrolled in a joint cross-university nursing programme in Pennsylvania (Ciesielka, 2008) came together online to engage in completion of a group project (http://614comm.pbworks.com/). Students in this project valued the opportunity to work with their peers and to be exposed to different viewpoints. Thus the wiki fostered collaborative learning, a key competency for the nurse practitioners enrolled in the programme. In both wiki case studies presented so far, academic staff carefully structured the wiki in advance to ensure success (Franklin & van Harmelen, 2007), thereby avoiding what some have described as the organic nature of wikis that can lead to a chaotic working space (Ciesielka, 2008).

A third case example of a wiki is Physiopedia (Lowe, Robertson, & Lowe, 2009), developed in order to provide an online reference source for health professionals, and a place where views of physiotherapists can be shared with each other. The owners also envisage that Physiopedia will be used by educators to support the learning of the physiotherapy students. Likewise, Kardong-Edgren et al. (2009) suggested that wikis could be used as a common place to post care plans or clinical worksheets for peer review Thus wikis support the work of online communities (Wenger, 1998), facilitating the exploration of ideas and the sharing of resources. Wikis are collaborative, with all engaging in the construction of knowledge (Boulos et al., 2006).

From the case examples we have provided for access, reflection and constructing knowledge, it is clear that ICTs can support fieldwork staff and students. It is important, however, also to consider some of the barriers and enablers of ICT use.

## BARRIERS AND ENABLERS TO USING ICTS

A number of studies cited in this chapter have identified the barriers and enablers to use of ICTs by students and fieldwork staff. We have organised these under structural and systemic, attitudinal, cultural and ethical use.

### Structural and Systemic

The ICTs discussed in this chapter are all computer-based. Ward and Moule (2007) found that nursing and allied health students often had little access to desktop computers during their fieldwork placements. Schaper and Pervan's (2007) survey of occupational therapists also identified inadequate access, with some respondents reporting that one computer was shared between up to 10 staff. Attitudes of staff to student use of shared resources can also act as a barrier (Ward & Moule, 2007), with students feeling reluctant or unable to ask for access. Even in situations where desktop computers are made available, their location appears the key to easy access. Gosling and Westbrook (2004) found that frequency of use of an online evidence system was higher by allied health professionals when the computers were located in close proximity to client treatment areas. Scott, Gilmour, and Fielden (2008) suggested that students modelled their behaviour on their fieldwork educators. If educators do not use ICTs in their everyday practice, it is unlikely that students will.

A separate but related issue which is little raised in the literature is the use of firewalls in health services and in some academic institutions to ensure the security of patient/client or other related data (Liu, May, Caelli, & Croll, 2007). These firewalls can prevent fieldwork staff and students using some of the Web 2.0 tools described in earlier sections of this chapter. Where access is a problem, one solution for student and fieldwork educator use may be the handheld personal digital assistant (PDA) (Bogossian, Kellett, & Mason, 2009), such as the Apple iPhone or Blackberry. However, for many countries the internet access costs when using PDAs are prohibitive. In such countries, students and fieldwork educators might be able to use their own private laptops in areas with wireless access within the facility.

### Attitudinal

Even in situations where access to ICTs is adequate, students and fieldwork staff may be reluctant users. Reluctance can stem from a lack of understanding of the relevance of ICTs to allied health professionals' practice (which includes fieldwork) (Levett-Jones et al., 2009) or because the health professional dislikes ICTs (Sandars & Schroter, 2007). In contrast, some may be aware of what is possible but still be reluctant because they have a lower self-efficacy (Schaper & Pervan, 2007; Levett-Jones, et al., 2009). People with lower self-efficacy expect to experience difficulty learning to use the tools, perhaps becoming so anxious that a barrier to learning is created as the learner feels overwhelmed and unable to learn. Still others may be aware of the possibilities but are hampered by a lack of skill (Lupiáñez-Villanueva, Mayer, & Torrent, 2009).

Although little can be done to address an individual's dislike of ICTs, exposure to what is possible and the advantages of ICTs may lead to a change in attitude. Articles in allied health professional newsletters, published research in academic journals, and chapters such as this can enhance readers' understanding not only of what might be possible and the benefits of use (Boulos & Wheeler, 2007), but also of how to get started. Hanson et al. (2008) helpfully described tools and strategies that Web 2.0 users can utilise to promote their digital content to those seeking these resources. Finally, a number of the articles cited in this chapter emphasise the need to embed digital information literacy in pre- and post-registration curricula with Skiba et al. (2008) calling for the merging of "informatics, telehealth, simulation and e-learning to create powerful learning environments" (p. 229).

*Cultural*

Allied health professionals may feel confident in the use of ICTs and have the necessary skills, yet they may question whether the time using ICTs is at the expense of working with the clients (Schaper & Pervan, 2007). Students have reported similar feelings, with Ward and Moule (2007) and Scott et al. (2008) finding that students felt guilty using ICTs, believing they should be engaged in hands-on learning while on placement. Students in the study of Bogossian et al. (2009) tended to limit their use of tablet PCs to when wards were quieter, usually during their night shift.

*Confidentiality and Privacy*

The last barrier to use is that of confidentiality and privacy. Allied health professionals (including students) are expected to maintain confidentiality of client information, but knowing how to do so online using some of the technologies introduced in this chapter can be challenging (Boulos et al.). The Healthcare Blogger Code of Ethics (2009, http://medbloggercode.com/) was designed to provide both readers and healthcare bloggers with a set of guidelines and standards for the maintenance of blogs. The presence of the Healthcare Blogger Code of Ethics logo on a blog assures the reader that the blogger aspires to a high ethical standard.

Privacy can be maintained by the use of usernames and passwords, providing restricted access (Erardi & Hartmann, 2008), or by using technologies such as wikis and blogs within proprietary learning management systems such as Blackboard, Moodle or WebCT. In these systems, online discussions can be made more secure as they can be accessed only by enrolled students and academic staff, but this can often exclude fieldwork educators. Finally, it falls to the "owner" or "editors" of these technologies to ensure that they know how to use the tools to manage the content posted (Boulos et al., 2006).

## SUMMARY

Although ICT use has proliferated in many professions, this has not been the case for health professionals who for the various reasons we have outlined, have given

ICTs minimal attention. As we have shown in this chapter, there have been few trials of the use of ICTs in fieldwork education, even fewer evaluations, and hence little evidence to inform ongoing developments. Thus our understanding of the value of these tools to support student learning in innovative or alternative fieldwork opportunities is definitely emergent (Skiba et al., 2008; Lemley & Burnham, 2009). In this chapter we have outlined and given examples of Web 1.0 technologies, along with the newer Web 2.0 tools. Where possible we have provided evidence for the value of these ICTs in supporting the learning community of students and fieldwork staff as they access information, reflect on what they are exposed to and construct new understandings. We have identified some of the structural or systematic, attitudinal, cultural and ethical barriers to use, and have also introduced enablers that can assist users to overcome the barriers. Finally, we close with the following quote from our medical colleague: "If the attitudinal wind of change is embraced and colleagues collectively combine their online knowledge, the clinical, educational, social and timely benefits are enormous" (Michael, 2009, p. 3). We hope that you will draw from this chapter to explore what is possible, to share it with your colleagues and to produce the research that will provide the evidence to support ongoing development.

## NOTES

1 Ethical approval granted by the Behavioural Research Ethics Board, University of British Columbia.
2 Development funded by British Columbia Ministry of Health through the Practice Education Innovation Fund, administered by the British Columbia Academic Health Council.

## REFERENCES

21st Century Information Fluency Project (2009). *21st Century information fluency*. Available: http://21cif. com/resources/difcore/index.html, accessed 20 October, 2009.

Abbott, P.A., & Coenen, A. (2008). Globalization and advances in information and communication technologies: The impact on nursing and health. *Nursing Outlook, 56*(5), 238–246.

Best, D. (2005). Exploring the roles of the clinical educator. In M. Rose & D. Best (Eds.), *Transforming practice through clinical education, professional supervision, and mentoring* (pp. 45–48). Edinburgh: Elsevier Churchill Livingstone.

Bogossian, F.E., Kellett, S.E.M., & Mason, B. (2009). The use of tablet PCs to access an electronic portfolio in the clinical setting: A pilot study using undergraduate nursing students. *Nurse Education Today, 29*(2), 246–253.

Boudreau, M.L. (2009). Is there a generation gap in occupational therapy? *Occupational Therapy Now, 11*(2), 16–18.

Boulos, M.N., Maramba, I., & Wheeler, S. (2006). Wikis, blogs and podcasts: A new generation of web-based tools for virtual collaborative clinical practice and education. *BMC Medical Education, 6*, 41.

Boulos, M.N.K., & Wheeler, S. (2007). The emerging Web 2.0 social software: An enabling suite of sociable technologies in health and health care education. *Health Information and Libraries Journal, 24*(1), 2–23.

Cadogan, M.D. (2009). Web 2.0 rollercoaster: A ride we should all take. *Emergency Medicine Australasia, 21*, 1–3.

Ciesielka, D. (2008). Using a wiki to meet graduate nursing education competencies in collaboration and community health. *Journal of Nursing Education, 47*(10), 473–476.

Erardi, L.K., & Hartmann, K. (2008). Blogs, wikis, and podcasts: Broadening our connections for communication, collaboration and continuing education. *OT Practice, 13*(9), CE-1-CE-7.

Franklin, T., & van Harmelen, M. (2007). *Web 2.0 for content for learning and teaching in higher education.* Available: http://staff.blog.ui.ac.id/harrybs/files/2008/10/web-2-for-content-for-learning-and-teaching-in-higher-education.pdf, accessed 26 October 2009.

Gosling, S.A., & Westbrook, J.I. (2004). Allied health professionals' use of online evidence: A survey of 790 staff working in the Australian public hospital system. *International Journal of Medical Informatics, 73*, 391–401.

Hanson, C., Thackeray, R., Barnes, M., Neiger, B., & McIntyre, E. (2008). Integrating web 2.0 in health education preparation and practice. *American Journal of Health Education, 39*, 157–166.

Healthcare Blogger Code of Ethics. (May 1, 2009). *Medical Blogs.* Available: http://medbloggercode.com/medical-blogs/, accessed 2 November 2009.

Kardong-Edgren, S.E., Oermann, M.H., Ha, Y., Tennant, M.N., Snelson, C., Hallmark, E., et al. (2009). Using a wiki in nursing education and research. *International Journal of Nursing Education Scholarship, 6*(1), 1–10.

Kassam, R., Drynan, D., MacLeod, E., Neufeld, L., & Tidball, G. (2008). *Contact.* Available: http://www.practiceeducation.ca/contact.html, accessed 30 October 2009.

Kessler, P., & Lund, C. (2004). Reflective journaling: Developing an online journal for distance education. *Nursing Education, 29*(1), 20–24.

Ladyshewsky, R.K., & Gardner, P. (2008). Peer assisted learning and blogging. A strategy to promote reflective practice during clinical fieldwork. *Australasian Journal of Educational Technology, 24*(3), 241–257.

Lemley, T., & Burnham, J.F. (2009). Brief communications: Web 2.0 tools in medical and nursing school curricula. *Journal of Medical Library Association, 97*(1), 50–52.

Levett-Jones, T., Kenny, R., Van der Riet, P., Hazelton, M., Kable, A., Bourgeois, S., et al. (2009). Exploring the information and communication technology competence and confidence of nursing students and their perception of its relevance to clinical practice. *Nurse Education Today, 29*(6), 612–616.

Liu, V., May, L., Caelli, W., & Croll, P. (2007). A sustainable approach to security and privacy in health information systems. *18th Australian Conference on Information Systems (ACIS '07).* Available: http://www.acis2007.usq.edu.au/assets/papers/51.pdf, accessed 31 October 2009.

Lowe, R., Robertson, E., & Lowe, T. (2009). *Physiopedia: About.* Available: http://www.physio-pedia.com/index.php5?title=Physiopedia:About, accessed 26 October 2009.

Lupiáñez-Villanueva, F., Mayer, M.A., & Torrent, J. (2009). Opportunities and challenges of Web 2.0 within the health care systems: An empirical exploration. *Informatics for Health and Social Care, 34*(3), 117–126.

McGee, J.B., & Begg, M. (2008). What medical educators need to know about "Web 2.0". *Medical Teacher, 30*(2), 164–169.

Michael, D.C. (2009). Web 2.0 rollercoaster: A ride we should all take. *Emergency Medicine Australasia, 21*(1), 1–3.

Oblinger, D.G., & Oblinger, J. (2005). Is it age or IT: First steps toward understanding the net generation. In D.G. Oblinger & J.L. Oblinger (Eds.), *Educating the net generation* (pp. 2.1–2.20). Available: http://www.educause.edu/ir/library/pdf/pub7101.pdf, accessed 30 October 2009.

Palloff, R., & Pratt, K. (2007). Online learning communities in perspective. In R. Luppicini (Ed.), *Online learning communities* (pp. 3–15). Charlotte, NC: Information Age Publishing.

Penman, M. (2008). The use of blogging to support professional learning. *Health Care and Informatics Review Online, 6.* Available: http://www.hinz.org.nz/journal/2008/6, accessed 26 October 2009.

Prensky, M. (2001). Digital natives, digital immigrants. *On the Horizon, 9*(5), 1–6. Available: http://www.marcprensky.com/writing/Prensky%20-%20Digital%20Natives,%20Digital%20Immigrants%20-%20Part1.pdf, accessed 30 October 2009.

Richard, L.F. (2008). Exploring connections between theory and practice: Stories from fieldwork supervisors. *Occupational Therapy in Mental Health, 24*(2), 154–175.

Sandars, J., & Haythornthwaite, C. (2007). New horizons for e-learning in medical education: Ecological and Web 2.0 perspectives. *Medical Teacher, 29*(4), 307–310.

Sandars, J., & Schroter, S. (2007). Web 2.0 technologies for undergraduate and postgraduate medical education: An online survey. *Postgraduate Medical Journal, 83*, 759–762.

Schaper, L.K., & Pervan, G.P. (2007). ICT and OTs: A model of information and communication technology acceptance and utilisation by occupational therapists. *International Journal of Medical Informatics, 76*(Suppl. 1), S212–S221.

Scott, S.D., Gilmour, J., & Fielden, J. (2008). Nursing students and internet health information. *Nurse Education Today, 28*(8), 993–1001.

Skiba, D.J., Connors, H.R., & Jeffries, P.R. (2008). Information technologies and the transformation of nursing education. *Nursing Outlook, 56*, 225–230.

Tapscott, D. (2009). *Grown up digital*. New York: McGraw Hill.

Villeneuve, M., Jamieson, M., Donnelly, C., White, C., & Lava, J. (in press). A comparison of interactive discussions and reflective blogs as methods to facilitate theory to practice learning. *Academic Exchange Quarterly, 13*(4), Electronic Publication #24. Available: http://www.rapid inte llect.com/AEQweb/redpast.htm#09win, accessed 8 January 2010.

Ward, R., & Moule, P. (2007). Supporting pre-registration students in practice: A review of current ICT use. *Nurse Education Today, 27*, 60–67.

Wenger, E. (1998). *Communities of practice: Learning as a social system*. "Systems Thinker". Available: http://www.co-i-l.com/coil/knowledge-garden/cop/lss.shtml, accessed 1 October 2009.

Young, P., Moore, E., Griffiths, G., Raine, R., Stewart, R., Cownie, M., et al. (2010). Help is just a text away: The use of short message service texting to provide an additional means of support for health care students during practice placements. *Nurse Education Today, 30*(2), 118–123.

*Merrolee Penman MA(Educ)*
*School of Occupational Therapy*
*Otago Polytechnic, New Zealand*

*Catherine Donnelly MSc*
*School of Rehabilitation Therapy*
*Queen's University, Canada*

*Donna Drynan Med OT*
*Occupational Science and Occupational Therapy Department*
*University of British Columbia, Canada*

LESTER E JONES, MERILYN MCKENZIE AND MAN-SANG WONG

# 15. THE USE OF VIDEOCONFERENCE TECHNOLOGY

*Creating Innovative and Interactive Fieldwork Education Experiences*

Health professional fieldwork experiences commonly involve a clinician supervising one or two students with occasional face-to-face support from university-based staff. Such experiences are resource intensive and increasingly unsustainable due to a high demand (Baldrey Currens & Bithell, 2003). As well, students often have limited exposure to rural and remote experiences, or highly specialised experiences, simply due to the lack of available fieldwork placements in these settings. Students on fieldwork placement may also feel isolated from the staff at the teaching institution, especially when it is difficult to organise face-to-face meetings for support or additional tuition.

In this chapter, we present two case studies that demonstrate the use of video-conference technology (VCT) to enhance, and in some cases, replace traditional fieldwork experiences. VCT provides a reliable and increasingly common mechanism for remote real-time communication. When applied to fieldwork experiences, a number of benefits become apparent. First, a large group of students can be exposed to the fieldwork environment simultaneously. This means that the students receive a relatively standardised experience which they can easily share. Second, students can obtain this experience within familiar surroundings and construct knowledge within an established learning "community". As well, university-based educators can adapt the learning experience to emphasise the integration of theory into practice.

The term eClinic is used here to describe fieldwork experiences where video-conference technology has been implemented to replace a traditional fieldwork placement or experience. The term could be used to describe other information and communication technology (ICT), but this is not explored in any detail in this chapter. The other use of VCT that is explored is for the enhancement of communication in a traditional practice placement. In particular, VCT can provide benefits to the relationships and interaction of university-based educators, students and the clinicians supervising the students.

CASE STUDY 1: USING VIDEOCONFERENCING TECHNOLOGY TO ALLOW
OBSERVATION OF A CLINICIAN/CLIENT INTERACTION BY STUDENTS
IN A DISTANT LOCATION (ECLINIC)

A successful model for fieldwork education using videoconferencing was developed in the School of Physiotherapy at La Trobe University, with funding from the

*L. McAllister et al., (eds.), Innovations in Allied Health Fieldwork*
*Education: A Critical Appraisal, 167–175.*

Clinical Placement Innovation Projects initiative (Victorian Government Department of Human Services, 2007). Twenty-two second year students located at the University's Bundoora campus experienced a number of real-time videoconference presentations. This involved a client being assessed and treated by a physiotherapist, over a period of a week, at the University's Bendigo campus, 150km away. Students had pre-assessment information emailed to them and were encouraged to make collaborative decisions about the structure of the client assessment, treatment selection and progression. The videoconference format enabled them to ask questions of the client and therapist to assist their decision making. Clinically-oriented tutorials were also provided and students were encouraged to keep a reflective journal to document and develop their learning. The experience was evaluated positively by students, academics and clinicians. The success of this project significantly reduced the burden on university-based and clinically-based staff. Normally they would have had to identify and resource 22 fieldwork placements. Students also benefited through reduced travel time and costs.

This approach to eClinic has proven sustainable and is continuing with larger groups. A recent implementation involved three clinicians, three clients and 135 students. The venue for the videoconferencing host site was a practical class-room equipped with resources to support the clinical interactions and mobile video-conferencing equipment. The remote site for the videoconferencing was a large lecture theatre with a large projection screen. Roving microphones enabled students to interact with the client and the clinician before, during, and at the end of the sessions. Seven real-time sessions, each lasting between 40 and 60 minutes, were delivered across a 4-day period. A staff member from the School of Physiotherapy operated the camera and positioned the microphone to capture clinician–client interaction during assessment and treatment. There was also at least one university-based educator at the remote site.

For students in the remote location, the videoconferencing sessions formed one part of their learning experience. In these sessions, they were able to witness the subjective assessment and physical examination for each client, and then at least one follow-up treatment session for each client. They then used breakout rooms to explore the conditions the clients had presented, document the assessment or treatment process they had witnessed, and search for supporting evidence. For this additional component to the eClinic, students worked in groups of six, each group having a laptop computer with a wireless connection to the University's intranet. Therefore they were able to access electronic library resources. It was important that students had a task to complete in response to the eClinic. The task set included a group submission of completed documentation of the assessment and treatment processes, and a reflective comment on the learning experience.

## ECLINICS AS A STRATEGY FOR EARLY FIELDWORK EXPERIENCES

### Gaining Fieldwork Experiences in a Safe and Familiar Environment

Early fieldwork experiences can be stressful and intimidating for students. Settling into a new environment can take time and often needs a considered socialisation process, as well as well-organised orientation to new process and surroundings (Worrall, 2007). Importantly, good learning environments create a sense of belonging in students (Worrall, 2007; Levett-Jones, Lathlean, Higgins, & McMillan, 2009).

An eClinic may reduce the stress of fieldwork experiences. Being exposed to the complexity of the fieldwork setting, with an established peer group, in a non-threatening environment, allows optimal learning to take place. The motivation and therefore the attention of the students can be directed and focused on clinical issues as opposed to socialisation issues such as feeling accepted (Levett-Jones & Lathlean, 2008).

*Learning to Integrate Theoretical Knowledge in Practice*

The integration of best research evidence into fieldwork is a common concern. Some authors have attempted to shed light on this conundrum by highlighting the changing influences on health professional education, and fieldwork, and the importance of non-propositional (or "craft") knowledge in developing practice (Higgs & Titchen, 2001; Higgs, 2009). The literature on evidence-based medicine stresses the need to consider best research evidence and clinical expertise, and the client's expectations and values (Sackett, Straus, Richardson, Rosenberg, & Haynes, 2000). The eClinic approach allows students to engage with the complexity of the clinical interaction, to begin to value the clinician's skill set and experience and, perhaps most importantly, to establish an insight into the client's expectations and values – all at a safe distance without the burden of responsibility for client care. They can then pursue the best evidence and debate how, or whether, it can be applied to the particular client they have encountered.

Advantageously, students can develop a culture of using best evidence to support clinical reasoning, using the time, resources and guidance available in a well-designed eClinic. In small teams, they can work through the cognitive process of deciding what to do next and can explore multiple options without the constraints caused by actually having to apply their ideas. Although this can lead to unrefined ideas, mainly due to the students' lack of fieldwork experience, it promotes the initiation of a reasoning process that incorporates best research evidence. As well, they can establish a clinical reasoning process that is not biased due the influence of the clinician's expertise and preference – which arguably does occur in face to face fieldwork education (for an interesting digression see Webb, Fawns, & Harré, 2009).

*Guiding Student Focus in Distant Fieldwork Experiences*

Observation of clinical interactions often forms an early part of a fieldwork place-ment, probably as a way of easing the student into practice. Arguably, this type of learning is more effective later when students are more aware of relevant cues. Early in a placement, the students may be distracted by the complexity of apparatus and equipment, or the novelty of noises and smells.

Staff prompts, prior to or during the sessions, can assist in establishing the focus of the learning experience. This can help the students to consider the relevant components of the process without being distracted by unimportant information. Indeed, the staff observing a session may provide a more comprehensive and objective review about an interaction than the clinician involved could do.

## Activities and Resources to Support Development of Knowledge and Skills

Resources to support student learning vary across fieldwork placements. Many sites still have limited computer availability and internet access. Opportunities for kinaesthetic learning – outside of direct client contact – may be limited due to space or the lack of a willing partner to model as a client.

To optimise the eClinics, opportunities can be created for students to pursue enquiries and to practise techniques. Students given well-defined tasks, relevant to the interaction they have witnessed, can explore important activities such as planning and recording assessments and treatments, considering differential diagnoses, writing referral letters and mastering clinical skills.

Lectures or "lectorials" can be timetabled around the videoconference transmissions to highlight supporting theoretical knowledge and to prime students for when particular principles or concepts might be relevant and important. Presentations might be generic, on topics such as clinical reasoning, evidence-based practice and outcome measures, or be condition- or disease-specific.

Furthermore, access to rooms for small group work, preferably with internet access, will support the learning process and allow students to explore their understanding through discussion. Sets of questions created by staff can be helpful for promoting the exploration of a topic, but allowing students the opportunity to pursue their own questions may engage them in deeper learning (Biggs & Tang, 2007). Set questions might best be used to set the scene, with the answers then forming the basis of a resource that can be developed during other fieldwork education experiences.

### eCLINICS NEED TO BE FLEXIBLE

## Creating a Flexible Learning Experience

One of the challenges of the eClinic process as a learning model is that it is based on real-time activities which are vulnerable to changing circumstances. Client or staff illness or technology problems can lead to planned transmissions being delayed. It is necessary, therefore, to develop learning activities that can be easily re-scheduled. As well, the students' level of knowledge about a health condition will depend on the stage of the curriculum they have completed. Thus the challenge is to prepare learning activities that are flexible enough to accommodate last-minute changes but remain meaningful and worthwhile.

Biggs and Tang (2007) applied an organisational climate theory to education, suggesting that a rule-based, highly structured learning experience can restrict student learning by raising students' anxiety. An approach that allows students collaborative time and the choice to swap between tasks gives them some decision-making power and the chance to explore how they will derive the most from the learning experiences. In terms of eClinics, this second approach allows an intrinsic flexibility in that the students can decide how best to spend the available time outside of the videoconference transmission. This may include some structured tasks that have been proposed by staff or the pursuit of something else the student or team of students identifies as more profitable. Evaluation of a recent eClinic highlighted the need to get this right. In that instance a client withdrew at the last moment, creating several timetable gaps that some students felt wasted their time.

*Staffing and Timetabling Issues*

To support a "fluid" timetable that might need to change suddenly, staffing needs to be considered carefully. At the transmitting site, someone other than the clinician should be responsible for the technology. At the receiving sites, a staff member should be present to instruct students, monitor their behaviour and monitor the video-link. Staff allocation for supervision of the group work provides the greatest challenge, as a sudden change to the timetable may mean that insufficient staff are available. Promoting independent learning among the student groups can resolve this problem to some degree.

When timetabling the sessions around the videoconference transmissions, it can be useful to create blocks of time that can be easily relocated. For example, transmission of a clinician/client/student interaction generally takes 60 minutes, so if other teaching tasks, such as small group work, are also planned for 60 minutes, there can be a direct swap as the need arises.

*Student Engagement*

Evaluation of an eClinic experience, involving approximately 90 students, indicated they perceived their interactions with both clinicians and clients to be positive (MacKenzie, unpublished data). This was confirmed by observations of student behaviour towards the client and clinician, with students being respectful and appropriate in their interactions, but also quite personable. As well, clients seemed quite responsive to student questioning and it was not uncommon for the client to include remarks that wished the students well in their studies. Although it might be an overstatement to suggest that this interaction is a representation of a learning community or community of practice (Wenger, 1998; Rogers, 2000), the shared responsibility of the students, the client and the clinician in supporting the learning experience may reflect an element of mutual engagement.

Advice on educational engagement suggests that students should be challenged to use their existing knowledge but also given opportunities to explore new contexts (Wenger, 1998). University-based educators could then take advantage of this experience and use the real-life examples from the eClinic when introducing students to the equipment or health conditions in the planned curriculum.

The opportunity to see a physiotherapist in practice was also considered to be beneficial for engaging students. For many, this opportunity to observe an expert may have been a new experience, as only some students had completed formal fieldwork placements. Students also reported that they found the opportunities for comparison of the their group tasks with clinicians' decision making particularly valuable (e.g., devising a treatment plan) (MacKenzie, unpublished data).

## ECLINICS ALLOW ACCESS TO A BROAD RANGE OF REAL-LIFE, REAL-TIME FIELDWORK

### Opportunities for Remote, Unique and Specialist Fieldwork Experiences

The eClinic approach need not be restricted to early fieldwork experiences. Through such experiences students could obtain an insight into the diversity of health care contexts that exist. For example, it has been reported that not all Australian physiotherapy students experience a rural placement. This is due to personal restrictions to living away from their city base and also due to the limited number of placements offered (Dean et al., 2009). The eClinic experience might also help to introduce and attract students to rural practice, where often there is a chronic shortage of health professionals (Dean et al., 2009). Similarly, specialist clinics have only a limited number of placements to offer. eClinics hosted by these sites would allow a greater number of students to experience the specifics of these often unique settings.

### A Prelude to Telemedicine and Telerehabilitation

There has been an increase in the use of videoconferencing technology and other ICT in rural and remote settings for health purposes. Growing areas of health service delivery include telemedicine and telerehabilitation. The videoconference transmissions with eClinics demonstrate to students the potential for interactive technology in healthcare transactions. Students attending eClinics may be more comfortable employing this technology in their future practice.

### Videoconferencing as a Strategy for Supporting Traditional Fieldwork Experiences

Where students are placed in remote fieldwork settings but linked to the University by VCT, it is reasonable to suggest that when problems arise, resolution can be promoted by timely interaction that can be facilitated between a university-based educator, the student and the fieldwork educator. This potential for early intervention means that students can have problems resolved quickly, reducing their stress and allowing them to re-engage with the important elements of the learning experience.

When university-based educators have ready access to real-time communication, opportunities arise for integration of university-based learning with clinic-based learning. Students involved in fieldwork experience can explore, in real time, how theoretical principles support fieldwork, by interacting with the academics who introduced the principles in lectures or tutorials.

CASE STUDY 2: USING VIDEOCONFERENCE TECHNOLOGY TO
PROMOTE COMMUNICATION BETWEEN UNIVERSITY AND FIELDWORK
EDUCATION UNIT IN THE TRAINING PROGRAMME FOR PROSTHETISTS
AND ORTHOTISTS AT THE HONG KONG POLYTECHNIC UNIVERSITY

As previously mentioned, incorporating theoretical concepts and principles into fieldwork approaches is a fundamental aim in the education and training of health professionals. There is concern, however, as to whether all students during their fieldwork placements are given quality time and enough clinical exposure to prepare them to practise competently and independently after their graduation. This case study describes an approach in which VCT was employed to enhance the integration of theory to practice, despite the limited duration of fieldwork placements and limited staffing. In particular, VCT was used to enhance the range of students' fieldwork experiences, their clinical reasoning and their problem-solving skills.

In this project, a telecommunication network system (multi-point communication unit, MCU) was set up to enhance clinical communications among students, fieldwork educators and university-based lecturers during the fieldwork placement periods. With the system in place, the physical distance between participants became irrelevant. The system allowed on-site student case presentations to be televised to university-based educators and to students and fieldwork educators located in different fieldwork education units (FWEUs).

To cover all the fieldwork placement locations, broadband connections were set up in the seven FWEUs located in seven integrated hospitals. Consideration of data protection and privacy issues was essential in consultation with hospital management and, to alleviate their concerns, the broadband connections were separated from the corresponding hospital systems. This enabled permissions to be granted.

Purchase of notebook computers and webcams, and installation of broadband connections were required. A multi-point communication unit (MCU) was then set up. First the NetMeeting software was trialled, providing the functions of audio–video, chat box, whiteboard, file sharing and transfer, but with relatively low security. The Information Technology Service of the university then suggested using Macro Media Flash, which could offer audio–video, chat box and swift file sharing. It provided fewer functions but with higher security, and was thus adopted.

A student leader selected from each FWEU was trained in using the software and taking care of the notebook computer. The leaders were also responsible for training the other students attached in the same FWEU. Students had to thoroughly prepare their cases in S.O.A.P. clinical documentation format (subjective, objective, action and plan of treatment) and submit PowerPoint presentations 2 days before the VCT transmissions. This allowed for conversion to swift files for compatibility with Macro Media Flash. The swift files were then shared on-line.

At the scheduled time, all students from the seven FWEUs would enter the on-line platform with known website address and password. Students were selected randomly to present a case on-line (approximately 10 cases at each teleconference). Each case lasted approximately 20 minutes (10 min for presentation and 10 min for discussion). The presenters were asked questions by other students, university-based educators and fieldwork educators. If necessary, students showed their own prosthetic/orthotic designs in front of the video camera. During the conferences, only the presenter's microphone was on, to prevent noisy echo, so questions had to be posted in the chat box. This made it easier for tracing the sequence of the questions to be answered. The presenters then replied verbally to the questions.

A purpose-designed student survey and a focus group discussion with student participants were conducted to evaluate the acceptance of the system. In this pilot study, the telecommunication network system was generally accepted by the students and teaching staff as adding value to the fieldwork.

The telecommunication system has now become a regular communication tool for fieldwork placements. Subsequently an eClinic was organised, where fieldwork educators in different FWEUs presented special clinical cases to the class. The system was also used among fieldwork educators and university-based educators for coordination of fieldwork placements and sharing of teaching experiences.

With advances in on-line technology, Adobe-Acrobat Connect Professional is currently used as it can provide even better audio and video quality. Moreover, it allows instant conversion of PowerPoint files, and no software installation is required. Users simply click on the provided URL at the scheduled time. This is proving to be more user-friendly and versatile.

## CONCLUDING COMMENTS

The benefits of fieldwork experiences for students include exposure to current practice, opportunity for integrating theory and practice, ability to develop competence in fieldwork performance, and the further enhancement of skills and confidence (Rodger et al., 2008). Well organised eClinics have the potential to offer experiences that target all these valued areas, but are naturally limited when compared to the specific benefits achieved through "hands on" experiences. In addition, teamwork, collaboration and peer-learning can be achieved through prescribed activities as part of an eClinic, but the development of autonomy and independence in practice needs fieldwork experience with direct responsibility of client care.

Our experiences so far suggest that eClinics are valuable for early fieldwork experiences. Videoconferencing offers university-based support to students who are placed at remote locations. Both these approaches contribute to safe, non-threatening learning experiences. Furthermore, both reduce the resource demand that these fieldwork experiences normally create.

There is clearly potential to use VCT to exploit the limited opportunities to observe and interact with specialist clinics. As well, VCT can provide reciprocal opportunities for city and rural educational and fieldwork institutions, to share their experiences and support.

## ACKNOWLEDGEMENTS

Thanks go to Andrea Bruder, Karen Donald, Rowena Jeans, Helen McBurney and Nora Shields, and to Janice McKay and Helen Edwards, for their contribution to the initial development and ongoing support of the eClinic experiences at La Trobe University, and the videoconferencing project at The Hong Kong Polytechnic

University, respectively. The authors would also like to acknowledge the funding agencies that supported the initial projects, namely the Victorian Government Department of Human Services and the University Grant Committee, Hong Kong.

## REFERENCES

Baldry Currens, J.A., & Bithell, C.P. (2003). The 2:1 clinical placement model: Perceptions of clinical educators and students. *Physiotherapy, 89*(4), 204–218.

Biggs, J., & Tang, C. (2007). Teaching according to how students learn. In J. Biggs & C. Tang (Eds.), *Teaching for quality learning at university* (pp. 16–49). Maidenhead: McGraw Hill.

Dean, C.M., Stark, A.M., Gates, C.A., Czerniec, S.A., Hobbs, C.L., Bullock, L.D., & Kolodziej, I. (2009). A profile of physiotherapy clinical education. *Australian Health Review, 33*(1), 38–46.

Higgs, J. (2009). Ways of knowing for clinical practice. In C. Delany & E. Molloy (Eds.), *Clinical education in the health professions* (pp. 25–37). Chatswood, NSW: Elsevier Churchill Livingstone.

Higgs, J., & Titchen, A. (2001). Rethinking the practice-knowledge interface in an uncertain world: A model for practice development. *British Journal of Occupational Therapy, 64*(11), 526–533.

Levett-Jones, T., & Lathlean, J. (2008). Belongingness: A prerequisite for nursing students' clinical learning. *Nurse Education in Practice, 8*, 103–111.

Levett-Jones, T., Lathlean, J., Higgins, I., & McMillan, J. (2009). Staff-student relationships and their impact on nursing students' belongingness and learning. *Journal of Advanced Nursing, 65*(2), 316–324.

Rodger, S., Webb, G., Devitt, L., Gilbert, J., Wrightson, P., & McMeekan, J. (2008). Clinical education and practice placements in the allied health professions: An international perspective. *Journal of Allied Health, 37*(1), 53–62.

Rogers, J. (2000). Communities of practice: A framework for fostering coherence in virtual learning communities. *Educational Technology & Society, 3*(3), 384–392.

Sackett, D.L., Straus, S.E., Richardson, W.S., Rosenberg, W., & Haynes, R.B. (2000). *Evidence-based medicine: How to practice and teach EBM* (2nd ed.). Edinburgh: Churchill Livingstone.

Victorian Government Department of Human Services (2007). *Clinical placement innovation projects initiative.* Available: http://www.health.vic.gov.au/workforce/placements/innovation/innovation-projects, accessed 25 August 2009.

Webb, G., Fawns, R., & Harré, R. (2009). Professional identities and communities of practice. In C. Delany & E. Molloy (Eds.), *Clinical education in the health professions* (pp. 53–69). Chatswood, NSW: Elsevier Churchill Livingstone.

Wenger, E. (1998). *Communities of practice: Learning, meaning, and identity.* Cambridge: Cambridge University Press.

Worrall, K. (2007). Orientation to student placements: Needs and benefits. *Paediatric Nursing, 19*(1), 31–33.

*Lester E Jones MScMed(PM) and Merilyn MacKenzie GradDip(ResMethods)*
*School of Physiotherapy*
*La Trobe University, Australia*

*Man-Sang Wong PhD*
*Dept of Health Technology and Informatics*
*Hong Kong Polytechnic University, Hong Kong*

# SECTION V: ALTERNATIVES TO PRACTICE
# IN THE FIELD

# 16. ALTERNATIVES TO FIELDWORK EDUCATION

*Including Service Learning and Case-Based Teaching*

In this chapter we examine service learning (SL) as an alternative to the traditional model of fieldwork education and case-based teaching as a possible substitute for fieldwork. Fieldwork education is seen as fundamental to the educational process that advances healthcare students from novice learner to entry-level practitioner who will ultimately achieve the seamless synthesis of conceptual knowledge and clinical reasoning which the "professional artistry" of the expert practitioner personifies (Paterson, Higgs, & Wilcox, 2005). Fieldwork education is typically exemplified as a student mentored by an experienced practitioner who models best practice and facilitates the integration of didactically acquired knowledge and clinical skills into professional behaviours and competent skills (Sherer, Morris, Graham, & White, 2006). However, the challenges of providing students with quality fieldwork education experiences have resulted in educators critically examining such education (American Physical Therapy Association (APTA), 1998; Casares, Bradley, Jaffee, & Lee, 2003; Kirke, Layton, & Sim, 2007; McAllister, 2007). The need to examine how field-work education needs are met is driven by a lack of placements due to workforce shortages and changes in healthcare staffing patterns and service delivery. This place-ment shortage is exacerbated by changes such as healthcare institutions expecting reimbursement for student supervision, increases in the number of programs and enrolments resulting in competition for a limited number of placements, and the narrow definitions of fieldwork education in accreditation and professional licensure requirements.

*Fieldwork Education and Pedagogical Models: Alternatives and Dilemmas*

There is no single solution to placement shortages. Some educators argue for a move away from the dependency on traditional practice areas for fieldwork education and direct mentoring of one practitioner per student (Martin & Edwards, 1998). Others recommend that students should have opportunities to develop practice competencies in more varied settings, and for greater continuity between the didactic and skills components of healthcare education (APTA, 1998; Stansfield, 2005). To be able to act on these recommendations it is useful to conceptualise allied health education as a continuum of university-based learning and fieldwork education, rather than maintain a contrived dichotomy between education in academic and fieldwork

*L. McAllister et al., (eds.), Innovations in Allied Health Fieldwork
Education: A Critical Appraisal, 179–188.*
© *2010 Sense Publishers. All rights reserved.*

education settings. This stance prompts us to be proactive rather than reactive to placement shortages, and less likely to view the traditional fieldwork education model as a gold standard. We are freed of the restraints imposed by how we currently conceptualise fieldwork education, to recognise that there are many potential educational activities that can achieve the learning objectives associated with fieldwork education. We also are more likely to acknowledge and explore more diverse learning environments.

Many initiatives in fieldwork education (e.g. different strategies, formats, and pedagogical models) can be used to facilitate the acquisition of skills and integration of knowledge and practice behaviours and skills. These can be divided into two broad categories: (i) alternative fieldwork education placements and (ii) classroom-based pedagogical models that are regarded as possible alternatives to fieldwork education.

*Alternative Fieldwork Education Placements: Service Learning (SL)*

Many initiatives have been developed to increase fieldwork education opportunities. These have included a restructuring of traditional placements by using different supervision models such as engaging students in peer to peer learning and group supervision (Farrow, Gaiptman, & Rudman, 2000; Aitken, Menaker, & Barsky, 2001; Stern & Rone-Adams, 2006). Similarly, university healthcare programs have developed clinical units that provide mainstream services within the university or a community agency to provide fieldwork education setting for students. However, the most innovative initiatives are the truly "alternative" fieldwork education placements that are diverse, often occur in emerging areas of practice, and are based on new pedagogical models such as SL. They are developed through community outreach programming and often involve services for at-risk populations (e.g. persons who are homeless, or underserved populations). Significantly, models such as SL placements represent a cognitive and organisational shift away from traditional fieldwork education.

Service learning is designed to "augment classroom teaching with real life experiences" through intentionally selected collaborative projects (Greene & Diehm, 1995, p. 54). It particularly meets the learning objectives of early and later levels of fieldwork. At an early level (initial), SL addresses students' introductory learning objectives of developing professional communication and interpersonal skills, having exposure to clinical populations and having opportunities to engage in basic clinical skills development. It is relevant again at an advanced level when students have demonstrated proficiency in basic skills and the emphasis of their learning has shifted to specific areas of expertise and more independent practice. The expectations of these students are that they will engage in relatively independent practice and advanced professional activities (e.g. advocacy), assume consultancy roles (e.g. program development or program evaluation), and seek positions of leadership. At the same time, SL contributes to a community, an agency, or underserved population and builds partnerships between universities and their communities (Cauley et al., 2001; Village, 2006).

*Principles and Format of SL*

The goal of SL is to provide optimal learning through the dynamic pursuit and integration of knowledge concurrently with application of that learning in a community setting (Cauley et al., 2001; Hansen et al., 2007). It pairs an academic course's learning objectives with a fieldwork education placement in which students meet a community need. The setting and learning activities reinforce and integrate the content of the academic course as well as provide learning related to core principles of healthcare practice such as cultural awareness, integrity and professionalism (Greene & Deihm, 1995; Seifer, 1998).

In SL the priority is students' learning goals (Greene & Deihm, 1995). It is this explicit focus on student learning and intentional selection of a community need to meet the objectives of a course that distinguishes SL from other experiential or community projects that are steeped in the philosophy of volunteerism. The first component of SL is the development of a syllabus and course learning objectives that would be significantly enhanced by experiential learning and would have previously been met in a traditional fieldwork education placement. Faculty/fieldwork educators, with community stakeholders, are responsible for identifying a need that also meets the course objectives, and this service is then embedded in the course. The order of course development is important; course content and objectives, then SL learning activities are developed, instead of making a community need fit into a course. It is important to ensure the parameters of the students' SL activities are clearly stipulated so that the experience meets the educational and accreditation specifications for fieldwork education hours.

A successful SL relationship between university and agency requires ongoing commitment by all involved and is usually formalised in a memorandum of understanding or affiliation agreement. It must be flexible and responsive to the needs of all stakeholders so that it can evolve with the inevitable changes that occur in both organisations. Attention to detail and being cognisant of the pedagogical principles of this model ensure the quality of both the students' learning experiences/ outcomes and the service provided.

The second component of SL is the teaching dimension. This involves attending to the educational processes that will facilitate students' learning of new knowledge and skills through classroom teaching and learning, and the application through service. Students engage in reflective exercises designed to link service experiences with course content. In these exercises they reflect on the clinical reasoning they use, their attitudes, and self-evaluation of their actions and interactions with community participants. These assignments and any evaluations must be congruent with the pedagogical model underpinning the program (Vroman & MacRae, 1999).

A core classroom activity that facilitates shared learning is student story-telling, a process akin to the narrative reasoning of practitioners who tell stories and reflect on their practice with peers. These learning activities deepen students' understanding, translating knowledge and principles of their profession into intentional tangible actions and behaviours that they will later associate with effective practice and self-evaluation. A critical outcome is a realisation that the professional knowledge used in practice is greater than the sum of the component parts described and learned in the classroom (Vroman et al., in press).

The third component of SL is service. It requires a mutual understanding of the education and service goals and deciding how and what services students can realistically provide that will also meet the learning objectives at their current educational level. Similarly the responsibilities of both parties need to be established. Clear expectations and definition of roles enhance the likelihood of success for all parties. The reciprocity of learning between students and service recipients challenges negative stereotypes, modifies attitudes, and subtly shifts the balance of power so that students realise that what they receive from the service recipients is greater than what they give. They experience mutuality and respect – the ingredients of the therapeutic relationship.

We provide here an exemplar of SL. It was introduced by the occupational therapy (OT) program at the University of New Hampshire and the Krempels Foundation, and now includes three other allied health professions (social work, speech language pathology and recreation therapy).

*A Multidisciplinary Consumer-Based Program for Adults with Acquired Brain Injuries (ABI)*

This SL program began as a collaborative project between the Krempels Foundation, whose mission is to support the needs of survivors of ABI, and the occupational therapy faculty. The OT program was looking for a community level I (first placement) SL program that would provide students with an opportunity to develop and lead groups. The Foundation had identified a need for services that would facilitate community re-integration for individuals with ABI. The outcome is a consumer-based program that emphasises the health, wellness, and empowerment of its members through meaningful participation in their community.[1] Members participate in structured groups and individual activities, 3 days a week. The groups are designed to improve communication, explore interests, build friendships, receive emotional support, connect with resources, and engage in advocacy and community education about ABI.

The OT SL program objectives include understanding individuals as occupational beings, needs assessment and program planning in community settings, group theory and group process, planning and implementing functional group activities, verbal and written communication skills, individual and goal setting, and group leadership skills, as well as the development/demonstration of professional behaviours.

Three teams of eight students spend one day a week for a semester at the community program working with individuals on goal setting, program development, and planning and facilitating groups that aim to improve independence, facilitate activities that promote community re-integration and improve quality of life. The reciprocity among members and students is a consistent and powerful outcome. Members gain self-esteem through their contributions (formal and informal) to students' learning (e.g. presentations to the students). Students gain respect for the members and discover client-centred practice as a tangible set of behaviours and attitudes.

These clinical hours meet the criteria of a level I fieldwork education placement. Initially supervision was provided by OT faculty. Now the program has an inter-disciplinary healthcare team (including two OTs) which provides group supervision to all the allied healthcare students. The faculty who provide the classroom-based teaching periodically observe students and attend supervision sessions and, in the case of the program's OTs, complete the American Occupational Therapy Association Level I fieldwork education student evaluation.

## Evidence in Support of SL and Challenges

SL programs have been shown to shape students' attitudes, increase interest in specific practice areas (e.g. geriatrics), enhance clinical reasoning and reflective practice, and expose students to both diverse and/or underserved populations (Hansen et al., 2007; Hoppes, Bender, & DeGrace, 2005). A variety of supervision models are used in SL; indeed, the uniqueness of many placements necessitates flexibility in how supervision is construed, such as onsite mentoring by a professional of a different discipline in collaboration with an offsite fieldwork educator or faculty member. The lack of direct supervision or on-site supervision by a professional of the same discipline is a source of criticism of SL fieldwork. The counter-argument is that students with more control and responsibility demonstrate more initiative, confidence, and independence (Baxter & Gray, 2001).

Students work closely with peers in SL, sharing and problem solving together in class and as teams in community settings. This process helps students to interpret the meaning of their collective experiences in the broader context of professional practice and facilitates professional acculturation. Both are important dimensions of fieldwork education. Also, interacting with students from other professions enhances their multidisciplinary awareness of respective roles in service delivery.

## CLASSROOM-BASED PEDAGOGICAL MODELS: SIMULATIONS AS AN ALTERNATIVE TO FIELDWORK

This second category is defined by initiatives that strengthen experiential learning in curricula. All represent a concerted attempt by academic programs to partner with practitioners and to infuse the behavioural elements of practice into the classroom through active, participatory, teaching and evaluation methods. They emphasise clinical reasoning and clinical skills competencies that explicitly integrate knowledge and practice throughout the curricula (Neistadt, 1998; Hoben, Varley, & Cox, 2007). Teaching strategies include case-based teaching (e.g. paper cases, simulated clients), and teaching in clinical skills classrooms equipped with observation mirrors, audio-visual recording technology and robotic simulators. They may also include curriculum designs such as problem-based learning. Given the limited availability of placements, these initiatives may be considered as alternatives to fieldwork education, especially if they are demonstrated to achieve the same educational outcomes.

In terms of its place in the overall scheme of students' education, classroom-based experiential learning is not considered "clinical hours" by professional accreditation agencies because the time typically does not involve hands-on or face-to-face client contact. It is, however, recognised as "focused clinical teaching", acceptable to some accreditation agencies, and intentionally moves students through the stages of novice learner to novice-in-transition through to developing practitioner ready to fully utilise traditional fieldwork.

Students learn from their perceptions of what they have observed or experienced (Moon, 1999), and clinical educators have the important role of shaping and facilitating these novice-in-transition learners' perceptions to avoid surface learning. As suggested by Eraut (1994):

> when happening in real time ... what is perceived will depend on the ability of the perceiver to notice and select the right information rapidly at the time of the encounter (p. 109).

Students are expected to learn from observing, especially observing others who are more experienced, and to learn from reflecting on their thinking and actions (i.e. metacognition). However, the clinical educator's dilemma of simultaneously being responsible for student learning and for quality healthcare to clients means that compromises are necessary in traditional fieldwork education, and the time to reflect on treatments often needs to be set aside in order to meet more pressing client-oriented demands. Thus, observation is not always seen as a learning objective in its own right in some fieldwork education settings. However, classroom exercises using computer-mediated simulations or videoed interactions are rich in opportunities to observe and process clinical interactions. The classroom provides the ideal context to support students and to make sense of their observations and experiences. Educators can slow down the pace of the learning activity, examine transactions between practitioner and client, and scaffold student understanding. Students undertake a common experience (e.g. videos which all watch) and they can capitalise on the fieldwork educator's contributions.

> Reflection has to take place after the event and may not be helpful without an experienced tutor who has observed the same incident and noted the significant evidence. (Eraut, 1994, p. 109)

Classroom-based models also enable faculty to purposefully manipulate the levels of Bloom's cognitive taxonomy (Krathwohl, 2002), and move students through the hierarchy from initial levels (i.e. students' ability to memorise, comprehend, and express their ideas in their own words) to midway levels (i.e. educational activities requiring students to demonstrate their ways of thinking through understanding, recognising examples and seeing relationships) to the highest level (where students apply what they have learned to create or act in novel situations in either the classroom-based model or actual fieldwork). Evidence from extracurricular classroom-based day workshops suggests that students make significant positive changes in various skills, and that educational activities need to specifically target Bloom's levels to achieve the higher-order thinking needed for clinical decision-making and reasoning (Cruice, 2005).

*A Classroom-based Model: An Example of Pre-Fieldwork Education Learning*

The following exemplar describes a classroom-based model for clinical skills learning. A safe learning environment is provided for students to develop clinical and communication skills with guidance from faculty (and peer feedback), supporting exploration and experimentation. The program provides quality teaching and demonstration opportunities, guiding students to critique and analyse the activities involved and to understand how they relate to clinical practice. The objectives of the program are to establish and develop students' core clinical skills in observation and reflection on others' actions, and for students to engage in self-reflection and discussion prior to their first fieldwork education experience. It is essential that students develop accurate observation skills as a prerequisite for all professional practice (interpretation, analysis, hypothesising, problem solving, and reflective practice) and it is equally important that students make sense of their learning and can communicate it to others.

*Pre-Fieldwork Education Clinical Skills Program*

This program at City University, London, began in 2008 and was implemented initially with subgroups of first year postgraduate students within the speech and language course. These students were "novices-in-transition" and participated prior to their first fieldwork education experience. The program was taught on campus by one faculty member with 20 students, in a normal university classroom setting. The first two years of this program ran as a response to insufficient placement offers for all students. Now the program is embedded into the core curriculum for all students, with increased faculty staff as clinical educators.

In addition to the core objectives described above, students gain an appreciation of different components of client session management (for example, goals, procedure, facilitation), and use theory to support observations and make clinical judgements. The program ran intensively over 5 consecutive days with 5 daily clinical sessions/slots. Students observed videoed interactions of 13 different cases of individuals with communication disorder (young child through to older adult) engaged in therapeutic activities or conversation with a speech language pathologist or a family member. The remaining 12 sessions were non-client, non-observation tasks, comprising self-evaluations, self-directed tasks, linking theory to client, session planning from videoed session, developing and presenting resources, and reflecting on learning. Students perceived great value in this alternative experience:

> ... it felt OK to talk ... make mistakes because it was a "safe" environment.
> I felt comfortable. I also feel I have gained confidence and will be much happier to start my next placement with many more skills under my belt.

*Evidence in Support of Classroom-based Experiential Learning and Challenges*

Developing students' observation skills can enhance and accelerate their learning (Stengelhofen, 1993), enabling novice-in-transition students to gain more from future fieldwork. Evaluation of the abovementioned skills program reveals that students made significant gains in core clinical skills, being better able to identify and describe relevant communication characteristics, discuss them with peers, and understand how what was happening in a clinical session impacted on the client. Such experiences also help students to effectively organise and store relevant information for later use, enhancing their reasoning and decision-making (Kim et al., 2006).

The challenge of classroom-based experiential learning is to convince others of its value: for students to value it as much as they value hands-on tasks and activities in traditional fieldwork, and for the wider allied health professional community and professional accreditation agencies to support such alternative learning models and champion their rightful place in student education. One of the greatest hurdles is knowing how and when classroom-based experiential learning best contributes to achievement of competence, among other models of clinical education. These questions are worthy of research in the healthcare professions.

## CONCLUSION

Alternative fieldwork education and classroom-based initiatives are not intended to fully replace traditional fieldwork education in mainstream domains of practice; after all, these are the settings in which most graduates still find employment. Instead, they complement, enhance, or expand learning associated with fieldwork. For example, transfer of learning, a perennial dilemma of education, is accentuated when students transfer knowledge and skills acquired in the classroom to real world contexts; classroom experiences are about optimising the transfer of learning and potentially reducing the time required in fieldwork. Exposure to different learning environments and a variety of educational approaches will produce students with a sense of professional identity, who are well prepared to demonstrate their knowledge and reasoning, translate them into skilled practice, and more fully appreciate the value of interventions and services for clients. Taking an alternative focus on fieldwork education encourages educators to re-examine the nature of students' learning and their transition to clinical competence. It assists in managing the crisis of placement shortages by providing learning experiences that are not "a lesser substitute for fieldwork", but instead are equally legitimate strategies to prepare students for practice.

However, a significant barrier for moving forward with alternative fieldwork education initiatives is that they do not meet accreditation and professional licensure guidelines for clinical hours. Acceptance of alternative fieldwork education models and classroom-based learning can be facilitated by empirically demonstrating that pre-fieldwork education experiential learning can result in a higher level of competency when students engage in fieldwork, and that alternative approaches can meet expected educational outcomes. In electing to pursue alternative approaches educators demonstrate their responsiveness to the changes occurring in healthcare delivery and their awareness of the need to prepare students for the diverse environments that are likely to be a reality in their careers.

Educators and organisations in the allied healthcare professions have the opportunity to model flexibility and openness to change in adopting alternatives to fieldwork education and exploring with others from within and across allied health-care professions. Changes in fieldwork education can be approached either by looking back and grieving the lack of traditional fieldwork education placements or can be a positive impetus for new initiatives (e.g. alternative strategies, formats, and pedagogical models for fieldwork).

## NOTES

[1]   http://www.unh.edu/engagement/partnerships/pdf/stepping-stones.pdf

## REFERENCES

Aiken, F., Menaker, L., & Barsky, L. (2001). Fieldwork education: The future of occupational therapy depends on it. *Occupational Therapy International, 8*, 86–95.

American Physical Therapy Association. (1998). *Dare to innovate: A consensus conference on alternative models of clinical education*. Alexandra, VA: APTA.

Baxter, S., & Gray, C. (2001). The application of student-centred learning approaches to clinical education. *International Journal of Language and Communication Disorders, 36*, 396–400.

Casares, G.S. Bradley, K.P., Jaffee, L.E., & Lee, G.P. (2003). Impact of the changing health care environment on fieldwork education: Perceptions of occupational therapy educators. *Journal of Allied Health, 32*, 246–251.

Cauley, K., Canfield, A., Clausen, C., Dobbins, J., Hemphill, S., Jaballas, E., et al. (2001). Service-learning: Integrating student learning and community service. *Education for Health, 14*, 173–181.

Cruice, M. (2005). Evidence for a structured approach to learning reflective practice skills in speech and language therapy. Paper presented at the Society for Research in Higher Education Annual Conference, Edinburgh, December.

Eraut, M. (1994). *Developing professional knowledge and competence*. London: Falmer Press.

Farrow, S., Gaiptman, B., & Rudman, D. (2000). Exploration of a group model in fieldwork education. *Canadian Journal of Occupational Therapy, 67*, 239–249.

Greene, D., & Diehm, G. (1995). Educational and service outcomes of service integration effort. *Michigan Journal of Community Service Learning, 4*, 54–62.

Hansen, A., Muñoz, J., Crist, P., Gupta, J., Ideishi, J., Primeau, L., et al. (2007). Service learning: Meaningful community-centered professional skill development for occupational therapy students. *Occupational Therapy in Healthcare, 21*, 25–49.

Hoben, K., Varley, R., & Cox, R. (2007). Clinical reasoning skills of speech and language therapy students. *International Journal of Language and Communication Disorders, 42*, 123–135.

Hoppes, S., Bender, D., & DeGrace, B. (2005). Service-learning is a perfect fit for occupational and physical therapy education: Commentary. *Journal of Allied Health, 34*, 47–50.

Kim, S., Phillips, W., Pinksy, L., Brock, D., Philips, K., & Keary, J. (2006). A conceptual framework for developing teaching cases: A review and synthesis of the literature across disciplines. *Medical Education, 40*, 867–876.

Kirke, P., Layton, N., & Sim, J. (2007). Informing fieldwork design: Key elements to quality in fieldwork education for undergraduate occupational therapy students. *Australian Occupational Therapy Journal, 54*, S13–S22.

Krathwohl, D. (2002). A revision of Bloom's taxonomy: An overview. *Theory into Practice, 41*, 212–218.

Martin, M., & Edwards, L. (1998). Peer learning on fieldwork placements. *British Journal of Occupational Therapy. 61*(6), 249–252.

McAllister, L (2007). Issues and innovations in clinical education. *International Journal of Speech Language Pathology, 7*(3), 138–148.

Moon, J. (1999). *Reflection in learning and professional development: Theory and practice.* Oxford: Routledge Falmer.

Neistadt, M.E. (1998). Teaching clinical reasoning as a thinking frame. *American Journal of Occupational Therapy, 52,* 221–229.

Paterson, M., Higgs, J., & Wilcox, S. (2005). The artistry of judgment: A model for occupational therapy practice. *British Journal of Occupational* Therapy, 68(9), 409–417.

Seifer, S.D. (1998). Service-learning: Community campus partnerships for health professions education. *Academic Medicine, 73,* 273–277.

Sherer, C., Morris, D., Graham, C., & White, L. (2006). Competency-based early clinical education experiences for physical therapy students. *Internet Journal of Allied Health Sciences and Practice, 4,* 1–4.

Stansfield, J. (2005). Issues and innovations in clinical education: Regulation, collaboration and communication. *Advances in Speech-Language Pathology, 7*(3), 173–176.

Stengelhofen, J. (1993). *Teaching students in clinical settings.* London: Chapman & Hall.

Stern, D., & Rone-Adams, S. (2006). An alternative model for first level clinical education experiences in physical therapy. *Internet Journal of Allied Health Sciences and Practice, 4.* Available: http://ijahsp.nova.edu.

Village, D. (2006). Qualities of effective service learning in physical therapy education. *Journal of Physical Therapy, 20,* 8–17.

Vroman, K., & MacRae, N. (1999). How should the effectiveness of problem-based learning in occupational therapy education be examined? *American Journal of Occupational Therapy, 53*(5), 533–536.

Vroman, K., Simmons, C.D., & Knight, J. (in press). Service learning can make occupation-based practice a reality: A single case study. *Occupational Therapy in Healthcare.*

*Kerryellen Vroman PhD*
*College of Health and Human Services*
*University of New Hampshire, USA*

*Madeline Cruice PhD*
*School of Community and Health Sciences*
*City University London, UK*

ROSEMARY LYSAGHT AND ANNE HILL

# 17. THE USE OF STANDARDISED PATIENTS AS AN ALTERNATIVE TO FIELDWORK EDUCATION

Standardised patients (SPs) are used widely in health science education as a means of student skill development. Often seen as a stepping stone to community-based fieldwork, SP encounters offer a number of unique educational opportunities, provide a bridge between classroom and community practice, and expand the range and number of practical learning experiences offered in an educational program.

*History of Simulation*

The use of simulation has been reported in a range of health professions. A key factor driving the move towards increased use of simulation over the past four decades has been the changing nature of health care delivery, which requires that students be prepared to meet the complex demands of diverse settings upon graduation (Bradley, 2006). This challenge means that students must be exposed to a broad variety of presenting health issues during their preservice training. Moreover, allowing students to have structured and "controlled" exposure to a broad range of cases helps build their self-confidence prior to encountering individuals with real-world problems (Lewis, Bell, & Asghar, 2008).

Simulation takes many forms. Models that replicate aspects of the human body have grown in sophistication and popularity since their introduction in the 1960s. These vary in presentation, from simple 3D models which, though inexpensive and mobile, allow limited training, to highly interactive patient simulators which provide a more realistic experience of the body's response to externally-driven factors. Computer-based simulations and virtual reality software are also used extensively and provide a relatively low-cost and somewhat interactive means to learn clinical skills. Yet they may be perceived by some students as an unrealistic representation of the patient.

*Standardised Patients*

SPs are another form of simulation. The terms "simulated" and "standardised" patients are variously used within the literature to describe actors or real patients who are trained to accurately portray a patient or an aspect of a patient's illness according to educational need (Barrows, 1993). Although these terms are used interchangeably, "simulated" is best used when referring to an actor portraying a patient, whereas

L. McAllister et al., (eds.), Innovations in Allied Health Fieldwork
Education: A Critical Appraisal, 189–198.

"standardised" can indicate either actors or real patients whose performance is standardised. Barrows and Abrahamson (1964) first described SPs in a report of a procedure to evaluate medical students undertaking clinical neurology examinations. Since that time, literature in medicine has abounded with references to the use of SPs in a wide variety of contexts to meet a range of educational objectives in both formative and summative assessment. The use of SPs within other health science programs has also gained momentum (e.g. Lewis et al., 2008; Hill, Davidson, & Theodoros, in press).

Although the majority of SP research focuses on the use of adults as SPs, literature reports the use of children (e.g., Brown, Doonan, & Shellenberger, 2005), adolescents (e.g., Blake, Gusella, Greaven, & Wakefield, 2006) and adults with intellectual disabilities (Thacker, Crabb, Perez, Raji, & Hollins, 2007) in SP roles. A "standardised family" has been reported as facilitating student learning in continuity of care, family dynamics and counselling behaviours (Clay et al., 2000).

## PRACTICAL ISSUES

### Recruitment

Recruitment of motivated and interested participants is imperative to maximise the success of a SP program. Previous acting experience is not considered essential. SPs must be carefully chosen so that their age, gender and physical presentation are all realistic in the context of the given scenario. To account for unanticipated absences, it is wise to recruit and train more SPs than are actually required. SPs may be recruited from an already established pool within the university and health sectors or from the local community, either through advertising or contact with local theatre organisations. Faculty, staff and senior students may be recruited if required for timing or financial reasons. Necessary human and financial resources should be in place prior to the establishment of such a program.

### Training Procedures

Rigorous training procedures for SPs contribute greatly to authenticity and standard-isation of presentation. The time required for training depends on the degree of difficulty or complexity of the simulation and whether or not feedback to students is required (Vu & Barrows, 1994; Chur-Hansen & Burg, 2006). Depending on the learning objectives for the encounter, training may take place individually or within a group.

The most common method of training is to formulate a scenario from an actual case history and prepare written notes for the SP that detail the role and scenario. Scenario formulation is an important stage of the program and should be completed by persons who are familiar with both case content and the learning objectives of the encounters. Involving community clinicians in case development can result in real or hybrid cases which include clinical test reports (with permission and elimination of identifying information) and strong sociocultural detail. Design of authentic cases can also be achieved by engaging volunteers living with health disorders or disabilities and drawing on their lived experiences (Nestel, Tierney, & Kubacki, 2008). Training notes should use lay rather than professional terminology to avoid possible misuse of professional terms by the SP. The inclusion of specified phrases to describe a presenting condition assists SPs to maintain a standardised presentation. SPs also benefit from review of videotapes of actual patients, to observe behaviours that are central to their role (Kurtz, Silverman, & Draper, 2005). SPs are encouraged to discuss their observations and practise putting into words their presentation of the scenario. The teaching and learning aims of the planned SP clinical encounters should be carefully communicated to the SP. Training also includes discussion of role responsibilities, how to manage their role during the encounter and how to provide effective and facilitatory feedback to students (Kurtz et al., 2005).

## METHODS OF PRESENTATION OF STANDARDISED PATIENTS

Although typical SP encounters are 1:1 interactions in an on-campus setting, alternative presentations allow the use of SPs in a range of educational contexts.

### Individual and Group Live Encounters

Beyond individual interactions, SPs have been used in group settings, in which a pair or small group of students interact directly with the SP. Such approaches are conducive to interdisciplinary education, and to early stage interventions in which students can support one another in conducting interviews or structured assessments, engaging in collaborative peer learning. An added advantage of team assessment is reduction in the number of SPs required for a learning module.

"Live" encounters with SPs can also be conducted using distance technology, such as telemedicine videoconferencing sites and Internet-based video communication tools. Although clearly well suited to distance learning programs, such modalities can also prepare on-campus students for clinical placements involving rural practice, where interactions are often conducted using distance technologies.

### Virtual Learning

Available technologies provide opportunities to use digital recordings of SPs engaged in interviews or other evaluative activities. Students can then access the videos as part of a web-based or DVD-loaded module, and engage in structured learning activities. These may take the form of asynchronous exercises, where students play video clips and identify questions they would ask of the patient or clinical actions they would take. This type of exercise is particularly beneficial in early learning, when clinical reasoning is less spontaneous, as it allows students to replay segments, process information, and reflect. It also provides student control over learning, as the time, place and length of the interaction can be individually tailored. Use of recorded SPs has been found effective in developing student clinical reasoning skills when compared with the use of live SPs (Liu, Schneider, & Miyazaki, 1997), and clearly allows increased flexibility in designing educational experiences.

Virtual SPs can also be used in synchronous learning. Web-based interaction involving learners, instructors and recorded SPs has been used as a means of honing interviewing skills in special education, occupational therapy and psychology students (Lysaght, 2002). The students review a case history prior to the interaction, and then conduct an "interview" by typing questions into an online "chat" platform. The instructor activates a suitable portion of a pre-recorded, comprehensive interview with the SP in response to questions asked. Following the session, students create a case report and recommendations based on the information gathered. Only portions of the interview that corresponded with questions asked would have been provided, and thus the quality and completeness of the interview can be readily determined. Following the exercise, students can be provided with the full recorded interview to discover what elements they have overlooked.

## USING STANDARDISED PATIENTS TO MEET EDUCATIONAL GOALS

SPs are used for a variety of teaching and assessment purposes. Development of an SP case profile and assignment requirements should be based on clear educational goals. In health professional education, SPs have been used to develop interview skills, teach physical examination and procedural skills, and to serve as a basis for intervention planning (Liu et al., 1997; Lysaght & Bent, 2005; Lewis et al., 2008; Cleland, Abe, & Rethans, 2009).

### Targeted Skill Development

SPs can be used to develop a range of clinical reasoning skills, such as interactive reasoning (understanding client needs, perspectives and goals through personal inter-action) or procedural reasoning (using critical thinking and intervention planning relative to clinical problems). Research shows that live interactions are one of the few means of developing interactive reasoning skills (van Leit, 1995; Lysaght & Bent, 2005; Lewis et al., 2008) and that such interactions are key to building student observational skills in physical examination (Panzarella & Manyon, 2007; Jansen, Thornton, & Szauter, 2008). The use of SPs in either context allows the educator to focus the encounter on the course unit goals.

### Developmental Skill Acquisition

Use of SPs can allow manipulation of case difficulty and targeting of the case to the level of student competency. Students early in their training can be provided with uncomplicated cases that present a limited number of problems, whereas more advanced students can be presented with more challenging and complex cases and assignments. For example, novice students might be required to conduct an interview only, and be guided through reflection on their skills in various aspects of information gathering and relationship building. In a later course, students might be required to conduct a comprehensive assessment and to develop an intervention plan.

*Non-Clinical Learning Goals*

SPs can also be used to present students with cases that challenge their thinking in a variety of non-clinical ways. SP cases may have certain socio-cultural elements embedded within them, such as diverse ethnic, socioeconomic, gender, age, sexual orientation and religious characteristics. This is particularly useful if learning takes place in a setting with limited diversity, or to ensure that all students have exposure to certain client differences. Cases might also present the students with challenging ethical dilemmas.

## USE OF FEEDBACK TO ENHANCE STUDENT LEARNING

Feedback to the student regarding the SP encounter may be provided in a variety of ways by the educator, peers, or the SP. Research indicates that these three sources of feedback are not equally useful or effective, and each has its own unique value (Jansen et al., 2008). Students often derive powerful lessons through self observation and reflection.

*Educator Feedback*

Feedback from the educator can be both formative and summative. Formative feedback is designed to provide specific information to students in order to encourage continuing growth in clinical performance. It is given in a positive, facilitatory manner. SP encounters, particularly those involving groups of students, benefit from the use of a "time-in, time-out" format which allows students and clinical educators to discuss the content and process in real time (Edwards, McGuiness, & Rose, 2000). During time out, discussion takes place about the nature of the student interviewer's questioning or actions and the response of the SP. Formative feedback is provided by the educator as to positive features and potential alternatives or improvements. The SP remains "frozen" in role during this time. This type of feedback and the opportunity to re-try a skill immediately have been reported by students to be effective in learning new skills (Kurtz et al., 2005; Chur-Hansen & Burg, 2006).

Summative feedback is provided at the end of SP encounters. This feedback is typically provided using an assessment checklist or rating scale. A form developed at the University of Queensland focuses on interpersonal and communication skills, interviewing skills and course-specific clinical skills. A Likert-type scale provides students with an easy-to-understand measure of their skill in each area. Clinical educators are trained in its use and report it to be effective in focusing and structuring their feedback both during and after SP interviews. It is imperative that students be familiar with the tool on which they will be assessed.

*Standardised Patient Feedback*

The provision of feedback to students is an essential aspect of the SP's role in most learning situations. Effective training provides SPs with information about the learning and assessment objectives of the activity in which they are engaged and an understanding of how formative feedback assists students in building skills towards these final goals. Targeted SP feedback is a rich form of learning for students as it encompasses a response to both content and emotional factors within a session, including how a client felt about certain questions asked or how the student's body language was perceived. As well as verbal post-session feedback, a written form that allows SPs to summarise their impressions by means of structured categories and/or scales can be valuable.

## Peer Feedback/Discussion

Students also benefit from discussion with peers about SP encounters. Peers can provide either a general overview of their impressions of an encounter or structured feedback using a formal rating scale. Providing students with clear guidelines about giving and receiving feedback reinforces to them the importance of their input to facilitating change in their colleagues. As peers are characteristically uncomfortable about providing critical feedback it is often helpful to provide examples of constructive, balanced, yet targeted feedback, encourage the use of examples, and reward thoughtful and reflective reviews.

## Student Reflective Exercises

Student skills and clinical reasoning can be enhanced through structured reflection on their SP encounters. The capacity of novice students to engage in critical reflection is limited (Newton, 2004), since they find it easier to reflect on an event after it has occurred rather than while it is occurring. Structuring reflection into clinical episodes helps students who are not natural "reflectors" engage in this process. SP encounters provide an environment in which students can build their reflective practice skills in safety. Students might be given a series of questions to guide reflection or might be able to reflect more freely on their experiences.

## UNIQUE CONTRIBUTIONS AND CHALLENGES OF USING STANDARDISED PATIENTS

Why are SPs a viable alternative and supplement to traditional placement experiences in the health sciences? They are not a substitute for "real" patients. Instead, their use is designed to complement a clinical program which provides real patient contact. SPs offer some important advantages to clinical education coordinators, which can be categorised into three main areas.

## Additional Teaching Opportunities

The above section highlights feedback as an integral part of SP programs. The capacity of clinical educators to present feedback to students both during and after interviews increases the number of available "teaching moments". Moreover, students benefit from discussion with SPs which focuses not only on the interview content but also on the impact of the student's questions and comments on the patient.

## Practice in Safe Environment

Students, particularly at a novice level, report anxiety about their performance in the clinical context. SPs support students in their learning by providing a safe environment (Black & Marcoux, 2002), with the luxury of being able to "try again" if a mistake is made. The interaction can be easily controlled to develop specific skills and manipulated to provide students with extra practice if required.

## Standardisation of Experience

Students' clinical experiences are often characterised as inequitable and arbitrary. Inequities can result from variations in client attendance and differences in type and severity of client presentation, due to the inability in natural settings to control these variables through client selection. The use of SPs allows for standardisation of experience, as all students can access the same information and deal with the same learning objectives (Vu & Barrows, 1994). Eliminating patient variability is conducive to more equitable assessment of competency (Ladyshewsky, Baker, Jones, & Nelson, 2000).

## Critical Comparison of SPs Relative to Other Methods of Instruction

Although the literature generally supports the inclusion of SPs in health science programs, some challenges are also reported. Increased cost, additional time and the need for a high level of organisational commitment are cited as major disincentives to using SPs. Administrative support is critical to the maintenance of a high quality program. It should be noted, however, that cost and demand are highest when initiating a new SP experience. Once a series of SP roles has been developed and a core set of actors identified, recruitment and preparation requirements are reduced. The skills of the SP actors can also limit success. Some SPs are naturally more skilled at portraying a case scenario and at maintaining the fidelity of the case across a number of student encounters.

The many advantages of SPs have been articulated throughout this chapter. The most critical of these may be enhanced instructor control over the student learning experience, given the ability to tailor the encounters to curricular goals. In one study that compared the use of SPs and real clients in an advanced clinical reasoning course, use of SPs heightened student challenge and allowed them to address a broader range of clinical reasoning skills (Lysaght, O'Connor, & Paterson, 2009). From an ethical standpoint, the use of paid SPs removes the level of risk presented to real clients, and allows for repetition of encounters with multiple students.

*Student Perceptions of SP Experiences*

Students have reported that they can relate well to SPs (Sanson-Fisher & Poole, 1980) and SPs are generally received positively by students in clinical teaching and assessment situations (Lane & Rollnick, 2007). For example, faculty in the Queen's University occupational therapy program, Canada, compared student feedback from two cohorts that completed the same clinical reasoning assignment, one with community volunteers with real disabilities, and the other with SPs. Among the students in the cohort that interviewed SPs, 70% reported that the interaction heightened clinical reasoning skills, compared with only 42% of students who interviewed volunteers. Although some of the students who worked with SPs indicated difficulty in exploring case intricacies due to constrained SP responses and their sense that it was not a "true" client, it was determined that these comments related to one or two of the SPs who were less skilled and confident in "living" the assigned role. The majority of students reported that the SPs were excellent actors who provided complex and comprehensive cases.

Bokken et al. (2009) identified valuable components of both real and SP encounters for medical students and recommended the inclusion of both in clinical programs. Although students in that study considered that real patient encounters were easier to undertake and more real, they also noted that SPs provided more effective feedback than real patients and offered a much-needed focus on discussion of students' communication skills. Other researchers (e.g., Rethans, Gorter, Bokken, & Morrison, 2007) have reported that students and practitioners did not detect incognito SPs and that they could not be reliably distinguished from real patients.

## SUMMARY

The use of SPs is a valuable addition to health science education programs, offering a wide range of options for skill development and evaluation. SPs can serve as a useful addition to traditional fieldwork, providing student exposure to a larger number and wider range of patients and facilitating targeted skill development and evaluation. Implementation of a quality SP program requires commitment of institutional resources and instructor creativity, but results in a rich and challenging educational experience.

## REFERENCES

Barrows, H., & Abrahamson, S. (1964). The programmed patient: A technique for appraising student performance in clinical neurology. *Journal of Medical Education, 39*, 802–805.

Barrows, H.S. (1993). An overview of the uses of standardized patients for teaching and evaluating clinical skills. *Academic Medicine, 68*, 443–451

Black, B., & Marcoux, B. (2002). Feasibility of using standardized patients in a physical therapist education program: A pilot study. *Journal of Physical Therapy Education, 16*, 49–56.

Blake, K.D., Gusella, J., Greaven, S., & Wakefield, S. (2006). The risks and benefits of being a young female adolescent standardized patient. *Medical Education, 40*, 26–35.

Bokken, L., Rethans, J.J., van Heurn, L., Duvivier, R., Scherpbier, A., & van der Vleuten., C. (2009). Students' views on the use of real patients and simulated patients in undergraduate medical education. *Academic Medicine, 84*, 958–63.

Bradley, P. (2006). The history of simulation in medical education and possible future directions. *Medical Education, 40*, 254–262.

Brown, R., Doonan, S., & Shellenberger, S. (2005). Using children as simulated patients in communication training for residents and medical students: A pilot program. *Academic Medicine, 80*, 1114–1120.

Chur-Hansen, A., & Burg, F. (2006). Working with standardised patients for teaching and learning. *The Clinical Teacher, 3*, 220–224.

Clay, M.C., Lane, H., Willis, S.E., Peal, M., Chakravarthi, S., & Poehlman, G. (2000). Using a standardized family to teach clinical skills to medical students. *Teaching and Learning in Medicine, 12*, 145–149.

Cleland, J.A., Abe, K., & Rethans, J-J. (2009). The use of simulated patients in medical education: AMEE guide no 42. *Medical Teacher, 31*, 477–486.

Edwards, H., McGuiness, B., & Rose, M. (2000). Using simulated patients to teach clinical reasoning. In J. Higgs & M. Jones (Eds.), *Clinical reasoning in the health professions* (2nd ed., pp. 262–269). Oxford: Butterworth-Heinemann.

Hill, A.E., Davidson, B.D., & Theodoros, D.G. (in press). A review of standardised patients in clinical education: Implications for speech-language pathology programs. *International Journal of Speech-Language Pathology*.

Jansen, C.W.S., Thornton, J.T., & Szauter, K.E. (2008). Use of a standardized patient with a frozen shoulder to test examination skills of physical therapy students: Student and faculty perspective. *Journal of Hand Therapy, 21*, 426.

Kurtz, S., Silverman, J., & Draper, J. (2005). *Teaching and learning communication skills in medicine* (2nd ed.). Oxford: Radcliffe Medical Press.

Ladyshewsky, R., Baker, R., Jones, M., & Nelson, L. (2000). Reliability and validity of an extended simulated patient case: A tool for evaluation and research in physiotherapy. *Physiotherapy Theory and Practice, 16*, 15–25.

Lane, C., & Rollnick, S. (2007). The use of simulated patients and role-play in communication skills training: A review of the literature to August 2005. *Patient Education and Counseling, 67*, 13–20.

Lewis, M., Bell, J., & Asghar, A. (2008). Use of simulated patients in development of physiotherapy students' interpersonal skills. *International Journal of Therapy and Rehabilitation, 15*, 221–227.

Liu, L., Schneider, P., & Miyazaki, M. (1997). The effectiveness of using simulated patients versus videotapes of simulated patients to teach clinical skills to occupational and physical therapy students. *The Occupational Therapy Journal of Research, 17*, 159–172.

Lysaght, R. (2002). *Development of a curriculum template for applied-problem solving in distance education learning communities – Final evaluation report.* Logan, UT: Western Institute for Research and Evaluation.

Lysaght, R., & Bent, M. (2005). A comparative analysis of case presentation modalities used in clinical reasoning coursework in occupational therapy. *American Journal of Occupational Therapy, 59(3)*, 314–324.

Lysaght, R., O'Connor, D., & Paterson, M. (2009, June). *Development of clinical reasoning skills through client interviews: Best practices.* Paper presented at Canadian Association of Occupational Therapists Annual Conference, Ottawa.

Nestel, D., Tierney, T., & Kubacki, A. (2008). Creating authentic simulated patient roles: Working with volunteers. *Medical Education, 42*, 1122.

Newton, J. (2004). Learning to reflect: A journey. *Reflective Practice, 5*, 155–166.

Panzarella, K.J., & Manyon, A.T. (2007). A model for integrated assessment of clinical competence. *Journal of Allied Health, 36*, 157–164.

Rethans, J., Gorter, S., Bokken, L., & Morrison, L. (2007). Unannounced standardised patients in real practice: A systematic literature review. *Medical Education, 41*, 537–549.

Sanson-Fisher, R.W., & Poole, A. D. (1980). Simulated patients and the assessment of medical students' interpersonal skills. *Medical Education, 14*, 249–253.

Thacker, A., Crabb, N., Perez, W., Raji, O., & Hollins, S. (2007). How (and why) to employ simulated patients with intellectual disabilities. *The Clinical Teacher, 4*, 15–20.

van Leit, B. (1995). Using the case method to develop clinical reasoning skills in problem-based learning. *American Journal of Occupational Therapy, 49*, 349–353.

Vu, N.V., & Barrows, H. (1994). Use of standardized patients in clinical assessments: Recent developments and measurement findings. *Educational Researcher, 23*(3), 23–30.

*Rosemary Lysaght PhD*
*School of Rehabilitation Therapy*
*Queen's University, Canada*

*Anne Hill B.Sp.Thy*
*The University of Queensland, Australia*

# SECTION VI: INTERPROFESSIONAL FIELDWORK EDUCATION

ANNE O'RIORDAN, MARGO PATERSON
AND JENNIFER MEDVES

# 18. INTERPROFESSIONAL FIELDWORK EDUCATION

## *Lessons Learned*

This chapter explores current ideas and approaches to interprofessional education (IPE) and interprofessional practice (IPP). We begin by providing key definitions and considering relevant literature from a systematic review. We discuss two projects from our programme of research including action research and a quasi-experimental research project. Within the discussion we explore lessons learned for enhancing collaborative interprofessional teaching and learning.

### KEY DEFINITIONS

The most frequently cited definition of interprofessional education is "when two or more health care professionals learn *with, from,* and *about* each other in order to improve collaboration and the quality of care" (CAIPE, 2002). The World Health Organization's *Framework for action on interprofessional education and collaborative practice* (2008) states that interprofessional collaboration in education and practice is a "necessary step in preparing a 'collaborative practice ready' health worker who has learned how to work in an interprofessional team and is competent to do so" (p. 8).

Collaborative practice is an interprofessional process for communication and decision making that enables the separate and shared knowledge and skills of care providers to synergistically influence the client care being provided while retaining the integrity of each profession (Way, Jones, & Busing, 2000). It is this process of collaboration that is most often discussed when talking about teamwork in healthcare. Collaborative practice occurs when health care providers from diverse backgrounds actively work together to optimise client care outcomes that reflect client- and family-centred goals and values (Way et al., 2000). It provides mechanisms for continuous communication among care providers, and optimises staff participation in clinical decision making (within and across disciplines), to ensure that clients receive care from the right person at the right time, and avoid duplication and gaps in care (HealthForceOntario, 2007). Respect and trust between team members are enhanced when health care providers develop a deeper understanding of each other's roles and responsibilities, with benefits to workplace cultures and morale (Suter et al., 2009). The culmination of these factors leads to improved clinical efficiencies

L. McAllister et al., (eds.), Innovations in Allied Health Fieldwork
Education: A Critical Appraisal, 201–213.

and client outcomes, as well as greater levels of workplace satisfaction and higher rates of staff recruitment and retention (HealthForceOntario, 2007). A Collaborative Learning Unit© (CLU) was adapted from the Lougheed and Galloway Ford definition for the purposes of our research and is defined as a "clinical unit where all members of the staff, together with students, patients/clients, family and community supports, work together to create a positive learning environment and provide high quality patient/client care" (Lougheed & Galloway Ford, 2005, p. 2).

However, placing health care providers of different professions or backgrounds into a team does not mean that they will have the knowledge and skills necessary to work together collaboratively to enhance client care. Professionals who have been educated and trained in practice settings modelled on traditional "siloed" approaches require education on how to work together collaboratively (Ferlie & Shortell, 2001; Canadian Health Services Research Foundation, 2006).

## LITERATURE

Interprofessional fieldwork education is essential if learners are to work in complex health care systems where teamwork is espoused as the best way to work together. It is not, however, a mandated component of curricula for most health care professional programs. Team-based healthcare and practice have been widely argued to provide not only improved efficiency and quality of service (Van Weel, 1994; Gair & Hartery, 2001; Reeves, 2001) but also cost reductions (Schmitt, 2001) and increased job satisfaction (Van Weel, 1994; Kyle, 1995; Gair & Hartery, 2001). As Carlisle, Cooper, and Watkins (2004) titled their paper "Do none of you talk to each other?", clients are also demanding a more integrated approach to health care. Challenges for educators in universities and colleges include historical reasons, as healthcare professionals are educated in "silos" and until recently have had little opportunity to interact. Gilbert (2008) described the education and professional organisation of health professionals as guilds, explaining that each profession has its own professional association and journal, subscribes to its own belief system and creates entry practices that ensure that others do not qualify. The guild system is then taught and demonstrated by educators and it is hard for others to access the knowledge. However, by learning together, new health care professionals should have a deeper understanding of each other's contribution to the overall care provided to clients. If practitioners do not understand the role of other professionals their ability to work together is compromised.

The development of a team does not necessarily mean that the team is interprofessional. But healthcare learners will acquire a deeper understanding of the roles of other professionals if fieldwork is designed to prepare them for interprofessional practice. Although interprofessional fieldwork education has multiple possibilities for learners, various factors affect the ability of educators to integrate it into professional programs (D'Amour & Oandasan, 2005).

Barriers for education programs are well recognised and include non-alignment of programs, difficulty in finding appropriate fieldwork settings; differing pedagogical approaches, assessment and evaluation of learners; and faculty who are not prepared to teach an interprofessional group of students (Canadian Health Services Research Foundation, 2006). Scheduling interprofessional fieldwork is not without difficulty: coordinating times in the curriculum has been identified as a major barrier, with logistics being so time-consuming that faculty abandon their efforts to bring learners together (Wilhelmsson et al., 2009). If and when these barriers can be overcome, preparing learners is the next challenge, as they may think they have insufficient knowledge of their own discipline to participate in an interprofessional experience. A major component of the fieldwork experience is collaborative work, defined by the Canadian Association of Occupational Therapists as "the positive interaction of two or more health professionals, who bring their unique skills and knowledge, to assist patients/clients and families with their health decisions" (CAOT, 2006, p. 188). West and Slater (1988) reported that to ensure effective collaboration, teams require explicit, appropriate tasks and goals and clear meaningful roles for each individual, criteria which could be met through the implementation of clear, systematic guidelines to assist in decision making.

The Linköping IPE model was the first example of an integrated model, where interprofessional groups of student learners provided all care within a clinical ward (Wahlström, Sandén, & Hammar, 1996). It provided learners with the opportunity to understand where their skill set was most useful, and to work with a team to define, with patient input, what care was required. Chapters 19 and 20 illustrate other examples of education programs that have adapted the Linköping IPE model. Analysis by students of interprofessional practice incidents has helped to determine when and how best practice in teamwork is demonstrated (Robson & Kitchen, 2007), indicating that there are still too many undesirable incidents, with the majority reported during informal ward communication.

Yet when interprofessional fieldwork occurs in a framework of understanding of the roles and responsibilities of each member of the healthcare team, learners experience well-organised teamwork with respect for each other. There are barriers to overcome, and if everyone remembers that care is about the client and they do not practise solely within their guild, there is a chance for learners to see best practice using teamwork to optimise best care for clients and their families.

It is important to understand the historical perspective that provided the impetus for the research described in this chapter. The Canadian federal government commissioned a report, *The future of health care in Canada* (Commission of the Future of Health Care in Canada, 2002), which led to a call for proposals from Health Canada for interprofessional education for collaborative patient-centred practice (IECPCP). Twenty projects were funded across Canada from 2005 to 2008. Interested readers can learn more about this work at the Canadian Interprofessional Health Collaborative website (www.cihc.ca).

We were fortunate to be funded initially by the federal government and later by the provincial government. Since these various research projects built upon each other as an overall programme of research at Queen's University, we describe two of them in chronological order, starting with the Queen's University Inter-Professional Patient-Centred Education Direction (QUIPPED) action research study, which occurred from 2005 to 2008, followed by a quasi experimental design research project, the

South Eastern Interprofessional Collaborative Learning Environment (SEIPCLE) project, which was carried out from 2008 to 2009.

## PROJECT 1: QUEEN'S UNIVERSITY INTER-PROFESSIONAL PATIENT-CENTRED EDUCATION DIRECTION (QUIPPED)

The QUIPPED action research project aimed to "create an interprofessional education environment that enhanced the ability of learners and faculty to provide patient-centred care, while recognizing the contribution of the health care team within a respectful and collaborative framework" (QUIPPED Annual Report, 2006, p. 4). The primary research question was: *How do interprofessional activities or experiences influence learner attitudes, skills and behaviours to contribute to enhancement of patient-centred care?*

The action research approach involved 48 co-researchers from seven disciplines, including 10 pre- and post-licensure student learners. We were trying to understand and promote interprofessional education in the Faculty of Health Sciences at Queen's University, Kingston, Ontario, Canada. Action research was chosen as the most appropriate methodology to study the transformation (Carr & Kemmis, 1997) of healthcare education to accommodate interprofessional learning opportunities for pre-licensure learners. Interprofessional teaching and learning activities are becoming increasingly common with the recognition of the value of teamwork in health care (Lemieux-Charles & McGuire, 2006).

We have published the findings of the QUIPPED project elsewhere (Medves et al., 2008; Paterson et al., 2008) and argued that as healthcare professionals share common competencies, teaching and learning together makes sense (Verma, Paterson, & Medves, 2006). The curricula in academic health sciences centres offer many opportunities for interprofessional teaching and learning; the challenge is to exploit them. We had a unique opportunity with external funding to develop interprofessional teaching and learning.

The process of developing the action research project through team building of faculty, and inclusion of students and patients, required an assessment of the status quo, an environmental scan, and a plan to transform beliefs, attitudes and behaviours through change processes. We perceived that within each professional silo specific customs had generated particular bodies of knowledge which no longer met the current needs of the health care system and the consumers who relied on it. As the research paradigm and methods adopted determine the form of knowledge generated, we chose the critical paradigm, which holds that knowledge is co-constructed in action with ongoing reflection. Through this process a shared culture continues to evolve to meet emergent needs. QUIPPED aimed to encourage this cyclical process through reflection on and change in the attitudes, beliefs and values held within the various professions, to initiate new ways of learning and acting together. We were successful in attaining our goals, which were to:
- Create an environment that was supported by stakeholders (including administration, clinicians, students, consumers, and faculty) at Queen's University and in the Kingston community.

- Create innovative opportunities at Queen's University and its outreach partners to ensure that pre- and post-licensure learners across the health professions were able to engage in interprofessional learning opportunities in theoretical and clinical courses and placements.
- Develop continuing professional development for all faculty and adjunct faculty to that ensure common interprofessional learning objectives were developed, provided to teachers and learners, and evaluated through courses and modules.
- Establish a sustainable Office of Interprofessional Education and Practice.
- Promote and share at the local level information, resources, and expertise related to teaching interprofessional concepts across healthcare professions.

Interprofessional activities and fieldwork education strategies changed and evolved over the course of the QUIPPED project and the initial stages of the Office of Interprofessional Education and Practice. Although each of these initiatives provided unique educational opportunities, strengths and challenges, there were common characteristics and lessons to be learned. We here delve more deeply into understanding and addressing the enablers and barriers to interprofessional collaboration and fieldwork education, building on our previous learning.

*Interprofessional Pilot Placements*

In the QUIPPED project we now discuss two pilot placements that took place with the Stroke Team and the Geriatric Team of our local rehabilitation facility. The aims were to enable students to:
- Have opportunities to learn together to enhance their understanding of the cooperative and collaborative nature of professional practice and to use group process in interprofessional decision making.
- Increase their understanding of the scope of practice of other professions in order to recognise, appreciate and utilise the competencies of other professionals.
- Develop the ability to effectively represent their own profession to patients and colleagues.
- Enhance their understanding of the role of the patient/client.
- Enhance critical analysis skills by increasing students' awareness of ethical aspects of patient care.
- Demonstrate effective communication and teamwork skills with student colleagues and team members.
- Develop essential skills, knowledge and behaviour relating to interprofessional education principles.

With financial support from the QUIPPED project and the partnership between the university and the clinical site, we were able to plan and implement the IP placements, study their impact, and consider carefully the logistics necessary for their success. We learned a great deal from this experience and drafted a variety of guiding documents for the IP components, which served us well in the clinical activities that followed. Key to the pilot placements' success was respecting the integrity and input of the clinical teams with whom we worked, and providing additional resources to ensure that the placement affected patient care and the workplace environment positively, despite requiring time and expertise of the preceptors and teams to supervise students. Funding allowed us to support a project coordinator and clinical site coordinator for the pilot placements. We found that the key components for both IP placements included: IP shadowing of professional colleagues, patient shadowing, IP tutorials, reflective journalling, and an IP group project, besides all the typical elements of a traditional clinical placement. Because the student placements were asynchronous, that is, following different time schedules, tutorials were organised in one of two ways: (1) spread out over a 4-month time period before the beginning of some of the participants' placements and during the placement for other participants; or (2) condensed into the shorter common or over-lapping time frames of all students. There were benefits and drawbacks for both scenarios. The longer time frame allowed relationships, communication and trust to develop gradually, but required a huge time commitment from students. The shorter time frame reduced the commitment required but created some stress in completing activities quickly and resulted in somewhat more superficial relationships.

The Stroke Team IP placement included five students representing the three disciplines of nursing, occupational therapy and physiotherapy, and took place over a 4-month period. The Geriatric Team placement involved seven students from the disciplines of medicine, nursing, occupational therapy, psychology, registered practical nursing, social work, and theology, and took place during the 4-week period in which all students were involved in their clinical education. For both projects, an IP project team, comprised of faculty educators from occupational therapy, physio-therapy, nursing and education, planned and implemented the IP components of the placement, including facilitating weekly tutorials, responding to student reflective journal entries and assisting students to complete their IP presentation. All the activities were made possible by the logistic support of the on-site clinical coordinator. Significant time and resources were invested in soliciting support from multiple levels of the stakeholder organisations at the university and the clinical site, ensuring that administrators, managers, clinicians, educators and students worked collabora-tively to support the initiation of IP clinical education.

The end result of the two projects was judged positive and worthwhile by everyone involved. For one participant, the most valuable aspect was *"the shadowing and reflections on the experience. Seeing other professions in action is a much better way to learn than in the classroom"*. Success was further evidenced by the following representative comments:

> *In my other placements I sort of wandered around treating people and working with them without ever understanding fully what the other professions were doing. In this placement, I have been able to actively figure out what I can do to be a more effective team member and this placement makes me wonder why all placements don't have this component.* (student)

> *I was floored by the students' depth of knowledge about the different scopes of practice [and the students] said that they now understand the roles of the other professionals much better, and that they wouldn't hesitate in other*

*settings to approach different professionals because of the experience that they had here.* (clinician)

*This was an energizing experience. We see it as doing the right thing for patients and clinicians. We need to support our current staff to engage in interprofessional education and activities.* (administrator)

The lessons learned from the QUIPPED IP pilot placements were:
– Diverse student groups lead to deeper discussions of values, roles, benefits and challenges in IPE.
– Diversity can include professional, institutional or geographic affiliation as well as gender, years of education, and professional work experience.
– IPE requires "thinking outside the box" to address key challenges (e.g. finding common tutorials to ensure face-to-face meetings for students despite asynchronous placement schedules).
– Supporting clinical environments through funding an on-site coordinator results in active engagement in IP collaboration.
– Clinicians and administrators are willing and eager to work toward enhanced IP teamwork if patient care is not adversely affected and funds are available.
– It appears that patient care is more fully understood and positively influenced by IP collaboration.
– Clinical sites that typically have difficulty recruiting professionals might find that offering IP clinical placements can be a positive recruitment strategy.

Despite this positive feedback, sustainability remains an issue as funds are not currently embedded in clinical site budgets for interprofessional fieldwork education. These pilot projects did, however, set the stage for ongoing IP placements within the research project that followed them. A similar planning and implementation team was adopted and the guideline documents developed within IP placements were utilised, namely for the IP shadowing activity.

## PROJECT 2: SOUTHEASTERN INTERPROFESSIONAL COLLABORATIVE LEARNING ENVIRONMENT (SEIPCLE)

The SEIPCLE project was a 15-month research study funded by HealthForceOntario to introduce and evaluate the use of educational modules and activities to enhance collaborative practice in three different clinical settings in southeastern Ontario. The project's stakeholders included Queen's University, three clinical sites, a community-based agency and patient representatives. The objectives of the project were to:

1. Develop a sustainable collaborative learning environment through the development of CLUs in several care settings.
– Create and maintain healthy work environments within the CLUs
– Develop and enhance CLUs to support caregiver recruitment and retention
– Develop and enhance IP clinical teams to model collaborative, patient-centred care
– Create IP placements for learners in multiple CLUs

- Enhance participation of patients, families, volunteers and community agencies in collaborative care
- Enhance collaboration with clinical and educational institutions and the community (Van Diepen, MacRae, & Paterson, 2007)

2. Evaluate process and outcomes systematically to better understand the components of IP education and care that support sustainability of existing CLUs and development of CLUs in other clinical settings.

The main goal of the project was to enhance collaborative practice within one clinical team at each of the participating sites. This goal emphasised learning about the barriers and enablers to collaborative practice faced by each team in its clinical setting, and the development of innovative educational interventions to increase levels of collaborative practice within the entire unit including all staff who interacted directly with and provided care to patients. The project aimed to provide a model of collaborative practice for pre-licensure students in clinical placements, but due to time constraints, the emphasis was placed on opportunities for students to shadow multiple preceptors from diverse professional backgrounds, enabling them to observe and learn about the roles and scopes of practice. A related goal of the project was to pilot and validate a tool for assessing team collaboration, previously developed through the QUIPPED project, with a view to making it publicly available and accessible.

The project chose to use the nursing preceptor model developed by Lougheed and Galloway Ford (2005) called the CLU. Rather than limiting membership to the traditional professional care team, the CLU was adapted to include all health care providers within the defined units who had close contact with patients. The CLU therefore included ward clerks, housekeeping/environmental services staff, and porters. Patients themselves were included as members of their own health care team participating in information sharing and decision making.

Led by the Office of Interprofessional Education and Practice, the project was guided by a steering committee made up of representatives from all stakeholders to ensure a voice at the table from researchers, educators, healthcare providers and patients. The steering committee met monthly and worked together to understand the current clinical environment, experience the advantages and barriers inherent in the processes of teambuilding and collaboration, and contribute to the scholarship and clinical application of the project. Key to the project's implementation was the funding of a project manager and the recruitment of a clinical site coordinator for each of the three units. The site coordinator was a person from within the organisation, known to and trusted by the CLU caregivers. These four individuals provided liaison between the research team and the clinical sites, helped with logistics, and detailed specific content for interventions required and requested by CLU members.

The SEIPCLE project was evaluated using a quasi-experimental design including pre- and post-tests matched with non-equivalent control groups (Shadish, Cook, & Campbell, 2002). Two teams were recommended by administrators from each of the three clinical sites. The project manager then met with the teams to provide detailed information about the project. We introduced a new quantitative survey tool, the Collaborative Practice Assessment Tool (CPAT), developed, piloted and validated by the QUIPPED project, to assess each team's perceived strengths and weaknesses related to collaboration. The CPAT asks respondents about their agreement levels with 56 closed-ended questions covering eight aspects of collaborative practice, namely mission, meaningful purpose, and goals; general relationships; team leadership; general role responsibilities, autonomy; communication and information exchange; community linkages and coordination of care; decision making and conflict management; and patient involvement. The CPAT also includes three open-ended questions that ask respondents about their team's greatest strengths, challenges, and needs in regards to collaborative practice. The CPAT served as the main outcome measure for levels of collaborative practice, and its results also helped to identify the teams' major roadblocks to collaborative practice and guided the development of educational materials used as part of the intervention. The teams also completed an Interprofessional Clinical Education Survey to gauge their preparedness for interprofessional student placements.

After completing pre-intervention surveys and focus groups, the treatment teams began a series of educational activities that consisted of online modules, face-to-face workshops, and real-time activities, which we defined as educational activities that are completed in parallel to work or within the same time-frame, and based upon prior knowledge and theory in combination with the results of each team's pre-assessment. The program included an initial online module that introduced a collaborative practice model and established common language and terminology for participants; a face-to-face workshop to assist with the planning and preparation of interprofessional student placements; an online module presenting the patient perspective and patient-centred care followed by a face-to-face workshop with a patient representative and project coordinator; a real-time activity that monitored each team member's interactions with selected patients (frequency of interactions, activities and roles, time commitment) to enhance understanding of roles and scopes of practice of each CLU member; and lastly a face-to-face workshop on compassion fatigue that brought together participants from all three sites. As the educational components were developed in response to each team's CPAT results and designed in part to suit their unique needs, a somewhat different sequence of intervention components was completed at each site.

Students engaged in IP shadowing with volunteer members of the CLU. At one of the sites, students' enthusiasm for this educational option resulted in students from other units contacting the clinical site coordinator to request involvement in the CLU. Two students summed up the IP shadowing experience by saying:

*By understanding the roles of other professionals, one can better understand how an interprofessional team is supposed to look and how we can work together.*

*It was a great experience. I gained an appreciation and understanding of what each member of the health care team does for the patient. I will feel more comfortable interacting with other team members and I am more inclined to learn the role of other members of the multi-disciplinary team. My collaboration abilities have begun to develop.*

The results of this project were dependent upon the length of time available to implement the educational activities. That is, the site involved for the longest time appeared to reap the most benefit in terms of the collaboration. Although analysis of the pre- and post-data did not yield statistically significant results, the outcomes were deemed educationally relevant and worthy of ongoing study. One clinician told us that the CLU:

> benefited from ongoing team building. Whenever there were face-to-face activities ... it really encouraged some of that team ... They were getting to know each other a little bit better ... that was a benefit I can see from my own perspective in the sense that it gave them other opportunities to get together that weren't always so formal.

The results were felt to be a true reflection of what was practical in the reality of a clinical health care setting where caseloads were high, resources were limited, and high turnover often existed within teams. The SEIPCLE project was exploratory in nature, and while one goal was to test the effectiveness of innovative interventions to enhance collaborative practice, another was to learn about the barriers and enablers to the development of collaborative practice in the health-care system. The lessons learned from the SEIPCLE project were:
− Clinical Site Coordinator roles were key to enabling the sites to participate effectively − funding for these positions was crucial.
− The Steering Committee actively modelled an IP approach and worked to understand the current clinical environment, resulting in a more deeply informed report for the government funder.
− IP shadowing was incorporated into the students' clinical placements with positive results.
− The CLU model of care was embraced by clinical sites at management, clinical and student levels.
− Institutional support was necessary for sustainability.
− Clinicians' involvement was limited by their ability to receive appropriate back-up to ensure that patient care was not affected.
− Educational activities with flexibility in their delivery and time commitment were appreciated;
− Hospital restrictions affected the use of electronic educational materials (firewalls, access to computers).
− Staff were eager for IP educational opportunities, as evidenced by their use of personal time to pursue educational activities.
− Blended learning activities were critical − electronic, reference material mixed with face-to-face "real-time" activities.
− Despite working effectively with other team members, often over many years, most professionals lacked a full understanding of other professions' roles and scopes of practice, in part due to traditional uniprofessional "silo" training.
− Communication between members of different professions remained a challenge due to lack of time to explore and understand roles and scopes of practice, an

absence of shared clinical reports within patients' medical records, different work schedules and absence of common work areas.

– Many IP teams focused on *content* in team meetings to the exclusion of *process*, a necessary component to team-building.

One general finding was clear to the project team from the beginning, that given their busy workloads, few if any teams would be able to set aside group time for process meetings. Although all teams scheduled regular meetings to discuss patient care, only one of six in the project was able to hold meetings dedicated purely to discussing team functioning in care giving, an important element in building collaborative teams. An unintentional effect of the project was that procedural time, required to discuss the project and conduct focus groups, was perceived by team members to be valuable as team process issues were addressed.

One of the most positive results of the project was the enthusiasm felt towards interprofessional student placements by clinicians and students. Although preceptoring students from other professional backgrounds required more time and effort by staff, the multi-preceptor placements were highly valued by students who were eager to sign up and universally appreciative of the opportunities they provided.

As the project manager for SEIPCLE, Anne spent considerable time reflecting about its goals, the resources developed, implementation strategies, and outcomes. Anne was struck by the number of personal connections that she witnessed across the three CLU sites and realised that this project had really been about building relationships through collaborative efforts: relationships between the members of the project Steering Committee as we led the project and engaged in team-building activities; relationships that grew between members of the Project Team who faced challenges and delays but also exciting progress coupled with innovative strategies; relationships that became stronger between healthcare providers in the clinical sites, who often took time from their evenings and weekends to complete the online educational modules; connections that were built through regular face-to-face meetings at the clinical sites as we debriefed about real-time activities and shared ideas for future steps; connections that developed with students who eagerly participated in the interprofessional shadowing opportunities which CLU participants were willing to offer.

Finally, Anne has reflected on the stories of the many patients/clients/family members who were the recipients of the enhanced care developed through the project, as well as the narratives and videos that were created with assistance from the project's patient representatives. Through these relationships and partnerships, the beginnings of enhanced collaboration are evident. Resources, now publicly available, are the tangible results of this project, representing the content that we envisioned at the very beginning of the initiative. But it is the relationships that have been fostered and strengthened that embody the process element of the project's objectives. Participants, having become more collaborative in their approach to working and caring, will advocate for a cultural shift toward collaborative practice in the long term, and will model this transformation in their everyday work, thereby ensuring that future patients, their families and healthcare providers themselves will experience a truly collaborative healthcare system.

## SUMMARY

In this chapter we have discussed two of the four projects in our program of research: the QUIPPED action research and the SEIPCLE quasi-experimental research project. We have explored some key issues, challenges and lessons learned for enhancing collaborative interprofessional teaching and learning. It is hoped that this review will inspire educators, researchers and clinicians to collaborate in the initiation of interprofessional fieldwork education opportunities for learners. This chapter provides a deeper understanding of the advantages, challenges and approaches that may be utilised in the implementation process.

## REFERENCES

Canadian Health Services Research Foundation. (2006). *Teamwork in healthcare: Promoting effective teamwork in healthcare in Canada*. Ottawa: Canadian Health Services Research Foundation. Available: http://www.chsrf.ca/research_themes/pdf/teamwork-synthesis-report_e.pdf, accessed 28 February 2009.

CAOT (2006). *Position statement: Occupational therapy and primary health care*. Available: http://www.caot.ca/default.asp?pageid=188, accessed 20 November 2007.

Carlisle, C., Cooper, H., & Watkins, C. (2004). "Do none of you talk to each other?" The challenges facing the implementation of interprofessional education. *Medical Teacher, 26*(6), 545–552.

Carr, W., & Kemmis, S. (1986). *Becoming critical: Education, knowledge and action research*. Geelong, VIC: Deakin University Press.

Centre for the Advancement of Interprofessional Education (CAIPE). (2002). *Interprofessional education - a definition*. Available: http://caipe.org.uk, accessed 19 October 2009.

Commission of the Future of Health Care in Canada. (2002). *Building on values: The future of healthcare in Canada: Final report*. Saskatoon, Saskatchewan: Commission on the Future of Health Care in Canada.

D'Amour, D., & Oandasan, I. (2005). Interprofessionality as the field of interprofessional practice and interprofessional education: An emerging concept. *Journal of Interprofessional Care, 19*(1), 8–20.

Ferlie, E.B., & Shortell, S.M. (2001). Improving the quality of health care in the United Kingdom and the United States: A framework for change. *Milbank Quarterly, 79*(2), 281–315.

Gair, G., & Hartery, T. (2001). Medical dominance in multidisciplinary teamwork: A case study of discharge decision making in a geriatric assessment unit. *Journal of Nursing Management, 9*, 3–11.

Gilbert, J.H.V. (2008). Abraham Flexner and the roots of interprofessional education. *Journal of Continuing Education in the Health Professions, 28*(S1), S11–S14.

HealthForceOntario. (2007). *Interprofessional care: A blueprint for action in Ontario*. Available: http://www.healthforceontario.ca/upload/en/whatishfo/ipc%20blueprint%20final.pdf, accessed 19 December 2009.

Kyle, M. (1995). Collaboration. In M. Snyder & M.P. Mirr (Eds.), *Advanced practice nursing: A guide to professional development* (pp. 169–81). New York: Springer.

Lemieux-Charles, L., & McGuire, W.L. (2006). What do we know about health care team effectiveness? A review of the literature. *Medical Care Research and Review, 63*(3), 263–300.

Lougheed, M., & Galloway Ford, A. (2005). *The Collaborative Learning Units© model of practice education for nursing: A summary*. Prepared for The Collaborative Learning Units Provincial Group, British Columbia.

Medves, J., Paterson, M., Schroder, C., Verma, S., Broers, T., Chapman, C., & O'Riordan, A. (2008). The constant cycle: Day to day of critical action of the QUIPPED project. *The Qualitative Report Journal, 13*(4), 531–543.

Paterson, M., Chapman, C., Medves, J., Schroder, C., Verma, S., Broers, T., & O'Riordan, A. (2008). Action research in health sciences: Inter-professional education *Journal Sociale Intervention, 17*(3), 3–19.

QUIPPED Annual Report. (2006). Prepared for Health Canada's Interprofessional Education for Collaborative Patient-Centred Practice Strategy.

Reeves, S. (2001). A systematic review of the effects of interprofessional education on staff involved in the care of adults with mental health problems. *Journal of Psychiatric Mental Health Nursing, 8,* 533–542.

Robson, M., & Kitchen, S. (2007). Exploring physiotherapy students' experiences of interprofessional collaboration in the clinical setting: A critical incident study. *Journal of Interprofessional Care, 21*(1), 95–109.

Schmitt, M.H. (2001). Collaboration improves the quality of care: Methodological challenges and evidence from US health care research. *Journal of Interprofessional Care, 15*(1), 47–66.

Shadish, W., Cook, T., & Campbell, D. (2002). *Experimental and quasi-experimental designs for generalized causal inference.* New York: Houghton Mifflin.

Suter, E., Arndt, J., Arthur, N., Parboosingh, J., Taylor, E., & Deutschlander, S. (2009). Role understanding and effective communication as core competencies for collaborative practice. *Journal of Interprofessional Care, 23*(1), 41–51.

Van Diepen, K., MacRae, M., & Paterson, M. (2007) Use of clinical placements as a means of recruiting health care professionals to underserviced areas in southeastern Ontario. Part 2: Community perspectives. *Australian Journal of Rural Health, 15,* 29–34.

van Weel, C. (1994). Teamwork. *Lancet, 344*(8932), 1276–1279.

Verma, S., Paterson, M.. & Medves, J. (2006). Core competencies for health care professionals: What medicine, nursing, occupational therapy, and physiotherapy share. *Journal of Allied Health, 35*(2), 109–15.

Wahlström, O., Sandén, I., & Hammar, M. (1996). The student ward at the University Hospital, Faculty of Health and Sciences, Linköping. *European Nurse, 1,* 262–267.

Way, D., Jones, L., & Busing, N. (2000). *Implementation strategies: Collaboration in primary care – Family doctors and nurse practitioners delivering shared care.* Toronto: Ontario College of Family Physicians.

West, M., & Slater, J. (1988). *Team working in primary health care: A review of its effectiveness.* London: Health Education Authority.

Wilhelmsson, M., Pelling, S., Ludvigsson, J., Hammar, M., Dahlgren, L-O., & Faresjö, T. (2009). Twenty years experiences of interprofessional education in Linköping – ground-breaking and sustainable. *Journal of Interprofessional Care, 23*(2), 121–133.

World Health Organization. (2008). *Framework for action on interprofessional education and collaborative practice.* Geneva: World Health Organization.

*Anne O'Riordan BScOT*
*School of Rehabilitation Therapy*
*Queen's University, Canada*

*Margo Paterson PhD*
*School of Rehabilitation Therapy*
*Queen's University, Canada*

*Jennifer Medves PhD*
*School of Nursing*
*Queen's University, Canada*

# 19. INTERPROFESSIONAL FIELDWORK EDUCATION IN PRACTICE

The provision of optimum health and social care to diverse communities in the twenty-first century is dependent to a large extent on well-functioning teams of professionals. Though some health and social care professionals might not be grouped together in "official" teams while interacting with the same clients and their families, we would expect them to adopt a client-centred approach, to work collaboratively and to learn together. The skills of team and collaborative working need to be learned, just like communication skills—they are not inherent within the fledgling health or social care professional. It seems logical, therefore, that students should be helped to develop these skills during their training and, moreover, that they learn with students from other professions on similar clinical placements, who are interacting with the same clients, through interprofessional learning (IPL) activities. In this chapter we explore the rationale behind IPL, describe interprofessional fieldwork education, both internationally and nationally, and consider the future direction of such programs.

## TEAMWORK AND EDUCATION

Health professional teams come in many guises, dependent on their membership, location and the clientele with whom they are working. They may also be defined by their ethos—the way the professionals work together. A *multiprofessional* team is characterised by practitioners working in parallel; each professional has a clear role definition and specified tasks. There are hierarchical lines of authority and high levels of professional autonomy within the team. The practitioners consult individually with clients, setting their own goals and management plans, to deliver a particular service (see Ivey, Brown, Teske, & Silverman, 1988). However, we advocate what is described as an *interprofessional* approach. This involves practitioners from different professional backgrounds delivering services and coordinating care programs to achieve different and often disparate client needs. Goals are set collaboratively through consensual decision making, and result in an individualised care plan which may be delivered by one or more professionals. This level of collaborative practice maximises the value of shared expertise while minimising the barriers of professional autonomy. In some instances there may be a recognised team (e.g. palliative care or primary care team), or the professionals might come together temporarily into a more fluid team. For both scenarios, collaboration is required.

L. McAllister et al., (eds.), Innovations in Allied Health Fieldwork
Education: A Critical Appraisal, 215–224.

Increasing numbers of IPL activities are being developed within higher education and healthcare institutions, to support the development of interprofessional collaborative practice. The widely accepted definition of interprofessional education (IPE) is that of the Centre for the Advancement of Interprofessional Education, based in the UK: "occasions when two or more professionals learn from, with and about each other to improve collaboration and quality of care" (CAIPE, 1997). In clinical environments, there are likely to be two or more health professional students from different courses doing fieldwork. IPE involves bringing them to learn together, with agreed learning outcomes based around teamwork, but also encompassing communication, ethical practice, respect, and knowledge of each other's roles and responsibilities.

## EXAMPLES OF INTERPROFESSIONAL FIELDWORK DURING PRE-QUALIFICATION EDUCATION

The growing IPE literature includes many examples of successful fieldwork placements, described in journals such as the *Journal of Interprofessional Care* and *Medical Education*. However, logistical and funding problems mean that many are not sustained. We give examples of some of the more longstanding and well-evaluated programs of which we have experience. The World Health Organization report *Learning together to work together* (1988) precipitated interest in IPE, leading to the development of activities that are still in place today.

Clinical educators in Sweden introduced the *interprofessional training ward*, now a feature of several Swedish health professions' courses. The first ward, which involved students from nursing, medicine, physiotherapy and other professions providing care to patients on an orthopaedic ward, was an initiative of the Faculty of Health Sciences of Linköping University (Areskog, 1994). A review of 20 years' experience with this ward has been published (Wilhelmsson et al., 2009). The learning outcomes for this fieldwork placement are: knowing the roles and capabilities of other professions; the ability to cooperate with other professionals; awareness of the skills and competences of other professionals; and an understanding of professional identity. Wilhelmsson et al. (2009) reported on the successes of the training ward in terms of statistics from the Swedish National Agency for Higher Education, showing that Linköping students were highly attractive in the labour market, easily finding employment. Doctors graduating from the university over the last 6 years who have been involved in IPL activities such as the training ward have reported significantly greater confidence in relation to interprofessional skills and the ability to cooperate with professions other than medicine from other faculties in Sweden. These results have been consistent for the last 6 years. There are similar wards at the Karolinska Institute (Stockholm), in Gothenburg and Vanersborg (Vyt, 2009), as well as one at St George's University of London with Kingston University (McKenzie et al., 2007).

Fieldwork also takes place in community settings. One example is the model of IPE developed by educators at the University of Leicester (UK). This fieldwork adopts an immersion strategy. Mixed groups of students visit clients in their homes in deprived areas of the city, talk to their health and social care workers and discuss biopsychosocial elements of the clients' health and conditions. They are encouraged to explore clients' ideas and expectations of health care and to reflect on the different ways in which professionals work to meet these expectations (Lennox & Anderson, 2007).

Elsewhere, Health Canada (2004) has financed the IPECPCP (the Interprofessional Education for Collaborative Patient-Centred Practice) project. The Canadian Health Services Research Foundation has reviewed and recognised the benefits of inter-professional collaboration in primary healthcare, including positive outcomes for clients, enhanced health professional satisfaction and skills, and cost benefits in some settings (Barrett, Curran, Glynn, & Godwin, 2007). This has stimulated more IPL activities and placements across the country.

At the University of British Columbia (UBC), in an interprofessional family medicine training centre (UBC Health Clinic) on campus, students from medicine, nursing, psychology and physiotherapy see clients, adopting a client-centred team based approach to diagnosis and management. Healthcare students (including medical, nursing and pharmacy) are also placed together in rural areas to learn clinical skills and experience primary care settings through the Interprofessional Rural Program of BC (Charles, Bainbridge, Copeman-Stewart, Art, & Kassam, 2006). The local community at the fieldwork sites helps decide which professions would be most appropriate to be placed to work there.

There have been a number of systematic reviews of the effects of IPE but these tend not to distinguish between classroom- and fieldwork-based IPE. The BEME (best evidence medical education) review (Hammick, Freeth, Koppel, Reeves, & Barr, 2007) concluded that IPE is generally well received, and that students learn knowledge and skills necessary for collaborative working. However, IPE does not influence as positively the attitudes and perceptions of learners towards others in the health service delivery team. The review emphasised that staff development was a major influence on the effectiveness of IPE for learners.

IPE AND FIELDWORK PLACEMENTS IN AUSTRALIA

The majority of reported Australian IPL fieldwork programs have taken place within rural settings (e.g. Dalton et al, 2003; Albert, Dalton, Spencer, Dunn, & Walker, 2004; McNair, Stone, Sims, & Curtis, 2005, Stone, 2006). We can speculate on reasons for this: the opportunity to promote the interprofessional benefits of rural practice, attracting practitioners to rural settings on graduation; enhanced opportunities to actively participate in interprofessional work activities; the existence of cohesive interprofessional teams to support student learning, a necessity for working in rural Australia. Moreover, because fewer students undertake rural placements overall there is more opportunity for the professions to mix, and they often stay in the same accommodation and socialise together.

There are fewer accounts of fieldwork IPL within the metropolitan setting. We provide a case study of one metropolitan university's experience of providing IPL experiences to healthcare students.

*Description of the IPL Clinical Program*

In early 2003, under the auspices of the Northern Clinical School, Faculty of Medicine, the University of Sydney, a working group was established at the Royal North Shore Hospital to investigate opportunities for pre-qualification students from nursing, medicine and allied health professions to learn with, from and about each other while undertaking fieldwork placements at the hospital. The working group included academic staff from the University of Sydney and the University of Technology, Sydney (a major provider of nursing students to the hospital) and fieldwork educator practitioners from nursing, medicine and allied health. Input was also provided by the Pam McLean Centre, affiliated with the University of Sydney, whose members have expertise in health professional teamwork, communication skills training and development. The strength of this working group was that it brought together academics and hospital practitioners from a range of health professions to work on a student placement project. Given the nature of the project, interprofessional collaboration was vital for its success. Working as a practitioner at the time, one of the authors (Gillian Nisbet) was a member of the working group and later became its project leader.

Based on a literature review, an IPL program was developed and piloted in mid-2004. Reaching this stage was not without its challenges. These were consistent with barriers noted by others (e.g. a systematic review by Davidson, Smith, Dodd, Smith, & O'Loughlan, 2008), and included alignment of fieldwork placement timetables across professions; matching of students based on stage in their courses; the voluntary nature of the program and the perception by students and some fieldwork supervisors that this was an "add-on" hence unimportant aspect of their placement; incorporating IPL activities into an already crowded placement curriculum; and establishing buy-in from individual fieldwork supervisors.

The educational design of the pilot program (Nisbet, Hendry, Rolls, & Field, 2008) involved senior year healthcare students from nursing, medicine and allied health professions, on fieldwork placement on the same hospital ward, coming together for structured IPL experiences focused on teamwork. The program ran over 4 weeks (approximately 1.5 hours face-to-face contact per week). Examples of IPL activities included an initial team building activity; observations of other professions' client interventions; student-run case meetings; and case presentations. Students were on placement primarily for their particular professional requirements, with the IPL activities integrated into the usual placement activities. In part, therefore, students formed their own interprofessional student team for interacting with and managing patients within the ward environment.

*Evaluation of the IPL Clinical Program*

Student feedback was very positive, with evaluations suggesting an increased understanding and appreciation of the roles of other professions in client care and increased confidence when interacting with other professions. As a result of pilot evaluations, further iterations of the program were implemented over the following years. Using Biggs' (2003) SOLO (Structure of the Observed Learning Outcomes) taxonomy,

students' levels of understanding of other healthcare workers' roles were evaluated pre- and post-program (Nisbet et al., 2008). The SOLO taxonomy focuses on the structure of students' understanding in describing the quality of their learning outcomes. Level of understanding is categorised as follows:
- pre-structural (no understanding demonstrated)
- uni-structural (minimal understanding/general definitions)
- multi-structural (increased detail/descriptions)
- relational (understanding of several components/application of knowledge)
- extended abstract (reflect/ theorise).

Students demonstrated greater depth of understanding of the roles of other professions on completion of the IPL program. Attitudes to teamwork were generally positive prior to starting the program and remained so on completion. However, negative attitudes towards doctors were voiced by some allied health students, with some students feeling intimidated by ward doctors.

## Critique of the IPL Clinical Program

Despite the overall positive evaluations, the IPL clinical program has not continued. Difficulties in up-scaling the program to include greater numbers of students (approximately 125 students took part in 2007), including equity issues in providing access to the program for all interested students, the associated costs with co-ordinating and facilitating the program, change in leadership, and curriculum challenges with having the program included as an assessed component of the fieldwork placement, could not be overcome.

The IPL clinical program model was reliant on healthcare students coming together and learning from one another within a structured timetabled IPL program. Challenges encountered in this program led the team to ask whether similar learning outcomes could be realised through alternative more flexible models of IPL, less dependent upon students coming together at set times. For example, could students develop interprofessional working attributes from existing health professionals? Could students be expected to find IPL experiences, rather than relying on supervisors to provide them?

## An Alternative Fieldwork Model

Using the above questions as a stimulus, an alternative model of IPL that provided a framework for students to capitalise on existing opportunities within their fieldwork placements was developed at the University of Sydney (IPL Research and Development Unit, 2008). This model embedded and integrated IPL outcomes into core curricula, linking them with the university's graduate outcomes. Learning outcomes fell under three broad IPL themes: interprofessional teamwork, professional roles and interprofessional communication (Table 19.1).

IPL activities were developed to provide students with opportunities to meet these learning outcomes. They were deliberately designed to allow flexibility in relation to incorporation into individual faculty and discipline curricula and to when,

*Table 19.1. IPL curriculum framework learning outcomes (IPL Research and Development Unit, 2008, p. 5)*

---

*1. Interprofessional Teamwork*

---

By graduation, students will be able to:
1.1 Recognise the rationale for interprofessional learning and working including the implications for patient safety.
1.2 Demonstrate the ability to work with, learn from and learn about other health and social care professions.
1.3 Demonstrate an understanding of how interprofessional collaboration can impact upon provision of care.
1.4 Contribute effectively as a member of the healthcare team, providing leadership when necessary and appropriate within the interprofessional team.
1.5 Recognise, evaluate and appropriately value and support the contributions and expertise of all healthcare team members, including the patient/client as a member of the team.

---

*2. Roles of Health and Social Care Professionals*

---

By graduation, students will be able to:
2.1 Recognise unique contributions, overlapping roles and inter-dependencies between different health professionals.
2.2 Recognise one's own scope of practice in patient care, and make appropriate referrals to other healthcare professionals.
2.3 Demonstrate understanding of and respect and support for the roles of all health professionals involved in patient care delivery.

---

*3. Interprofessional Communication*

---

By graduation, students will be able to:
3.1 Identify and discuss the key characteristics of effective communication strategies within interprofessional teams.
3.2 Communicate effectively and ethically within interprofessional teams, through appropriate verbal, written and visual formats with the aim of providing optimal patient care and safety.
3.3 Detect deficiencies in communication between IP team members in the workplace and be able to suggest solutions to correct these deficiencies.
3.4 Analyze, raise and challenge differences of opinion within an interprofessional team in the interests of patient safety.

---

where and how students completed the activity. For example, one activity required students to observe another profession's intervention and then reflect on implications for their future practice, client care and interprofessional teamwork. This might involve observation of another student or of a qualified health professional. Students were asked to reflect on similarities and differences in roles and approaches to care in comparison with their own role and to consider overlaps in roles. In 2008, the Faculty of Nursing included this activity as an assessment task within a unit of study that had a fieldwork component. Students were expected to complete the task while on placement, regardless of the location and setting. In 2009 other health faculties followed similar implementation processes.

Shadowing of another profession has been suggested as a potential opportunity for students to gain an appreciation of roles and responsibilities of fellow healthcare professionals (Bainbridge, 2008). This is a relatively easy activity to instigate, though it does require support and willingness from healthcare professionals within the workplace. Reflection on team processes within a team meeting is another IPL activity that can be easily implemented, allowing students to develop insights into the complexities of interprofessional team functioning. Reflective questions draw out issues around team communication, participation, leadership and conflict management. More advanced activities involve students providing a client assessment or intervention with another health professional, ideally another student who is on placement at the same time. Similarly, mapping a client's journey provides an opportunity for students to come together and learn from each other as well as identify ways in which the client's journey could be improved through greater collaboration.

*Assessment and Evaluation*

Assessment of IPL is a recognised component of student acceptance of IPL participation (Morison, Boohan, Jenkins, & Moutray, 2003). Students are quick to judge the need to participate in IPL by whether or not it "counts" towards their overall grades. Ideally, assessment of an IPL activity would be the same across participating faculties and disciplines, but this requires considerable negotiation and curriculum adjustment. The University of Sydney IPL framework proposes a portfolio-based assessment as a means of demonstrating that learning outcomes have been met. Students may be exposed to different IPL experiences throughout their course, which can be included as evidence of learning with reflection.

As of December 2008, implementation of the IPL curriculum framework within individual faculties and disciplines at the University of Sydney had been partially achieved. Objective evidence of its impact on knowledge, attitudes and behaviours of students was not available. However, anecdotally, coordinators reported positive reception by students and insightful reflective assignments. We cannot say, therefore, whether this alternative model is as effective in meeting IPL outcomes. However, we suggest that pragmatics need to come into play when designing and delivering IPL programs for pre-qualification healthcare students.

FUTURE DEVELOPMENT AND APPLICATIONS OF THE INNOVATION

The IPE research literature is expanding rapidly as government and university policy shifts in favour of IPE and interprofessional practice. In Australia, recent documents have highlighted the importance of teamwork and collaborative practice. In *Towards a national primary health care strategy* (2008), the Australian Department of Health and Ageing recommended that "the current and future primary health care workforce is provided with high quality education (undergraduate, postgraduate and vocational) and clinical training opportunities that support interdisciplinary learning." However the document also declared: "concerns have been raised regarding whether standards for training and education are keeping pace with ... the importance of interdisciplinary learning opportunities given the growing importance of team work in the community setting" (p. 41). The 2008 Garling report on conditions in the hospitals of New South Wales included:

> Recommendation 37: that clinical education and training should be undertaken in a multi-disciplinary environment which emphasises interdisciplinary team based patient centred care; that the education and training be delivered by the most appropriate and suitable person regardless of the profession or specialty of the individual, and including, where appropriate, non-clinically trained personnel. (p. 43)

So how do we as educators create successful IPE opportunities? Findings from a comprehensive review into IPE found that authenticity, customisation and the use of adult learning principles were important for a positive experience for participants of IPE (Hammick et al., 2007). On the basis of our experiences, we suggest that these mechanisms may be adapted specifically for designing successful IPE fieldwork programs with:
- explicit interprofessional learning outcomes, for example, learning about each other's roles;
- alignment of IPE learning outcomes with authentic and relevant learning activities and student assessment;
- active learning activities that align with students' professional roles and responsibilities and also require them to work collaboratively;
- supportive workplace cultures at all levels, including staff development in the facilitation of IPE.

Sustainability of IPE is an important concern. As demonstrated in the case study described here and in the literature (Hammick et al., 2007) resources such as time, space and management support are key determinants in establishing and sustaining IPE initiatives. In the Sydney case described, circumventing problems with such resources led to a redesign of fieldwork education placements, with a widening definition of IPE, where students learned from practising health professionals as well as from other students.

Evaluating IPE outcomes is challenging (Freeth, Hammick, Reeves, Koppel, & Barr, 2005). The majority of papers tend to report on short-term participant attitudinal outcomes rather than longer-term evaluation of how any attitudinal shifts translate into changes in the workplace (Barr, Freeth, Hammick, Koppel, & Reeves, 2005). Measuring behaviour change is an important future direction for IPE research, in particular considering that IPE is complex and time-consuming to coordinate and sustain (Kilminster et al., 2004).

CONCLUSION

Fieldwork education offers an ideal opportunity for IPE due to alignment of authentic learning activities and settings with proposed outcomes of IPE that ultimately focus on improved client outcomes and care. Despite the challenges, there is a proliferation of programs that offer IPE, with evidence in support of continued innovation.

## REFERENCES

Albert, E., Dalton, L., Spencer, J., Dunn, M., & Walker, J. (2004). Doing it together: The Tasmanian interdisciplinary rural placement program. *Australian Journal of Rural Health, 12*(1), 30–31.

Areskog, N-H. (1994). Multi-professional education at the undergraduate level - The Linköping model. *Journal of Interprofessional Care, 8*(3), 279–282.

Australian Government – Department of Health and Ageing. (2008). *Towards a national primary health care strategy.* Available: http://www.health.gov.au/internet/main/publishing.nsf/Content/PHS-DiscussionPaper, accessed 1 November 2008.

Bainbridge, L. (2008). *The power of prepositions: Learning with, from and about others in interprofessional health education.* Unpublished PhD thesis, University of British Columbia.

Barr, H., Koppel, I., & Reeves, S., Hammick, M., Freeth, D. (2005). *Effective interprofessional education: Argument, assumption and evidence.* Oxford: Blackwell Science.

Barrett, J., Curran, V., Glynn, L., & Godwin, M. (2007). *CHSRF synthesis: Interprofessional collaboration and quality primary healthcare.* Ottawa, ON: Canadian Health Services Research Foundation. Available: http://www.chsrf.ca/research_themes/documents/SynthesisReport_E_FINAL.pdf, accessed 17 May 2009.

Biggs, J.B. (2003). *Teaching for quality learning at university: What the student does* (2nd ed.). Buckingham: The Society for Research into Higher Education and Open University Press.

Centre for the Advancement of Interprofessional Education (CAIPE). (1997). *Interprofessional education - a definition. CAIPE Bulletin, 13*, 19.

Charles, G., Bainbridge, L., Copeman-Stewart, K., Art, S.T., & Kassam, R. (2006). The interprofessional rural program of BC (IRPbc). *Journal of Interprofessional Care, 20*(1), 40–50.

Dalton, L., Spencer, J., Dunn, M., Albert, E., Walker, J., & Farrel, G. (2003) Re-thinking approaches to undergraduate health professional education: Interdisciplinary rural placement program. *Collegian, 10*, 17–21.

Davidson, M., Smith, R.A., Dodd, K.J., Smith, J.S., & O'Loughlan, M.J. (2008). Interprofessional pre-qualification clinical education: A systematic review. *Australian Health Review, 32*(1), 111–120.

Freeth, D., Hammick, M., Reeves, S., Koppel, I., & Barr, H. (2005). *Effective interprofessional education: Development, delivery and evaluation.* Oxford: Blackwell Publishing.

Garling P. (2008). *Final report of the Special Commission of Inquiry into Acute Care Services in NSW Public Hospitals.* Available: http://www.lawlink.nsw.gov.au/lawlink/Special_Projects/ll_splprojects.nsf/pages/acsi_finalreport, accessed 1 November 2009.

Hammick, M., Freeth, D., Koppel, I., Reeves, S., & Barr H. (2007). A best evidence systematic review of interprofessional education: BEME Guide no. 9. *Medical Teacher, 29*(8), 735–51.

Health Canada. (2004). *Interprofessional education for collaborative patient-centred practice.* Available: http://www.hc-sc.gc.ca/hcs-sss/hhr-rhs/strateg/interprof/index_e.html, accessed 17 May 2009.

IPL Research and Development Unit. (2008). *A curriculum framework for the integration of interprofessional learning (IPL) into health and social care curricula.* Sydney: The University of Sydney. Available: http://www.edsw.usyd.edu.au/learning_teaching/resources/Framework Document March08.pdf, accessed 6 October 2009.

Ivey, S., Brown, K., Teske, Y., & Silverman, D. (1988). A model for teaching about interdisciplinary practice in health care settings. *Journal of Allied Health, 17*, 189–195.

Kilminster, S., Hale, C., Lascelles, M., Morris, P., Roberts, T., Stark, P., et al. (2004). Learning for real life: Patient-focused interprofessional workshops offer added value. *Medical Education, 38*, 717–726.

Lennox, A., & Anderson, E. (2007). *The Leicester model of interprofessional education: A practical guide for implementation in health and social care.* University of Newcastle: Higher Education Academy Subject Centre for Medicine, Dentistry and Veterinary Medicine.

McKenzie, A., Craik, C., Tempest, S., Cordingley, K., Buckingham, I., & Hale. S. (2007). Interprofessional learning in practice: The student experience. *British Journal of Occupational Therapy, 7*, 358–361.

McNair, R., Stone, N., Sims, J., & Curtis, C. (2005). Australian evidence for interprofessional education contributing to effective teamwork preparation and interest in rural practice. *Journal of Interprofessional Care, 19*(6), 579–594.

Morison, S., Boohan, M., Jenkins, J., & Moutray, M. (2003). Facilitating undergraduate interprofessional learning in healthcare: Comparing classroom and clinical learning for nursing and medical students. *Learning in Health and Social Care, 2*, 92–104.

Nisbet, G., Hendry, G.D., Rolls, G., & Field, M.J. (2008). Interprofessional learning for pre-qualification health care students: An outcomes-based evaluation. *Journal of Interprofessional Care, 22*(1), 57–68.

Stone, N. (2006). The rural interprofessional education project (RIPE). *Journal of Interprofessional Care, 20*(1), 79–81.

Vyt, A. (2009). *Exploring quality assurance for interprofessional education in health and social care.* Antwerp: Garant.

WHO. (1998). *Learning together to work together.* Technical Report Series No. 769. Geneva: World Health Organization.

Wilhelmsson, M., Pelling, S., Ludvigsson, J., Hammar, M., Dahlgren, L-O., & Faresjö, T. (2009). Twenty years experiences of interprofessional education in Linköping – ground-breaking and sustainable. *Journal of Interprofessional Care, 23*(2), 121–133.

*Jill Thistlethwaite PhD*
*Institute of Clinical Education*
*The University of Warwick, UK*

*Gillian Nisbet MMEd*
*(Formerly) Faculty of Health Sciences*
*The University of Sydney, Australia*

*Rola Ajjawi PhD*
*Office of Medical Education*
*The University of Sydney, Australia*

# 20. INTERPROFESSIONAL STUDENT TEAMS IN PRACTICE

Interprofessional education (IPE) in health and social care has become an important part of pre-qualification education in the United Kingdom. Much of it has been implemented in the university or classroom setting, with few examples in the client care setting. It is rare, for example, for a team of students from several professions to take over the responsibility for caring for a group of in-patients in a hospital ward. This chapter presents an innovation in South West London that embodies this type of interprofessional learning. It includes a discussion of how student teams worked together, what changes were made as a result to the placement, the organisation of patient care and staff development.

The chapter draws on the perspectives of those participating in the Interprofessional Practice Placement (IPP) at Queen Mary's Hospital, Roehampton, London, together with some longer contributions from an individual occupational therapy (OT) student. The IPP was evaluated annually over 5 years by means of a student questionnaire and group feedback meetings. The exact structure of the questionnaire varied from year to year, although it essentially requested the same qualitative information about the most and least useful aspects of the placement in relation to interprofessional learning, as well as free comments.

## BACKGROUND

The "interprofessional student ward" was first created at Linköping in Sweden (Wahlström, Sandén, & Hammar, 1997; Fallsberg & Wijma, 1999; Fallsberg & Hammar, 2000) and then implemented at the Karolinska Institute in Stockholm (Ponzer et al., 2004). In 1996 it was introduced to the UK at the Royal London Hospital (Reeves, Freeth, McCrorie, & Perry, 2002) and this was followed in 2003–2004 by a pilot, solely for graduate-entry medical students, at Queen Mary's Hospital, Roehampton, London. From 2004, the pilot was developed to include medical and physiotherapy students from St George's, University of London, nursing students from Kingston University and OT students from Brunel University (Mackenzie et al., 2007).

## HOW THE PLACEMENT WAS ORGANISED

The SW London IPP (formerly the "interprofessional training ward") was designed to last 3 weeks and take place six or seven times a year. In between times, the ward

*L. McAllister et al., (eds.), Innovations in Allied Health Fieldwork*
*Education: A Critical Appraisal, 225–233.*

continued to run with staff replacing the student teams. The placement occurred in an elderly rehabilitation setting with a mixed patient group.

## Student Teams

For each placement a total of 30 students from medicine, nursing, OT and physio-therapy were allocated by faculty to the placement. They were split into three equal teams, with each team working shifts: late, early, then day off. To maximise the opportunity for relationships to develop, team membership was fixed and students were not permitted to swap shifts. Students were required to work over the two weekends and to attend a group induction day on the first Monday and a presentation afternoon on the final Friday.

During the course of their time on the ward, students were expected to assume responsibility for the care of the 14 patients allocated to the team, and to make collective decisions within their capabilities, in collaboration with the patients and under the supervision of ward staff. They were encouraged to engage with their team colleagues to jointly provide basic patient care and to appreciate the care given by all professions, both unique to a particular profession and common or shared. When providing care specific to their own profession, students demonstrated expertise to the others within their team, thereby generating understanding of the different roles. They were also expected to attend all multidisciplinary meetings, medical ward rounds, nursing handovers, teaching and reflective sessions.

## Supervision, Facilitation and Assessment

Members of staff on the ward facilitated the learning for all students, regardless of profession. They were strongly encouraged to facilitate rather than teach the students. They guided and supported the students whenever necessary and during the formal handover session from the late to early shift. Furthermore, one or two inter-professional facilitators, recruited from the participating professions, supported the ward staff supervising both the students' work and the day-to-day running of the ward. They arranged for teaching sessions to augment the students' learning and reflective sessions to encourage students to critically reflect on their team-work.

Interprofessional and professional progress was assessed by the interprofessional facilitators, in collaboration with ward staff, in accordance with the placement learning objectives which were set by the participating universities.

## DISCUSSION

The following discussion was generated from a retrospective examination of students' written and spoken comments. Five years of data were fragmented and sorted, and from this process several categories emerged, to which further comments from an individual OT student have been added.

*Learning about Each Other's Roles*

Students identified the sharing of roles on the placement as the most useful aspect of interprofessional learning. They enjoyed participating in and being able to ask about the roles of other professionals. "Being able to interact with other staff and gain rationale for some of the things that you are asked to do and experiencing how they work" (nursing student, 2007–8) was recognised as important for improving the quality of care that they sought to provide for the patients. They differentiated this from the shadowing of jobs that some of them had experienced before, "[I had the] chance to make [my] own decisions on patients and talk it through with other professions rather than following or shadowing" (nursing student, 2006–7).

However, the need for adequate preparation to appreciate the various roles was underlined by an OT student: "I was unsure what to expect. This was only my second practice placement and I lacked some confidence in my OT skills. I was also apprehensive about how I would defend my profession if challenged. I was keen to understand the influence and impact of different health professionals' roles on each other and the service provided to patients. I already understood how occupational therapists and physiotherapists often work closely to develop plans for rehabilitation, but I was not as aware of the interaction between and with nursing and medical staff on a daily basis" (OT student, 2007–8).

*Learning in Mixed Student Teams*

Teamwork on the ward received exclusively positive feedback, "I think this is an excellent way of breaking down the barriers between the different professionals and thus, changing attitudes towards each other" (nursing student, 2006–7). Students felt that this was a particularly important aspect of their learning, "It was a good opportunity to learn how to effectively delegate jobs among our team and demonstrate efficient team working skills and ability to cooperate" (medical student, 2007–8).

Students stated that they learned the most from other students in their teams, rather than from the ward environment or the qualified staff, "I think working as a group and arranging the care between the group really worked and we were able to learn skills from each other" (nursing student, 2008–9). If a particular student profession was not represented, due to time-tabling constraints, the interprofessional nature of the placement became limited, along with the specific learning of that role. When attempts to replace these learning opportunities were made by qualified staff, students felt that it was not as useful as learning directly from a student.

Students further commented that learning from informal discussions during breaks and in shared ad hoc experiences was as valuable as that from the structured sharing of work on the ward. "The social interaction was contributory to clinical co-operation, as by getting to know and enjoying each other's company on breaks, it was easier to open up and share ideas" (nursing student, 2007–8). "Discussing patients' care in an informal setting with the medical team was very useful" (physiotherapy student, 2007–8). "Having lunch together as a team was very good for group morale. I believe equal opportunity for contact was very positive and did not create hierarchical interactions" (OT student, 2006–7).

When there was an unequal balance of student numbers it affected the workload for the remaining students, making them feel that explicit interprofessional activities were limited. Occasionally "the ratio of medical students to therapy staff and the lack of nursing students meant the interprofessional team was not balanced" (OT student, 2007–8). "Working with a team towards common patient goals was very productive and satisfying in most cases. But as the sole therapy student on my team and rotation at times I felt a little isolated, as there was limited opportunity for peer support and it was not always a positive experience. I do not deal with confrontation well, but was forced to defend myself, on numerous occasions successfully. I learned to establish myself as an OT student within a team and realised that I can offer something different to others whilst still contributing to a common goal for the care of patients. I became an advocate for my profession; defending and believing in the values of therapy" (OT student, 2007–8).

*Learning in Structured Events*

Although students often commented that day-to-day working with other students was most useful for interprofessional learning, it was frequently reported that structured events in the day were also enjoyed and provided good learning opportunities. These included ward rounds, handover meetings, tutorials and reflection times. "Handover and MDT [multi-disciplinary team] meetings were very informative for understanding specific roles and how individual disciplines come together to share a common goal for each patient" (OT student, 2007–8).

There are several possible reasons why students on the one hand liked the informal sharing of learning but then also valued the structured sessions. Firstly, their own roles in the latter were clear, and this gave them more opportunity to consider the roles of others. Secondly, the sessions ensured that there were equal opportunities for all students to contribute. Thirdly, students were encouraged to question or debate patient care plans, something they would not normally be invited to do. "Handovers were useful for clinical reasoning, increasing knowledge on roles of team members, making decisions as a team and discussing issues/conditions as they arise" (nursing student, 2007–8).

However, at times, the structured sessions could be overly long, "sometimes there seemed to be endless handovers and meetings. We should have learned to be more concise and manage our time more effectively" (medical student, 2007–8). Meetings were also sometimes felt by therapists to be medical- or nursing-biased.

*Becoming Independent Practitioners*

Although for some, "being part of a student team with responsibility for patient care was initially quite overwhelming" (OT student, 2007–8), many students reported enjoying the independence they were given for patient care on the ward. "The balance of supervised and unsupervised work was excellent. I felt supported but also given the space and responsibility to achieve tasks independently" (OT student, 2007–8).

Students stated that it increased their confidence in their individual abilities and their own roles, "[there was a] good balance of supervision and freedom to learn from experience in a supportive environment and build confidence working independently" (OT student, 2007–8). This was particularly useful as most students were in the final year and about to qualify for practice, "I was able to expand my role as a student nurse, as the qualified staff had faith in us to 'run' the ward while making it clear that they were there to help if needed" (nursing student, 2006–7).

Other students, however, commented that the responsibility they carried for their profession-specific work limited the experience they could obtain with the other professions. "Because I spent a lot of time off the ward (especially during the week when I was with my facilitator) I did not feel I worked as hard as nursing students" (OT student, 2005–6).

The following is an example of times when interprofessional relations influenced the emotional involvement with patients and challenged a student's concept of the therapeutic relationship: "I quickly came to appreciate the reasons why a patient may be too tired or unenthusiastic to participate in therapy. For example, less than favourable experiences with nursing or medical staff may lead them to distrust physiotherapists or occupational therapists and vice versa. I enjoyed developing a therapeutic relationship with patients but this brought problems as well as benefits and I found some situations particularly emotionally challenging. Despite providing good levels of care I sometimes felt the attitudes of nursing staff to be quite detached. As an OT student my aim was to develop a therapeutic relationship with patients ... but I came to recognise my tendency to be emotionally involved. Although having this tendency helped me empathise with patients it also became a source of personal distress. I understand now that I need to protect my own wellbeing while also developing an effective therapeutic relationship" (OT student, 2007–8).

## The Balance between Interprofessional and Profession-Specific Work

Students commented both positively and negatively on the split between profession-specific work and interprofessional working. "There was [an] appropriate level of unique work; you can't impose investigations and procedures on patients that don't need them" (medical student, 2007–8). But there were "some role conflict problems – i.e. preparing for the ward round instead of doing the nursing care – felt like [we] weren't sure how much we were expected to be working and how much expected to be learning" (nursing student, 2006–7).

Sometimes, time for interprofessional work competed with profession-specific time: "between sharing roles and jobs it sometimes became difficult to organise personal profession-specific work" (physiotherapy student, 2005–6). This was somewhat dependent upon the patient load but could also be influenced by the year of study or by the individual learning objectives prescribed by the university. For example, therapy students needed more time with a qualified therapist than the other students because for them the IPP was included within a short therapy placement, which had its own profession-specific learning needs. Although positive for the therapist, "supervision with an experienced OT was very productive and I was

229

actively encouraged to be proactive in planning interventions with numerous patients and to develop my clinical reasoning skills when prioritising my workload" (OT student, 2007–8), a perception of extra attention could lead to a sense of inequality by other students: "medical and OT students had more time with qualified staff so received more mentorship support and their knowledge was quizzed more" (nursing student, 2007–8).

## Shift Working

Aspects of the placement that received negative feedback were the shift patterns and sharing care. Students generally did not enjoy working shifts, and there were often difficulties with attendance, particularly at weekends. "The shifts are awful, late followed by early, when I live such a far distance; I get home after 9 and have to go straight to bed! No two days off in a row; no way of swapping shifts if you have tutorials or an appointment" (nursing student, 2008–9). This was not universally felt. "The shift system worked well and it was good to see the ward at different times of the day, also to follow patients over two consecutive days" (medical student, 2007–8).

Every year this was raised as a problem and in some years it contributed to a few students receiving a poor grade for the placement. In addition "working outside normal hours of therapy (i.e. early morning and late evenings) was physically demanding and challenged the team to work interprofessionally. This sometimes resulted in confrontations between students when some team members appeared less committed" (OT student, 2007–8).

It was felt that changing the shift pattern would compromise the continuity of students' care, an essential feature of the placement recognised by some, "[the] shift system worked well – [it] gave sense of ownership and responsibility for our patients as a team" (medical student, 2008–9). Changing the shifts would also reduce the number of students that could be accommodated on each rotation.

## Sharing Basic Patient Care

During the interprofessional placement, students were expected to share the provision of basic patient care, which included, but was not limited to, the washing and dressing of patients, support over mealtimes, and the addressing of day-to-day concerns. Some students commented that they did not want to work as "healthcare assistants". Nevertheless, basic patient care was an important activity to which all team members could contribute. It helped students get to know and appreciate each other and better understand the patient experience. Some students recognised this and commented positively on the value of their shared role in providing care, "patient washing and dressing is a good exercise in moving and handling and more so in helping a patient to maintain dignity" (medical student, 2007–8).

"The learning experience required that all student team members take part in the daily routine of nursing care on the ward, experiencing the physical and mental demands of dealing with patients. It was satisfying to work with nursing and medical students who were genuinely keen to understand the role of an occupational therapist and how we could work together towards common goals" (OT student, 2007–8).

Not all students, however, felt that this helped with mutual appreciation: "although some [students] were keenly aware of the benefits of therapy in rehabilitation, others considered my input much less important and demonstrated little respect for OT" (OT student, 2007–8).

### Administrative Work

Another area for comment was the administrative aspect of healthcare delivery. Although most students seemed to be aware of paperwork, form filling and background organisation, many had not previously appreciated the time these tasks would take. For some, this was the first time they experienced the more mundane but realistic areas of their jobs, "there was no induction for completing paperwork i.e. referral letters. That was very time consuming and for which we were not the most appropriate people" (medical student, 2006–7). For others the ward provided a "good opportunity to see how medics' time is taken up with paperwork and referrals" (nursing student, 2005–6).

The volume of nursing administration received both negative and positive comment, "I felt that the nursing administration took over so I didn't manage to get as involved with other disciplines' work as I would have liked" (medical student, 2007–8). "It was good to practise referrals and all the paperwork side of nursing" (nursing student, 2008–9).

Involvement with administrative tasks helped students understand the influence they could have on the smooth management of a patient's stay, "it made me more aware that it is the small things that patients notice – sorting out small non-medical problems is more important to the patient than chasing results/appointments etc. It really has made me aware to treat the person, not the medical problem" (medical student, 2008–9).

### IMMEDIATE CHANGES TO THE PLACEMENT

Evaluations from the students and staff on site provided insight into the placement while it was being implemented, enabling changes to be made immediately. These generally involved alterations to the induction day in order to better prepare students for the 3 weeks. For example, training in basic moving and handling was added to ensure that all students were competent to help patients with basic care or able to recognise when help was needed. Secondly, induction from different professions helped bridge the gap between the different professional discourses. Thirdly, students were split into their teams during induction so they could start to bond with their new colleagues immediately.

Students commented on the overlap between the early and late shifts where there were more students, and roles and responsibilities were less clear. "There is usually a lull from about 12pm – 3pm when two teams are on the ward and there is confusion as to what to do" (medical student, 2008–9). As a result, a formal tutorial slot was initiated for this time.

Other ongoing problematic issues reported by students were not amenable to immediate change. For example, provision of a generic student uniform could help break down cultural differences between the professions. But this would need finance that was not available. "It would be nice if all students could wear scrubs to make everybody the same, as the uniforms segregate the students" (nursing student, 2008–9). Many tasks required student computer access, which, particularly coinciding with the introduction of new IT systems, was not always possible.

## CHANGES TO WARD WORKING

Although not yet formally analysed, the IPP highlighted areas in the day-to-day running of the ward that could be improved. Hosting a unique placement carried implications that were not truly appreciated before the start of the project. Some of these became apparent during the setting up of the placement and others developed over the years of implementation. Changes successfully implemented included the interprofessional integration of patient notes, the sharing of more information between all the professions, and new nursing shift patterns. A structured interprofessional staff development module was also developed and instigated. More subtle changes came about as ward staff facilitated student learning; they learned more about their colleagues' roles and built new connections and closer working relationships that persisted even when the students were not there.

The successful implementation of the innovation was made possible in the first place by the organisational infrastructure of Queen Mary's Hospital. This was supported by inspired leadership from a senior podiatrist within the Trust (Wandsworth, TPCT) who was able to steer the faculty/practice partnership through some of the trickier issues in the early days and continued to sustain and develop the IPP. Continuity of support for the students and staff over the 5 years was provided by the same clinical facilitator (one of the co-authors of this chapter) who provided commitment to the interprofessional ideals of the project and embodied the shared experience of the developing placement.

## THE FUTURE

With the introduction of a new medical curriculum in 2009, the school leaver and graduate entry medical streams were merged. If the IPP were to continue, places would be needed for over 300 medical and a corresponding number of nursing and therapy students. As the student experience was overwhelmingly positive, steps were taken to extend the number of placements by introducing interprofessional wards to further sites. During the last year an IPP based upon the original model was established in the hospice setting, and at the time of writing further sites were being sought for interprofessional development.

## ACKNOWLEDGEMENT

With thanks to Bethan Dickson, OT student.

## REFERENCES

Fallsberg, M.B., & Hammar, M. (2000). Strategies and focus at an integrated, interprofessional training ward. *Journal of Interprofessional Care, 4(4)*, 337–350.

Fallsberg, M.B., & Wijma, K. (1999). Student attitudes towards the goals of an interprofessional training ward. *Medical Teacher, 21(6)*, 576–581.

Mackenzie, A., Craik, C., Tempest, S., Cordingley, K., Buckingham, I., & Hale, S. (2007). Interprofessional learning in practice: The student experience. *British Journal of Occupational Therapy, 70(8)*, 358–361.

Ponzer, S., Hylin, U., Kusoffsky, A., Lauffs, M., Lonka, K., Mattiasson, A., et al. (2004). Working and learning together: Interprofessional training in the context of clinical practice: Goals and students' perceptions on clinical education wards. *Medical Education, 38*, 727–736.

Reeves, S., Freeth, D., McCrorie, P., & Perry D. (2002). "It teaches you what to expect in future...": Interprofessional learning on a training ward for medical, nursing, occupational therapy and physiotherapy students. *Medical Education, 36*, 337–344.

Wahlström, O., Sandén, I., & Hammar, M. (1997). Multiprofessional education in the medical curriculum. *Medical Education, 31(6)*, 425–429.

*Lynda D'Avray DHC*
*Centre for Medical and Healthcare Education*
*St George's, University of London, UK*

*Sarah Forrest MB ChB*
*Centre for Medical and Healthcare Education*
*St George's, University of London*
*Queen Mary's Hospital, Roehampton, London, UK*

# 21. COLLABORATIVE FIELDWORK EDUCATION

*Exploring the Intraprofessional and Interprofessional Context*

There has been an increased focus on interprofessional education within the health professions, with the premise that students in the health professions will increase their understanding and appreciation of each other's roles and this will ultimately lead to more collaborative teamwork. The importance of collaborating *intra*professionally has largely been ignored, and we therefore consider here the complexities of *intra*-professional and *inter*professional education within the context of the changes in healthcare and the political and professional environments. The rationale for this focus is that competencies are needed for collaboration both within and between professions rather than examining them as distinct concepts. Both approaches are important to educate practitioners for safe, ethical, and competent practice.

Intraprofessional education is an educational activity that occurs between two or more professionals within the same discipline, with a focus on the participants to work together, act jointly and cooperate (Hayden-Sloane, 2005). Interprofessional education is described as occasions when two or more professions learn with, from and about each other to improve collaboration and quality of care (Barr, Koppel, Reeves, Hammick, & Freeth, 2005). The key element in both is the importance of collaboration. This chapter provides a brief overview of the literature on intra- and interprofessional fieldwork education and describes the evolution in support personnel education in the province of Ontario, Canada. The objective is to highlight the important elements of intra- and interprofessional education, to assist faculty in developing fieldwork education opportunities which prepare our students for practice that embraces collaboration. It is worth noting that many terms are used to describe the role designation of the individual who provides intraprofessional support for the therapist. The terms include support personnel, support worker, support staff or aide, therapist assistant and rehabilitation assistant. In this chapter we use the term *support personnel* broadly to include the occupational therapist assistant (OTA) and physiotherapist assistant (PTA) roles. Lawson (2004, p. 227) referred to collaboration as involving the development of a new relationship between two or more entities, which is evident when

> … interdependent, autonomous stakeholders with their respective competency domains mobilize resources, and both harmonize and synchronize their operations to solve shared problems, meet common needs, capitalize on important opportunities, and obtain prized benefits.

*L. McAllister et al., (eds.), Innovations in Allied Health Fieldwork*
*Education: A Critical Appraisal, 235–243.*

There is evidence that collaboration results in improved quality of care, efficiency of care, and health outcomes for clients (Carpenter, 1995; Van der Horst et al., 1995; Tryssenaar, Perkins, & Brett, 1996; Clark, 1997). Freeth and Reeves (2004) identified collaborative practice as a core aspect of professional practice, which should be a focus of professional education. Their educational model facilitates the development of collaborative competencies. It considers the context for learning, the characteristics of both educators and learners, and the approaches to learning and teaching. They suggested a grading process for collaboration, through the introduction of uniprofessional activities as preparation for interprofessional learning. Learners can develop increased confidence through learning within their profession which can enhance their ability to learn with and from others. In their systematic review of interprofessional education, Barr, Freeth, Hammick, Koppel, and Reeves (2006) recommended that there is a need for a career-long continuum of integrated uniprofessional and interprofessional learning.

Miller and Ishler (2002) followed four student groups that included OT, PT, physician assistant, and public health students as they participated in a non-traditional community placement. The students identified benefits such as gaining interprofessional team knowledge and skills, and having direct client contact. Solomon and Jung (2006) described a model of fieldwork education in which an OT and a PT student worked together to develop roles in the management of human immunodeficiency virus (HIV) in a community health centre. They concluded that an interprofessional model of fieldwork education could be successfully implemented with organised planning and selection of students. Norman (2005) reflected that the positive effects of interprofessional education were most likely to occur in the clinical practice setting where pre-registration students from different professions work together on client-focused problems.

Salvatori (2001) suggested that shared clinical learning experiences would facilitate the development of collaborative relationships prior to graduation. Higgins (1998) used a collaborative model with OT and OTA students in fieldwork which allowed students to learn about each other's respective roles, simulated the realities of clinical practice, provided a sense of teamwork among all students, and decreased the need for individual supervision. Clinical educators had experience in supervising both student OTs and student OTAs and had knowledge of national documents and practice requirements related to OT and OTAs. The educational programs also needed to have flexibility within their curricula to allow the students to start placements on alternative dates to coordinate the student pairs. A case study by Mostrom, Ribesky, and Klukos (1999) paired a PT and student PTA in a 6-week clinical placement and found benefits of expanding opportunities for teamwork and collaboration. A challenge encountered was the inequitable division of attention from the clinical educator to each student. More recently, in a study of student OTs and OTAs, Jung, Salvatori, and Martin (2008) identified that intraprofessional learning experiences prior to graduation prepared students for collaborative practice. They introduced weekly tutorials led by both an OT and an OTA. The tutorial allowed students to consolidate new knowledge, address potential conflicts and practise team problem solving. The placement helped the students to develop respectful and trusting relationships with peers, understand their own roles and the roles of others, develop collaboration skills, and explore complementary practice.

*Support Personnel Education in Canada*

Education of support personnel in Canada has received significant attention in the professions of OT and PT over the last 20 years. There is a growing appreciation and recognition of the importance of support personnel in the service delivery of health care. For these direct clinical service workers, who may work with and be accountable to a number of different health care professionals, education in collaboration is critical to supporting and delivering services. Most of the training has been through an apprenticeship model where support personnel received their training on the job in a given discipline following completion of secondary school or some level of postsecondary education (Hagler et al., 1993). Formal support personnel education is now offered in 20 provincial community colleges across Canada, with half of these located in Ontario.

Guiding documents prepared by professional associations, governments and regulatory colleges, and use of advisory committees linking colleges to employer/ vocational relevance, have influenced curriculum review and development (CAOT, 2007a, 2007b). In these documents collaboration with colleagues, peers and other professions is clearly and prominently identified as a core requirement (OCUPRS, 2009). Students and health care professionals need to consider collaboration as a competency that traverses many domains of interactions. Nationally, the Canadian Association of Occupational Therapists (CAOT) and the Canadian Physiotherapy Association (CPA) in partnership with the Canadian Alliance of Physiotherapy Regulators have published profiles for support personnel which represent the essential broad-based competencies for practice. The introduction of the competency profiles provides guiding documents for classification and clear utilisation of support personnel in multiple roles in the area of client service and student teaching (The Alliance & CPA, 2002; CAOT, 2009). This has led to collaboration between professional national accreditation bodies within Canada to develop a combined OTA and PTA accreditation assessment process of support personnel education programs.

Since 2003, Mohawk College and McMaster University have collaborated to provide education within the academic and clinical settings for OT, OTA, PT, and PTA students. Collaboration has included cross-faculty appointments and cross-teaching between the two educational institutions. Working together and sharing resources are critical to successful management of the programs. Developing intra- and inter-fieldwork education opportunities was a natural extension of the collaboration, fieldwork education being an essential component of all curricula. Intra-professional fieldwork education has occurred over the last 8 years whereby student OTs and OTAs are assigned in pairs to clinical settings (Jung, Sainsbury, Grum, Wilkins, & Tryssenaar, 2002; Jung, Salvatori, & Martin, 2008). Current initiatives involve student pairs of OTs and OTAs, and PTs and PTAs, assigned to clinical settings. A tutorial facilitated by two educators who represent an OT and a support person is held weekly to address objectives related to collaborative practice, team building and conflict management.

*Implications for Intraprofessional Fieldwork Education*

*Student values.* Students become socialised to their professional roles by acquiring the knowledge and skills needed for practice within their chosen field. Grounding in the knowledge and skills unique to their profession is a key component to their development of professional identity (Weideman, Twale, & Stein, 2001). It can be a challenge for students to look outside their own profession while they perceive that they may not have the knowledge and skills to truly understand their own profession. Some may think that inter- and intraprofessional education are not critical to their education and that content learning is a priority to gain competence for practice. The challenge here relates to the values that students place on collaborative professional education. The plethora of literature related to the importance of IPE suggests that students are beginning to place value on collaboration from the IPE perspective (Tunstall-Pedoe, Rink, & Hilton, 2003). However, changing values can be difficult. Students may enter their courses with pre-formed and stereotyped views of their own and other professions (Horsburgh, Lamdin, & Williamson, 2001), creating barriers to the development of collaborative learning and practice. In the area of intraprofessional learning there has been little research exploring students' values in relation to working with each other. Jung et al. (2008) reported that OT and OTA students who had placements together gained new appreciation of intraprofessional learning.

*Role expectations of the educators.* Therapist educators may encounter a number of challenges. The first is related to the lack of clarity regarding their professional expectations to educate student support personnel. There are clear guidelines from the Canadian PT and OT national bodies that being an educator is one of the key competencies for practice (The Alliance, CPA, ACCPAP, CUPAC, 2004; CAOT, 2007b). It is expected that therapists will educate students within their own professions. However, the professional responsibility to supervise student support personnel is less explicit.

Secondly, most educators have limited skills in educating multiple students in the clinical setting. They need to understand the curricula from different programs, frame the learning environment to meet the educational needs of all the students, utilise collaborative models of supervision, and dedicate individual evaluation time to students. Discussing learning needs and entry-level preparation in the United States, Crist, Brown, Fairman, Whelan, and McClure (2007) identified three broad areas of commonality in the interventions provided by OTs and OTAs: preparatory and ADL-related; motor and posture skills; and mental functions. These core areas should be applicable to the fieldwork learning experiences of both sets of learners and would be helpful for educators in planning intraprofessional placements. Professional behaviours and skills are also important for all learners in the health care system. Palladino and Jeffries' (2000) assessment tool for OT and OTA students addresses relevant skills such as communication, cooperation, dependability, professionalism and initiative that are linked to education standards. Selection of teaching and evaluation strategies should be based on the domains of learning and level of learner (Cranton, 2000) to reflect the OTA focus on technical expertise and the OT focus on theory and evidence-based practice.

The third challenge relates to the comfort and skill of the therapist educator in supervising support personnel. With the evolution of the education of support personnel, clinicians may have difficulty keeping pace with the assistant role and how such personnel can be utilised within their practice setting. In physiotherapy, recommendations were identified in the late 1990s by Loomis et al. (1997, 1998) regarding the need to educate professionals and to establish and standardise supervision requirements of support personnel. Nancarrow and Mackey (2005) reported that ambiguous supervision and accountability relationships existed between support personnel and their supervisors. They noted that occupational therapists did not automatically have the skills to supervise support personnel, and stressed that it is important to provide interactions with support workers during OT education. If therapists have unclear supervisory approaches with the support personnel within their practice setting they may be less inclined to offer placements to student support personnel and student therapists at the same time. The last challenge is related to liability. Ultimately therapists are responsible for the actions of all the students they supervise. Jung, Solomon, and Cole (2005) reported that clinical educators were concerned with their liability when overseeing role-emerging placements that have less clear structures and role definition.

National competency profiles also address the role of support personnel in education (The Alliance & CPA, 2002; CAOT, 2009). The expectation is that they will contribute to the educational experience of students by acting as a resource, following the clinical objectives of the educational programs, and providing feedback and evaluation within their classification. Support personnel can play a significant role in the education process of both the student support personnel and the student therapist and can be a powerful influence in their entry to practice. However, role utilisation strategies need to be clearly identified, in concert with the therapist, to support effective and efficient teaching while delivering service. The challenges facing support personnel are thus related to developing the knowledge and skills in teaching their scope of practice, using supervision models and communicating feedback.

*Power Relationships*

Although the power relationship between professions and within professions impacts on daily practice it is often an unspoken issue in health care. Making it explicit and transparent to the learners can be the first step in promoting collaboration and relationship building.

The power relationship is different in the intraprofessional relationship than in an interprofessional relationship. As professionals, we work collaboratively with other professions, but we are neither responsible nor accountable to each other's professional groups. The relationship between the assistant and the therapist, moreover, is a closer one that is still evolving. In Canada, therapists are responsible for the actions of the assistants and as such have a supervisory position of real power and authority with the assistant. The relationship involves both interdependency and dependency. Despite the difference in power, Hagler and McFarlane (1997) have suggested that assistants and professionals who worked in effective partnerships emphasise collaboration as an important element of their relationship. However, Kumar, Nyland, Young, and Grimmer's (2006) systematic review identified that support personnel can still be marginalised and not recognised as being integral to the team. Jung et al. (2002) reported that the term *supervisor* seemed to set up barriers to the development of effective working relationships for some student OTs and OTAs on placement. The students were more comfortable working in environ-ments where the learning *partnership* concept was stressed rather that the supervision aspects.

## Recommendations and Future Directions

A number of areas warrant further exploration and action from the following stake-holders. Further refinement of competency profiles and role expectations to guide practice and education for educators and students in both inter- and intraprofessional education and collaboration is needed. The shift in the educational preparation of OTAs and PTAs from certificate to diploma degree will force all stakeholders to redefine and re-examine what constitutes rehabilitation service, how this service is delivered, and by whom. Although there are guidelines to assist OTs and PTs in working with support personnel (The Alliance & CPA, 2002; CAOT, 2009) their status within *professional associations and regulatory bodies* is still being defined and clarified. Over the next decade the role of the OTA and PTA in Canada will be enhanced in scope of practice and expertise. and professional organisations and regulatory bodies should be poised to take a leading position in facilitating this transition.

*Education programs* play a primary role in the socialisation process of students into their professions (Weideman et al., 2001). The programs have a responsibility to educate students in the knowledge, skills and behaviours required for collaborative roles. Areas of curriculum focus directed at the student can include (1) changing preconceived attitudes and stereotypes about other professionals; (2) ensuring opportunities for intra- and interprofessional learning; and (3) preparing students for practice realities within a system that is hierarchical, focusing on accountability and responsibility (scope of practice) vs power differences. The programs also have a responsibility to train and support clinical educators for their pivotal roles in teaching students. Role-modelling exemplary collaboration can be a powerful influence on students' future practice.

From an *individual perspective*, each therapist and support person should assume the responsibility to educate students both within and beyond their profession. We need to reconsider the traditional thinking of each profession having exclusive domain over unique knowledge and skills (Larson, 1977), and embrace a more open learning environment that supports learning which will benefit the client in the area of excellent service delivery. Ultimately clients do not really care what profession we are; they just want to have the best health care possible by the best people.

The current focus on interprofessional education provides an opportunity for educators to focus on collaboration between professions. However, in the enthusiasm to support interprofessional collaboration we should not forget the need for intra-professional education and collaboration. Academic and clinical educators need to provide learners with the knowledge, skills and attitudes to embrace a future where working together is a key expectation and competency in practice both between and within professions.

## REFERENCES

Barr, H., Koppel, I., Reeves, S., Hammick, M., & Freeth, D. (2005). *Effective interprofessional education: Argument, assumption and evidence.* London: Blackwell Publishing.

Barr, H., Freeth, D., Hammick, M., Koppel, I., & Reeves, S. (2006). The evidence base and recommendations for interprofessional education in health and social care. *Journal of Interprofessional Care, 20*(1), 75–78.

Canadian Alliance of Physiotherapy Regulators [The Alliance] & Canadian Physiotherapy Association [CPA]. (2002). *Competency profile: Essential competencies of physiotherapist support workers in Canada.* Toronto, ON: Authors.

Canadian Alliance of Physiotherapy Regulators [The Alliance], Canadian Physiotherapy Association [CPA], Accreditation Council for Canadian Physiotherapy Academic Programs [ACCPAP] & Canadian Physiotherapy Association and the Canadian Universities Physical Therapy Academic Council [CUPAC] (2004). *Essential competency profile for physiotherapist in Canada.* Toronto: National Physiotherapy Advisory Group.

Canadian Association of Occupational Therapists [CAOT]. (2007a). *Background paper: Development of a practice profile for support personnel in occupational therapy in Canada: Environmental scan.* Ottawa: CAOT Publications ACE.

Canadian Association of Occupational Therapists [CAOT]. (2007b). *Profile of occupational therapists of Canada.* Ottawa: CAOT Publications ACE.

Canadian Association of Occupational Therapists [CAOT]. (2009). *Practice profile for support personnel in occupational therapy.* Ottawa: CAOT Publications ACE.

Carpenter, J. (1995). Interprofessional education for medical and nursing students: Evaluation of a program. *Medical Education, 29*, 265–272.

Clark, P.G. (1997). Values in health care professional socialization: Implications for geriatric education in interdisciplinary teamwork. *The Gerontologist, 37*(4), 441–451.

Cranton, P. (2000). *Planning instruction for adult learners* (2nd ed.). Toronto: Wall & Emerson.

Crist, P.A., Brown, L.I., Fairman, A., Whelan, L., & McClure, L. (2007). Entry-level OTR and COTA intervention utilization derived from NBCOT practice analysis: Implications for fieldwork experiences. *Occupational Therapy in Health Care, 21*(2), 71–89.

Freeth, D., & Reeves, S. (2004). Learning to work together: Using the presage, process, product (3P) model to highlight decisions and possibilities. *Journal of Interprofessional Care, 18*(1), 43–56.

Hagler, P., & McFarlane, L. (1997). *Collaborative service delivery by assistants and professionals (revised). A manual for occupational therapists, physical therapists, speech-language pathologists and assistants.* Prepared for the Alberta Association of Registered Occupational Therapists, Alberta Physiotherapy Association, College of Physical Therapists, and Speech-Language and Hearing Association of Alberta. Edmonton, Alberta: Alberta Rehabilitation Coordinating Council.

Hagler, P., Madill, H., Warren, S., Loomis, J., Elliott, D., & Pain, K. (1993). *Role and use of support personnel in the rehabilitation disciplines.* Final report on Project #6609-1730-RP to the National Health Research and Development Program. Edmonton, AB: University of Edmonton Press.

Hayden-Sloane, P. (2005). Collaborative models of treatment. In A. Wagenfeld & J. Kaldenberg (Eds.), *Foundations of pediatric practice for occupational therapy assistants* (pp. 23–32). Thorofare, NJ: Slack.

Higgins, S. (1998). The OT/OTA collaborative model of fieldwork education. *OT Practice,* October, 41–44.

Horsburgh, M., Lamdin, R., & Williamson, E. (2001). Multi-professional learning: The attitudes of medical, nursing, and pharmacy students to shared learning. *Medical Education, 35,* 876–883.

Jung, B., Sainsbury, S., Grum, R., Wilkins, S., & Tryssenaar, J. (2002). Collaborative fieldwork education with student occupational therapists and student occupational therapist assistants. *Canadian Journal of Occupational Therapy, 69*(2), 95–104.

Jung, B., Salvatori, P., & Martin, A. (2008). Intraprofessional student fieldwork education: Occupational therapy and occupational therapist assistant students learning together. *Canadian Journal of Occupational Therapy, 1,* 42–50.

Jung, B., Solomon, P., & Cole, B. (2005). Role-emerging placements in rehabilitation sciences. In P. Solomon & S. Baptiste (Eds.), *Innovations in rehabilitation sciences education: Educating leaders for the future* (pp. 39–58). Berlin: Springer-Verlag.

Kumar, S., Nyland, L., Young, A., & Grimmer, K. (2006). Final report on the systematic review of the literature on the utilisation of support workers in community based rehabilitation. Available: http://www.health.qld.gov.au/qhcrwp/docs/qh_final_report.pdf, accessed 21 December 2009.

Larson, M.S. (1977). *The rise of professionalism: A sociological analysis.* Berkeley: University of California Press.

Lawson, H. (2004). The logic of collaboration in education and the human services. *Journal of Interprofessional Care, 18,* 225–237.

Loomis, J., Hagler, P., Forward, J., Wessel, J., Swinamer, J., & McMillan, A. (1997). Current utilization of physical therapy support personnel in Canada. *Physiotherapy Canada, 49,* 284–291.

Loomis, J., Hagler, P., Forward, J., Wessel, J., Swinamer, J., & McMillan, A. (1998). Future utilization of physical therapy support personnel in Canada. *Physiotherapy Canada, 50,* 17–24.

Miller, B., & Ishler, K. (2001). The rural elderly assessment project: A model for interdisciplinary team training. *Occupational Therapy in Health Care, 15,* 3–34.

Mostrom, E., Ribesky, C., & Klukos, M. (1999). Collaboration in clinical education: Use of a 2:1 student physical therapist–student physical therapist assistant model. *Physical Therapy Case Reports, 2* (2), 45–57.

Nancarrow, S., & Mackey, H. (2005). The introduction and evaluation of an occupational therapy assistant practitioner. *Australian Occupational Therapy Journal, 52,* 293–301.

Norman, I. (2005). Inter-professional education for pre-registration students in the health professions: Recent developments in the UK and emerging lessons. *International Journal of Nursing Studies, 42,* 119–123.

Ontario Council of University Programs in Rehabilitation Sciences [OCUPRS]. (2009). Essential skills and competencies required for the study of speech-language pathology, audiology, physiotherapy, occupational therapy. Toronto: OCUPRS.

Palladino, J., & Jeffries, R. (2000). *The occupational therapy fieldwork manual for assessing professional skills.* Philadelphia: F.A. Davis.

Salvatori, P. (2001). The history of occupational therapy assistants in Canada: A comparison with the United States. *Canadian Journal of Occupational Therapy, 68*(4), 217–227.

Solomon, P., & Jung, B. (2006). An interdisciplinary role-emerging placement in HIV rehabilitation. *International Journal of Therapy Rehabilitation, 13,* 59–64.

Tryssenaar, J., Perkins, J., & Brett, L. (1996) Undergraduate interdisciplinary education: Are we educating for future practice? *Canadian Journal of Occupational Therapy, 63(4),* 245–251.

Tunstall-Pedoe, S., Rink, E., & Hilton, S. (2003). Student attitudes to undergraduate interprofessional education. *Journal of Interprofessional Care, 17*(2), 161–172.

Van der Horst, M., Turpie, I., Nelson, W., Cole, B., Sammons, S., Sniderman, P., et al. (1995). St. Joseph's Community Health Center model of community-based interdisciplinary health care team education. *Health & Social Care in the Community, 3,* 33–42.

Weidman, J.C., Twale, D., & Stein, E.L. (2001). *Socialization of graduate and professional students in higher education: A perilous passage?* ASHE-ERIC Higher Education Report, 28(3). San Francisco: Jossey-Bass.

*Bonny Jung MEd*
*School of Rehabilitation Science*
*McMaster University, Canada*

*Patty Solomon PhD*
*School of Rehabilitation Science*
*McMaster University, Canada*

*Adele Martin Dip. P & OT*
*Mohawk College of Applied Arts and Technology, Canada*

# SECTION VII: STUDENT ASSESSMENT IN FIELDWORK EDUCATION

SUE MCALLISTER, MICHELLE LINCOLN, ALISON FERGUSON
AND LINDY MCALLISTER

# 22. DILEMMAS IN ASSESSING PERFORMANCE ON FIELDWORK EDUCATION PLACEMENTS

There are many approaches that aim to assess students' ability to practise competently in the workplace. The reliability and validity of these assessments, their ability to predict professional performance in the workplace, and their often paradoxical negative impact on learning present dilemmas that have been discussed widely in the health education literature. In the meantime, the "real" challenge remains – assessment of actual performance in real workplaces (Wass, van der Vleuten, Shatzer, & Jones, 2001). It is this challenge that we embraced when we embarked upon the process of developing a competency-based assessment of speech language pathology students' observed performance in the workplace in 2001 (McAllister, 2005). This program of research has resulted in the development of COMPASS®: Competency assessment in speech language pathology (McAllister, Lincoln, Ferguson, & McAllister, 2006). Projects have also been undertaken to support the adoption of COMPASS® across all speech language pathology programs in Australia and New Zealand as well as in Singapore and Malaysia (Ferguson, Lincoln, McAllister, & McAllister, 2008; Lincoln, Ferguson, McAllister, & McAllister, 2008). Our understanding of the assessment of observed performance using a competency-based framework continues to be developed through participation in research and collaborative benchmarking projects. We believe this experience in assessment is applicable to the assessment of performance across the allied health professions.

In this chapter we draw upon this experience to share some frameworks we have used to manage dilemmas arising in competency-based assessment in the workplace and to guide decision making in assessment design and application. These include addressing fairness, and its interaction with objectivity and subjectivity and relationship to reliability, and choosing assessment formats and processes that are both feasible and support valid assessment – see Table 22.1 for a summary of these in relation to the approach to assessment with which we have been involved. Assessment also impacts on learning and involves competing agendas of certification for practice and guiding of students' learning and development. These considerations need to be balanced with issues of authenticity – are we really assessing what we want to assess? To this end we need to understand the nature of competence in allied health professional practice.

*L. McAllister et al., (eds.), Innovations in Allied Health Fieldwork*
*Education: A Critical Appraisal, 247–260.*

*Table 22.1. Dilemmas and examples of strategies*

| Dilemma | Examples of strategies (from COMPASS®) |
| --- | --- |
| Learning and competence | Assessment includes relevant generic and occupational competencies<br>Competencies emphasise principles and qualities of practice, rather than being checklists of isolated skills |
| Fairness | Assessment design and process supports quality judgment<br>Rating format includes clear rating criteria<br>Manual provides examples of observable behaviours<br>Rating scale is validated<br>Measurement model focuses on quality assessment<br>Students involved in development and assessment process<br>Judgment based on multiple assessments over student's placement<br>Rated by person who best knows student's typical performance |
| Authenticity | Competencies developed with reference to profession's understanding of nature of practice<br>Assessment conducted in the workplace to reflect complexity, scope of practice, integrated demonstration of variety of competencies<br>Performance rated by real practitioner on real tasks with real people |
| Impact on learning | Developmental pathway is described and subsequent assessments build on this (e.g. summative assessment becomes formative for the start of the next placement)<br>Assessment is non-graded and criterion-based not normative<br>Detail in assessment resource allows for developing learning goals at formative assessment and planning for learning |

## Nature of Competence

Given that fieldwork education placements are about learning the doing of allied health practice, competency-based approaches align well with developing criteria for teaching and assessment of that doing. However, the nature of professional competency and the appropriate definitions to support development of teaching and assessment approaches have become the focus of protracted debate. The dilemma central to this debate is development of a definition of competency that includes both specific skills as well as the ability to practise in a range of complex and dynamic workplace environments.

## Competency Frameworks

The most dominant competency paradigm in health professional education has its origins in medical education. It takes a reductionist approach that aims to describe every skill that has to be competently performed for the professional to be deemed competent. As a result, many competency frameworks have presented detailed mapping of professional practice. This approach has been criticised as unwieldy in practice and as neglecting the integrative aspects of competency (i.e. the whole of professional practice is more than the sum of its parts (Gonczi, 1992). Hodges (2006) has highlighted that the discourse, or world view, espoused by this type of reductionist competency-based education model risks creating professionals who have isolated skill sets that are not integrated with the knowledge to create complex meaningful performance in the workplace.

Reductionist approaches have resulted in large curriculum documents and assessment approaches that "slice and dice" (Albanese, Mejicano, Anderson, & Gruppen, 2008, p. 7) competency into smaller and smaller units and neglect holistic aspects of professional practice. The dilemma seems to be that the harder a profession tries to define competency for teaching and assessment, the further it moves away from what it understands as real professional competency. Students' overall competence is assumed to be represented by adding together performances measured by assessments of subsets of competencies using different stand-alone formats and processes that appear to bear little relationship to each other. One example, cited by Epstein (2007), uses history taking and examination (MiniCEX) + overall performance in placement (in training assessment forms) + specific technical skills (Direct Observation of Procedural Skills or DOPS) + communication skills (360 degree feedback form) and so forth = overall level of competence.

The challenge is to reflect an understanding that professional practice involves the "competent exercise of complex professional judgment across all tasks and contexts of the profession" (McAllister, 2005, p. 107). An alternative combined framework for conceptualising competence has emerged in allied health, particularly in Australia. These frameworks differ from those previously described in two major respects. First, competencies are framed as active processes of professional practice that interact with each other. For example, physiotherapy and speech language pathology (among others) identify professional practice as including processes of assessment, interpretation and analysis of assessment findings, planning intervention, implementing intervention, and professional development (Speech Pathology Association of Australia, 2001; Dalton, Keating, & Davidson, 2009). In this view, competencies are processes involved in the practice of our professions, or "the things we do" when working with patients or clients. This is different from static skills-based competencies (things we have) and roles (things we are). Professional action therefore is seen as arising from the integration of aspects of knowledge, skill and personal qualities to form these processes or practices, rather than from a collection of separate discrete components of competency. Second, this process or "doing" orientation is understood as including generic competencies, those aspects of professional practice that enable us to coordinate and integrate occupational competencies holistically. This approach to defining competencies may also reflect differences in understanding of the nature of learning and assessment between medicine and other health disciplines. Allied health practitioners appear to view learning as a process, unlike the more dominant Western paradigm that views learning as a product to be acquired (Hager, 2004).

For example, in speech language pathology research, practitioners, educators and students all identified integrative generic aspects of practice as important for inclusion in any assessment of performance in fieldwork education placements (McAllister, Lincoln, Ferguson, & McAllister, 2010). As a result, assessment items representing four groups of generic competencies were included for assessment in COMPASS®: reasoning, lifelong learning, communication and professional behaviour (McAllister et al., 2006). These four competencies are seen as critical for integrating holistic professional action across the occupational competencies (McAllister et al., 2010). Other competency frameworks, for example in physiotherapy, have included generic competencies such as communication and professional behaviour, and these are represented in their assessment of students' observed performance in fieldwork education placements (Dalton et al., 2009).

The allied health focus on integrative and process aspects of competency also facilitates the development of clear descriptors and exemplars of performance that are indicative of the competencies of interest. Qualities of these performances can also be described across a continuum of development, allowing for competency to be vertically integrated over time across practice and across the scope of practice. For example, COMPASS® includes three levels of behavioural descriptor to guide ratings against each of the competencies: novice, intermediate, and entry-level (McAllister et al., 2010). The development of these descriptors was guided by combining concepts of managing complexity, transforming knowledge into practice, and degree of support/guidance required to perform (McAllister et al., 2010). The pharmacy profession in Australia has recently begun describing levels of performance across curriculum against pharmacy competencies with reference to five qualities: skills development, level of support, time taken, clinical reasoning and focus on self versus client (personal communication, Ieva Stupans, 2009).

Basing workplace performance assessment on these principles also allows the development of more manageable frameworks that can be reliably and validly used by fieldwork educators to assess student performance. For example, fieldwork educators can validly assess a student's performance across 11 competencies on COMPASS® (McAllister et al., 2006) and across seven competencies on the *Assessment of Physiotherapy Practice* (Dalton et al., 2009). These frameworks also permit this brief, feasible assessment format to be supported by resources providing more detail when more difficult assessment judgments are to be made, a need strongly identified by fieldwork educators (McAllister, 2005).

## Conflicting Theories of Learning and Competence

However, as is to be expected when discussing dilemmas, there are alternative viewpoints. Including generic competencies requires specification of tacit understandings within practice which may not be amenable to description. Yet this may not be as great a barrier as previously anticipated, as validation of the COMPASS® assessment indicated that the generic competencies were well described and understood by fieldwork educators and students (McAllister, Lincoln, Ferguson, & McAllister, 2004). The process approach to competency accepts that judgment is central to assessment, and aiming for objectivity through the use of specific (or reductionist) checklists of items is counterproductive. Process-based competencies mean that specific prerequisite skills that must be acquired before graduating into the profession are not specified as individual items of assessment on placement. This view of competence as processes rather than products may at times clash with other unarticulated and commonly held reductionist views of learning and how it should be assessed.

## FAIRNESS

To paraphrase the art connoisseur, surely "we know competence when we see it" – so where do the dilemmas lie? Why are so many of us able to empathise with Chapman's experience of "agonising" about assessment of students' performance in fieldwork education placements (Chapman, 1998, p. 157)? Although "agony" may be too strong a word for some of us, there is no doubt that the process of assessing students' fieldwork performance has an affective element for fieldwork educators (Duke, 1996; Ilott & Murphy, 1997). Notions of fairness are central to these tensions (Chapman, 1998). We wish to be fair to our students, clients, profession, workplace, and ourselves as assessors. Fair assessment is a subjective concept and therefore involves the same ethical and attentive processes of judgment that inform our daily practice as allied health professionals (Hager, 2000). Fair assessment can be considered from the different perspectives of those who hold a stake in the outcome: the student, the university and the fieldwork educator.

From the student perspective, fairness is a key condition for any assessment. By fairness, students generally refer to a constellation that includes unbiased judgments (the educator is not prejudiced), clear performance criteria (all students are measured against the same criteria with the same expectations), equal opportunity (all students have the same level of access to learning opportunities) and assessment tools that match the learning and assessment tasks. From the university perspective, a fair assessment is one that can be used reliably (different assessors generate the same marks or decisions), is a valid measure of performance (it assesses what it sets out to assess), minimises the degree of subjective judgment required (promotes objective measures), differentiates well between levels of student performance, conforms to the university's assessment policies and procedures, and possibly even helps meet accreditation requirements. From the fieldwork educator perspective, a fair assessment is one that manages problems related to variance in amount of exposure to learning opportunities, complexity of learning opportunities, and degree of support provided or needed in completing assessment tasks. Competency assessment that occurs in real-world situations also needs to incorporate a duty of care for the person or situation where the assessment is situated. Given the diverse perspectives of students, university and fieldwork educators and the characteristics required of assessment (Table 22.2) it is not surprising that achieving fairness in competency assessment is a dilemma. In the following section we discuss some of the issues central to achieving fair assessment: objectivity and subjectivity, judgment, validity and reliability.

*Table 22.2. Characteristics of fair assessment (adapted from Hager et al., 1994)*

| Characteristics of fair assessment | Examples of strategies (from COMPASS®) |
|---|---|
| Does not disadvantage particular students (i.e. equitable for individuals and groups of students) | Observed performance is assessed, not how the student reached a decision on a particular course of action. |
| Assessment procedures and criteria for judging performance are made clear to students | Students are provided with copies of the assessment form and manual and provided with familiarisation sessions; fieldwork educators are asked to involve students in the assessment process. |
| Assessment procedures support learning | COMPASS® is validated on the basis of a detailed formative assessment conducted at the half-way point of every placement. |
| There should be a participatory approach | It is recommended to fieldwork educators that the student is involved in the assessment process and students are informed that this is the expectation. The formative assessment component supports this process. |
| Information and opportunities must be provided for students to challenge assessments and there must be provision for reassessment | The COMPASS® Technical Manual recommends that (a) assessments are used as part of the usual university assessment process, allowing opportunities for students to challenge assessment results, (b) COMPASS® results are interpreted in the light of all relevant information on the student's performance, and (c) students are involved in the assessment process. |

## OBJECTIVITY AND SUBJECTIVITY IN ASSESSMENT

As identified in the introduction, assessment of performance in the workplace can be considered the "gold standard" for determining competency to practise (Wass et al., 2001), as opposed to decontextualised assessment strategies with unproven links to real-life performance in the workplace (Rethans et al., 2002). Workplace assessments have generally relied on subjective evaluations by supervising clinicians, self, and peer assessments. This reliance on workplace-based evaluations, often by the same person who is responsible for teaching the student(s) on a day-to-day basis, is common practice across allied health professions. Such assessments are faced with threats to validity and reliability, on the basis, for example, of their vulnerability to subjective bias (Epstein & Hundert, 2002). In particular, concern has been expressed about the use of subjective judgment in determining whether students' performances are at a particular level (Alexander, 1996; Chapman, 1998). This concern has been echoed by fieldwork educators who are concerned that their judgment is influenced by irrelevant personality factors (Duke, 1996).

*Judgment*

The concern that the subjective judgmental nature of assessment unduly affects the evaluation of students' performance is not well supported in the literature. In generalisability studies that use a matrix to examine the influence of various factors upon the scores received by the students, the judgment of raters has in fact been found to be a relatively small source of error. These studies have found that raters' or judges' behaviour generally had a much smaller effect on scores than other factors such as assessee knowledge and tasks sampled (Shavelson, Gao, & Baxter, 1993; Govaerts, van der Vleuten, & Schuwirth, 2002; Keen, Klein, & Alexander, 2003). This is in fact not surprising, given that professional judgment of client performance is central to practice; therefore fieldwork educators are typically experienced and expert at making judgments based on observed behaviours. This ability to make reliable judgments of performance is exemplified in the literature that has identified that global ratings based on qualities of performance tend to have higher reliability than specific ratings based on checklists (Cohen, Rothman, Poldre, & Ross, 1991; Govaerts et al., 2002).

We contend that judgment is both inevitable in and integral to the design and use of any valid assessment tools. Competency-based assessment of performance in the workplace does not appear to be any more disadvantaged by the need for judgment than any other assessment strategy. Ultimately, as for any assessment approach, issues related to generalisability and fairness of performance assessment must be attended to during assessment design, and the related sources of error must be controlled for and evaluated, or indeed, judged (McAllister, 2005). Strategies to do so include supporting a "rich" understanding of competence and performance (Jones, 2000). COMPASS® provides this richness through exemplars of aspects of observed performance that would identify where a student lies on the continuum from novice to entry-level on each of the competencies, as well as formative assessment strategies that are described later in this chapter.

A final consideration regarding judgment is that quality judgment of performance needs to be based on multiple observations of performance. Multiple observations underpin reliability and validity of all assessment (Schuwirth et al., 2002), but are usually the result of a number of different people (examiners) making one-off observations and judgments of the student's performance. Workplace-based integrated assessment by fieldwork educators working directly with students ensures that assessment is based on multiple observations and judgments about students' ability to learn and practise their profession. This enhances the perception of fairness, as fieldwork educators can identify whether performance is representative of a student's overall competence.

## VALIDITY

It is likely that validity of competency assessment means different things to students, fieldwork educators and university assessors. For students it might mean, "Does the assessment actually measure my competency development or is it measuring something else like my personality or interpersonal skills?". Fieldwork educators might question whether the assessment tool can accurately capture the range and complexity of their workplace and caseload and the competencies needed to work in the area. University assessors might be concerned with whether decisions made regarding students' ability to progress in their university program are based on sound measurement tools that have known measurement properties and manage potential sources of bias.

The model of validity that most strongly guided our development of COMPASS® was that of Messick (1996). This model has largely replaced the previously dominant model of content, criterion-related and construct validity (American Education Research Association, 1999). Messick's (1996) model incorporates reliability as one of six aspects of validity to be considered when designing fair assessments (Table 22.3). This ensures that reliability is not privileged at the expense of validity (Norman, van der Vleuten, & de Graaff, 1991).

The process of determining the validity of a competency assessment involves accumulating evidence to provide a sound scientific basis for the proposed score interpretations (American Education Research Association, 1999). It is the development and articulation of this scientific basis for score interpretation that promotes fairness of assessment.

*Table 22.3. Aspects of validity (based on Messick, 1996)*

| Aspects | Focus |
| --- | --- |
| Content validity | Is the content relevant and representative of allied health competencies? |
| Substantive validity | Is the assessment consistent with theoretical models of competency development? |
| Structural validity | Does the rating scale accurately measure a range of competent performance? |
| Generalisability | Can the assessment results be generalised across the student's whole performance in this placement, or even across other fieldwork placements and caseloads? |
| External validity | Does the assessment yield similar results to other assessments of competence? |
| Consequences | Are the assessment results a good basis for action (e.g. passing or failing the student)? |

## RELIABILITY

We contend that students, fieldwork educators and university assessors may share ideas about fairness in relation to reliability. Essentially they are all concerned that any fieldwork educator would assign a student similar marks or ratings. This can be seen in students' comments that some fieldwork educators are "easy" or "hard" markers, or students' beliefs that they would have passed a fieldwork placement or done better if they had had a different fieldwork educator.

Traditional reliability analysis focuses on identifying and quantifying the inevitable errors that occur during measurement (i.e. quantifying the inconsistency and consistency of examinee performance). It acknowledges that human performance is variable and that this will affect test scores due to a variety of factors. Factors include variations in physical and mental efficiency of the test taker, uncontrollable fluctuations in external conditions under which the assessment is undertaken (e.g. client complexity), tasks required by the assessment that may favour one individual over another, and inconsistencies in the judgment of assessors. As already mentioned, basing assessment on multiple observations by a fieldwork educator familiar with the student's usual range of performances is important. Furthermore, using a competency model that reflects the fieldwork educator's understanding of competency and provides information for guiding ratings will assist with reliability. Finally, using a scoring system that identifies and makes allowance for variability in ratings will support the reliable use of an assessment (McAllister et al., 2010). These strategies are thought to have supported the high inter-rater reliability found in the validation trials of the COMPASS®.

To summarise, notions of reliability and error of measurement are important components of the overall validity of an assessment to the extent that they contribute to an understanding of a justifiable interpretation of test scores. From a fairness perspective it is important that competency assessments have acceptable reliability for students to be confident in the feedback that the assessment provides. Acceptable reliability also allows fieldwork educators to make confident judgments of competency development.

## AUTHENTICITY

In this section we widen the discussion of validity and defining competence to consider the notion of authenticity; that is, the extent to which we are assessing students doing the task that they will be expected to do as graduate health care professionals. As argued already, fieldwork settings provide multiple opportunities to observe the performance of students as they participate within the authentic delivery of care. Their participation might vary in the degree to which they are centrally involved in client care. Beginning students might be involved in assisting with simple tasks, and even advanced students would typically be well supported in their participation in decision making regarding client discharge (Lave & Wenger, 1991). So real-world settings provide opportunities for assessment of students across a range of complexity of performance. It is this very complexity that creates dilemmas.

The learning and assessment environment of real workplaces cannot be controlled to ensure that all students receive the same opportunities and are assessed in the same context. This has driven university programs to retreat to controlled assessments such as objective structured clinical examinations or "standardised patients" conducted in controlled environments separate from the workplace. The paradoxical effect is to sacrifice validity for reliability. Similarly students' performance needs to be evaluated relative to the complexity of their tasks, their prior learning and the complexity of the workplace. Both these issues can only be resolved by employing an ethical and attentive judgment approach to assessment that allows for these factors to be considered during the learning and assessment process. This can be supported by provision of assessment criteria that allow for these sources of variability. For example, the description of levels of performance applied to any competency in COMPASS® (McAllister et al., 2006) requires the fieldwork educator to factor in the complexity of the client, the workplace and the student's previous experience when deciding what level of supervision is representative of intermediate or entry-level performance. Therefore a student requiring a moderate degree of supervision with a complex client would be judged as performing at a similar level to a student requiring little supervision with a client who has a simpler condition or with whom he/she has experience.

Assessments are ideally developed with close consultation and collaboration within the professional community of practice to ensure authenticity (Wenger, 1998). However, communities of practice are dynamic. Changes to practice occur at the boundaries of disciplinary expertise, raising dilemmas when defining practice to be assessed (Wenger, McDermott, & Snyder, 2002). Authentic assessments should incorporate the flexibility to reflect up-to-date practice and enable fieldwork educators to recognise a range of practice options as appropriate. Assessments based on process-oriented competencies provide flexibility by avoiding specifying particular skills and domains of practice that can change over time. As already identified in this chapter, this approach needs to be balanced against the recognition that there are core skills that students must be able to demonstrate in the workplace before graduating. However, assessments such as COMPASS® also lend themselves well to development of site-specific exemplars of each competency for each level of performance.

When assessments are not closely aligned with the expectations of the community of practice, the engagement of educators and students with the tool may lessen (Cross, Hicks, & Barwell, 2001). This lack of engagement would affect both the learning associated with assessment (Boud, 2000) and the validity and reliability of the assessment tool. Indeed, Neary (2000) found that both fieldwork educators and nursing students chose to not use an assessment tool as intended if it was perceived as irrelevant to the placement experience. Hence, authenticity is a strong influence on both perceived validity of assessment tools and reliability through correct tool usage.

There are broader sociocultural issues in communities of practice that impinge on determining a performance representative of entry-level competence. Fieldwork educators' expectations can drift over time, or they may be unwilling to identify a student's performance as entry level in case the student sees it as denoting excellence and becomes demotivated. Fieldwork educators, students and university educators may also differ in what they recognise as learning in fieldwork and university settings. Hamilton (2005) described a fundamental distinction between the expectations of the two settings, with universities expecting students to display their ability to "know what", and workplaces expecting students to show that they "know how" (Habermas, 1972). Le Maistre and Pare (2004) identified a related issue where students need to transform the object of learning assessed at university (e.g., theories of language development) into a tool to enable them to perform competently in fieldwork education placements (e.g., assessing a child with a language delay).

*Impact on Learning*

Authentic assessments have a positive impact on learning, as fieldwork educators and students value their relevance to students' future practice. But assessment usually does "double duty", both certifying students as fit to practise and at the same time attempting to support to the learning process (Boud, 2000). The dilemma here is that assessment for certification, or summative assessment, tends to exclude students from the learning process by placing responsibility for judgment about learning with fieldwork educators and/or the university (Boud, 2000). Formative assessment, on the other hand ,is a process of collaborating with students to identify how they can engage in the learning required to develop competency.

Many educationalists have pointed out that all types of assessment affect learning (often described as the "backwash" or "washback" effect (Wall, 1997)), in that assessment can drive teaching, which can have positive or negative consequences. When assessment is formative in nature, it typically involves a greater degree of interaction between the educator and the learner. This interaction provides opportunities for feedback about the learner's performance (e.g. "You need to use more open questions"), and feedback about ways they can enhance their performance (e.g. "After you've completed this reading today, try practising asking open questions in a role play with me tomorrow"). This interaction provides the opportunity for an approach that may align more with the individual learner's style. For example, provision might be made for unobserved practice in non-fieldwork settings for a learner who experiences some level of performance anxiety, or a learner might suggest that the educator provide detailed feedback about particular aspects such as communication skills (McNeilis, 2001).

Summative assessment is a "snapshot" of the learner's abilities and performance at one point in time, usually at the end of the placement. This focus changes the type of feedback from assessment in important ways, and we might expect a different "washback" from the two different foci. Students who are formatively assessed are likely to critically and constructively reflect on their performance and to generate a plan for continued development. Summative assessment is often less informative for developing learning plans. It is important to keep in mind the purpose of the assessment and consider the potential impact upon students' learning behaviours. Given that fieldwork educators are concerned with learning as well as with ensuring that students are safe and effective practitioners, designers of workplace competency assessments should consider including both formative and summative components.

Assessments that describe performance as a developmental continuum provide further support to both formative and summative aspects of competency development. The developmental continuum maps the learning pathway or next steps in the process of developing competency for both the students and fieldwork educators. Identifying the end of that pathway (entry-level performance) provides students and fieldwork educators with a clear description of end goal of the fieldwork learning process.

## SUMMARY

Our students value fieldwork placements and their fieldwork educators highly. They enter our university programs with the goal of joining us in our practice.

Competency-based assessment based on observed performance of students in the real world of the workplace is highly authentic and motivating for all. As described in this chapter, this assessment practice raises a number of dilemmas, many of which are common with any kind of assessment. However, valid and reliable competency-based assessments with positive impacts upon learning can be developed through careful thought and attention to the processes and content required to support fieldwork educators' judgments and the students' learning.

## REFERENCES

Albanese, M.A., Mejicano, G., Anderson, W.M., & Gruppen, L. (2008). Building a competency-based curriculum: The agony and the ecstasy. *Advances in Health Sciences Education*, Available: http://www.springerlink.com/content/102840/?Content+Status=Accepted, accessed 14 December 2009.

Alexander, H.A. (1996). Physiotherapy student clinical education: The influence of subjective judgements on observational assessment. *Assessment & Evaluation in Higher Education, 21*(4), 357–366.

American Educational Research Association. (1999). *Standards for educational and psychological testing*. Washington: American Educational Research Association.

Boud, D. (2000). Sustainable assessment: Rethinking assessment for the learning society. *Studies in Continuing Education, 22*(2), 151–167.

Chapman, J. (1998). Agonising about assessment. In D. Fish & C. Coles (Eds.), *Developing professional judgment in health care: Learning through the critical appreciation of practice* (pp. 157–181). Oxford: Butterworth-Heinemann.

Cohen, R., Rothman, A.I., Poldre, P., & Ross, J. (1991). Validity and generalizability of global ratings in an objective structured clinical examination. *Academic Medicine, 66*(9), 545–548.

Cross, V., Hicks, C., & Barwell, F. (2001). Exploring the gap between evidence and judgment: Using video vignettes for practice-based assessment of physiotherapy undergraduates. *Assessment & Evaluation in Higher Education, 26*(3), 189–212.

Dalton, M., Keating, J., & Davidson, M. (2009). *Development of the assessment of physiotherapy practice (APP): A standardised and valid approach to assessment of clinical competence in physiotherapy*. (Australian Learning and Teaching Council Final report PP6-28). Brisbane: Griffith University.

Duke, M. (1996). Clinical evaluation - difficulties experienced by sessional clinical teachers of nursing: A qualitative study. *Journal of Advanced Nursing, 23*(2), 408–414.

Epstein, R. (2007). Assessment in medical education. *The New England Journal of Medicine, 356*(4), 387–396.

Epstein, R.M., & Hundert, E.M. (2002). Defining and assessing professional competence. *Journal of the American Medical Association, 287*(2), 226–235.

Ferguson, A., Lincoln, M., McAllister, L., & McAllister, S. (2008). *COMPASS® directions: Leading the integration of a competency based assessment tool in speech pathology learning and teaching*. Sydney: Australian Learning & Teaching Council Ltd, an initiative of the Australian Government Department of Education, Employment and Workplace Relations.

Gonczi, A. (1992). *A guide to the development of competency standards for the professions*. Canberra: National Office for Overseas Skills Recognition.

Govaerts, J.J.B., van der Vleuten, C., & Schuwirth, L.W.T. (2002). Optimising the reproducibility of a performance-based test in midwifery education. *Advances in Health Sciences Education, 7*, 133–145.

Habermas, J. (1972). *Knowledge and human interests* (J.J. Shapiro, Trans.). London: Heinemann Educational.

Hager, P. (2000). Know-how and workplace practical judgment. *Journal of Philosophy of Education, 34*(2), 281–296.

Hager, P. (2004). Metaphors of workplace learning: More process, less product. *Fine Print, 27*(3), 7–10.

Hager, P., Athanasou, J., & Gonczi, A. (1994). *Assessment technical manual.* Canberra: Australian Government Publishing Service.

Hamilton, H. (2005). New graduate identity: Discursive mismatch. *Contemporary Nurse, 20,* 67–77.

Hodges, B.D. (2006). Medical education and the maintenance of incompetence. *Medical Teacher, 28*(8), 690–696.

Ilott, I., & Murphy, R. (1997). Feelings and failing in professional training: The assessor's dilemma. *Assessment and Evaluation in Higher Education, 22*(3), 307–316.

Jones, A. (2000). The place of judgment in competency-based assessment. *Journal of Vocational Education and Training, 51*(1), 145–160.

Keen, A.J.A., Klein, S., & Alexander, D.A. (2003). Assessing the communication skills of doctors in training: Reliability and sources of error. *Advances in Health Sciences Education, 8,* 5–16.

Lave, J., & Wenger, E. (1991). *Situated learning: Legitimate peripheral participation.* New York: Cambridge University Press.

Le Maistre, C., & Pare, A. (2004). Learning in two communities: The challenge for universities and workplaces. *Journal of Workplace Learning, 16*(1–2), 44–52.

Lincoln, M., Ferguson, A., McAllister, L., & McAllister, S. (2008). *Benchmarking clinical learning in speech pathology to support assessment, discipline standards, teaching innovation and student learning.* Sydney: Australian Learning & Teaching Council Ltd, an initiative of the Australian Government Department of Education, Employment and Workplace Relations.

McAllister, S. (2005). *Competency based assessment of speech pathology students' performance in the workplace.* Unpublished PhD thesis, The University of Sydney, Australia.

McAllister, S., Lincoln, M., Ferguson, A., & McAllister, L. (2004). User evaluation of the content and processes of an assessment of student performance in workplace settings. Paper presented at the IALP World Congress, Brisbane.

McAllister, S., Lincoln, M., Ferguson, A., & McAllister, L. (2006). *COMPASS®: Competency assessment in speech pathology.* Melbourne: Speech Pathology Association of Australia Ltd.

McAllister, S., Lincoln, M., Ferguson, A., & McAllister, L. (2010). Issues in developing valid assessments of speech pathology students' performance in the workplace. *International Journal of Language and Communication Disorders, 45*(1), 1–14.

McNeilis, K. S. (2001). Analyzing communication competence in medical consultations. *Health Communication, 13*(1), 5–18.

Messick, S. (1996). Validity of performance assessments. In G.W. Phillips (Ed.), *Technical issues in large-scale performance assessment* (pp. 1–18). Washington: National Center for Education Statistics.

Neary, M. (2000). Supporting students' learning and professional development through the process of continuous assessment and mentorship. *Nurse Education Today, 20,* 463–474.

Norman, G., van der Vleuten, C., & de Graaff, E. (1991). Pitfalls in the pursuit of objectivity: Issues of reliability. *Medical Education, 25,* 110–118.

Rethans, J.-J., Norcini, J., Baron-Maldonado, M., Blackmore, D., Jolly, B. C., LaDuca, T., et al. (2002). The relationship between competence and performance: Implications for assessing practice performance. *Medical Education, 36,* 901–909.

Schuwirth, L.W.T., Southgate, L.J., Page, G.G., Paget, N., Lescop, J., Lew, S.R, et al. (2002). When enough is enough: A conceptual basis for fair and defensible practice performance assessment. *Medical Education, 36,* 925–930.

Shavelson, R.J., Gao, X., & Baxter, G. (1993). *Sampling variability in performance assessments: CSE Technical Report 361.* Santa Barbara: University of California National Center for Research on Evaluation, Standards, and Student Testing.

Speech Pathology Association of Australia. (2001). *Competency-based occupational standards for speech pathologists (Entry level).* Melbourne: Speech Pathology Association of Australia Ltd.

Wall, D. (1997). Impact and washback in language testing. In C. Clapham & D. Corson (Eds.), *Encyclopedia of language and education: Language testing and assessment,* (Vol. 7., pp. 291–302). Dordrecht: Kluwer.

Wass, V., van der Vleuten, C., Shatzer, J., & Jones, J. (2001). Assessment of clinical competence. *The Lancet, 357*, 945–949.
Wenger, E. (1998). *Communities of practice: Learning, meaning, and identity.* Cambridge: Cambridge University Press.
Wenger, E., McDermott, R., & Snyder, W.M. (2002). *Cultivating communities of practice: A guide to managing knowledge.* Boston, MA: Harvard Business School Press.

*Sue McAllister PhD*
*Speech Pathology*
*Flinders University of South Australia, Australia*

*Michelle Lincoln PhD*
*Discipline of Speech Pathology*
*The University of Sydney, Australia*

*Alison Ferguson PhD*
*Humanities and Social Science*
*The University of Newcastle, Australia*

*Lindy McAllister PhD*
*School of Medicine*
*The University of Queensland, Australia*

TARA L. WHITEHILL, KAREN YU, LORINDA KWAN
AND DIANA W.L. HO

# 23. PEER, SELF AND SUPERVISOR ASSESSMENT

*Piloting a Reflective Week in Fieldwork Education*

In this chapter, we present a pilot experience: a "reflective week", scheduled mid-way through a 10-week fieldwork placement. The initiative incorporated several components that have received attention in the literature on fieldwork education, namely reflection, student-directed learning, peer learning and supervision, and "no-client-contact" fieldwork learning opportunities. The context for the study was a speech language therapy program; we believe the concept and results have implications for allied disciplines.

*Reflection* is considered a crucial component of learning (e.g. Kinsella, 2000; Baxter & Gray, 2001; Baird & Winter, 2005). Mandy (1989) proposed a reflective model of clinical supervision. Although her model focused on incorporating reflection in the regular cycle of supervision, she also suggested delayed watching of videos of sessions, to assist in the reflective process. Mandy made several suggestions as to how the reflective model could be adapted, particularly for more clinically experienced students. One suggestion was that "students may engage in the reflective process with peers" (p. 91). Other authors have highlighted the variety of activities which can be employed to facilitate reflection for student clinicians, including sharing a critical incident, presenting a case, and writing a journal (McAllister & Lincoln, 2004; Baird & Winter, 2005).

*Student-directed learning* has received much attention in the literature on student learning (e.g. Boud, 1981). In fieldwork education this may be conceptualised or termed differently. For example, several authors have advocated the use of contracts to guide learning (e.g. McAllister & Lincoln, 2004). Although our project involved students in their first fieldwork attachment, a student-directed model is consistent with our program's problem-based learning (PBL) curriculum. The students involved in this study had already experienced four blocks (semesters) of PBL, an explicitly student-directed model of learning (Barrows & Tambyln, 1980; Boud & Feletti, 1997).

A traditional model of fieldwork education involves one-to-one student-client sessions, and one-to-one student-supervisor supervision (Baxter, 2004). However, several authors have argued that students learn better with *peer interactions* in fieldwork settings (Lincoln, Stockhausen, & Maloney, 1997; Grundy, 2004; McAllister & Lincoln, 2004; McAllister, 2005). By watching, questioning, criticising, praising

*L. McAllister et al., (eds.), Innovations in Allied Health Fieldwork*
*Education: A Critical Appraisal, 261–270.*

and instructing one another, students can constructively learn among themselves (Robertson, Rosenthal, & Dawson, 1997). Another form of peer involvement is the employment of more clinically-experienced students as peer-supervisors of more junior students. This model is commonly employed in medical education but has been less frequently reported in speech language pathology (Rosenthal, 1986).

One issue attracting considerable recent attention is the use of *non-client-contact* fieldwork learning experiences (e.g. Bearman, Cesnick, & Liddell, 2001; Kneebone & Apsimon, 2001). Many speech and hearing sciences programs world-wide apparently employ such opportunities. However, there has been little study of the effect of this innovation on fieldwork learning in the speech language pathology profession. One recent study indicated that 80% of speech language pathology students needed more than 180 hours of face-to-face clinical experience to reach entry-level clinical competency (McAllister, 2006, p. 51). However, this is one of the few substantiated claims surrounding this issue.

In the following sections we introduce a novel fieldwork education activity that addressed the concepts raised in this introductory section.

CONTEXT

The education of speech therapists at the University of Hong Kong is undertaken in a four-year undergraduate course. About 12 years ago, we converted our traditional curriculum to a PBL model. Details of this program have been previously described (e.g. Whitehill, Stokes, & MacKinnon, 1997; Whitehill, 2006). As with all PBL programs, we emphasise student-directed learning, in a peer-learning context, supported by a tutor. Another emphasis of our PBL program is reflection, which is realised in a number of ways including requiring students to engage in reflection at the close of every PBL session and to submit a reflective journal at the end of each PBL problem. This culture of reflection (Whitehill, 2006) was one impetus for the pilot reflective week described and evaluated in this chapter.

Direct client contact does not begin for our students until their second year. The second-year fieldwork attachment takes place in our university clinic, and focuses on paediatric cases. The students work in groups of six, with two Year 4 peer supervisors and one experienced fieldwork supervisor per group. Students are assigned one client but observe all other sessions. Each 3-hour clinic is followed by a group discussion session, in which students are asked to summarise, critique and reflect upon their session. This is followed by feedback from their second-year peers, the fourth-year peer supervisor and the fieldwork supervisor.

PILOT STUDY: THE REFLECTIVE WEEK

*Background*

In 2008, our second-year fieldwork education placement had to be suspended mid-way due to a flu outbreak. Rather than cancelling or postponing the clinics we implemented a contingency plan, involving non-client-contact learning. Although driven by practical necessity, the contingency plan also addressed a troubling perception we had, that Year 2 students were so overwhelmed with the routine tasks of clinic (preparing sessions plans and reports, preparing materials for sessions, etc.) that they had little time for reflection on their developing clinical skills. At the end of this first reflective week, feedback was collected from the students and supervisors. The feedback was so positive (in particular from the supervisors) that we decided to implement the reflective week as an ongoing component of our program.

## Description of the Reflective Week

After attending 5 weeks of clinic, all Year 2 students are involved in a reflective week. They then continue with their client-contact clinics in weeks 7 to 10. The reflective week involves a heavy component of student-directed learning. At the beginning of the week, all students are asked to reflect upon their previous fieldwork sessions, to write down particular difficulties they experienced as well as their self-perceived strengths and weaknesses. Following this, the students are asked to write a "contract": goals they wish to achieve in the reflective week as well as methods to achieve the goals. The students circulate their contracts among each other and discuss the goals with their supervisors.

The groups are encouraged to employ videotapes of their fieldwork sessions from the preceding 2 weeks. Each group determines how they wish to use the videos to achieve the goals identified in their contracts. For example, one group might elect to view a preselected segment from each student's prior session, and focus on individual contracts. Another group might select only two or three videos from the group, focusing on common learning issues. Some groups pause the video and engage in role-play, to illustrate how a particular interaction might have been better managed. Although the supervisor and Year 4 peer supervisor are present for these activities, the activities themselves are student-led. Finally, the students are asked to write an approximately 200-word "reflective journal", focusing on their learning and performance in the week.

## Data Collection and Analysis

Thirty-nine students participated in this reflective week. Our evaluation of the experience was based on data from several sources:

1. Formal course evaluation (Year 2 students, n = 37; Year 4 peer supervisors, n = 14). All students completed a modified version of the course evaluation form used throughout our program. As shown in Table 1, the questionnaire includes two self-evaluation items, eight program-specific items and two overall summary items. The forms were submitted anonymously.
2. Reflective journal (Year 2 students, n = 22; Year 4 peer supervisors, n = 12). Qualitative analysis of the journals was undertaken by two investigators (TW and DH). We followed analysis procedures outlined by Strauss and Corbin (1998) and as employed in a previous study of our PBL program (Stokes,

MacKinnon, & Whitehill, 1997). More specifically, exploratory analysis was conducted by each investigator independently, noting points that appeared to stand out. Main themes were identified by each investigator. Consensus agreement was used to consolidate themes (for example, to recognise similar themes with different labels) and to identify illustrative quotations for each theme. The number of students who included a particular theme in their journal was calculated.

3. Feedback from the supervisors was not analysed systematically, but provided an additional informal source of feedback on the experience.

## EVALUATION OF THE PILOT STUDY

### "Course" Evaluation

*Second year students.* The results of the questionnaire are shown in Table 23.1. For the first summary item (Item 11), relating to the effectiveness of the program, the mean score was 75.7% (SD 18.7), equivalent to a rating of "good". For the second summary item, referring to the effectiveness of the supervisor, the mean score was 80.7% (SD 19.4), a rating between good and excellent. For the remaining 10 items, mean scores ranged from 64.6 to 88.3%. The most highly rated item (Item 5) related to video watching. The lowest rated item (Item 4) referred to the writing of personal learning contracts. The two self-evaluation items (Items 1 and 2) received mean scores of 72.2% and 80.1%, respectively.

*Fourth year students.* The evaluations from the Year 4 peer supervisors (also shown in Table 23.1) were generally poorer. For the summary items (Items 11 and 12), mean scores were 63.5 % (SD 9.88) and 68.8% (SD 8.3), respectively. Scores for the remaining items ranged from 58.3% to 82.3%. The highest scores were for the items referring to opportunities to ask questions (Item 9, 80.21%) and responses to questions (Item 10, 82.3%).

*Table 23.1. Results of student questionnaire to evaluate the reflective week*

| Section Titles and Item Descriptions | Year 2 Mean (SD) | Year 4 Mean (SD) |
|---|---|---|
| Student Evaluation of Self | | |
| 1. I was well prepared for the clinical program | 72.2 (16.6) | 63.5 (9.9) |
| 2. I was attentive and participated in the clinical program | 80.1 (17.4) | 75.0 (0) |
| Program-Specific Items | | |
| 3. The program content was relevant to the stated objectives and clinical learning | 78.8 (9.1) | 75.0 (5.9) |
| 4. The writing of (Commenting on Year 2 students') personal learning contracts helped my learning. | 64.6 (16.9) | 61.5 (16.8) |
| 5. The focused clinical learning (video watching and discussion) helped my learning | 88.3 (12.7) | 68.8 (14.7) |

*Table 23.1. (Continued)*

| | | | |
|---|---|---|---|
| 6. | The writing of (Commenting on Year 2 students') personal learning objectives helped my learning. | 70.6 (14.1) | 58.3 (11.3) |
| 7. | The writing of (Commenting on Year 2 students') critiques helped my learning | 71.3 (15.3) | 58.3 (9.3) |
| 8. | The relative amount of time for discussion, tasks and exercises was appropriate | 77.1 (19.6) | 72.9 (3.0) |
| 9. | Opportunities to ask questions were sufficient | 86.5 (13.6) | 80.2 (8.0) |
| 10. | Responses to questions were useful | 78.8 (9.1) | 75.0 (5.9) |
| Overall Summary Items | | | |
| 11. | All things considered, the overall effectiveness of the program in helping me learn clinical skills was | 75.7 (18.7) | 63.5 (9.9) |
| 12. | All things considered, the overall effectiveness of the supervisor in helping me learn clinical skills was | 80.7 (19.4) | 68.8 (8.3) |

Notes: The questionnaire employed a 5-point Likert scale where 1 = strongly disagree, 2 = disagree, 3 = neutral, 4 = agree, 5 = strongly agree, except for the last two items where 1 = poor, 2 = fair, 3 = satisfactory, 4 = good, and 5 = excellent. The Year 2 and Year 4 students completed slightly different versions of three items; the adaptations for the Year 4 students appear in brackets for those items.

## Reflective Journal (Year 2 Students)

Six themes were identified. Below, we provide illustrative quotations for each theme, extracted from the journals, together with the number of students contributing to each theme (in square brackets). English is a second language for our students; we have preserved the original quotations, except for ensuring consistent use of the term "reflective week", which was used inconsistently. Six students appeared to misunderstand the purpose of the reflective journal, as they commented on their fieldwork education work over the entire past 5 weeks, rather than concentrating on the reflective week only. Therefore, the data are based on 16 student journals.

*Theme 1: The value of the supervisor* [n=12 students].
Although the reflective week was designed as a student-directed activity, supervisors were present and involved. Of the 16 students, 12 included comments referring to the role and value of the supervisor. Example: "The ideas and experiences shared by the supervisor also gave me insight as to how to improve on my clinical skills." [Student #3]

*Theme 2: The value of peers* [n=10].
Ten students included comments focusing on the value of peers in their learning: Example, "We can learn together and share each other's cases to discuss. In this way, not only can I learn more about my case, but also other type of cases." [#8]

265

*Theme 3: The value of video viewing* [n=14].
Although our students have opportunities to watch videos of their sessions during the regular fieldwork placement, group viewing of videotapes during the reflective week appeared to be a powerful learning experience for participants: "I think the session that the whole group reviewed videotapes of previous clinical sessions was most inspiring to me." [S#2]; "I found video viewing beneficial because it helped us match things we discussed with our own positive and negative examples." [#8]

*Theme 4: The development of "microskills"* [n=11].
Many students commented on specific clinical skills that were addressed during the reflective week. Example: "We were provided very useful information and suggestions about pre- and post-treatment baseline, technique to draw client's atten-tion to final consonants, cues to stimulate or elicit target behaviors, feedbacks to the client's productions and procedures of implementation of increase and decrease steps." [#6]

*Theme 5: The timing of the reflective week* [n=5].
Although only five students commented on the timing and duration of the reflective week, this gave us valuable information in terms of future planning. Also, it demo-nstrated our students' willingness to be frank about the planning aspects of our curriculum. Example: "I think that the reflective week may be arranged earlier during the clinical program (for example, after the third week or the fourth week). Since the first few weeks are tougher for us and we have come across with more difficulties, the reflective week organised earlier will help us to realise our weakness earlier and make modifications earlier. This will facilitate our learning and also the progress of the client." [#7]. Another student (#3) wrote that the reflective week was too short.

*Theme 6: General comments about the value of the experience* [n=11].
Most of the students included summary statements on the overall value of the reflective week. Example: "I think the gap week provides me with a very good chance to really sit down and reflect what I had done in the past few sessions. Many times after the session, many feelings and ideas concerning clinic popped up into my mind, but gradually disappeared due to tiredness. The gap week allows me to recall what I had encountered and wanted to know" [#3].

*Reflective Journal (Year 4 students)*

Four primary themes emerged from the 12 peer supervisors who submitted reflective journals:

*Theme 1: Role of the supervisor* [n=7 students].
Although the Year 4 students had a peer-supervisor role, comments from the journals indicated the leadership role of the supervisor. Example: "Under the guidance of

the supervisor, we were able to think of different possible... ways to deal with some difficult situations." [Student B]

*Theme 2: Peer supervision in general* [n=5].
Several students commented on aspects of peer supervision throughout the regular fieldwork placement, rather than focusing on the reflective week only: Example: "If I had the chance, I would prefer handling the cases myself and directly commented by the supervisors on my clinical skills." [Student F]

*Theme 3: Critique of reflective week* [n=4].
Like their Year 2 peers, several Year 4 peer supervisors were frank in their criticism of the reflective week. Examples: "However, I think it is valuable to have one more week of direct client contact so Year 2 students can have more opportunities to practice and improve their clinical skills. It would be better if the reflective week did not replace one week of direct clinical contact but rather as an extra..." [Student D]; "I do not think I benefit much in the reflective week... but I do think Year 2 students could learn..." [Student F]

*Theme 4: Praise for the reflective week* [n=8].
Several comments pointed out the advantages of the reflective week from the perspective of the peer supervisors: Example: "Through discussion on different learning goals... Year 2 students and peer supervisors learnt to have more in-depth evaluation of their clinical skills. These also helped me to develop more critical and independent self-evaluation skills... I understand more about my strength and weakness in evaluation of... clinical skills." [Student H]

*Supervisor Comments*

Six supervisors were involved in this pilot scheme (one supervisor managed two groups). Although we did not systematically collect feedback from the supervisors, we learned informally that most supervisors found the experience useful. They commented that the reflective week helped overcome the time constraints faced in the regular supervision sessions, that learning issues were raised by the students rather than by the supervisor, and that they were learning new information alongside the students. In an email she shared with us, one supervisor commented: "I think it's particularly good for my group, since most of them are too willing to accept comments but yet they would follow suggestions even without understanding the concepts behind thoroughly. Through formulating the learning issues by themselves [they] could let me know what they are still in doubt [about]."

## REFLECTIONS

In summary, feedback received from the Year 2 students on the course evaluation form was generally positive. We were able to identify components of the experience that the students found particularly useful to their learning as well as components that they found less helpful. This feedback will be invaluable as we modify the reflective week in the future. Course evaluation feedback from the Year 4 peer supervisors was generally less positive. Although this group of students found some aspects of the experience useful, many other components of the reflective week did not receive very positive feedback, in terms of enhancing their own learning. We discuss the issue of peer supervisors further, below.

Analysis of the reflective journals provided another perspective on the experience. The Year 2 students identified both the supervisor and their peers as making valuable contributions to their learning. The opportunity to discuss videos of previous sessions with the group was a particularly powerful learning experience. Some students gave suggestions for improving the reflective week, particularly in terms of timing (earlier, longer). The reflective journals from the Year 4 students raised concerns about the role of peer supervisors in the reflective week as well as more generally in our fieldwork education program. Although these students found the supervisor helpful to both the year 2 students and their own clinical learning, a strong peer supervision role was not apparent.

We had suspected that novice students can become so overwhelmed by routine clinical work that they have little time to reflect and process. The results of this study indicated that novice clinicians benefit from a "reflective week" in the middle of their first fieldwork placement. The structure of the reflective week was consistent with our commitment to student-directed learning (e.g. individual learning contracts, group consensus on strategies for achieving those objectives). However, feedback obtained from the journals suggested that the supervisor played a strong leadership role in the reflective week. With students experienced in PBL, we might have expected a less strong role of the supervisor. However, we know from previous literature that novice clinicians generally require a large degree of input from their supervisors at this stage of their development (e.g. Anderson, 1988). The pattern observed in our pilot week appears to reflect this developmental model, and is consistent with the principles incorporated in the teacher-manager model developed by Romanini and Higgs (1991).

This project was not designed specifically to determine the efficacy of non-client-contact fieldwork education. Nevertheless, the results of this study have implications for this concept. For many health education programs world-wide, opportunities for direct client contact are diminished. For both practical and pedagogical reasons, therefore, it is important to explore and to systematically evaluate non-contact learning opportunities.

This study had a number of limitations: we evaluated a pilot experience after only the second year of implementation, the total number of participants was relatively small, and we did not have a systematic comparison group. Nevertheless, we have provided preliminary quantitative and qualitative results of an innovative initiative, the provision of a mid-block reflective week for students beginning their fieldwork education practice. We are not aware of previous studies where a "break" in the regular fieldwork education program was built in, to provide greater opportunity for reflection. This may be particularly valuable for novice clinicians, coping with all the demands of a new learning experience.

## REFERENCES

Anderson, J.L. (1988). *The supervisory process in speech-language pathology and audiology*. Boston, MA: College-Hill.

Baird, M., & Winter, J. (2005). Reflection, practice and clinical education. In M. Rose & D. Best (Eds.), *Transforming practice through clinical education, professional supervision and mentoring* (pp. 143–159). Edinburgh: Elsevier Churchill Livingstone.

Barrows, H.S., & Tamblyn, R.M. (1980). *Problem-based learning: An approach to medical education*. New York: Springer.

Baxter, S. (2004). Fit for practice: New models for clinical placements. In S. Brumfitt (Ed.), *Innovations in professional education for speech and language therapy* (pp. 116–141). London: Whurr.

Baxter, S., & Gray, C. (2001). The application of student-centred learning approaches to clinical education. *International Journal of Language and Communication Disorders, 36*, 396–400.

Bearman, M., Cesnick, B., & Liddell, M. (2001). Random comparison of "virtual patient" models in the context of teaching clinical communication skills. *Medical Education, 35*, 824–832.

Boud, D. (Ed.) (1981). *Developing student autonomy in learning*. New York: Nichols Publishing.

Boud, D., & Feletti, G. (Eds.) (1997). *The challenge of problem-based learning* (2nd ed.). London: Kogan Page.

Grundy, K. (2004). Peer placements. In S. Brumfitt (Ed.), *Innovations in professional education for speech and language therapy* (pp. 51–77). London: Whurr.

Kinsella, E.A. (2000). *Professional development and reflective practice: Strategies for learning through professional experience: A workbook for practitioners*. Ottawa, ON: CAOT Publications ACE.

Kneebone, R., & Apsimon, D. (2001). Surgical skills training: Simulation and multimedia combined. *Medical Education, 35*, 909–915.

Lincoln, M., Stockhausen, L., & Maloney, D. (1997). Learning processes in clinical education. In L. McAllister, M. Lincoln, S. McLeod & D. Maloney (Eds.), *Facilitating learning in clinical settings* (pp. 99–129). Cheltenham, UK: Stanley Thornes.

Mandy, S. (1989). Facilitating student learning in clinical education. *Australian Journal of Human Communication Disorders, 17*(1), 83–93.

McAllister, L. (2005). Issues and innovations in clinical education. *Advances in Speech-Language Pathology, 7*(3), 138–148.

McAllister, L., & Lincoln, M. (2004). *Clinical education in speech-language pathology*. London: Whurr.

McAllister, S.M. (2005). *Competency based assessment of speech pathology students' performance in the workplace*. Unpublished PhD thesis, The University of Sydney, Australia.

Robertson, S., Rosenthal, J., & Dawson, V. (1997). Using assessment to promote student learning. In L. McAllister, M. Lincoln, S. McLeod & D. Maloney (Eds.), *Facilitating Learning in Clinical Settings* (pp.154–184). Cheltenham, UK: Stanley Thornes.

Romanani, J., & Higgs, J. (1991). The teacher as manager in continuing and professional education. *Studies in Continuing Education, 13*, 41–52.

Rosenthal, J. (1986). Novice and experienced student clinical teams in undergraduate clinical practice. *Australian Communication Quarterly, 2*, 12–15.

Stokes, S.F., MacKinnon, M., & Whitehill, T.L. (1997). Students' experiences of PBL: Journal and questionnaire analysis. *The Austrian Journal for Higher Education, 27*(1), 161–179.

Strauss, A., & Corbin, J. (1998). *Basics of qualitative research: Techniques and procedures for developing grounded theory* (2nd ed.). London: Sage Publications.

Whitehill, T.L. (2006). Converting to PBL: Problem-Based Learning in speech and hearing sciences: Review, reflection and renewal. Invited keynote presented at the Conference on Problem-Based Learning in Speech-Language Pathology Programmes, Linkoping, Sweden, 18–20 May.

Whitehill, T.L., Stokes, S.F., & MacKinnon, M.M. (1997). Problem based learning and the Chinese learner. In R. Murray-Harvey & H.C. Silins (Eds.), *Learning and teaching in higher education: Advancing international perspectives* (pp. 129–146). Adelaide: Flinders Press.

*Tara L. Whitehill PhD*
*Division of Speech & Hearing Sciences*
*Faculty of Education*
*University of Hong Kong, Hong Kong*

*Karen Yu Med*
*Division of Speech & Hearing Sciences*
*Faculty of Education*
*University of Hong Kong, Hong Kong*

*Lorinda Kwan Med*
*Division of Speech & Hearing Sciences*
*Faculty of Education*
*University of Hong Kong, Hong Kong*

*Diana W.L. Ho PhD*
*Division of Speech & Hearing Sciences*
*Faculty of Education*
*University of Hong Kong, Hong Kong*

# 24. ASSESSING IN PRACTICE

*The Challenges of Authenticity*

In this chapter we describe research that analysed the extent to which an oral assessment in the context of fieldwork education placements is authentic to real practice and might complement performance assessment. Oral assessment is defined as "assessment in which a student's response to the assessment task is verbal" rather than written (Joughin, 1998, p. 367). The research context is an undergraduate physiotherapy program in the United Kingdom (UK). The assessment is examined through the lens of authenticity, which is "defined by its resemblance to the real world; to the professional real world" (Gulikers, Bastiaens, & Kirschner, 2004, p. 4). Authentic assessment requires students "to demonstrate the same (kind of) competencies, or combinations of knowledge, skills, and attitudes, that they need to apply in the criterion situation in professional life" (Gulikers et al., 2004, p. 5).

Given contemporary challenges impacting on fieldwork placement assessment, including increased emphasis on efficiency, we acknowledge that the oral assessment providing the focus for this chapter might be deemed impractical and lacking objectivity. The tendency to adopt a reductionist approach to assessment in an effort to "cut down on pen-pushing" (Martell, 2005, p. 8) and emphasis on assessment based on behavioural learning outcomes has become the norm in the UK. Therefore, the practicalities of arranging time out for a three-way discussion between fieldwork educator, visiting lecturer and student might be viewed as a disincentive. Notwithstanding these points we will illustrate how an oral assessment component in conjunction with a performance assessment component together provide a means of gaining a holistic impression of students' learning in the practice setting, which students believe reflects the realities of professional practice. We describe how the assessment has been evaluated and provide insight into findings. Using a framework of "five dimensions of authenticity" developed by Gulikers et al. (2004) we explore the elements that contribute to the perceived authenticity of the assessment. We conclude by suggesting that despite authenticity being subjective, students appear to perceive the oral assessment as authentic; an important factor that drives and positively influences learning (Radinsky, Boullion, Lento, & Gomez, 2001). On the basis that oral communication dominates most fields of professional practice, we advocate the use of oral assessment in qualifying programs in health and social care.

*L. McAllister et al., (eds.), Innovations in Allied Health Fieldwork*
*Education: A Critical Appraisal, 271–280.*

*The Concept of Authentic Assessment*

The notion of authentic assessment is not new. Archbald and Newman (1988) used the term *authentic achievement*. However, it was Wiggins (1989) who coined the phrase "authentic assessment". Authenticity is defined as "resembling students' (future) professional practice" (Gulikers et al., 2004, p. 3). Gulikers, Bastiaens, Kirschner, and Kester (2008) suggested that if students perceive an assessment to be authentic it will have a positive effect on their learning, as well as preparing them for the labour market. However, their research identified differences in perceptions of authenticity between students and teachers, with teachers rating most assessment characteristics more authentic than students.

The relationship between performance assessment and authenticity was explored by Cumming and Maxwell (1999), who suggested that the two complement one another when the execution of a task or activity that requires the integration of knowledge and holistic applications is contextualised so that the task appears real., Authentic assessment, therefore, is not simply assessment of performance but assessment that emphasises the realistic value of the task and the context (Herrington &

*Table 24.1. Dimensions of authenticity (adapted from Gulikers et al., 2004)*

| Dimensions of Authenticity | Assessment Characteristics |
| --- | --- |
| Task | Meaningfulness, typicality and relevance in the students' eyes<br>Degree of ownership of problem and solution space<br>Degree of complexity<br>Criterion situation at the students' educational level<br>Structure (well-defined/ill-defined)<br>Domains (monodisciplinary/multidisciplinary |
| Physical context | Similarity to professional workplace<br>Availability of professional resources (methods/tools)<br>Similarity to professional timeframe (thinking/acting) |
| Social context | Similarity to social context of professional practice<br>Individual work/decision-making<br>Group or collaborative work/decision-making |
| Result/Form | Demonstration of competence<br>Presentation to others<br>Multiple indicators of learning |
| Criteria | Based on criteria used in professional practice<br>Related to realistic products/processes<br>Transparent and explicit<br>Criterion-referenced leading to profile score |
| **Assessors** | **Based on who should develop and use assessment criteria and standards** |

Herrington, 1998). Reeves and Okey (1996) also identified the fidelity of the task and the conditions under which the performance would normally occur as paramount in making an assessment authentic. However, in developing what might be termed an authentic assessment it is important to identify what students need to learn or develop in order to function in real life situations (Gulikers et al., 2004). Similarity to cognitive real-life demands is clearly fundamental (Savery & Duffy, 1995). However, the development of professional thinking skills, including problem-solving skills and critical-thinking skills, must be complemented by metacognitive skills, such as reflection and social competences, such as communication and collaboration (Birenbaum, 1996).

Gulikers et al. (2004) reviewed the literature on authentic assessment, deriving five dimensions of authenticity, which they then tested: the task, the physical context, the social context, the assessment result or form and the criteria (see Table 24.1). Within this framework of dimensions, levels of authenticity can vary.

The sixth "assessors" dimension was added by Gulikers et al. (2004) following research with students and teachers from a nursing college, and therefore is included in the framework. Although they describe this dimension as a sub-element of the criteria dimension we include it in the table as a dimension in its own right as our data suggest it is of comparable importance. Gulikers et al. suggested that the task, form and criteria are the most important aspects of assessment, whereas the physical and social contexts appear less critical overall.

## Development of the Oral Assessment Rationale

The aim of our research project was to develop competent professionals able to enter the workplace "fit for practice". We were keen to develop an assessment strategy, in addition to the performance assessment, that would be flexible enough to accommodate all levels of fieldwork placement experience from first to final placement, in the wide range of settings in which students experienced the different facets of physiotherapy practice. A range of competencies that students might be expected to exhibit wherever they are placed can be identified.

Although we were relatively comfortable with the longstanding approach to assessing competence through performance assessment and we recognised the importance of ensuring high standards in this respect, we also wished to gain insight into the thinking processes in which students were engaging, given awareness of the limitations of observed performance (Clouder & Toms, 2008) and students' capacity for impression management (Alexander, 1996; Clouder, 2003). We wished to assess what both Gardner (1993) and Wiggins (1993) termed "performances of understanding" through which students' depth of understanding can be gauged by their ability to apply knowledge. This aspiration resulted in the adoption of an oral assessment component.

Oral assessment has both advocates and critics. Critics highlight issues of low reliability due to inconsistency between assessors, use of non-standardised questions, and student anxiety and variability in verbal fluency (Nayer, 1995). Case specificity (Swanson, 1987) and practical difficulties associated with creating a relaxed yet questioning atmosphere and a lack of written evidence of the interaction (Gibbs, Habershaw, & Habershaw, 1988) represent further problems. However, Joughin (1999) emphasised the ability of oral assessment to test knowledge, understanding, problem-solving capacity and the ability to think on one's feet, as well as challenging students' interpersonal skills. In fact, Joughin's research suggests that students respond positively to oral assessment, making greater efforts to meet its demands, and as a result improve assessment outcomes.

## The Combined Assessment Strategy in Focus

The combined approach of observation of performance and an oral assessment seemed to provide an assessment with a sense of resemblance to real life situations with which early career professionals might be confronted, and hence a taste of future demands. Both components must be passed successfully. The first component focuses on observed performance of the student over a 5-week period, at the end of which the fieldwork educator is responsible for completing a summative assessment of performance. This component relies on both objective and subjective judgement and is criterion-referenced.

The second assessment component, which is the focus of this discussion, involves a clinical reasoning viva voce (CRV) that occurs during the final stages of each placement. This component involves the fieldwork educator and university visiting tutor in assessing students' capabilities through a formal discussion of clients with whom the student has been involved. Questioning can be as wide as is appropriate to the chosen cases, and involves the testing of anatomical, physiological and pathological knowledge as well as insight into the individual client's social circumstances and psychological as well as physical needs. The emphasis is on the student's ability to justify interventions. Students identify the clients for discussion and the assessors choose the cases on which to focus the discussion. Clearly this means that students are able to prepare for the assessment; for instance, anticipating questions that they might be asked, although because questioning can be very wide students must be extremely well prepared to offer reasoned responses and to think on their feet. The assessment duration is 45 minutes for year 2 students and 60 minutes for year 3 students. Again, the assessment is criterion-referenced. Following a brief discussion between the fieldwork educator and visiting tutor the student receives a mark and immediate feedback.

## The Research Study

The aim of the full study was to explore the validity of the Coventry University assessment process of fieldwork placement, particularly the CRV, and to develop an increased understanding of the contribution of both elements of assessment to our overall insight into student capability (for a full account of research findings see Clouder & Toms, 2008).

A qualitative methodology was most appropriate for exploring perspectives, with semi-structured interviews deemed the method of choice when a researcher knows most of the questions to ask but cannot predict the answers (Morse & Field, 1996, p. 76). A purposive sampling method was used to recruit all parties involved in the assessment process under exploration. This resulted in 55 participants, as outlined in Table 24.2. Ethical approval was obtained, consent sought and data transcribed and analysed (Clouder & Toms, 2008).

The primary focus for the research was on whether the two assessment components were necessary. It was found that all participants supported the relevance of the performance element of the assessment as a given. More of a surprise was the over-whelming support for the inclusion of the oral assessment, with the two assessment components together being seen as complementary and offering a more *rounded* assessment process.

Student support for the CRV was particularly surprising as it was perceived, by all participant groups, as making assessment of fieldwork placement *tougher* than placement assessment strategies of other programs. All assessment stakeholders described different ways they believed the CRV reflected *what happens in real life in the NHS*. Recognition by the authors that the apparent authenticity of the CRV may have been an important factor in its acceptance and as a motivator to drive learning led to scrutiny of the data against this concept. As a result the current discussion is based on the findings of secondary data analysis, during which the data were reviewed in the context of authenticity with respect to the CRV only.

*Table 24.2. Research participants*

| Role in Assessment | Number | Female: Male ratio | Description | Details |
|---|---|---|---|---|
| Physiotherapy student | 18 | 14: 4 | Final year, having completed all 6 placements | Mean marks for each assessment component for this group close to mean marks of year group |
| Fieldwork educator | 19 | 15: 4 | Hospital-based physiotherapist | 18 months to 8 years experience |
| Visiting tutor | 18 | 15: 3 | University-based physiotherapy educator | 1 year to several decades experience |

## The CRV and Authenticity

Gulikers et al. (2004) discussed authenticity as a dimension of assessment to consider prior to devising an assessment process. Here authenticity and the CRV are considered retrospectively. Each dimension of authenticity is explored against (a) the process of the CRV, (b) what was said about it by participants, and (c), where appropriate, how its development may have contributed to authenticity. The importance of gaining students' perspectives regarding assessment was emphasised by Gulikers et al. (2004), so where appropriate student comments are used to illustrate points made, although it was found that very often all three groups of participants were in agreement and raised similar points (Clouder & Toms, 2008).

*Task*

An authentic task is one that confronts students with activities also carried out in professional practice. Numerous comments by students demonstrated recognition that this was the case, comparing the CRV to a variety of potential work situations and the need for professional accountability, not least with respect to *the legal environment* that was viewed as *increasingly a part of practice*. Comments such as *professionals spend a lot of time justifying to each other why they have chosen different treatments* and *as a junior you are going to be questioned about the patients you are treating* were typical. One student described the CRV as reflecting a funda-mental aspect of practice in *help[ing] you get used to articulating how you have assessed the patient ... why you are doing a treatment*. Another student saw it as a tool for developing the thinking skills behind the action:

> *To some extent it's possible to be a practitioner without really thinking but the opposite occurs through the clinical reasoning exam ... it does just make you think and that's good training for the future.*

The fact that students were able to choose the clients to be discussed during the CRV was viewed positively, as it gave them a sense of being able to take control and influence the viva by *thorough preparation*, according with the sense of ownership of the task fundamental to perceived authenticity (Gulikers et al., 2004).

*Physical Context*

This dimension relates to the similarity between the assessment context and the professional workplace, regarding not only the environment but also the resources available and the similarity to the professional timeframe of thinking and acting. The CRV takes place in a quiet room away from the fieldwork environment and the client but within the fieldwork placement timeframe. It was interesting to note that Gulikers et al. (2004) found that physical context and social context were perceived by all as less important than other dimensions such as task; therefore, being away from the actual fieldwork environment may not greatly affect perception of authenticity. However, students did appreciate the fieldwork placement timing of the CRV and valued the opportunity to come back and *put your hands on* following the preparation and the exam.

The nature of the CRV, and its timing at the end of placement, means that it potentially allows weeks of preparation. During this time students can draw on placement resources, yet what they have prepared is delivered in a succinct time frame away from those resources. This is authentic to practice and was perceived to reflect the need to be able to *think on the spot* as, regardless of prior preparation, assessors may take the CRV down a path as yet unprocessed by the student, which involves *thinking under pressure*.

## Social Context

Authentic assessment is deemed to embrace social processes that reflect the practices of the professional culture. The three-way discussion that characterises the CRV was seen by one student as *like having a chat about your patients*; a common element of professional culture, albeit uni-professional rather than including other professionals who might be present in the workplace. Nevertheless, reflecting the complexity of practice through the need to *know every aspect of your patient ... a holistic view*, the students had had to draw on the expertise of others in preparing for the CRV, reflecting how expertise is shared in practice. Yet the individual nature of the student's final conclusions about a client, as brought to the exam, is typical of clinical decision-making processes in practice, as is the scrutiny that then follows. One fieldwork educator emphasised the importance of the *why* behind the *doing* and the *evidence behind things*, which is *what we are forever being asked to [provide] in practice*, highlighting the social context in which practice occurs.

## Assessment Result/Form

Gulikers et al. (2004) discussed the authenticity of the form of assessment with respect to whether it allows students to demonstrate their competence and present their ideas to others, and whether it pays attention to multiple indicators of learning. We have already illustrated the way in which the CRV offered students opportunity to present and defend their thinking to their colleagues in a performance similar to real life. It might be argued that the learning tasks which students have completed in preparing for the CRV and indicators of learning are in some respects implicit in the students' interventions with clients and thought processes that they describe. Aware that they were showing their *thought processes* students described how the CRV encouraged them to be more *holistic, pull[ing] it all together* and *know[ing] every aspect of your patient*. To do so students recognised the requirement to draw on diverse sources of evidence, from talking to clients and carers to accessing current research evidence. One student suggested: *it's kind of unlimited, the amount you can learn [about your CRV patients] and show you have learnt.* Visiting tutors emphasised their role in checking whether students had completed the necessary learning tasks in suggesting that the CRV *allows you to test deep learning* and *intellectual capability* and whether students had a *wider understanding, for example of the psychosocial aspects[of the case].*

## Criteria

Authentic criteria should include relevant professional competencies and be based on criteria used in real life (Gulikers et al., 2004). The CRV is criterion referenced and adopts what is considered by fieldwork educators to be a *standardised format* that takes away the *fear of assuming*, providing clear demarcation between student knowledge and prompting by assessors. The general rather than specific criteria allow for flexibility where needed and assessment of the performance as a whole, as advocated by Biggs (2003). The criterion referenced scheme was originally developed in collaboration with approximately 200 fieldwork educators over an 18 month period and has since been adapted slightly in the light of feedback. Students are assessed with respect to their ability to communicate effectively and with confidence, to portray a professional demeanour, to demonstrate good background knowledge, adopting a questioning approach to their practice, and their ability to synthesise and analyse information and to translate their clinical reasoning into an action plan. Such attributes are consistent with professional standards with which students are familiar; as a consequence students recognise the value in being able to articulate their ideas during the CRV, which as one student suggested gives an increased sense of *confidence in [my] competence.*

*Assessors*

Our findings support the notion that it is vital that assessment criteria are developed and used by those most capable of passing opinion on students' fitness for practice if assessment is to be authentic. Innovation and change in healthcare provision is so rapid that collaboration between fieldwork educators and university visiting tutors provides a means of ensuring that knowledge of the most up-to-date advances in everyday practice is combined with academic and research-based knowledge. Not-withstanding the need for the thorough induction of new staff, students and staff enjoy the opportunity offered by the CRV and experience some mutual gain from discussions. In fact, it seems that fieldwork educators see their own preparation for the CRV as beneficial for their continuing professional development, and one suggested that there is *the bonus that you are learning as well during the viva.*

*Reflections on Authentic Assessment*

We have discussed the merits of including an oral component in the protocol for assessing fieldwork placement learning in health and social care programs, based on our own experience and research of combining oral assessment with the assessment of observed performance. We argue that complementing a traditional performance assessment with an oral component increases insight into student capability, as well as increasing student motivation for learning. Our findings extend Joughin's (1999) support for oral assessment on the grounds that students respond positively to it and make greater efforts to meet its demands, by suggesting that for health and social care students oral assessment is perceived as authentic because oral communication is fundamental to professional practice.

We have used the "five dimensions of authenticity" framework developed by Gulikers et al. (2004) to consider the extent to which our oral assessment component might claim to be authentic, and have provided evidence mainly from the student perspective that supports this claim. As practice changes, so too must assessment, necessitating regular review. For instance, interprofessional education highlights a need for assessment that recognises the interprofessional nature of practice if it is to be authentic. However, as Gulikers et al. (2004) have reminded us, there is more to assessment than authenticity alone. In considering authenticity we have tangentially considered validity, but reliability is clearly an additional factor that is of extreme importance. Affordability and timeliness are also highly influential factors. Yet if we believe that assessment drives learning we might reflect on the importance of messages that we send future students in choosing assessment approaches that reveal what we most value. Resorting to confining assessment to a skills-based competency approach undervalues the potential learning that can occur in practice-based settings. The alternative is to embrace oral communication as the essence of professional practice and let students speak for themselves to prove their fitness for purpose.

## REFERENCES

Alexander, H.A. (1996). Physiotherapy student clinical education: The influence of subjective judgements on observational assessment. *Assessment and Evaluation in Higher Education, 21*(4), 357–366.

Archbald, D.A., & Newman, F.M. (1988). *Assessing authentic academic achievement in the secondary school*. Reston, VA: National Association of Secondary School Principals.

Biggs, J.B. (2003). *Teaching for quality learning at university: What the student does* (2nd ed.). Buckingham: Open University/Society for Research into Higher Education.

Birenbaum, M. (1996). Assessment 2000: Towards a pluralistic approach to assessment. In M. Birenbaum & F.J.R.C. Dochy (Eds.), *Alternatives in assessment of achievements, learning processes and prior knowledge* (pp. 3–29). Boston, MA: Kluwer Academic.

Clouder, L. (2003). Becoming professional: Exploring the complexities of professional socialisation in health and social care. *Learning in Health and Social Care, 2(4)*, 213–222.

Clouder, L., & Toms, J. (2008). Impact of oral assessment on physiotherapy students' learning in practice. *Physiotherapy Theory and Practice, 24*(1), 29–42.

Cumming, J.J., & Maxwell, G.S. (1999). Contextualising authentic assessment. *Assessment in Education, 6*(2), 177–194.

Gardner, H.W. (1993). Educating for understanding. *The American School Board Journal, July*, 20–24.

Gibbs, G., Habershaw, S., & Habershaw, T. (1988). *53 interesting ways to assess your students*. Bristol: Technical and Educational Services.

Gulikers, J.T.M., Bastiaens, T.J., & Kirschner, P.A. (2004). Perceptions of authenticity: Five dimensions of authenticity. Paper presented at the Second Biannual Joint Northumbria/EARLI SIG Assessment Conference, Bergen.

Gulikers, J.T.M., Bastiaens, T.J., Kirschner, P.A., & Kester, L. (2008). Authenticity is in the eye of the beholder: Student and teacher perceptions of assessment authenticity. *Journal of Vocational Education and Training, 60*(4), 410–412.

Herrington, J., & Herrington, A. (1998). Authentic assessment and multimedia: how university students respond to a model of authentic assessment. *Higher Education Research and Development, 17*(3), 305–322.

Joughin, G. (1998). Dimensions of oral assessment. *Assessment and Evaluation in Higher Education, 23*(4), 367–378.

Joughin, G. (1999). Dimensions of oral assessment and student approaches to learning. In S. Brown & A. Glasner (Eds.), *Assessment matters* (pp. 146–156). Buckingham: Society for Research in Higher Education/Open University.

Martell, R. (2005). Student placement tool cuts down on pen-pushing. *Physiotherapy Frontline, April 20*, 8.

Morse, J.M., & Field, P.A. (1996). *Nursing research: The application of qualitative approaches*. London: Chapman Hall.

Nayer, M. (1995). The assessment of clinical competency: An overview and preliminary report of Canadian physiotherapy programmes. *Physiotherapy Canada, 47*, 190–199.

Radinsky, J., Boullion, L., Lento, E.M., & Gomez, L.M. (2001). Mutual benefit partnership: A curricular design for authenticity. *Journal of Curriculum Studies, 33*, 405–430.

Reeves, T.C., & Okey, J.R. (1996). Alternative assessment for constructivist learning environments. In B.G. Wilson (Ed.), *Constructivist learning environments: Case studies in instructional design* (pp. 191–202). Englewood Cliffs, NJ: Educational Technology Publications.

Savery, J.R., & Duffy, T.M. (1995). Problem based learning: An instructional model and its constructivist framework. In B.G. Wilson (Ed.), *Constructivist learning environments: Case studies in instructional design* (pp. 135–148). Englewood Cliffs, NJ: Educational Technology Publications.

Swanson, D.B. (1987). A measurement framework for performance-based tests. In I.R. Hart & R.M. Harden (Eds.), *Further developments in assessing clinical competence* (pp. 13–45). Montreal: Can-Heal Publications.

Wiggins, G.P. (1989). A true test: Toward more authentic and equitable assessment. *Phi Delta Kappan, 70*, 703–713.

Wiggins, G.P. (1993). *Assessing student performance*. San Francisco: Jossey-Bass.

*Lynn Clouder PhD*
*Centre for Interprofessional E-learning*
*Coventry University, UK*

*Jane Toms MSc*
*Department of Physiotherapy and Dietetics*
*Coventry University, UK*

# SECTION VIII: PREPARATION AND SUPPORT OF FIELDWORK EDUCATORS AND MANAGERS

# 25. EDUCATING FIELDWORK EDUCATORS AND MANAGERS

Coming together is a beginning. Keeping together is progress. Working together is success. (Attributed to Henry Ford)

For over 20 years, our team has run interprofessional fieldwork supervision courses for fieldwork educators in the health professions. These continuing education courses are recognised as a postgraduate subject in some programs. The collaboration and the courses have been among the highpoints of our professional careers, producing a best-selling text (Rose & Best, 2005). In this chapter we outline the thinking behind our courses, discuss how we run the courses, and look at the team's expansion over time. We also discuss a recently developed advanced program for managers of fieldwork education and the advent of online delivery options. Finally, we analyse what we have learned through the process and posit advice for people trying to set up similar courses.

How did we begin? More than 20 years ago, a chance conversation in a staff tea room revealed that three academics from different health professions were each preparing courses for their fieldwork educators. They decided to collaborate in providing courses in rural areas and brought in an education development professional to work with them in the development of an interprofessional course. Thus, an interprofessional aspect was embedded from the beginning, albeit that it was driven more by practical than by theoretical or value considerations.

We came to the project of developing and presenting interprofessional courses for fieldwork educators with formative and strong experiences, and with personal values extending beyond any individual profession or fieldwork setting. We believe it is this core of experience and values that has held the team process together, shaped the courses we ran and allowed progress and expansion. The eclectic mix of values and experience included, in no particular order: a lack or arrogance; an assumption that we might not know something; open minds; critical inquiry; willingness to learn from each other; enthusiasm; valuing of diversity. But above all, a focus on relationship, the importance of emotions and time for process were seen as paramount. These values have remained through our 20 years of course development and expansion. Over this time, over 30 professionals have become members of the team for a period, representing 12 different professions. They are mainly academics but include people with responsibility for organising supervision in fieldwork settings. Some, including the authors of this chapter, have been involved for most of the period.

*L. McAllister et al., (eds.), Innovations in Allied Health Fieldwork*
*Education: A Critical Appraisal, 283–296.*
© *2010 Sense Publishers. All rights reserved.*

It's worth noting that at the time of our first course in 1990 the role of the field-work education person in the academic departments was predominantly to organise fieldwork placements. Fieldwork education had not yet emerged as a legitimate area of study/discipline, so the group had to build its own theoretical perspective. The group has always fostered and encouraged research, both in what it presents and in the learning projects that participants undertake. Much work, including several PhDs, has emerged from the group.

Over time the principal course has developed, been restructured, and remodelled. Throughout, the focus on relationship has always been, we believe, the key to the success of the group and its courses, along with its strong theoretical base, its eclectic mix of teaching and learning approaches, and the importance of the team modelling good practice. The following section provides details of the underlying learning principles we believe assist in preparing fieldwork educators.

## PRINCIPLES FOR PREPARING FIELDWORK EDUCATORS

Ten years ago we suggested that preparation for the role of fieldwork educator could be based on seven principles (Rose, Best, & McAllister, 1999). It is interesting to review these principles a decade later and realise that although their implementation may have altered over time, these principles continue to be relevant, and they underpin our current educational programs. The following section reviews and updates the original list and adds two new principles.

### 1. Develop Multiple Pathways

Our original suggestions for preparing fieldwork educators included readings in fieldwork education, group discussions, reflection on supervisory practice through journals, portfolios, debriefing, professional and peer supervision, mentoring, self-evaluation, student feedback and formal student evaluation. Short workshops and formal certificate courses have now been extended to include the considerable amount of material available online, as well as a number of university higher degrees in field-work education. The development and implementation of an online interprofessional course is described later in this chapter.

### 2. Begin Early at the Undergraduate Level

The considerable changes in health sciences curricula in the last decade include the incorporation of reflective practice and evidence-based practice, clinical reasoning processes and client education principles. Many entry-level professional courses include peer teaching, case-based or problem-based teaching opportunities, and learning contracts or agreements for some components. In addition, graduates of Masters entry-level courses often bring more sophisticated skills and maturity to the fieldwork education workplace. Therefore, even if only through a passive acculturation process, recent graduates are likely to be more aware of basic educational principles and more skilled in teaching others. Some modification of fieldwork education course material is required to address this increased skill level of some recent graduates. However, there are still course participants with considerable clinical expertise who have not experienced recent educational processes. In fact, the participants of our current courses reflect more diversity than our earlier courses and this must be planned for.

## 3. Understand Social Learning and the Importance of Modelling

Our ongoing experience, confirmed by more recent sociocultural learning theories, highlights the powerful influence on student learning of the opportunity to actively participate in practice with professionals in healthcare workplaces (Lave & Wenger, 1991; Billet, 2001; Sheehan, Wilkinson, & Billet, 2005). Workplace learning highlights the importance of orienting the learner into the social workplace and affirms and expands the importance of role modelling in learning in the clinical environment. We emphasise the fundamental requirement that any fieldwork education preparation initiative provides the exemplar for effective student learning. We also acknowledge the indirect influences of learning through professional and social activities.

## 4. Model a Person-Centred Approach

Although person-centred learning is widely promoted, the conflicts created by economic rationalism have created a climate where "telling" may be seen as more time efficient than taking the time to get to know learners and exploring the experience of others before modifying and tailoring programs to individual learning needs. The importance of a humanistic approach and the fundamental requirement of an effective relationship in facilitating learning are reinforced by more recent research (Sheehan et al., 2005; Higgs & McAllister, 2006). We believe it is important to apply such a learner-centred approach to participants of all fieldwork education preparation activities and as emphasised in the principle above, essential that such characteristics are modelled by presenters/educators.

## 5. Provide Time and Flexibility for Experiential Learning

Planning and delivering experiential learning programs for today's health care professionals requires absolute confidence that the time spent in experiential learning activity is justified. Learning in the fieldwork environment is complex, and creativity is required in balancing the limited time and reductionist pressures of the workplace with a conviction of the central importance of the fieldwork educator in effective student learning. It is critical that fieldwork educators have the knowledge and skills to facilitate optimal student learning in their fieldwork placements. The principles we follow and the broad themes identified in the following section require time for personal participation. In our experience, time spent exploring, experiencing and reflecting on assumptions and tacit knowledge is time well spent.

## 6. Incorporate Adult Learning Principles

"Tell me what to do and how to do it" was a frequent response of clinicians involved in fieldwork education 30 years ago (Best & Rose, 1996). If participants were pressed further, there were usually requests for strategies for dealing with time pressures or for managing the difficulties associated with "marginal students". Consistent with adult learning principles, we usually began workshops with a negotiation phase of the workshop content, which was usually a fairly brief section. Responses to a recent informal survey sent out to participants prior to a one-day fieldwork education workshop were received from nine health professions and resulted in a total of 71 individual learning goals! After analysis these were reduced to a more manageable list, although it far exceeded the time available. It is interesting to note that although the learning objectives were more detailed and diverse than 30 years ago, there were still many requests for strategies for managing time and dealing with individual challenges. Empowering clinicians to have the confidence and skills to develop strategies specific to their own challenges remains an essential component of all fieldwork education preparation.

## 7. Continue to Learn from Teaching Experience, from Learners and from Research

Personal and group reflection, feedback and participant evaluation have always been essential principles of our fieldwork educator preparation programs. This topic is discussed in the evaluation section later in the chapter. We have now updated and expanded this principle to explicitly include research. Our programs have always been research-based, and it is surprising now with the influence of evidence-based practice in the past decade to realise that this was implicit in our original principles. Two examples of current research which have informed and guided our more recent fieldwork education programs are:

– In a rigorous 5-year phenomenological narrative enquiry into the experience of being a fieldwork educator of speech language pathologists, McAllister highlighted the importance of the affective domain in fieldwork education. She identified that successful fieldwork educators have self-knowledge and a deep understanding of themselves and their relationship with others, as well as professional craft knowledge (Higgs & McAllister, 2005, 2006).

– Rafferty, Llewellyn-Davies, and Hewitt (2007) developed a provisional standard for clinical supervision using a Delphi technique with a large population of nurses. Although these performance indicators were specifically developed for supervision in the workplace they provide, with minor adaptation, a useful structure for fieldwork education. These authors too highlight the importance of a supportive learning environment and the relationship between learner and educator. They propose a constructivist reflective approach in order to encourage the development of personal meaning of professional practice and the use of critical appraisal in improving practice. The standards also recommend the use of learning agreements or contracts for negotiating and documenting individual learning goals with the available organisational resources and support.

We further update the original list of seven, adding the following two principles:

## 8. Foster, Promote and Support Fieldwork Education Research Evidence

Without a specific body of literature, early courses incorporated principles from the fields of education and management, as well as humanistic, cognitive, behavioural and organisational psychology. Today fieldwork education has developed its own theoretical framework, with ongoing research informing practice (Brown, Esdaile, & Ryan, 2004; Rose & Best, 2005; Higgs, Jones, Loftus, & Christensen, 2008; Delaney & Molloy, 2009). Fostering, promoting and supporting critical enquiry related to clinical learning is an emergent principle for our fieldwork educator preparation courses. Negotiating a learning contract and completing a small project remains an important learning activity in our courses. In some cases this leads to a more sustained research activity or a published article (e.g. Jukes, 2007).

## 9. Utilise an Interprofessional Approach

Our early beginnings as an interprofessional team were described in the introduction to this chapter. The opportunity to work together came as an informal opportunity and was something we wanted to do as individuals. We thought it would be easier and strategic to combine our endeavours. We were right, and were more than rewarded for our persistence. At that time there was little recognition of the importance of interprofessional education and certainly no foresight that this topic would develop its own extensive international body of literature (Freeth, Hammick, Reeves, Koppel, & Barr, 2005; Davidson, Smith, Dodd, Smith, & O'Loughan, 2008). Finding a time to meet when we were all available was difficult. A recent systematic review of the interprofessional literature identifies scheduling and timing as one of the greatest barriers to interprofessional fieldwork education (Davidson et al., 2008). Developing a shared understanding of basic terminology (Rose & Best, 2005) and purposes takes longer than expected and is not without some debate – on occasions leading to frustration and irritation for some team members. Yet the collaboration, sharing of expertise and opportunity for discussion between professions has enriched the learning of participants and presenters, and whenever possible we promote and encourage interprofessional courses. These nine principles provide the framework for the courses we design and facilitate. They identify the way we do things. The next section presents the essential course content of our beginner and more advanced fieldwork education courses.

## CONTENT AND PROCESSES OF BEGINNER AND ADVANCED FIELDWORK EDUCATION COURSES

### Beginner-Level 3- Day Course

Our early workshop content was structured on the roles of fieldwork supervisors as presented by Turney, Cairns, Eltis, et al. (1982) in the field of education: manager, instructor, counsellor, observer, giver of feedback, assessor. The workshops emphasised experiential learning (Kolb, 1984) and reflection (Schön, 1987). Exploring the educative roles of a fieldwork educator provided an opportunity for microteaching key activities such as managing the learning program and orienting learners to the workplace, instructing, observing, giving feedback and assessing student performance.

The current 3-day course (Advancing Clinical Education) is loosely structured to reflect activities required in different stages of the clinical experience. Day one explores assumptions about being a fieldwork educator, managerial issues such as orientation and planning, and highlights the importance of the learning relationship and the need to understand and accommodate individual learning preferences. The second day presents theoretical frameworks for learning and professional expertise, supervision styles, and experiential learning activities in teaching, observing and giving feedback. The final day uses case-based teaching to explore the complexities and challenges associated with learning in the fieldwork environment, as well as assessment and program evaluation. Opportunities for personal learning and reflection are provided in parallel small group discussions and in the selection and negotiation of a learning contract to be submitted at a later date.

*Advanced-Level 3-Day Course*

Over time, it became increasingly clear that there was a group of people who required a different and more advanced course, especially for those who manage the field-work education process and the fieldwork educators. The latter group includes staff based in fieldwork settings who have responsibility for organising and overseeing fieldwork education of students, either in a single fieldwork setting or for a group of fieldwork settings in a region or a network. Often these people no longer undertake direct supervision of students but are responsible for organising and supporting the staff who work directly with students. The group includes people with joint appointments between a fieldwork setting and a university, and university staff with the responsibility for organising fieldwork education.

Developing a course for this group was challenging and fun. Again we were resolved to apply our previously discussed nine guiding principles to course development. Thus there was a strong focus on process, and on valuing and building on participants' experience. At the same time there was an underlying theoretical basis to all content and activities. We identified five themes that we saw as crucial for managers of fieldwork educators. These themes emerged through brainstorming, discussion, reflection on our practice, and feedback from earlier courses for beginning practitioners. They also drew from and are congruent with published material (e.g., Higgs & McAllister, 2005, 2006):

1.  *Exploring Professional Practice Expertise*
    Professional practice is complex. Fieldwork educators need to be able to articulate components of professional practice expertise and relate them to their own practice in order to assist others in the development of professional knowledge and skills.

2. *Identifying Educational Expertise*

Relating learning theory to the fieldwork environment as a means of explaining or predicting learning outcomes provides fieldwork educators with confidence and skills in addressing the challenges of the fieldwork environment.

3. *Creating Learning Relationships*

The centrality of the learning relationship in effective fieldwork education outcomes warrants an exclusive theme related to creating and managing individual relationships appropriate to the level and maturity of the student or new graduate clinician.

4. *Managing Learning Programs and Resources*

Effective and efficient fieldwork education demands managerial skills and models appropriate to the individual professional workplace.

5. *Focusing on Personal Knowledge*

Developing awareness of personal knowledge provides course participants with an increased sense of self and reinforces the importance of tailoring learning opportunities to individual learners. It also helps to sustain ongoing involvement in fieldwork education.

The five themes formed the skeleton of the course, and around them we developed content. We wove through the teaching and learning processes discussed earlier in the chapter. We expect managers of fieldwork education to come to the advanced level course with skills and knowledge of health professional practice and to be able to supervise students. These skills remain at the heart of what they are trying to achieve through their practice as managers. But also they have to work at a "meta" level, to provide the conditions for good fieldwork education to occur and to support fieldwork educators who work directly with students.

We chose NOT to rely on management theory or to ask managers of fieldwork educators to apply it. Rather, we chose to continue to emphasise the importance of relationships, this time between the manager and those directly supervising students. The humanistic and interpersonal skills that lead to trusting and supportive relationships were encouraged. The theoretical bases of educational processes were emphasised, especially constructivism and reflection. Participants were encouraged to share their experience, professional knowledge and practical tips. The word "management" was limited to "managing learning programs and resources".

We designed a 3-day course. Day one focuses on sharing experiences and reflecting on practice, especially in the area of clinical reasoning. The second day focuses on learning in the workplace and the need to acknowledge and respond to diversity. It also introduces the syndicate groups that give participants the opportunity to explore a topic in depth. Syndicate groups are formed across disciplines and across workplace locations. The third day of the course is scheduled 3 months later, when participants have the opportunity to present their syndicate group results. The group presentations are combined with developing oral and written feedback skills and understanding assessment.

Teaching the course is complex. A wide variety of educational strategies and methods are used, including narrative story telling, case studies, small group discussion, brainstorming, presentation, reflection, practice skill development and self- and peer assessment. We also use PEARLS – personally arranged learning sessions (Schwartz & Heath, 1985) – that give participants the opportunity to follow areas of their particular interest.

People undertaking the course are expected to have at least 5 years' experience as fieldwork educators and normally to have a role organising fieldwork programs and managing and supporting fieldwork supervisors. Facilitators for the course are experienced, and embody and demonstrate the principles underlying the course. For example, they use educational processes that enhance student learning; have a capacity to work effectively and are comfortable in the affective domain; and have personal knowledge and attributes that provide a strong positive role model for participants. For both participants and facilitators there is an emphasis on interdisciplinary knowledge and expertise.

## ONLINE FIELDWORK EDUCATION PROGRAMS

Attendance at face-to-face courses is valued by many fieldwork educators, but for some, such as rural and remote fieldwork educators, it is simply not a viable option. Prior to the advent of computer and teleconference technologies, it was often possible for university programs to send academic staff into the field to provide fieldwork education short courses in rural and remote areas. In Australia, funding for such outreach support activities became scarce in the early 1980s, and university educators searched for creative and cost-effective solutions to the challenge of adequately preparing fieldwork educators. Advances in information and communication technologies offered the opportunity to improve the quality, reduce the costs, and increase the accessibility and flexibility of fieldwork education preparation programs for rural, remote, and metropolitan fieldwork educators.

Online education programs provide many benefits, including reducing barriers to learning from gender and cultural differences (Standish, 2002), offering freedom to learners who are time-poor and require greater timetabling flexibility, and providing more comfortable learning contexts for learners who are shy or have oral communication difficulties (Hodgson & Reynolds, 2005). However, online programs are not without its critics. Research concerning learner perceptions of online courses has uncovered a variety of responses, with some students reporting stress and anxiety associated with the use of the technology (Lee, Hong, & Ling, 2001). Attention to how and how often learners relate to their teachers and learning peers during online modes of learning seems important. It may be possible, for example, that online learning actually increases the learner's sense of disconnection, because use of the technology can be a depersonalising experience (Papastephenou, 2005). For some learners in remote locations access to online technologies is still limited by poor broadband access, and they request additional CR-ROM downloads to supplement their poor or fluctuating Web access (Taylor et al., 2007).

In 2004, the Australian Consortium for Clinical Education was formed by a group of academics from five Australian universities with direct representation from the fields of nursing, pharmacy, speech language pathology, and physiotherapy. This group initially developed and trialled an online preceptor education program for pharmacy preceptors, with considerable success (Marriott et al., 2005; Dalton et al., 2007). In 2006, the group developed the inter-professional online Australian Clinical Educator Preparation Programme and have trialled and enhanced it. The latter program is currently being made available to fieldwork educators from a wide range of medical, nursing and allied health professions (http://www.clinicaleducation. info). The program consists of six education modules: Exploring clinical education (considers the roles of a fieldwork educator and the importance of fieldwork education in developing professional competence); Focus on learning (principles of learning, learning styles); Focus on being a clinical educator (roles of fieldwork educators and personal factors that impact on the roles); The relationship between the learner and the clinical educator (emphasises the importance of and how to develop effective learning relationships); Learning in the workplace (link between theory and practice in the workplace, social learning theory, legal and ethical issues); and Mentoring. Modules are cross-linked and can be undertaken separately or as an entire package. The course contains a core educational program providing information and activities relevant to being a fieldwork educator, a contemporary evidence base, self-assessment and reflective activities, and an online discussion forum. The course is run with the assistance of an online moderator who enrols the learners, introduces them to their peers, and moderates online discussion and facilitates course progression. Self-assessment activities are designed to assist participants to determine their own learning needs.

Although research is emerging that supports positive changes in knowledge following online precepting and fieldwork education programs (e.g., Parsons, 2007), learner perceptions and preferences for online versus face-to-face modes of delivery for fieldwork educator preparation remain under-researched. In experimental studies we carried out during the trial of the online Australian Clinical Educator Programme, moderated and un-moderated groups were compared in terms of their self-reported learning outcomes (Rose et al., in preparation). One hundred fieldwork educators from physiotherapy, speech language pathology, occupational therapy, podiatry, radiography, dietetics and orthotics enrolled in an 8-week trial of the program and, following completion of a pre-course online survey, were randomly assigned to one of 10 moderated or 10 un-moderated groups. Following completion of the course, participants were requested to complete an online post survey. Levels of self-reported confidence, preparedness and enthusiasm for the role of fieldwork educator all significantly improved following the program. Participants in the un-moderated groups identified the need for moderation as an improvement strategy, citing lack of timely and relevant discussion board activity as a major negative attribute of the course. This result is consistent with previous suggestions concerning the importance of social interaction and sense of belonging in online learning situations (McAllister & Moyle, 2005). There are encouraging results in the literature in terms of offering online modes of fieldwork education preparation programs. However, the face-to-face courses we and our colleagues continue to run remain well attended and positively rated, suggesting the need for several mode options to meet the varying needs of today's learners.

## EVALUATION OF OUR COURSES: PROCESS AND OUTCOMES

Our evaluation focus has been on reflection on practice and quality improvement, using reactions from participants and reflection by presenters. We try both to demonstrate effectiveness and to review practice. The presenting team is the main client for the evaluation and our approach is qualitative rather than quantitative. For most of the history of our courses, participants have completed an evaluation sheet immediately at the end of the course. A typical sheet contains open ended questions and a rating scale, with an indication of the respondent's profession:
– What did you like best about the course?
– What improvements would you suggest?
– What will you take with you from this course into your fieldwork teaching/ education practice?
– Overall how would you rate the course – 5 point Likert scale, very good to very poor
– Would you recommend this course to a colleague Yes; Yes with reservations; No
– Any other comments.

Responses over the years from more than 2,500 participants have been remarkably positive and it is to our shame that we have not published the results. Readers interested in a more detailed approach to educational evaluation in the area of fieldwork supervision could consult Fish (2005). We can assert that participants in our courses appreciate
– the interprofessional nature of the course and participants
– the enthusiasm and professionalism of the presenting team
– the applicability of the concepts and strategies contained in the course
– the variety of teaching methods with emphasis on interactivity
– the opportunity to try skills e.g., giving feedback
– the open discussion

Suggestions for improvements are as varied as there are learning styles and preferences in the group. If one theme emerges it is around "condensing" the course into 2 days. Such suggestions reflect the pressure people are under and maybe a lack of understanding of the time necessary to get to a point where practice might change and learning contracts can be meaningfully developed.

As well as receiving feedback from participants, presenters do their own reflection and evaluation. On conclusion of each day of the course there is a short debriefing session. At the end of the final day there is a longer structured reflection and the opportunity for presenters to scan the evaluation responses from all participants. The evaluation replies are later collated, typed and circulated.

It is still fairly unusual for a team of teachers to see each other present and facilitate as we do, to take time to openly discuss results and difficulties and to agree on suggestions for change and improvement. People new to the presenting team tend to focus on results from their profession and to note comments from the area(s) they directly presented. They also tend to focus far more on negative than on positive comments. This focus on self gradually diminishes over time, and with encouragement from the more experienced members, individuals can learn to value the positives.

We are now experimenting with online evaluation using "Survey Monkey" instead of the handwritten responses. It is cheap and fast. Response rates are not as good, since participants do it after returning to their workplaces rather than at the end of the course and the presenters do not have the immediate feedback. Actually handling the handwritten responses and discussing their content with the team gives a more personal ownership of the evaluation results. It is worth noting that most of our major changes come not from evaluation results but more from external events such as an influx of new members into the team, availability of teaching space, research being undertaken, or quite simply the need for change.

## LESSONS LEARNED

We have learned many lessons along the way and are happy to share them. But we also caution that times have changed since we began and it may not be possible to create the time, space and circumstances in which such an exciting and effective group might emerge.

A key aspect of working in an interprofessional team is willingness to learn from outside your discipline. In the beginning we faced a lack of shared understanding, differences of terminology and, in retrospect, no real sense of community. We advise new course developers to attend to these three aspects as early as possible. The task at hand involved multiple professions, different learning needs and contexts. A group was needed to develop such a course. In our experience, an individual cannot develop an interprofessional course. It was important for us also that it was a grassroots, flat structure group – not a top-down organisation. Equally important is the acknowledgement that developing an interprofessional course is a complex task that requires time and space. There needs to be a commitment to the nature of the process as well the content of the course.

As the team grows and expands, changes occur. Such changes need to be monitored and accommodated. The underlying values and principles of the group and the course need to be made explicit to new members. Often it seems to be such a smoothly operating process and team that newcomers are unaware of the depths underpinning the process. Indeed, it's not unlike the iceberg model of professional practice that appears in many publications, beginning with Fish and Coles (1998). In that model, the "doing" seen on the surface is underpinned by the "unseen" experience, knowledge, feelings, expectations, assumptions, attitudes, beliefs and values. Over the years, our team has tripped up on some of these hidden aspects, particularly unspoken expectations and assumptions.

The group needs to be able to change in order to accommodate new people, new professions and new ideas. Over the years we have learned to fit courses into shorter time periods – moving from 6 days back to 3. We have introduced new teaching methods and perspectives to address the ever-changing sophistication and needs of participants, and on occasion, accommodated a team member's latest passion. Our courses have been the foundation for developing an on online learning course, as outlined earlier. Online learning might seem a long way from our focus on personal interaction and relationship. Yet those principles were applied and the importance of having a moderator was established.

As life in Australian universities has become more pressured over the years, it has been harder to find the time and space to be together and to bond into a cohesive work group. The "old timers" believe such bonding among the team is the underpinning of a good course. The newcomers have never known such "luxury" and may not see its value, even if they were able to find the time to do it.

A positive learning and outcome for us has been opportunity for publishing. Many chapters and books have been based on our courses (e.g. Best & Rose, 1996; Higgs & Edwards, 1999; Rose & Best, 2005). In all cases publications were practical and experienced-based and followed successful implementation of courses. The act of preparing material for publication ensured that we kept our courses grounded in theory as well as making them process-driven and friendly. Writing also provided opportunities to reinforce and develop the team's sense of community and purpose.

Readers are reminded this chapter is an edited version of the discussion and reflections of three people who have worked together for many years. We hope it offers some useful ideas and practical support to those developing courses for fieldwork educators. It has provided us with deeper personal insights of our own journeys. It has also reminded us of the importance of being responsive to change within the clinical workplace and modifying past practices for future learning opportunities, as well as the deep satisfaction to be found in true collaboration!

## REFERENCES

Best, D., & Rose, M. (Eds.) (1996). *Quality supervision: Theory and practice for clinical supervisors.* London: WB Saunders.

Billet, S. (2001). *Learning in the workplace: Strategies for effective practice.* Crows Nest, NSW: Allen & Unwin.

Brown, G., Esdaile, S., & Ryan, S. (2004). *Becoming an advanced health care practitioner.* Edinburgh: Butterworth-Heinemann.

Dalton, L., Bull, R., Howarth, H., Marriott, J., Taylor, S., Leversha, A., Best, D., Galbraith, K., Simpson, M., & Rose, M. (2007). Evaluation of a national pharmacy preceptor education program. *Australian Journal of Rural Health, 15,* 159–165.

Davidson, M., Smith, R.A., Dodd, K.J., Smith, J.S., & O'Loughan, M.J. (2008). Interprofessional pre-qualification clinical education: A systematic review. *Australian Health Review, 32*(1), 111–120.

Delaney, C., & Molloy, E. (2009). *Clinical education in the health professions.* Chatswood, NSW: Churchill Livingstone.

Fish, D. (2005). The anatomy of education evaluation in clinical education, mentoring and professional supervision. In M. Rose & D. Best (Eds.), *Transforming practice through clinical education, mentoring and professional supervision* (pp. 327–342). Edinburgh: Elsevier.

Fish, D., & Coles, C. (Eds.) (1998). *Developing professional judgement in health care: Learning through the critical appreciation of practice*. Oxford. Butterworth-Heinemann.

Freeth, D., Hammick, M., Reeves, S., Koppel, I., & Barr, H. (2005). *Effective interprofessional education: Development, delivery and evaluation*. Oxford: Blackwell Publishing.

Higgs, J., & Edwards, H. (Eds.) (1999). *Educating beginning practitioners: Challenges for health professional education*. Oxford: Butterworth-Heinemann.

Higgs, J., & McAllister, L. (2005). The lived experience of clinical educators with implications for their preparation, support and professional development. *Learning in Health and Social Care, 4(3)*, 156–171.

Higgs, J., & McAllister, L. (2006). Being a clinical educator. *Advances in Health Science Education, 12*(2), 187–200.

Higgs, J., Jones, M., Loftus, S., & Christensen, N. (Eds.) (2008). *Clinical reasoning in the health professions* (3rd ed.). Oxford: Butterworth-Heinemann.

Hodgson, V., & Reynolds, M. (2005). Consensus, difference and "multiple communities" in networked learning. *Studies in Higher Education, 30*, 11–24.

Jukes, S. (2007). Developing a positive supervision framework from negative student experiences. *ACQ Acquiring Knowledge in Speech Language and Hearing, 9*(2), 71–73.

Kolb, D.A. (1984). *Experiential learning: Experience as the source of learning and development*. Englewood Cliffs, NJ: Prentice Hall.

Lave, J., & Wenger, E. (1991). *Situated learning: Legitimate peripheral participation*. Cambridge: Cambridge University Press.

Lee, J., Hong, N., & Ling, N. (2001). An analysis of students' preparation for the virtual learning environment. *The Internet and Higher Education, 4*(3-4), 231–242.

Marriott, J., Taylor, S., Simpson, M., Bull, R., Galbraith, K., Howarth, H., Leversha, A., Best, D., & Rose, M. (2005). Australian national strategy for pharmacy preceptor education and support. *Australian Journal of Rural Health, 13*, 83–90.

McAllister, M., & Moyle, W. (2005). An online learning community for clinical educators. *Nurse Education in Practice, 6*(2), 106–111.

Papastephanou, M. (2005). Difference-sensitive communities, networked learning, and higher education: Potentialities and risks. *Studies in Higher Education, 30*(1), 81–94.

Parsons, R. (2007). Improving preceptor self-efficacy using an online education program. *International Journal of Nursing Education Scholarship, 4*(1), 1–17.

Rafferty, M., Llewellyn-Davies, B., & Hewitt, J. (2007). Setting standards for the practice of clinical supervision: A Welsh perspective. In J. Driscoll, *Practising clinical supervision* (2nd ed., pp. 217–241). Edinburgh: Balliere Tindall Elsevier.

Rose, M., & Best, D. (2005). *Transforming practice through clinical education, professional supervision and mentoring*. Edinburgh: Elsevier.

Rose, M., Best, D., & McAllister, L. (1999). Becoming a clinical educator. In J. Higgs & H. Edwards. (Eds.), *Educating beginning practitioners: Challenges for health professional education* (pp. 271–277). Oxford: Butterworth-Heinemann.

Rose, M., Marriott, J., Galbraith, K., Bull, R., Best, D., Dalton, L., Leversha, A., Howarth, H., & Simpson, M. (in preparation). A randomized control trial of the effectiveness of moderated versus un-moderated online education for health professional clinical educators.

Schön, D.A. (1987). *Educating the reflective practitioner: Towards a new design for teaching and learning in professions*. San Francisco: Jossey-Bass.

Schwartz, P.L., & Heath, C.J. (1985). PEARLS (Personally arranged learning session): An alternative to presentations of free papers. *British Medical Journal, 290*(9), 453–454.

Sheehan, D., Wilkinson, T., & Billet, S. (2005). Interns' participation and learning in clinical environments in a New Zealand hospital. *Academic Medicine, 8*(3), 302–308.

Standish, P. (2002). Euphoria, dystopia and practice today. *Educational Philosophy and Theory, 34*, 407–412.

*SurveyMonkey.com*. Available: http://www.surveymonkey.com, accessed 11 November 2009.

Taylor, S., Best, D., Marriott, J., Dalton, L., Bull, R., Leversha, A., Galbraith, K., Howarth, H., Simpson, M., & Rose, M. (2007). Participant views of an online program supporting rural pharmacy preceptors. *Focus on Health Professional Education, 9*(3), 44–56.

Turney, C., Cairns, L.G., Hatton, N., Towler, J., Eltis, K.J., Thew, D.M., & Wright, R. (1982). *Supervisor development programmes: Role handbook.* Sydney: Sydney University Press.

*Miranda Rose PhD*
*School of Human Communication Sciences*
*La Trobe University, Australia*

*Helen Edwards PhD*
*Consultant Higher and Health Professional Education*
*Faculty of Health Sciences, (Adjunct)*
*La Trobe University, Australia*

*Dawn Best MEd*
*Health Professional Education Consultant*
*School of Physiotherapy (Adjunct)*
*La Trobe University, Australia*

# 26. USING MENTORING AND PEER SUPPORT IN THE DEVELOPMENT OF NEW FIELDWORK EDUCATORS

A great deal of the success of clinical education rests on the shoulders of clinical educators, their own abilities and personal attributes and the preparation and support they receive. (Higgs & McAllister, 2005, p. 156)

*Why Do We Need to Educate Our Educators?*

Fieldwork education is widely recognised as a key component in health professional training programs. The need for training of fieldwork educators is emerging as a key consideration for both educational facilities and workplaces undertaking fieldwork education. The Allied Health Professionals Australia in 2006 called for increased recognition of and training for clinicians who undertake fieldwork education. In their discussion of fieldwork education from an international perspective, Rodger et al. (2008) recommended a comprehensive program of informal and formal education to support fieldwork educators and noted, "clinical expertise does not necessarily translate into supervisory expertise, reinforcing the importance of clinical [fieldwork] educator training" (p. 58).

Literature related to the area of fieldwork educator training approaches the issue from a number of perspectives. Yeates, Stewart, and Barton (2008) described the attributes important to fieldwork educators; others have examined roles and competencies and their development within different frameworks. Prideaux et al. (2000) suggested that a key component of good clinical teaching in medicine was the provision of role models of good practice. They described seven roles that provide a framework for fieldwork educators. Landmark, Hansen, Bjones, and Bohler (2003) described three areas of importance identified by nurses in the development of competence and skills in fieldwork education: didactic factors such as integration of theory and practice, reflection and goal setting; role function factors associated with the fieldwork educator role; and organisational framework factors particularly around planning and expectations. Kilminster, Jolly, and Van der Vleuten (2002), discussing fieldwork educator training in medicine, identified the need to base training on accepted understandings about learning processes and supervisory models combined with empirical data, which they acknowledged to be sparse in this area.

In the area of speech language pathology a model of six interactive and dynamic dimensions was presented by Higgs and McAllister (2007) as a basis upon which to develop fieldwork educator training, and which the authors suggested might be

*L. McAllister et al., (eds.), Innovations in Allied Health Fieldwork*
*Education: A Critical Appraisal, 297–305.*

of benefit to other disciplines. Although all these reports provide insights into the attributes, attitudes and skills of fieldwork educators, and provide some understanding of the developmental process from novice to expert for fieldwork educators, they do not necessarily provide specific guidance as to how to gain the required skills or attributes or how to develop training programs. Moreover, although there is substantial literature providing insights into a range of learning processes supporting the development of competency in students, application of these or other learning processes to fieldwork educators is less frequently explored but certainly supported in the existing literature.

## How Do We Educate Our Fieldwork Educators?

Reflection is acknowledged as a key means of facilitating learning, and underpins many of the learning processes used routinely with students in the context of fieldwork education. Learning processes that support reflective practice include self-evaluation, journalling, peer learning and feedback. As fieldwork educators we require our students to regularly and actively reflect retrospectively on their performance. Indeed, in the field of speech language pathology, with the assessment tool Competency Assessment in Speech Pathology (COMPASS®; McAllister, Lincoln, Ferguson, & McAllister, 2006), students are rated on lifelong learning with a strong emphasis on reflection. As practising clinicians and experienced fieldwork educators, however, we are more likely to undertake reflection as an automatic process and while in the midst of practice. Schön (1983) described retrospective reflection as reflection-on-action, and that described for practising clinicians is reflection-in-action. For clinicians new to fieldwork education, the process of reflection-on-action needs to be encouraged and facilitated as it supports the integration of theoretical knowledge and that gained through practice. As suggested by McAllister and Lincoln (2004), reflection is a means by which professional artistry in fieldwork education can be developed.

Much has been written about the benefits of peer learning for students in both fieldwork education and general education contexts. The literature also provides some reference to peer support as an effective mechanism for fieldwork educators, with the suggestion that it is critical for both student and fieldwork educators to allow time to engage in peer learning (McAllister & Lincoln, 2004). The benefits of peer learning for all involved were described by Boud, Cohen, and Sampson, (2001, p. 3) who suggested that "peer learning should be mutually beneficial and involve the sharing of knowledge, ideas and experience between the participants".

Prideaux et al. (2000, p. 820) asserted that "good clinical teaching is concerned with providing role models for good practice, making good practice visible and explaining it to trainees". They described seven roles of the medical fieldwork educator: medical expert, communicator, collaborator, manager, advocate, scholar and professional. This role modelling function of fieldwork educators was also detailed by Landmark et al. (2003) in their study of factors influencing competence and skill development on fieldwork education in the nursing profession.

*An Opportunity for Capacity Building in Fieldwork Education*

The establishment of a student unit (hereafter referred to as the Unit) dedicated to educating speech language pathology students within a public health network provided an opportunity for capacity building in fieldwork education, with specific focus on the opportunity for more experienced fieldwork educators to support development in clinicians with little or no fieldwork education experience.

The Unit was established within the authors' speech language pathology department, which is part of a major health care provider serving both metropolitan and rural areas in Victoria, Australia. It was established through a formal agreement between the health service and a university providing a speech language pathology degree program. Our department has the equivalent of 18 full-time staff working across three streams: adult acute care, sub-acute care and paediatrics. Staff are based in seven geographically separate sites, providing a range of services to adult and paediatric populations. These services are co-ordinated and managed as a whole department, offering unique opportunities in terms of networking and peer support for staff and the co-ordination of programs and projects. The Unit was co-ordinated by the first author, a designated Senior Clinician - Clinical Education, who was able to provide operational support, clinical leadership and strategic direction. The department structure lent itself to the provision of varied placements across a wide range of service delivery models, caseloads and service development opportunities within a whole-of-department approach.

## PROVIDING A SUPPORTIVE CONTEXT FOR LEARNING

To sustain the Unit and meet the objective of capacity building in fieldwork education we developed a model of support for experienced and new fieldwork educators. This model utilised elements of the frameworks and models described above, as well as the learning processes previously identified as supporting the development of competency. That is, we adopted approaches of reflective practice, peer support, role modelling and mentoring. We also built on the speech language pathology department's strong commitment to lifelong learning and professional development for all staff. The existing culture of support was enacted primarily through a coaching program in which every staff member had a specific coach with whom they developed individual professional development plans. This was not a traditional supervisory relationship but one in which the agenda was set primarily by the person being coached. This coaching program provided an ideal backdrop for the upskilling of staff in fieldwork education. The integration of these accepted learning processes into the existing culture was designed to ensure that we adequately prepared and supported all clinicians engaged in fieldwork education.

We incorporated fieldwork educator peer learning as a key component of the support model. This included peer learning not only *within* the separate peer groups of novice and experienced educators but also *between* the two. A specific forum in the form of fieldwork educator support groups (known as "clinical educator catch-ups") was established, facilitating shared learning of all fieldwork educators within a safe and supportive environment essential to effective learning (Hutchinson, 2003). These sessions were facilitated by the Senior Clinician - Clinical Education, who had recognised skills in facilitation and mentoring. Fieldwork educators were given the opportunity to benefit from the experiences and strategies used by others at a similar level in fieldwork education and to engage in productive reflection and self-evaluation. In addition to the formalised groups we all took advantage of informal peer support opportunities utilising networks within the department.

The student supervision model used in the Unit was adapted from Rosenthal (1986) and involved the pairing of an experienced and a developing fieldwork educator with individual or multiple students. This model had a number of advantages. One was the provision of opportunities for role modelling. Experienced fieldwork educators could model specific skills such as the provision of feedback, development of learning agreements and teaching of clinical skills to students, as well as exploration of professional issues, time management and self-care. It also provided opportunity for explicit, real-time feedback to the developing fieldwork educator that was meaningful and immediately of benefit in changing practice. This was provided in a safe and supportive environment. Another advantage was the opportunity for "down time". Both experienced and developing fieldwork educators were given time away from students, allowing completion of tasks not related to fieldwork education as well as providing further opportunity for active reflection.

Formal continuing professional development opportunities were accessed within the workplace and through workshops for fieldwork educators at nearby universities. The external sessions were seen by many as more of an adjunct than a key component of the support model, which had a strong focus on experiential learning. As the Unit evolved we utilised some of the clinical educator catch-ups for specific professional development, covering topics such as feedback and working with challenging students.

## EVALUATION AND OUTCOMES

Introduction of the model of support within the newly established student unit provided us with the opportunity to undertake two qualitative studies of the experiences of fieldwork educators from the perspectives of: (1) less experienced clinicians developing their skills as speech language pathologists, while simultaneously learning to be fieldwork educators, and (2) experienced fieldwork educators supporting and mentoring the new fieldwork educators as well as supervising students. The studies allowed in-depth exploration of our model of support, positive and negative aspects in fieldwork educator training, and the model's role in ongoing development and sustainability of the Unit.

Participants from both studies were speech language pathologists with clinical experience ranging from one to 20 years. The two separate groups identified were experienced fieldwork educators and those for whom this was a new role. Those in the novice fieldwork educator group were all women, with an average age of 24 and an average of two years' clinical experience as speech language pathologists. Those in the experienced fieldwork educator group were all women, with an average age of 30 and an average of 10 years' clinical experience as speech language pathologists. Data relating to their experience of mentoring and peer support was collected within a phenomenological approach (Minichiello, Sullivan, Greenwood, & Axford, 2004) across the first 12 months of the Unit. This approach was deemed appropriate because the aim of the study was to describe the lived experience of the two groups of fieldwork educators. Data was collected through participants' reflective writings, summaries from clinical educator catch-ups, and two focus groups. The primary researchers for these studies (the authors of this chapter) were an experienced and a developing fieldwork educator, who were also focus group participants. Although this gave the potential for participant bias, this was managed by having independent facilitators conduct the groups. The advantage of participant/ researcher crossover was the ability to conduct rigorous member checking during data analysis, allowing for accurate and detailed interpretation of data. Data from the focus groups underwent thematic analysis. Initial or first order analysis (Shekedi, 2005; Fereday & Muir-Cochrane, 2006) was conducted by each researcher/participant independently listening to the recording of the focus groups and recording verbatim significant statements or key words and phrases of the participants, relating the experiences of fieldwork educators. These statements were grouped according to semantic categories and related sub-themes.

To further extrapolate meaning from the data, the researchers compared their independently grouped data and discussed interpretation of key statements. This permitted rigorous participant checking and accurate use of extracts from the data. Overarching themes were identified and agreed upon by all researchers. A primary goal in naming the themes was to use the researcher-participants' language from the transcripts, thus adding detail and depth to the discussion of results.

A range of themes arose from these two studies relating to the experience of fieldwork education from the different perspectives of experienced and developing clinical educators (Bourke, Gilmore, & Sargent; 2008; Van Beek, Healey, & Sawicki, 2008). Although a number of themes were unique there was commonality between the groups. The themes concerning support for fieldwork educators from both perspectives are the focus of the discussion in the rest of this chapter.

*Mentoring and Support*

For both experienced and developing fieldwork educators the theme of support and mentoring reflected the points described previously in the support model used within the Unit. These included the coaching program, peer support, clinical educator catch-ups, reflection, the student supervision model and infrastructure or operational supports. The formal coaching program was seen by participants as providing significant support to the developing fieldwork educators. Participants described benefits in having a formal program focused specifically on skill development which was built in to clinical position descriptions. Moreover, the developing fieldwork educators did not have to feel they were burdening their seniors. For the experienced fieldwork educators, their own coaching offered the opportunity to target either specific aspects of fieldwork education or, for some, the role of mentoring the developing fieldwork educators. It also offered an effective time management strategy, as the clinicians coaching developing fieldwork educators could use the formal sessions as a means of "quarantining" time. We encouraged staff to wait to raise concerns and ask questions until their coaching session, allowing for individual reflection and problem solving in the meantime.

All the fieldwork educators described the benefits of peer support. These were identified from both formal and informal peer support processes. The clinical educator catch-ups, reported as being of benefit to all fieldwork educators, were particularly so for the developing educators. This group described the value of being listened to with sympathy and non-judgmentally, with one participant describing the experience as "cathartic." For the experienced fieldwork educators the formal support groups provided less opportunity for peer support, with one participant suggesting "we never got to switch off from teacher mode". These sessions did, however, provide the impetus for reflection for all the clinicians. The experienced clinicians gained more peer support through informal networks.

The student supervision model of pairing an experienced and developing fieldwork educator with students was considered positive by all fieldwork educators. Opportunities for role modelling were highly valued by the developing fieldwork educators, particularly in the initial stages of placements. The benefit of down time from the supervisory role was recognised by all, but it seemed in the early stage that greater advantage was taken of it by the developing fieldwork educators, reflected in the recurring themes of the experienced fieldwork educators of time management, juggling and self care. With the various demands on these more senior clinicians, including departmental roles, fieldwork education, managing student projects and supporting the developing fieldwork educator, having enough time was a challenge.

The need for infrastructure, including robust operational processes and systems prior to and throughout the Unit's operation, was identified by both experienced and developing fieldwork educators. Although this incorporated some aspects of support and mentoring, it extended to areas such as specific resources and the more operational and administrative aspects of fieldwork education. This area of operational support was one which was not fully developed when we commenced placements, so had required immediate attention.

> "It was hard – trying to do your preparation and organising yourself while the students were already there."

One of the areas within this theme of mentoring and support identified more by experienced fieldwork educators than those new to the role was that of maintenance of professional development goals outside of fieldwork education. This group felt it was not only important for themselves but should also be encouraged in the developing fieldwork educators.

*Steps to Success*

> "No bad experience that I had would take away the benefits I've gotten from this [having a student]. The sense of confidence and the joy that I have in my job and being able to share it with other people, that won't be taken away."

Fieldwork education is emerging as a topic of discussion in recent literature and many studies have explored the benefits, challenges and barriers involved in taking on the role of fieldwork educator (Kathard, 2005; Lincoln & McCabe, 2005; Rodger et al., 2008). Research is also beginning to focus on supports and learning needs for developing fieldwork educators. Whereas many researchers have detailed the experiences of clinicians taking on a student supervisory role, we took the unique opportunity that was presented to explore the implementation of specific formal and informal support mechanisms within our Unit.

This chapter has discussed the successfully implemented model of fieldwork education within our Unit which supported and facilitated the development of field-work educators across a range of experience and involvement. The use of reflective practice during and between student placements allowed us to take a responsive approach to both the support model and operational aspects of the Unit itself. There was continual improvement and development as opportunities for change were identified and acted upon. The success of the model was validated by the positive responses from all the clinicians involved, also reflected in the analysed data. Some of the factors contributing to success of this model are summarised in Box 26.1.

Fieldwork education can be daunting, difficult, stressful and challenging, but also highly rewarding. The benefits can be lost on clinicians who are not supported and educated in this role, to the detriment of clinicians, students and whole departments. The implementation of structured formal and informal supports such as outlined in this chapter can create successful, positive, beneficial experiences for fieldwork educators. As participant researchers in this model of support for fieldwork education we learned a lot as clinicians and fieldwork educators. Our data shows that this was also the case for other participants in the studies. We urge other clinicians and field-work educators to further contribute to the body of knowledge that is emerging in this area.

*Box 26.1. Steps to Success*

1. Formalised department support program such as a coaching program
2. Formalised fieldwork educator support groups to facilitate peer support and reflective practice for both experienced and developing fieldwork educators
3. A student supervision model that permits experiential learning for developing fieldwork educators while offering a supportive learning environment through pairing with experienced fieldwork educators
4. The expectation and opportunity for reflection by all fieldwork educators
5. Access to continuing professional development opportunities both within and beyond the workplace

## ACKNOWLEDGEMENTS

The initiative described in this chapter was made possible by the collaboration of staff from the Speech Pathology Program at Charles Sturt University and the staff of the Peninsula Health Speech Pathology Department who acted as co-researchers on the project reported here by the two lead researchers.

# REFERENCES

Allied Health Professions Australia. (2006). *Solving the crisis in clinical education for Australia's health professions: A proposal for funding and other changes.* Available: http://www.ahpa.com.au/ pdfs/Clinical_Education_Proposal_Nov06.pdf, accessed 13 December 2009.

Boud, D., Cohen, R., & Sampson, J. (2001). *Peer learning in higher education: Learning from and with each other.* London: Kogan Page.

Bourke, N., Gilmore N., & Sargent, M. (2008). Providing a supportive context for learning: Mentoring new clinical educators. Paper presented at the Speech Pathology Australia/ New Zealand Speech Therapy Association National Conference, Auckland, May.

Fereday, J., & Muir-Cochrane, E. (2006). Demonstrating rigor using thematic analysis: A hybrid approach of inductive and deductive coding and theme development. *International Journal of Qualitative Methods, 5*(1), 1–11.

Higgs, J., & McAllister, L. (2005). The lived experiences of clinical educators with implications for their preparation, support and professional development. *Learning in Health and Social Care, 4*(3), 156–171.

Higgs, J., & McAllister, L. (2007). Educating clinical educators: Using a model of the experience of being a clinical educator. *Medical Teacher, 29*(2), e51–e57.

Hutchinson, L. (2003). ABC of learning and teaching in medicine: Educational environment. *British Medical Journal, 326*, 810–812.

Kathard, H. (2005). Clinical education in transition: Creating viable futures. *Advances in Speech Language Pathology, 7*(3), 149–152.

Kilminster, S., Jolly, B., & Van der Vleuten, C. (2002). A framework for effective training for supervisors. *Medical Teacher, 24*(4), 385–389.

Landmark, B., Hansen, G., Bjones, I., & Bohler, A. (2003). Clinical supervision: Factors defined by nurses as influential upon the development of competence and skills in supervision. *Journal of Clinical Nursing, 12*, 834–841.

Lincoln, M., & McCabe, P. (2005).Values, necessity and the mother of invention in clinical education. *Advances in Speech-Language Pathology, 7*(3), 153–157.

McAllister, L., & Lincoln, M. (2004). *Clinical education in speech-language pathology.* London: Whurr.

McAllister, S., Lincoln, M., Ferguson, A., & McAllister, L. (2006). *COMPASS®: Competency assessment in speech pathology.* Melbourne: Speech Pathology Association of Australia Ltd.

Minichiello, V., Sullivan, G., Greenwood, K., & Axford, R. (Eds.) (2004). *Handbook of research methods in nursing and health science.* Sydney: Pearson/Prentice Hall.

Prideaux, D., Alexander, H., Bower, A., Dacre, J., Haist, S., Jolly, B., et al. (2000). Clinical teaching: Maintaining an educational role for doctors in the new health care environment. *Medical Education, 34*(10), 820–826.

Rodger, S., Webb, G., Devitt, L., Gilbert, J., Wrightson, P., & McMeeken, J. (2008). Clinical education and practice placements in the allied health professions: An international perspective. *Journal of Allied Health, 37*(1), 53–62.

Rosenthal, J. (1986). Novice and experienced student clinical teams in undergraduate clinical practice. *Australian Communication Quarterly, 2*, 12–15.

Schön, D.A. (1983). *The reflective practitioner: How professionals think in action.* London: Temple-Smith.

Shekedi, A. (2005). *Multiple case narrative: A qualitative approach to studying multiple populations (Studies in narrative).* London: John Benjamins.

Van Beek, C., Healey, J., & Sawicki, D. (2008). Teaching and learning at the same time: Experiences of developing clinical educators. Paper presented at the Speech Pathology Australia/ New Zealand Speech Therapy Association National Conference, Auckland, May.

Yeates, P., Stewart, J., & Barton, J. (2008). What can we expect of clinical teachers? Establishing consensus on applicable skills, attitudes and practices. *Medical Education, 42,* 134–142.

*Noni Bourke BAppSci*
*Improving Care for Older People*
*Peninsula Health, Australia*

*Christie Van Beek BHlthSci(SpPath)*
*Peninsula Health, Australia*

# SECTION IX: PREPARATION AND SUPPORT OF STUDENTS FOR FIELDWORK EDUCATION

JULIE BALDRY CURRENS

# 27. PREPARING FOR LEARNING TOGETHER IN FIELDWORK EDUCATION PRACTICE SETTINGS

## INTRODUCTION

Fieldwork education placements are extremely challenging. At best, they prove to be exciting and rewarding; students enjoy feeling stretched, their confidence grows as their skills develop and theory begins to unite with practice. At worst, the clinical workplace is experienced as a hostile and unforgiving environment, in which a student feels isolated, fearful, inadequate and disempowered. In such situations students describe being uncertain of what to expect of the situation, their educators and of themselves, and often feel as if they are all at sea or "drowning". In keeping with the nautical metaphor, the presence of a fellow student, a peer, being "in the same boat" may provide reassurance, offset tensions and allay fears.

Peer learning draws from a rich theoretical base which locates learning as a socially constructed activity involving sociocognitive and sociocultural development (Piaget, 1926; Vygotsky, 1978). Aspects of social interaction, cognitive challenge, skill development, modelling, reinforcement and dialogue (Bandura, 1971; Johnson & Johnson, 1987; Wertsch, 1991; King, 1999; Renshaw; 2004) all contribute to the success of the process. In fieldwork education settings, influences on peer learning are multifaceted. These include individual conceptions of learning and performance; prior experiences of learning with and from others; relationships with peers, and student attitudes to learning together; the approach taken by fieldwork educators; and the format and process of assessment. This chapter explores the components of preparation that are necessary to facilitate effective peer learning experiences. It identifies key aspects of the peer learning process in fieldwork, and considers how this information can be used to assist with both managing expectations of peer learning and facilitating effective engagement in the process. Issues of companionship, collaboration, comparison, competition and conflict are considered. This work derives from doctoral research (Baldry Currens, 2008).

## EXPECTATIONS AND GROUND-RULES

Presentation to students and university staff of the importance and value of peer learning is critical to the success of peer learning programs in fieldwork education and must signal its relationship to professional, autonomous practice. The effectiveness of peer learning and the preparation of the individual for competent autonomous practice is just as important as the social and collaborative goals of peer learning.

*L. McAllister et al., (eds.), Innovations in Allied Health Fieldwork*
*Education: A Critical Appraisal, 309–317.*

Effective engagement in peer learning offers outcomes that are relevant to building the social skills necessary for appropriate collegiate relationships and teamwork. It offers learning experiences that are not dependent upon the presence of a more senior "other" who will show a learner what to do in a given situation. It emphasises reflective, experiential learning, shared with others at a similar level of experience. And it allows students to gain competence and confidence in self and peer evaluation.

Healthcare students usually report eager anticipation for fieldwork education placements, since they provide a taste of authentic practice. Yet such experiences, especially those occurring early in the degree, may also be filled with uncertainty. Initial considerations inevitably relate to the nature of the placement itself, its area of specialty, the hospital or service in which it is hosted and its location, the types of clients and the extent to which students feel prepared for the conditions they may encounter. Secondary concerns usually relate to particular fieldwork educators, their reputation regarding the extent to which they support students' learning, and relationships with the student with whom a placement will be shared. Students can worry that a difficult relationship with a fellow student might add significant stresses to their fieldwork education, and may anticipate a placement with anxiety. Issues of personal compatibility feature highly in students' concerns regarding peer learning (Ladyshewsky, 1993; Triggs Nemshick & Shepard, 1996; Martin & Edwards, 1998; Baldry Currens & Bithell, 2003; Baldry Currens 2003a).

Some programs incorporate many opportunities for peer learning, teaching and assessment into all aspects of the degree, both in university-based and field-work education components. If expectations of the latter are coloured by negative experiences of peer learning in the former, particular support in the preparation phase will be required. Other students may have specific concerns related to learning with peers during client-contact activities. In large cohorts it is quite possible that students may have never met the peer with whom they will be placed, have only a vague awareness or even an unfavourable impression of that peer.

Regardless of any prior knowledge of each other, it is advisable for students to meet before commencing their placement and begin to build a relationship that will support later learning. Formal or informal meetings, facilitated by academics, can offer reassurance, particularly if peers can appreciate that the fellow student has concerns similar to their own. A suitable agenda for such meetings could include:
– introduction of peers and discussion of any relevant work experience
– sharing and consideration of available information and resources
– discussion of practicalities such as travel
– reflection on any previous related experiences
– sharing of specific concerns or anxieties
– identification of any preferences regarding learning and desired outcomes.

Once the placement is under way, educators should ideally facilitate similar discussion of expectations and concerns, and ensure that any ground-rules and proce-dures related to learning and working together are made explicit during induction to the placement. Information regarding when and where peers can practice together and engage in discussion is vital, along with clarification that these are valued aspects of fieldwork learning. Learning outcomes that require evidence of effective peer learning and working, such as joint case presentations, must be explained with opportunity for questions. Practical examples and guidance on how to work together are helpful. For example, joint treatment of a client might be led by one student, agreed and planned beforehand, with the other student undertaking an "assistant" role.

Appropriate professional communication between student peers should be emphasised. It is crucial both to acknowledge that peers may experience interpersonal tensions and to emphasise that seeking guidance from the educator without fear of judgment or penalty in these situations is expected. If problems occur it is essential that the fieldwork educator is perceived as approachable and as one who will not apportion blame or penalty. Many students are reluctant to acknowledge difficulties of this sort for fear of being perceived as a poor communicator or team player. Serious difficulties such as these are relatively uncommon, and rarely require separation of students. Facilitated discussion of differences in a mature and professional manner, without blame, emphasising collegiality and reflection, will usually suffice.

## COMPANIONSHIP

### Familiarity, Solidarity and Compatibility

When students, particularly those new to fieldwork education, feel overwhelmed or disoriented in the practice setting, a friendly face and a sense of companionship is important (Baldry Currens, 2003b). An intimacy of the type that exists within a close friendship is unnecessary here. Merely being a student from the same program may be sufficient to offer a sense of reassurance. A sense of the "known" counters feelings of insecurity and enhances a sense of comfort, safety and connection.

Through discussion of their experiences, students discover they are not alone in finding situations that are stressful, demanding or frightening; they voice concerns and share emotions and insecurities. Through a mutual recognition of the similarity of their position and experiences, students learn to accept their responses to the challenges of fieldwork education as normal. Allegiances develop, anxiety lessens as confidence grows, and daunting situations are mediated through sharing and identifying with a peer. Through discussion, students begin to develop the reflective, interpretative and problem-solving processes that are crucial to their professional skill set.

In preparing students for learning together in the fieldwork education setting, it is important that professional companionship between peers is presented as desirable and achievable for all students. Prerequisities that need to be made explicit are:
- a sense of trustworthiness in the peer
- being able to respect a peer and his/her interactions with colleagues and clients
- a degree of personal compatibility, such that peers can feel broadly comfortable with one another
- a capacity for mutual tolerance within the shared experience.

Peers need not be at exactly the same level of academic ability and achievement, although a substantial difference in the level of knowledge and practice can become awkward, resulting in dependency or feelings of burden (Tiberius & Gaiptman, 1985; Zavadak, Dolnack, Polich, & Van Volkenburg, 1995; Martin & Edwards, 1998;

Baldry Currens & Bithell, 2003). Effective peer learning does not require similar life experiences. Many students report that despite having little in common with a peer learner, they are pleasantly surprised to discover a degree of compatibility which is sufficient to engender effective peer learning activities, even though their life experience, gender, age or ethnicity may differ significantly. Neither is friendship a necessary prerequisite for successful professional companionship. Pre-existing friendship patterns can sometimes act as hindrance, particularly if the dynamics constrain the learning relationship. Many students report developing satisfactory and fulfilling working relationships with a peer whom they will not, once the placement is finished, chose to meet socially.

Adequate preparation for effective peer learning should stress the importance of developing companionship as a means by which distress can be alleviated. It reassures peers, and helps facilitate a relaxed atmosphere with conditions conducive to learning. Peer interaction can enhance learning through emotional expression, where the relative safety of a peer is more supportive and less judgmental (Lincoln & McAllister, 1993). Peers help mediate difficult emotions, and in so doing adjust the emotional landscape in preparation for learning.

## COLLABORATION AND PEER LEARNING

Students are frequently unaware of the components of peer learning in the field-work education setting. Making these explicit prior to participation facilitates understanding and participation. Adequate preparation helps students understand that they will engage in a learning paradigm which differs from traditional methods of teaching and learning. They are likely to be more familiar with a paradigm in which teaching is undertaken by one who is more capable and experienced, often an expert practitioner and an accomplished teacher. In contrast, peer learning during fieldwork education utilises a discovery-based approach, in which a significant commitment to experiential and reflective learning is essential. Although some learning experiences may be facilitated and prepared by the educator, far more are spontaneous and unscripted (Baldry Currens, 2008). Learning occurs through participation in a variety of reciprocal and interactive activities (e.g. Tiberius & Gaiptman, 1985; Ladyshewsky, 2000, 2002, 2004, 2006; Zavadak et al., 1995; Triggs Nemshick & Shepard, 1996; Martin & Edwards, 1998; Baldry Currens & Bithell, 2003; Moore, Morris, Crouch, & Martin, 2003). Broadly, it is helpful to identify two sets of collaborative learning behaviours: dialogic and activity-based collaboration (Baldry Currens, 2003b, 2008). In both sets of behaviours, a peer is cast as a learning and practice partner and critical friend. These activities are described separately below, but they commonly occur together, in combinations which differ according to individual situations.

### Dialogic Collaboration

Within *dialogic collaboration,* peers engage in a range of activities involving conversation. They include questioning, clarifying, exchanging and participating in rich co-constructive dialogues (Baldry Currens, 2008).

*Questioning.* Peers ask each other questions of variable levels of complexity. At their most simple, these are uncomplicated requests for information, to which a simple answer suffices. Students often regard these as "stupid questions" which need not involve their educator. Intermediate level questions may be answered by one student, or developed as a result of discussion. Higher level questions and answers are more complex, and may require consultation with others.

*Clarifying.* Speaking aloud assists with clarifying one's thoughts through reframing the question and reducing its complexity. Through expression, students are able to make better sense of ideas, situations or concepts.

*Exchanging.* This involves sharing and transferring knowledge, information and resources in a collegial manner. Generosity, reciprocity and sometimes trading activities ("I'll help you with that if you help me with this") are involved. Students help each other form connections between different situations. A wider range of experiences, ideas and approaches are accumulated than would be achieved alone.

*Rich, co-constructive dialogues.* These are dynamic, complex and highly interactive dialogues in which students elaborate ideas. Peers probe and challenge each other through different, sometimes conflicting, perspectives. Resolution of cognitive conflict facilitates deeper understanding, new meanings and altered conceptions. Hypothesis generation and testing, broader clinical reasoning (Ladyshewsky, 2002) and reflection are all supported.

## Activity-Based Collaboration

Peers also learn through engagement in a range of behaviours which involve learning through activity. These include modelling, rehearsing, reviewing, and tutoring (Baldry Currens, 2008).

*Modelling.* Students learn through observing practice which they consider to be both good and poor. They emulate successful behaviours modelled by the peer, and learn to avoid unsuccessful approaches.

*Rehearsing.* Students practise treatment and assessment approaches, often repeatedly in order to master techniques and processes, both verbal and physical, before using them with clients. They receive feedback from their peer and consider how they might adapt techniques to suit individual needs. A less formal and more relaxed atmosphere (than with an educator) is particularly valued.

*Reviewing.* Practice is first observed and then discussed. Learning is enhanced through the giving and receiving of feedback. Mental rehearsal also occurs during observation, in which one's intended approach is compared with that which is observed. If feedback is offered by a supportive, not overly critical peer, separated from formal assessment procedures, the process becomes a mutually owned fact-finding process in which critique is permissioned. Skills related to facilitating self and peer reflection and the provision of non-judgmental feedback are developed.

*Tutoring.*   Students demonstrate and teach one another techniques and strategies in an informal and reciprocal arrangement. Tutees gain a wider repertoire of treatment techniques and can ask questions about delivery. Tutors gain opportunities to clarify knowledge, consolidate understanding and reinforce skills.

Preparation for peer learning in fieldwork education settings requires adequate explanation of the different types of activity that might be involved. Practice of some activities can be helpful, particularly offering constructive and focused feedback. It is helpful to emphasise that the learning is flexible and is developed according to the needs and preferences of the learners and the clinical context in which they are placed.

COMPARISON, COMPETITION AND CONFLICT

Issues of comparison and competition are a frequent source of concern for students undertaking peer learning (Tiberius & Gaiptman, 1985; Martin & Edwards, 1998; Baldry Currens & Bithell, 2003). Each is explored below.

*Comparison*

Although individual programs vary, it is usual for students to negotiate specific learning outcomes with their educator for the period of their placement as part of a learning contract. Despite facilitated reviews of progress, many students find self-evaluation difficult, and doubt their own judgement. Students acknowledge that comparing their own ability with that of a peer aids self-assessment. Although some may discuss this, a private and internalised process is more usual, in which students quietly make a personal assessment of their peer's ability and compare it to their own. Students consider first how they expect themselves to fare, and then how they are actually faring, in comparison. In this way, they use the peer as a "mirror" through which a clearer view of their performance, knowledge, and skills may be attained (Baldry Currens, 2003b, 2008).

Although the subjective and normative nature of these comparisons is inevitably limited, shortfalls in students' own performance may be identified. Peers rarely discuss such observations, and students may consider it poor etiquette to do so, unless disclosure permissions are discussed. Comparisons are private, since the desire is to better one's own ability, rather than to outdo the peer.

In contrast, comparison of performance between students by a fieldwork educator is a source of great concern (Tiberius & Gaiptman, 1985; Ladyshewsky, 1993; Triggs Nemshick & Shepard, 1996; Martin & Edwards, 1998; Baldry Currens & Bithell, 2003). Students accept that their educator's assessment of their abilities is based on knowledge and experience gained from many previous students of different levels and abilities. However, comparison with the current student peer raises concerns that the process will favour one student over another. Having someone against whom an immediate comparison may be made may cause individual weaknesses to be enhanced. Some students experience considerable pressure in this regard, diverting their focus from learning. Educators should reassure students that assessment of individuals is always against identified criteria and agreed learning outcomes, rather than through comparison with other students, and should avoid inadvertent comments such as "Ah yes, [named peer] had the same difficulties yesterday".

## Competition

Although intentions to enhance individual performance are acceptable to students, intentions to appear better than a peer are not. Competition is a significant concern for students (Tiberius & Gaiptman, 1985; Martin & Edwards, 1998; Baldry Currens & Bithell, 2003) and one which leads to individualistic learning rather than effective peer relationships (Ladyshewsky, 2006). Perceptions of competition are highly personal. For some, it is perceived as a natural, healthy phenomenon that enhances motivation. A peer may spur greater efforts than might occur when learning alone or with a non-competitive partner. Sparring is light hearted, manageable and good natured. Conversely, competition is destructive when a conscious and blatant desire to out-perform a peer is present. "One-up-manship" and other behaviours which undermine the achievement of a peer are damaging and may strain a learning relationship beyond tolerance.

Fieldwork education preparation should support students' reflections on their attitudes towards motivation, performance and competition. Students with differing attitudes towards competition may be encouraged to seek a positive approach, and competitive peers encouraged to avoid excess. Effective peer learning relationships will contain learning outcomes that require sharing and interdependence (Ladyshewsky, 2006).

## Conflict

Students acknowledge that peer relationships are not always successful, and may deteriorate. Although these situations occur rarely, they are a significant concern and may become dysfunctional. Several factors may contribute: poor communication, lack of personal compatibility, a highly aggressive and competitive approach by one or both peers, or a blatant disregard for the sensibilities by one peer for the other (Baldry Currens, 2007. In some instances, despite severe difficulties, students can be loth to discuss matters with their educator, even when a third party might be of help. They fear judgment and exposure, worrying that a situation might become common knowledge. They may experience a range of difficult and painful emotions which include doubting themselves and their abilities, feeling hurt, angry, resentful, frustrated, despondent and isolated. Conflict places a burden on the learning experience, since the students usually continue to work together unless separated. They acknowledge minimal engagement in peer learning, because the inadequate and potentially volatile relationship usually causes them to reject opportunities to participate in collaborative learning activities. As with competition, the importance of acknowledging difficulties must be emphasised. It is essential that students are prepared for the fact that relationships can deteriorate if problems are not addressed at an early stage.

## CONCLUSION

The extent to which students engage in peer learning activities varies immensely, and is dependent upon a variety of interpersonal, environmental and situational contexts. These are influenced by individuals' attitudes, beliefs and preferences, and the dynamics of their relationships.

Disabling attitudes and behaviours include reluctance to engage in or negotiate a mutual and reciprocal learning experience; a preference for individualistic learning, instruction-oriented and expert-centred approaches to teaching; a focus on competence and performance rather than learning and development; condescending and overly competitive attitudes; and significant differences in ability, such that one peer is heavily dependent upon another.

Enablers include positive, facilitative and proactive attitudes towards peer learning by academics and fieldwork educators who understand both the collaborative learning paradigm and the processes involved; fieldwork educators who are willing to withdraw and enable students to explore their own creative collaboration; learning outcomes that require peer collaboration; sufficient resources such as space and time; similar levels of commitment to the shared learning process; a readiness to support the development of a peer; a willingness to pool ideas without expectations of gain for self alone; and an understanding of the concepts and practices involved.

Effective preparation is essential if students are to realise the potential of peer learning for self and others. Peer learning offers a valuable contribution to fieldwork education since it helps students gain confidence in their own analytic and reflective processes, strengthens confidence and competence, and facilitates professional social practices.

## REFERENCES

Baldry Currens, J.A., & Bithell, C.P. (2003). The 2:1 clinical placement model: Perceptions of clinical educators and students. *Physiotherapy, 89*(4), 204–218.

Baldry Currens, J.A. (2003a). The 2:1 clinical placement model: Review. *Physiotherapy, 89*(9), 540–554.

Baldry Currens, J.A. (2003b). Physiotherapy student perceptions of peer assisted learning. Paper presented at 14th World Confederation for Physical Therapy Conference, Barcelona.

Baldry Currens, J.A. (2007). Student perceptions of peer learning in the practice setting: A Q-methodological study. Paper presented at 15th World Confederation for Physical Therapy Conference, Vancouver, June.

Baldry Currens, J.A. (2008). *Peer learning in the practice setting: Issues of companionship, collaboration and contrast*. Unpublished PhD thesis, Institute of Education, University of London.

Bandura, A. (1971). *Social learning theory*. New York: General Learning Press.

Johnson, D.W., & Johnson, R.T. (1987). *Learning together and alone: Cooperative, competitive and individualistic learning*. Englewood Cliffs, NJ: Prentice-Hall.

King, A. (1999). Discourse patterns for mediating peer learning. In A.M. O'Donnell & A. King (Eds.), *Cognitive perspectives on peer* learning (pp. 87–115). Mahwah, NJ: Lawrence Erlbaum.

Ladyshewsky R.K. (2006). Building cooperation in peer coaching relationships: Understanding the relationships between reward structure, learner preparedness, coaching skill and learner engagement. *Physiotherapy, 92* (1), 4–10.

Ladyshewsky, R. (1993). Clinical teaching and the 2:1 student-to-clinical instructor ratio. *Journal of Physical Therapy Education, 7*(1), 31–35.

Ladyshewsky, R. (2000). Peer assisted learning in clinical education: A review of terms and learning principles. *Journal of Physical Therapy Education, 14*(2), 15–22.

Ladyshewsky, R. (2002). A quasi-experimental study of the differences in performance and clinical reasoning using individual learning versus reciprocal peer coaching. *Physiotherapy Theory and Practice, 18*(1), 17–31.

Ladyshewsky, R. (2004). The impact of peer coaching on the clinical reasoning of the novice practitioner. *Physiotherapy Canada, 56*(1), 15–25.

Lincoln, M., & McAllister, L. (1993). Peer learning in clinical education. *Medical Teacher, 15*(1), 17–25.

Martin, M., & Edwards, L. (1998). Peer learning on fieldwork placements. *British Journal of Occupational Therapy, 61*(6), 249–252.

Moore, A., Morris, J., Crouch, V., & Martin, M. (2003). Evaluation of physiotherapy clinical education models: Comparing 1:1, 2:1 and 3:1 placements. *Physiotherapy, 89*(8), 489–501.

Piaget, J. (1926). *The language and thought of the child.* New York: Harcourt Brace.

Renshaw, P.D. (2004). Dialogic learning, teaching and instruction: Theoretical roots and analytical frameworks. In J. van der Linden & P. Renshaw (Eds.), *Dialogic learning: Shifting perspectives to learning, instruction and teaching.* Dordrecht: Kluwer Academic Publishers.

Tiberius, R., & Gaiptman, B. (1985). The supervisor-student ratio: 1:1 versus 1:2. *Canadian Journal of Occupational Therapy, 52,* 179–183.

Triggs Nemshick, M., & Shepard, K. (1996). Physical therapy clinical education in a 2:1 student-instructor education mode. *Physical Therapy, 76*(9), 968–981.

Vygotsky, L.S. (1978). *Mind in society: The development of higher psychological processes.* Cambridge, MA: Harvard University Press.

Wertsch, J.W. (1991). *Voices of the mind: A sociocultural approach to mediated action.* Cambridge, MA: Harvard University Press.

Zavadak, K.H., Dolnack, C.K., Polich, S., & Van Volkenburg, M. (1995). Collaborative models. *Magazine of Physical Therapy, 3*(2), 46–54.

*Julie Baldry Currens PhD*
*Learning, Teaching and Assessment*
*University of East London, UK*

LUCIE SHANAHAN, LINDA WILSON,
ANNA O'CALLAGHAN AND TANYA DAWE

# 28. INVOLVING STAKEHOLDERS IN A CLINICAL EDUCATION PROGRAM

*An Action Research Study*

## PROJECT AIM

This chapter explores a key issue in clinical or fieldwork education: the involvement of stakeholders in the development, implementation and quality review of clinical education programs. The topic is examined through an action research project conducted to develop and evaluate the clinical education program of the Speech Pathology Department at Albury Hospital (AH). The hospital is located in Albury, New South Wales, Australia. The hospital provides clinical education placements for several undergraduate and Masters entry level speech language pathology programs from across two states. On average, the department hosts students for 30 calendar weeks per year and, as students usually attend placements in pairs or groups of three, the department provides up to 70 placement weeks of clinical education per year.

The impetus for this research and development program was an emerging awareness among the clinical educators (CEs) in the department that students from each of the universities arrived at AH with varying levels of theoretical and clinical knowledge, competencies, and methods of engaging in clinical education. In other words, they arrived with differing "clinical-cultural" backgrounds. This meant that the CEs frequently felt the need to adapt their approaches to clinical education in order to accommodate students' different needs and backgrounds. However, in the absence of sufficient theoretical knowledge or a practical framework to guide them, adaptations to these variations by the CEs were ad hoc and reactive. The CEs began to feel frustrated and disillusioned in their clinical education roles, and began to lose confidence in their skills. They expressed a desire to identify a theoretical basis for clinical education within the department, with a view to quality improvement of the program and developing research skills. This chapter describes the action research project which has begun to target these goals.

## LITERATURE REVIEW

A brief review of the literature pertinent to clinical education in speech language pathology identified that the concerns, issues and challenges faced by the AH Speech Pathology Department were echoed by researchers and authors. For example,

L. McAllister et al., (eds.), *Innovations in Allied Health Fieldwork*
*Education: A Critical Appraisal, 319–328.*

McAllister (2005) identified that one of the challenges clinicians faced in providing clinical placements was the increasing diversity of student cohorts, thus necessitating greater flexibility in modes of clinical education. Other authors have similarly discussed this (and other) challenges (McAllister & Lincoln, 2004; Cruice, 2005; Lincoln & McCabe, 2005; Pickering, 2005; Stansfield, 2005).

The need for innovative models of clinical education has also been clearly highlighted in the literature. Pleasingly, some of the approaches suggested by McAllister (2005) had already been adopted at AH. For example, the department's preference for concurrent placements (involving multiple students from different disciplines) created opportunities for peer learning and supervision, and ensured efficient use of CE time. However, some of the practices indicated as outdated, such as heavy emphasis on direct supervision of student-client interactions, were still used by the department. The Teacher as Manager model (Romanini & Higgs, 1991), advocated as a solution for better management of clinical placements (McAllister & Lincoln, 2004; McAllister, 2005), was identified as fitting the department's conception of the framework needed.

In the Teacher as Manager model, CEs are viewed as facilitators of students' learning in an adult learning environment. As managers of the learning program, CEs encourage student participation in educational tasks, group processes and individual student development. Students are viewed as contributors to the learning program rather than subordinates. Emphasis is placed on the interaction of all participants in the learning program, and interdependence between CEs and students is valued. CEs encourage students to develop increasing levels of self-direction and responsibility for their own learning. This means that CEs are required to change their role over time in response to the phases of the placement and the students' changing needs and capabilities (Romanini & Higgs, 1991). According to the model, it is useful to think of placements in terms of three phases and to think of the CE's role as managing each of these phases so as to maximise students' learning. The three phases outlined in the model are preparation, implementation and evaluation. Table 28.1 presents definitions of the three phases, and their conceptualisation within the current research program.

The articulation of the three phases within the model led the CEs to reflect on their current practices, specifically the preparation phase of the placement. The CEs identified that the orientation program in use could be improved to better prepare students for the "learning and development" phase of their placements. This chapter focuses on Stage One of an ongoing quality improvement process: the development of a new orientation package and the process and outcomes of the action research program used to evaluate it.

## DESCRIPTION OF THE PROJECT

### Methodology

This project adopted an action research methodology for several reasons. Firstly, it suits the complex nature of investigating clinical/professional practice and the

*Table 28.1. Conversion of Romanini and Higgs (1991) phases to AH program phases*

| Teacher as Manager phase | Description | AH phase | Placement timing (10 weeks) |
|---|---|---|---|
| Preparation | Preparation for a learning task: teacher's prior planning and preparation, initial encounter of teacher and learner, exploration of learning goals and strategies, assessment of learner readiness, and preparatory activities. | Orientation | Weeks 1 and 2 |
| Implementation | Activities related to completion of the learning tasks: planning and review of learning goals and strategies, learning experience, ongoing review of progress. | Learning and development | Weeks 3 to 8 |
| Evaluation | Evaluation of the learning program and outcomes; determination of any subsequent action: evaluation of program input, process and outcomes, application beyond the direct context, entering a new learning cycle. | Evaluation | Weeks 9 and 10 |

inextricable relationship between practice and reflection. It also fits with the Teacher as Manager model, allowing discrete evaluation of each phase of the clinical placement (Orientation, Learning and development, Evaluation) in the AH context. Finally, it is a method of research readily understood by clinicians who are novice researchers.

A project plan and various learning resources were developed following a semi-structured group interview with CEs at AH in April 2007. The resources are described in the following section. The project has involved all staff members of the department and the majority of final year speech language pathology students who have completed a clinical placement at AH since May 2007. The project commenced by trialling the learning resources with the first student cohort (student placement one; SP1). Evaluative feedback about the satisfaction of students and CEs with the resources and structure of the Orientation phase was obtained via semi-structured interviews at the end of this phase (i.e. Week 1). Semi-structured interviews were conducted again with students during the final week of placement, and with CEs one week after the completion of placement. The purpose of this second interview was to ascertain whether the focused Orientation phase had influenced the students' experience during placement, and whether students perceived that the learning activities had influenced their learning throughout the placement. Each interview was audio recorded and the content was transcribed.

Recommendations from these interviews were incorporated, and the subsequent revised learning package was trialled with student placement two (SP2). Again, semi-structured interviews were used to collect data from students and CEs at the two designated time points, and further fine-tuning of the Orientation phase was completed. Recommendations from this round of data collection were incorporated for student placement three (SP3). Following this placement, no recommendations for change were made for the Orientation phase. To ensure that a robust and sustainable Orientation phase had been developed, the Orientation program implemented for SP3 was replicated for student placement four (SP4), and results confirmed that both CEs and students were satisfied with the Orientation program. The research focus then shifted to Stage Two of the project, the Learning and development stage, the results of which are not presented in this chapter.

*Student Learning Package*

Stage One of the project focused on developing activities and tools that enabled CEs to more effectively identify students' learning styles, needs, goals and preferred supervision methods. It also aimed to provide students with a coordinated and structured start to placement, with the goal of reducing students' anxiety while encouraging them to take responsibility for their learning. CE consultation during the planning stage of this project had identified these as the greatest needs and concerns. A learning package (see Table 28.2) is now emailed to all students at least two weeks prior to the commencement of placement.

*Table 28.2. Student learning package*

| Component | Description |
|---|---|
| Research project | Information sheet and consent form. |
| Learning styles | Information provided about: a) what learning styles are and types of learning styles; b) activities to help students identify how they perceive, process and plan or organise information; c) Honey and Mumford (1989) learning styles activity; d) Suggestions for how to develop non-dominant learning styles |
| Learning styles summary sheet | Captures and summarises results of activities outlined above; used as the basis of discussion with CE. |
| Challenge test | 40 questions that reflect primary areas of clinical practice. Students are asked to rate their knowledge and confidence in relation to each question. Used in first discussions with CE about learning goals. Students are expected to work to develop their knowledge and confidence before the end of the Orientation phase of the placement. |
| Learning agreement | Standard agreement to be used in the absence of a university-specific agreement. Provides a framework for developing learning goals, discussing type and frequency of feedback, and negotiating dates for reviewing the learning agreement. |

## FINDINGS

The findings of the research are summarised in Table 28.3. By the end of SP3, the feedback received from students and CEs was positive and consistent. That is, all participants independently identified similar features of the program as facilitators of learning. The aspects that enabled a smooth and focused start to placement were: development of a shared understanding of learning styles and needs, knowledge of expectations and time frames for clinical documentation, and knowing when CEs would be available for consultation or feedback. The challenge test was also well received. Both students and CEs commented that it helped with students' preparation for the caseload they would be working with and identification of learning goals for the placement. After SP3 participants did not identify any aspects or features that required further improvement. A welcome finding was that no CE commented on compromised client care during the Orientation phase. Identical feedback was obtained at the end of SP4, indicating that the findings were robust. We acknowledge that a formal orientation phase, as used in this project, takes time and human resources but our experience is that the benefits far outweigh these costs.

## FUTURE DEVELOPMENT

With the completion of the Orientation phase we have shifted our focus to Stage Two of the project, the Learning and development phase. We are continuing to use action research in this endeavour. Following conference presentations, another speech language pathology service has adopted the Teacher as Manager model and the Orientation framework, and has adapted the challenge test to reflect the clinical caseload. This site has agreed to participate in action research to evaluate and develop this ongoing project. A key challenge for the department will be sustaining this new approach to clinical education in light of staffing changes. New staff will need to be educated about the Teacher as Manager model and to be supported in implementing it within their practice. It is hoped that this will lead to maintenance of a consistent approach to clinical education within the department.

*Table 28.3. Project findings*

| Time point/ Participants | Findings | Examples of data | Actions arising from findings |
|---|---|---|---|
| Pre-SP1/ CEs | Adaptations were ad hoc and reactive; CEs felt frustrated, disillusioned with their clinical education roles, and were losing confidence in their skills; they expressed a need to identify a theoretical basis for clinical education and a desire to develop research skills. | "You look at the feedback from the last students and set up the next placement in response to that … and the hope is that that makes the next placement better"<br>"It's hard because I'm finding that I'm trying to adjust to fit, and I wonder how much is reasonable? … Sometimes I feel like I'm not being an effective CE"<br>"For me, teasing out communication styles versus professionalism versus initiation and learning styles, that's the hard part … I think it links into how I interpret their professionalism … and it might be something totally different"<br>"I think we need to be more directive at the start of place-ments so students know exactly what the expectations are" | Consultation with researcher;<br>Identified action research as the methodology;<br>Undertook a literature review;<br>Adopted Teacher as Manager model;<br>Identified a need for students to assume responsibility for learning;<br>Established a focus on learning styles;<br>Developed Version 1 of the Orientation package → trialled in SP1. |

*Table 28.3. Project findings (Continued)*

| Time point/ Participants | Findings | Examples of data | Actions arising from findings |
|---|---|---|---|
| End of SP1/ CEs | Pleased with the structure provided by the Orientation phase; felt they needed to develop their skills to more effectively discuss learning styles with students and use this information to assist with tailoring education strategies to students; felt that more structure was needed for later phases of the placement. | "One of the glitches with [the challenge test] could be [the student's] self perception, but I think the student was generally over-confident and that was reflected in that tool … It also allows you to look at their ability to reflect on their skills, so that straightaway said to me 'OK, that student is perhaps not great at evaluating their performance' and so, I need to watch that and help them develop those skills" "I don't think I know enough about learning styles to be able to use all the information well enough" "[the student and I] made a specific time to look over all the paperwork … at the end of Week 1, and it … made a difference to setting … learning goals and talking about [placement] expectations" | CEs undertook professional development related to adult learning principles and learning styles; Developed timetables showing CEs' availability for direct supervision and student consultation; Modified the Orientation package → Version 2 i. Orientation phase of placement was extended from 1 to 2 weeks; ii. Consolidated into one document the AH site orientation package and orientation to learning package, removing repetition. |
| Students | Liked the Orientation phase, as it helped them settle in; there was too much information in the Orientation package; the case study was large and difficult to complete in the timeframe. | "The learning styles … activities have just made it really obvious to me and [CE] what I need" "The challenge test … really helped me see what type of patients I might be seeing here" "There was just too much in the case study" "Overall the orientation was good, but that first week was still really busy" | iii. Added theoretical information about learning styles to provide contextual information for students; iv. Added learning styles summary sheet; Extended timeframe for completion of the case study. |

*Table 28.3. Project findings (Continued)*

| Time point/ Participants | Findings | Examples of data | Actions arising from findings |
|---|---|---|---|
| End of SP2/ CEs | Had met their need to be able to more effectively discuss learning styles and needs; the timetable was working well; wanted the hypothetical case study removed from the Orientation package as the workload was too high; realised that they had begun to implement the Teacher as Manager model at the micro level. | "I felt more comfortable discussing learning styles with the students this time ... I don't think I'm adapting my teaching style necessarily, but I am more consistently aware of how each student learns"<br><br>"I liked [the challenge test] because it was very visual and I could just scan down and look at what she had rated 1, 2 and 3, and what I did was just highlight the 1s and the 3s so I knew the things she was competent and confident with and the things she wasn't ... And ... after I had observed her with patients to check that I thought her ratings were fair, I felt confident when I knew it was something she had rated as being competent in ... It really helped with my time management 'cause I didn't need to be there all the time I knew she'd be OK" | The case study was removed from the Orientation package and deferred until a later phase of the placement → Orientation package Version 3;<br><br>CEs began to think of other learning activities that might be suitable for later phases but no changes were made as yet;<br><br>CEs decided to work through the Challenge Test with students at the time of setting learning goals and to use information from the Challenge Test to identify learning goals. |
| Students | Very satisfied with Orientation; felt well supported; liked the learning activities; didn't complete the hypothetical case study in the timeframe required; suggested placement information be emailed out in two sections. | "The challenge test ... good ... And it was ... good chatting through it ... because I could say 'This is how competent I feel, this is my level of independence in this area'"<br><br>"I think the case study would be good to talk through"<br><br>"This has just been a really great placement and looking back now I think ... the orientation process was ... what gave me the smooth transition through the placement" | Student recommendation of sending pre-placement information in two emails was implemented. Email 1: placement dates, site requirements, necessary theoretical background, etc.; Email 2: CE Project information with explanation that time will be allocated in Week 1 to complete tasks. |

*Table 28.3. Project findings (Continued)*

| Time point/ Participants | Findings | Examples of data | Actions arising from findings |
|---|---|---|---|
| End of SP3/ CEs | All positive: better placement coordination and transition of students across placement; CEs satisfied with their roles and competence; placement experiences are student driven and goal focused. | "What I did this time was actually go through the challenge test and ... set some goals around that ... This helped move away from generic goals like assessment"<br><br>"It was good for the students to go through [the learning styles] ... because they both had such outgoing personalities, they thought they were activists, and they were both certainly more reflector. So then we had to set some goals around that"<br><br>"Placements are now more student directed than clinician directed and I am really aware of making that very, very clear at the beginning" | No changes needed to Orientation package. Therefore, a decision was made to retain Orientation package Version 3. |
| Students | Perceptions of greater independence within place- ments; evidence that students were using components of the Orientation package as tools to negotiate their needs. | "The learning styles activities are great because they give you more direction and then you can say exactly what you need help with. It made negotiating with the CE heaps easier"<br><br>"It helps you justify: Instead of saying 'I'd like to watch', you can say why and how it will help your confidence and what you're going to do while you're watching to make sure you're learning" | |
| End of SP4/ CEs and students | All positive. | "It's definitely been worth it. I am going to speak to my previous CE and tell them that ... Albury Hospital ... had this orientation thing and it's all worked out ... on Day 1" | Switched attention to second phase of the research, Learning and development. |

## REFERENCES

Cruice, M. (2005). Common issues but alternative solutions and innovations. *Advances in Speech-Language Pathology, 7*(3), 162–166.

Honey, P., & Mumford, A. (1989). *The manual of learning styles* (2nd ed.). Berkshire: Peter Honey Publications.

Lincoln, M., & McCabe, P. (2005). Values, necessity and the mother of invention in clinical education. *Advances in Speech-Language Pathology, 7*(3), 153–157.

McAllister, L. (2005). Issues and innovations in clinical education. *Advances in Speech-Language Pathology, 7*(3), 138–148.

McAllister, L., & Lincoln, M. (2004). *Clinical education in speech-language pathology.* London: Whurr.

Pickering, M. (2005). Issues and innovations in clinical education: A view from the USA. *Advances in Speech-Language Pathology, 7*(3), 167–169.

Romanini, J., & Higgs, J. (1991). The teacher as manager in continuing and professional education. *Studies in Continuing Education, 13,* 41–52.

Stansfield, J. (2005). Issues and innovations in clinical education: Regulation, collaboration and communication. *Advances in Speech-Language Pathology, 7*(3), 173–176.

*Lucie Shanahan PGDip (Rural Health)*
*Albury Hospital*
*Albury Wodonga Health, Australia*

*Linda Wilson PhD*
*School of Community Health*
*Charles Sturt University, Australia*

*Anna O'Callaghan PhD*
*Albury Hospital*
*Albury Wodonga Health, Australia*

*Tanya Dawe BAppSc (SpPath)*
*Albury Hospital*
*Albury Wodonga Health, Australia*

# 29. SUPPORT FROM NON-ACADEMIC UNITS FOR FIELDWORK EDUCATION

Professional entry education is not simply a relationship between learners and teachers, whether they are classroom, distance or fieldwork educators. Supporting teaching and learning are many systems, strategies, departments and staff that are sometimes called non-academic or support teams. These individuals and teams include student administrators, student services officers, librarians, educational developers, information technology specialists, communication system managers, campus managers, counsellors, ombudsmen, finance and travel officers, course administrators and fieldwork education administrators.

In this chapter we focus on services provided by such teams and units in support of curriculum planners, fieldwork education managers, students and educators. We acknowledge that there are many employees of industry partners who participate in fieldwork education, providing such services as the onsite facilitation of student placements, technical and library support in industry locations, coordination with university staff in fieldwork program organisation, and transmitting communications across participants in fieldwork education. However, here we concentrate on university employees and departments to address the question: How do non-academic support and administrative staff employed by universities provide support to educators, practitioners and students participating in fieldwork education? Given the coverage of related topics in other chapters (such as on-campus clinics, fieldwork education management, peer and self-directed learning and flexible teaching and learning) we concentrate here on fieldwork education placements that are conducted off-campus for blocks of time in real/actual workplaces. Examples in this chapter are provided from Charles Sturt University (CSU) in Australia. Other universities would have their stories and examples of ways of supporting fieldwork education.

## CHALLENGES STUDENTS FACE REGARDING FIELDWORK PLACEMENTS

Administrative and learning support units and systems at universities play an essential role in helping students learn and effectively navigate the challenges of being a university student. These challenges include:
- developing learning competencies such as information literacy skills alongside mastery of core curriculum content
- managing time to learn, live and earn income (and perhaps deal with loss of income during placements while paying rent at "home" and at the clinical site)
- coping with curriculum scheduling and location expectations (including attending off campus placements)

*L. McAllister et al., (eds.), Innovations in Allied Health Fieldwork*
*Education: A Critical Appraisal, 329–338.*
© *2010 Sense Publishers. All rights reserved.*

- buying or borrowing resources such as laptop computers to access university administration and learning resources systems while learning on campus, in distance mode and on placements
- accessing learning resources (e.g. library media, including during placements)
- dealing with university administration requirements.

Fieldwork education placements pose particular problems and challenges for students. Students are often required to relocate temporarily to another town, district or even offshore to undertake their fieldwork. The stress involved in finding somewhere to live, arranging childcare and organising transport, coupled with isolation from supportive networks, can sometimes have a detrimental impact on the overall success of the fieldwork experience. Accessing the information resources and services to support the student's endeavours can be a major stress. Libraries, learning support and information units, and student support systems (e.g. financial, travel, resources schemes) are often established in universities to help students cope with these challenges and stressors.

In parallel with the challenges that students *face*, are the challenges today's generation of students *pose* for universities. For instance,

- they are time-poor, juggling jobs, family and study
- they are more literate in advanced technological communication skills than previous generations and utilise many second generation communication technologies, particularly small portable devices, in many areas of life
- they expect rapid responses and service
- they expect information, teaching and supplementary materials to be online, and for online access to be readily available
- they use the Internet for social activity as well as study.

How universities cope with these expectations is just as much part of 21st century higher education as are the widespread demands for accountability to external stakeholders (e.g. governments, professional associations, accreditation authorities). Universities need to ask how their pedagogy and their student support services and infrastructure can cope with the current and future generations of students. In workplace learning there are many stakeholders, including practitioners, clients, managers, senior members of the professions and workplace regulators, whose attitudes to students may well differ from those of universities, seeing them as novice practitioners or workers who are expected to demonstrate behaviours more akin to professionalism and accountability than students' learning preferences. Part of the preparation of students for fieldwork education in real workplaces is helping them to understand these workplace expectations.

## CURRICULUM AND EDUCATIONAL DEVELOPMENT

Historically, many curricula educating students to enter professions or practice-based occupations adopted an apprenticeship approach. Students learned "at the feet of the master", practised skills demonstrated by the master and learned the master's practice knowledge. As learning moved from the workplace into learning institutions, many of the notions and practices of learning from skilled practitioners remained, with a strong separation between classroom and fieldwork learning. Classroom learning was regarded as the theory, and the teaching of practical skills and fieldwork was regarded as the opportunity to practise in the real world what was already learned. There are obvious flaws in this model from today's perspective. First, the divide between theory and practice is artificial and unhelpful. Practice is a means of generating knowledge and theory, and theory is a support for practice. Second, learning occurs both in the practice world (or "field") and in the classroom. To limit the view of fieldwork education to a place where prior learning and skills are practised is vastly to underestimate and devalue the richness of this world as a vital source for learning not just the knowledge and skills needed for practice but also the nature of practice, professionalism, the people who participate in practice and the professional identity. A key challenge for any program that prepares students for working in practice is to design a curriculum that (a) integrates all modes and learning venues (on campus, fieldwork education, distance learning), (b) values fieldwork placements as means of learning and not just practising, and (c) brings sound educational principles and practices to the design, implementation and evaluation of learning in all these areas of the curriculum.

Curriculum design involves a complex range of tasks and roles. Universities frequently maintain educational development and support units with staff who can support curriculum design, particularly at the overall curriculum level for both on campus and distance education, and who work with academic staff with disciplinary and professional backgrounds to tailor curricula to the needs of the particular profession. Less commonly do educational developers have expertise in fieldwork education design, and there is a tendency for academics to focus on fieldwork education at the broad level of goals and curriculum architecture (e.g. how many subjects, hours, broad content areas are needed, and where they should be placed in the curriculum). In many situations the actual learning and teaching that occur in fieldwork education are the responsibility of the fieldwork educator. Although this is to some extent desirable – these are the people "on the job" who can take best advantage of the unpredictable learning opportunities (e.g. availability of clients/ patients) – it is important to remember that these people are practitioners rather than trained educators (generally) and students can therefore receive quite varied learning experiences and learning outcomes of variable quality. We conclude that: curriculum design needs flexible consideration of the whole curriculum; and staff development for educational developers, academic curriculum designers and fieldwork educators needs to include educational preparation for fieldwork education design, teaching, learning and assessment.

## NETWORKS AND SERVICES TO SUPPORT TEACHING STAFF

In schools and faculties that conduct fieldwork education programs there are staff who organise fieldwork education placements. This is often a complex and difficult task. It commonly relies heavily on collaboration with industry partners, with implications for workload, resourcing and funding for both parties. Moreover, industry partners commonly provide support to fieldwork placements in the form of practitioners and other professionals who act as fieldwork educators. University and industry staff require support and training to help them organise and facilitate effective fieldwork education.

Universities commonly have learning and teaching centres that provide support and training to university staff in relation to curriculum development, design of learning and teaching resources, student assessment, curriculum evaluation, training in use of educational technologies and related matters. Staff induction and development programs are important for assisting staff to understand the needs and expectations of current students, to learn how to design, manage and organise fieldwork education placements, and to collect and interpret course evaluation data.

One of the problems faced by fieldwork education staff is that university staff development commonly focuses on the needs and preparation of academic staff generally, whereas fieldwork education staff are often left to fend for themselves. Two strategies and support systems at Charles Sturt University (CSU) provide exceptions to this rule. The Fieldwork Education Network is a staff support network of fieldwork education academic and general staff who provide advice, support, education and information to each other, sharing their expertise, specialist knowledge and collaboration in recognition of the significant challenges of these roles. The Education For Practice Institute conducts research, staff education, leadership and strategic development input across the university to enhance the practices and outcomes of practice-based education and fieldwork education at CSU. The Institute is facilitating the expansion of staff development for fieldwork education staff, quality assurance and review of practice-based education and fieldwork education.

## LIBRARY SERVICES AND SUPPORT FOR STUDENTS

Many Australian university libraries have developed a range of strategies to assist students with challenges they face in participating in fieldwork education. At CSU students may be located large distances from their home campus (see Chapter 8). The CSU Library's motto is "anywhere, anytime", promising to provide prompt services to clients (particularly staff and students) wherever they are located. Making this a reality for students engaged in fieldwork experience and placements across Australia and internationally is a challenge. This is a multifactorial problem: location, availability of local resources, adequate communication networks, restrictions on software and resources licensing agreements, and the cost of resources for multiple locations, each with its own student cohort ranging from single students in isolated inland areas to groups in town or city centres. Different, but equally difficult, problems arise for distance students studying or endeavouring to schedule virtual workplace learning at night when most of the support and academic staff are not on duty.

*Library Services – Preparation for Placements*

In the period leading up to fieldwork education, students need to acquire the knowledge, abilities and the library resources and access tools they will need during their placement. Of particular importance are students' information literacy skills. At CSU an Information Literacy Portal has been set up on the library's website to allow students to pursue self-directed learning via podcasts, interactive tutorials, video, guides and blogs. An online information literacy tutorial is also available that can be embedded into web-based learning programs.

In relation to library resources, CSU librarians have found that, despite the increased provision of online library resources such as e-books and journals, the demand for physical resources in some disciplines has not decreased. This is particularly the case for education students who are heavy borrowers of kits, picture books, games and teaching aids.

*Library Services – During Placements*

Most university libraries provide extended loan periods for students on fieldwork education to enable them to borrow resources up to a week before they leave for their placements and retain them for the duration of the placement plus a week to allow time for the student to return home. CSU's library provides a distance education service for students undertaking fieldwork education. For the duration of the placement students' status is changed to distance education (DE) and they receive a full DE service which includes the dispatch of materials by post or courier. This service is appreciated by students who find themselves in a fieldwork location where there are limited resources or where they are denied access to resources at the local institution. The latter is a common experience of health science students. The CSU Library also scans documents on request and delivers these via email.

During placements students frequently require advice and support on library matters. This support can include assistance with terminology, help with finding resources for a presentation or paper, advice on information technology matters, and training in the use of particular resources. Many libraries provide free telephone access for students who are located off campus. This service is vital for students in remote locations without access to the Internet. At CSU Library team members regularly take phone calls from students on placement. The library also provides a chat service and a web-based information service, and these services enable students to obtain quick responses to queries. Figure 29.1 illustrates a video on the CSU Library website[1] that provides information for students on placements.

CSU's website statistics show that a small but growing number of students utilise mobile devices to access the library's online services and resources. Victoria University[2] has a mobile (cell phone) friendly version of its library catalogue. Curtin University and CSU are developing pages that provide access to most library services and resources via a handheld device. Currently CSU provides access to videos, podcasts and some journal databases. In some areas, particularly rural and remote regions, limitations in telecommunication infrastructure have a negative impact on the effectiveness of this service.

The CSU Library has a practice of privileging online over print media for the delivery of resources such as books, journals and video, and in general Australian academic libraries are shifting away from print to online delivery for journal and book resources. Delays associated with postage and couriers are removed at the click of a finger, with virtually instant access to resources. Regardless of location, students on fieldwork placements can access these resources at any time.

The CSU Library understands the difficulties many students face when involved in practicum placements.

*Figure 29.1. Library video for students on placements.*

## LEARNING SUPPORT SYSTEMS

Universities have many systems for supporting students' learning outside the classroom and formal learning programs. One example is on-campus learning centres that students can access for assistance with learning, technological support and Internet usage, as well as advice on learning concerns. The Learning Commons at CSU is one such example. It is a learning space – both real and virtual – beyond the classroom, which supplements classroom learning experiences and helps to prepare students for distance, fieldwork and independent learning. The Commons is a learning hub that provides seamless access to the University's information resources, supports flexible learning methodologies and provides an integrated work environment for students and academics. Its learning spaces and technologies support learning theory principles, and it provides a single point of access to services such as information literacy, learning support, research support and IT support. The Commons is built on the principles of cooperation, co-location and collaboration. It seeks to facilitate social-isation as well as learning and to suit the ways that many of today's students learn and behave. The Learning Commons provides new spaces for learning including:
- an environment which surrounds students with multiple format scholarly materials from print to Web
- student-focused spaces
- group spaces and single spaces
- quiet spaces and noisy spaces
- flexible spaces and furniture that students can move to suit the needs of the group at the time
- access to refreshments
- 24/7 access within the bounds of security requirements.

Study skills programs are valuable student resources. As well as assisting students, study skills teams can work with academic staff to embed the learning of academic literacy and learning skills into curricula. Linking study skills development with discipline-specific learning can help students acquire knowledge and literacy skills more deeply and with greater relevance.

The concept of *the student experience* has been the focus of much endeavour in recent years. The Student Experience Program at CSU focuses on enhancing the quality of services to students. One of the projects within this program is designed to improve transitioning into university, pathways for technical college and Indigenous students, final year practices, and orientation. Another has led to the establishment of Student Central. Located in the Learning Commons, Student Central offers a range of services to students from a single point, as well as providing virtual support by phone and online. Students can access the knowledge management system for responses to common questions.

Another program designed to assist students in their transition to university is CSU's STUDY LINK. Developed for distance students, this is a flexible delivery, enabling program comprising 18 self-paced units aimed to build confidence, skills and knowledge in a supportive and non-threatening environment prior to the commencement of university study. An important aspect of the STUDY LINK program is that it provides the same opportunities to acquire the necessary competencies to study successfully at university to distance education students as to on campus students. This access has been particularly important for specific cohorts such as enrolled nurses and prospective policing students, who often need to continue to work and maintain family responsibilities while completing preparatory studies.

## STUDENT ADMINISTRATIVE AND SUPPORT SERVICES

Administrative services needed for students range from enrolment to regulations, examination results, timetabling, and university requirements for fieldwork education, e.g. police checks, vaccination records. Students may also have specific queries about their circumstances during a placement, e.g. insurance cover.

Student support and welfare services include assistance with both on-campus residences and accommodation linked to fieldwork placements (e.g. at hospitals). Students may also be able to apply for assistance with the cost of travel to placements and employment, the latter helping students to fund their education including the costs of fieldwork education. Students with special needs (linked to disabilities, language, living away from home) and Indigenous students are also supported at many universities by assistance with enrolment and with participation in fieldwork education. Support programs offered at CSU, for example, include:
- Professional Placement Equity Grants to assist undergraduate students to attend fieldwork education placements
- Residential School Equity Grants to assist distance education students attend residential schools
- Disability Support through Study Access Plans that include access to liaison staff, teaching resources, alternative format study materials and assistive technologies
- Indigenous Student Services providing Indigenous students with study and social skills development, dedicated tutorial support and computer access.

## COMMUNICATION TECHNOLOGY AND INFRASTRUCTURE

A particular difficulty for fieldwork education students is the variable availability of reliable Internet connections and computing facilities. Some students discover that their placement organisation will not allow them to use local computing facilities or access the Internet. Other students located in remote areas may find that tele-communication services are slow and unreliable. Students on remote or offshore placements often face acute telecommunication problems due to poor or non-existent infrastructure and services.

Figure 29.2 shows a Web page[3] illustrating ways to access library resources via mobile devices that can be taken on placements.

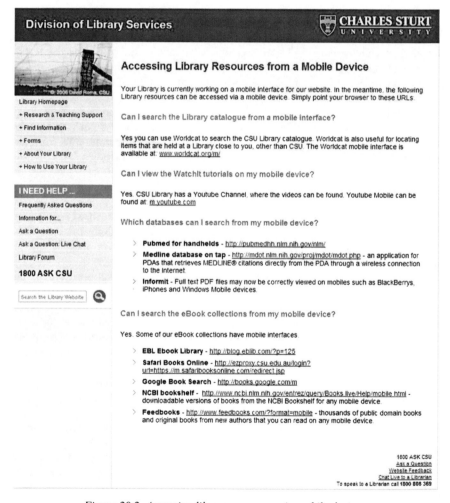

*Figure 29.2. Accessing library resources via mobile devices.*

Services and resources provided by universities can help to overcome these problems for students on placements. At CSU the online learning environment Interact provides support for distance learning, allowing students to interact at any time and in any place. Students can also teleconference with staff, and use Web 2.0 social web technologies (including blogging, podcasting, social bookmarking, social networking, wiki writing or virtual worlds) and online environments. Students can borrow laptop computers from the CSU Library to take with them on placements.

Essential support services for staff involved in managing fieldwork education placements are technical support, infrastructure resources and staff development linked to computerised systems for the organisation of student placements. There are many challenges associated with managing fieldwork placements, including difficulty in finding sufficient places and industry partners to place and supervise students, lack of reliability of these arrangements (e.g. linked to workplace staff absences and variable workloads) and competition among universities for limited places. Computerised systems must be flexible, able to cope with many variables in terms of workplaces and student data recording, and able to deal with the demands of different courses. University teams that support these management systems and infrastructure need to understand the management tasks as well as the capacity of the computer program/hardware to cater for the data processing.

## REFLECTIONS

The importance of strong and coordinated support for students' fieldwork education by administrative/non-academic/support divisions and units is likely to increase, due to several trends. One is recognition of the importance of fieldwork education in courses for professionals who will practise with confidence and sound knowledge of their workplaces. Another is growing recognition of the importance of *the student experience*, that is, the ways in which students engage broadly and experience their interactions with the university. A third is the increasing recourse to online delivery of learning and of student support services. Fieldwork placements must be seen as integral components of courses and supported accordingly, and support must aim to be just as effective while students are undertaking fieldwork as when they are on campus.

For non-academic services, it is likely that there will be an increasing emphasis on improved communication with students about how they can expect to be supported during fieldwork. This will in turn require a more integrated view of non-academic services and consolidation of information, with its more effective delivery online.

Challenges for support services include maintaining currency with what is required across the range of academic programs on offer at any one time, identifying those requirements that are generic and those that are course-specific and tailoring support accordingly; ensuring that different student cohorts (on-campus, distance education, etc.) are, as far as possible, provided with equivalent service and support; ensuring that program delivery takes advantage of evolving technological opportunities; and always maintaining close alignment with academic program objectives and effective communication and liaison with academic staff. Such alignment will continue to be essential to the development and delivery of non-academic support for fieldwork education.

## NOTES

[1]  http://www.csu.edu.au/division/library/how-to/services-videos.html
[2]  http://w2.vu.edu.au/library/airpac/
[3]  http://www.csu.edu.au/division/library/how-to/faq/mobile-device.html

*Joy Higgs AM PhD*
*The Education For Practice Institute,*
*Charles Sturt University, Australia*

*Kerryn Amery*
*Division of Library Services*
*Charles Sturt University, Australia*

*Lyn Gorman PhD*
*Charles Sturt University, Australia*

# CONTRIBUTORS

*Rola Ajjawi PhD*
*Office of Medical Education*
*The University of Sydney, Australia*

*Julaine Allan PhD*
*Centre for Inland Health*
*Charles Sturt University, Australia*

*Kerryn Amery*
*Division of Library Services*
*Charles Sturt University, Australia*

*Julie Baldry Currens PhD*
*Learning, Teaching and Assessment*
*University of East London, UK*

*Jean-Pascal Beaudoin M.A.P.*
*Formation clinique - ergothérapie*
*Université d'Ottawa, Canada*

*Ruth Beecham DEd*
*Consultant, Yackandandah, Australia*

*Dawn Best MEd*
*Health Professional Education Consultant*
*School of Physiotherapy (Adjunct)*
*La Trobe University, Australia*

*Christine Bithell MA(Educ)*
*Faculty of Health and Social Care Sciences*
*St George's, University of London and Kingston University, UK*

*Noni Bourke BAppSci*
*Improving Care for Older People*
*Peninsula Health, Australia*

*Wendy Bowles PhD*
*School of Humanities and Social Sciences*
*Charles Sturt University, Australia*

*Carol Burgess MEd*
*School of Teacher Education*
*Charles Sturt University, Australia*

CONTRIBUTORS

*Nicole Christensen PhD*
*Department of Physical Therapy*
*Samuel Merritt University, USA*

*Lynn Clouder PhD*
*Centre for Interprofessional E-learning*
*Coventry University, UK*

*Madeline Cruice PhD*
*School of Community and Health Sciences*
*City University London, UK*

*Michael Curtin PhD*
*School of Community Health*
*Charles Sturt University, Australia*

*Lynda D'Avray DHC*
*Centre for Medical and Healthcare Education*
*St George's, University of London, UK*

*Tanya Dawe BAppSc (SpPath)*
*Albury Hospital*
*Albury Wodonga Health, Australia*

*Marijke Denton CPSP*
*Albury Community Health Centre*
*Greater Southern Area Health Service, Australia*

*Catherine Donnelly MSc*
*School of Rehabilitation Therapy*
*Queen's University, Canada*

*Donna Drynan Med OT*
*Occupational Science and Occupational Therapy Department*
*University of British Columbia, Canada*

*Helen Edwards PhD*
*Consultant Higher and Health Professional Education*
*Faculty of Health Sciences, (Adjunct)*
*La Trobe University, Australia*

*Alison Ferguson PhD*
*Humanities and Social Science*
*The University of Newcastle, Australia*

*Sarah Forrest MB ChB*
*Centre for Medical and Healthcare Education*
*St George's, University of London*
*Queen Mary's Hospital, Roehampton, London, UK*

*Lyn Gorman PhD*
*Charles Sturt University, Australia*

*John Hammond MSc*
*Faculty of Health and Social Care Sciences*
*St George's University of London and Kingston University, UK*

*Julian Hargreaves MSc*
*School of Health and Bioscience*
*University of East London, UK*

*Joy Higgs AM PhD*
*The Education for Practice Institute*
*Charles Sturt University, Australia*

*Anne Hill B.Sp.Thy*
*The University of Queensland, Australia*

*Diana W.L. Ho PhD*
*Division of Speech & Hearing Sciences*
*Faculty of Education*
*University of Hong Kong, Hong Kong*

*Jill Hummell PhD*
*Community Integration Program*
*Westmead Brain Injury Rehabilitation Service, Australia*

*Lester E Jones MSc MEd(PM)*
*School of Physiotherapy*
*La Trobe University, Australia*

*Bonny Jung MEd*
*School of Rehabilitation Science*
*McMaster University, Canada*

*Jenny Kent PhD*
*Institute for Land Water and Society*
*Charles Sturt University, Australia*

CONTRIBUTORS

*Lorinda Kwan MEd*
*Division of Speech & Hearing Sciences*
*Faculty of Education*
*University of Hong Kong, Hong Kong*

*Richard Ladyshewsky PhD*
*Graduate School of Business*
*Curtin University of Technology, Australia*

*Michelle Lincoln PhD*
*Discipline of Speech Pathology*
*The University of Sydney, Australia*

*Rosemary Lysaght PhD*
*School of Rehabilitation Therapy*
*Queen's University, Canada*

*Merilyn MacKenzie GradDip(ResMethods)*
*School of Physiotherapy*
*La Trobe University, Australia*

*Adele Martin Dip. P & OT*
*Mohawk College of Applied Arts and Technology, Canada*

*Jennifer Medves PhD*
*School of Nursing*
*Queen's University, Canada*

*Lindy McAllister PhD*
*School of Medicine*
*The University of Queensland, Australia*

*Sue McAllister PhD*
*Speech Pathology*
*Flinders University of South Australia, Australia*

*Susan Mulholland MScRehab*
*Department of Occupational Therapy*
*University of Alberta, Canada*

*Gillian Nisbet MMEd*
*(Formerly) Faculty of Health Sciences*
*The University of Sydney, Australia*

*Anna O'Callaghan PhD*
*Albury Hospital*
*Albury Wodonga Health, Australia*

*Bridget O'Connor BPT*
*School of Community Health*
*Charles Sturt University, Australia*

*Peter O'Meara PhD*
*Centre for Inland Health*
*Charles Sturt University, Australia*

*Anne O'Riordan BScOT*
*School of Rehabilitation Therapy*
*Queen's University, Canada*

*Margo Paterson PhD*
*School of Rehabilitation Therapy*
*Queen's University, Canada*

*Claire Penn PhD*
*Department of Speech Pathology and Audiology*
*University of Witwatersrand, South Africa*

*Merrolee Penman MA(Educ)*
*School of Occupational Therapy*
*Otago Polytechnic, New Zealand*

*Rodney Pope PhD*
*Centre for Inland Health*
*Charles Sturt University, Australia*

*Miranda Rose PhD*
*School of Human Communication Sciences,*
*La Trobe University, Australia*

*Susan Ryan PhD*
*School of Health Sciences*
*University of Newcastle, Australia*

*Lucie Shanahan PGDip (Rural Health)*
*Albury Hospital*
*Albury Wodonga Health, Australia*

*Patty Solomon PhD*
*School of Rehabilitation Science*
*McMaster University, Canada*

CONTRIBUTORS

*Yda Smith MOT*
*Division of Occupational Therapy*
*University of Utah, USA*

*Megan Smith PhD*
*School of Community Health*
*Charles Sturt University, Australia*

*Jill Thistlethwaite PhD*
*Institute of Clinical Education*
*The University of Warwick, UK*

*Jane Toms MSc*
*Department of Physiotherapy and Dietetics*
*Coventry University, UK*

*Christie Van Beek BHlthSci(SpPath)*
*Peninsula Health, Australia*

*Sandra Van Dort MA (SLP)*
*Department of Audiology and Speech Sciences*
*University Kebangsan, Malaysia*

*Kerryellen Vroman PhD*
*College of Health and Human Services*
*University of New Hampshire, USA*

*Tara L. Whitehill PhD*
*Division of Speech & Hearing Sciences*
*Faculty of Education*
*University of Hong Kong, Hong Kong*

*Linda Wilson PhD*
*School of Community Health*
*Charles Sturt University, Australia*

*Man-Sang Wong PhD*
*Dept of Health Technology and Informatics*
*Hong Kong Polytechnic University, Hong Kong*

*Karen Yu MEd*
*Division of Speech & Hearing Sciences*
*Faculty of Education*
*University of Hong Kong, Hong Kong*

LaVergne, TN USA
23 September 2010
198070LV00002B/8/P